The Complete

DATABASE MARKETER

Tapping Your Customer
Base to Maximize Sales
and Increase Profits

Arthur M. Hughes

PROBUS PUBLISHING COMPANY
Chicago, Illinois

Authorization to photocopy items for internal or personal use, or the internal or personal use of specific clients, is granted by PROBUS PUBLISHING COMPANY, provided that the US$7.00 per page fee is paid directly to Copyright Clearance Center, 27 Congress Street, Salem MA 01970, USA; Phone: 1-(508) 744-3350. For those organizations that have been granted a photocopy license by CCC, a separate system of payment has been arranged. The fee code for users of the Transactional Reporting Service is: 1-55738-192-5/91/$0.00 + $7.00

Hughes, Arthur Middleton.
    The complete database marketer : tapping your customer base to
maximize sales and increase profits / Arthur M. Hughes.
        p.   cm.
    Includes bibliographical references and index.
    ISBN 1-55738-192-5 : $34.95
    1. Data base marketing.   I. Title.
HF5415.126.H84   1991
658.8'4--dc20   91-15706

    CIP

Printed in the United States of America

BB

        3   4   5   6   7   8   9   0

For Helena

Acknowledgements

I have interviewed and quoted scores of people in the process of writing this book. Most of them are quoted by name. But there are some others to whom I owe a special debt of gratitude for working with me, providing leadership, and helping me to understand this exciting new marketing method. Among these people are:

Robert Smith, President of Targeted Communications Corporation, who had the vision to understand database marketing in the early years, and built a successful company around the concept.

Larry Rinaldi, Vice President and General Manager of Ogilvy & Mather Direct in Los Angeles; one of the creative geniuses who has the ability to dream up successful database concepts and sell them to company managements.

Paul Shoemaker, Brand Manager, The Carnation Company, a role model for the Database Administrator: a hands-on, can-do, successful administrator of a marketing database.

Skip Andrew, Executive Director of the National Center for Database Marketing, whose organizational skills and drive have made a profession out of an idea.

Ernie Schell, President of the Communications Center, who reviewed this book and provided valuable insights for improving it and keeping it within bounds.

Ben Spaisman, President of ACS, Inc., who started with a small direct mail service bureau and turned it into a major player in the modern database marketing world.

Arthur M. Hughes

Contents

Part Four: Reaching Out to Prospects

Part Five: Operating a Marketing Database: Two Case Studies

Part Six: Economics and Corporate Relationships

Part Seven: Concluding Words

Glossary

Appendix: How to Keep Up with Database Marketing

Index

Introduction

The Old Corner Grocer

Sally Warren was surprised. She was used to getting commercial messages in the mail, but this one was different. The St. Paul Luggage Company was writing her to congratulate her on her son David's upcoming graduation from Hobart. In the letter, they suggested that she and Dan consider giving David luggage as a graduation present. The letter included a small colorful catalog featuring St. Paul luggage. But the letter suggested that she could probably beat the listed prices through sales in the three stores in Rochester that carried the famous St. Paul brand. The store names were listed along with the direct dial number of the luggage departments. The topper was a $5 rebate check good at any of the three stores, or also good if she ordered the luggage direct using an 800 number.

Sally Warren's relationship with the St. Paul company went back more than a year, when she and Dan bought their first set of matched luggage for a trip to Florida. Included in the package was an owner registration form offering a $5 rebate from St. Paul's for filling it out and returning it. She did so, and received her check. Six weeks later she also received a nice telephone call from a customer service rep at St. Paul asking, "How did you like your trip to Disney World?" They had a nice talk about Disney World, her family and her job, but not much about luggage.

Six months after that first call, when Sally's daughter, June Baumgartner, gave birth to Sally's first granddaughter, Sally received another letter from St. Paul's congratulating her on becoming a grandmother and suggesting either a St. Paul's Stroller or Car Seat as a useful gift. St. Paul was becoming a household word for the Warrens!

What Sally doesn't know yet, because it is still in the future, is that before she and Dan take that long planned vacation to Spain (which she told the St. Paul's customer service representative about), she will get another letter from St. Paul's wishing them well in Spain, suggesting that they both might want to take along two matching overnight bags specially designed to fit into an airplane overhead compartment.

Sally Warren was experiencing database marketing, the way that business will be conducted in the future. It is a system that sees in every customer an opportunity for a long-term relationship. In past years, marketing aimed at making a sale; database marketing begins with the sale and aims at establishing a lifetime friendship.

Our mythical St. Paul Luggage Company has established a Customer Marketing Database: an interrelated series of computer records about the Warren household that enables St. Paul to know and retain a hundred useful facts about this household and to bring them to bear at the right time.

This is what the corner grocer did in the old days. He knew that the Warren's daughter was having a baby and that their son was graduating from Hobart and, if he was successful, he used this information in his work. That was why his customers kept coming back to him, even though the supermarket down the street had lower prices. But the corner grocer is no more. The rising tide of mass markets and discounted prices did him in. Stores in the Sixties, Seventies and Eighties became impersonal warehouses where no one knew anyone, and clerks were impossible to find.

Database marketing exists today because of one important development: every year, the price of storing and using information has become cheaper and cheaper. The constant improvement in microchips means that vital facts about 800 customers that the grocer used to keep in his head can now be maintained on 8,000,000 St. Paul customers on a mainframe computer.

St. Paul's has set up an integrated system of software, direct mail, telemarketing, rebate checks and intercompany data exchange which is coming closer and closer to recreating the marketing technique of the corner grocer.

Think about it: from what Sally told them on their first telephone call, they learned that Sally's daughter June was recently married to Jack Baumgartner and that the couple were living in Oswego. They stored that information in Sally Warren's file.

Once a month, St. Paul's Stroller and Baby Car Seat Department gets a list of expectant mothers. They were able to link expectant mother June Baumgartner in Oswego with Sally Warren in Rochester and know that they had a proud grandmother who was in the market for the perfect gift. The corner grocer would have done this effortlessly. St. Paul required a lot of advance planning, organization and software, but they did it. And what's more, if they hadn't done it, they wouldn't have been able to maintain market share in the face of modern competition!

That is what this book is about—database marketing, as defined by the National Center for Database Marketing:

> Managing a computerized relational database system, in real time, of comprehensive, up-to-date, relevant data on customers, inquiries, prospects and suspects, to identify our most responsive customers for the purpose of developing a high quality, long-standing relationship of repeat business by developing predictive models which enable us to send desired messages at the right time in the right form to the right people—all with the result of pleasing our customers, increasing our response rate per marketing dollar, lowering our cost per order, building our business, and increasing our profits.

SOME BASIC DEFINITIONS

We need to distinguish a number of terms: let's begin with direct marketing and distinguish it from general advertising.

Direct marketing is any marketing activity in which you attempt to reach the consumers directly, or have them reach you:

- A television or radio ad which features a telephone number to call for information or to order the product.

- A print ad with a coupon, an order solicitation or a telephone number to call.

- Any direct mail piece or catalog sent to a household, designed to sell a product or service.

General advertising measures its success by whether possible customers are aware of or can recall your message. Direct marketing measures its success by whether the profits from direct sales exceed the cost of producing these sales. General advertising aims at projecting an image, positioning the product, increasing general awareness; direct marketing aims at sales and generating leads.

Direct marketing has been around for a long time, but has been growing very fast in comparison with other forms of marketing. It has consistently grown at twice the rate of the United States' gross national product. It is and will continue to be the hottest growth area in advertising for the foreseeable future.

Database marketing is derived from direct marketing: the advertiser maintains an active list of customers and prospects which is updated on a regular basis with information about the customer's response to your message. It is the newest and fastest growing part of direct marketing. It has these features:

1. A list (database) of customers and prospects is maintained on a computer using software which permits ongoing revisions of information about each person.

2. The database is actively used by several different people at the same time to:

   - add names of customers and prospects to the database;
   - enhance these names with demographic and lifestyle information;
   - correct and clean the name and addresses;

> plan marketing strategy using information from the database;
> select names for mail or telephone contact, developing source codes for each different marketing package or message;
> post each customer's record with his or her response to direct marketing with dates, amounts and source codes, and new information specifically requested in the outgoing message;
> prepare frequent reports on the results of marketing efforts and survey questionnaires and
> use the information in the database in a continuing, planned program which builds relationships with the customer and promotes sales.

INDIVIDUAL MARKETING

Direct marketing attempts to reach groups of potential customers. You screen media and mailing lists to concentrate on those most likely to reach groups of people who will respond and buy.

Database marketing attempts to talk one-on-one with people about whom you already know a lot. You want to make customers feel you have a product just for them. You build their loyalty to your product and service because you have demonstrated that you have taken the trouble to learn and remember their past purchases, past requests, past complaints, their lifestyles and interests. They feel that you know them and understand them.

I recently spent a night in a Hyatt Hotel in San Francisco. About 9:30 P.M., I pushed the button on the telephone marked "In-Room Dining" to order a hamburger. The operator said, "Hello, Mr. Hughes. What would you like to eat this evening?" I was surprised and pleased. It sounded as if she had been sitting by the phone all evening, hoping that I would call!

A week later, I stayed in another very new, very large and very expensive hotel in San Francisco. I again pushed the button for room service. The operator did not know my name. He asked me what room I was in. I had to go to the dresser to look at my room key to be sure. He didn't know!

The Hyatt had a marketing database which permitted the operator to know my name as soon as I picked up the phone. I had only checked in one hour before the call, yet they already had my name on their system. A small matter, but enough to make me remember the Hyatt. I have forgotten the name of the other hotel.

THE IMPORTANCE OF COMPUTERS

Of necessity we will spend much time in this book talking about computers: what you can do with them, and what they will do for your business. There is no getting around it—database marketing owes its existence to the dramatic cost reductions and efficiencies made possible by what has happened to mainframe computers in the last ten years. Most of the techniques we will be discussing were possible, but not cost-effective, a few years ago. The way computers are developing, some techniques in this book may be obsolete ten years from now. We are on a very fast track. The race will go to the swiftest: the companies that learn these new techniques, and learn how to adapt their businesses to them.

If you are not computer literate, do not worry. There is nothing in this book that you can't understand or that will force you to consult some other book or expert. This is a book for marketing professionals, not for computer experts. As we introduce concepts that involve computers, we will explain what we mean in layman's language. Those who already know computers can skip these brief definitions.

THE CIRCLE OF PROFITS

If you took the time to study the old-fashioned, successful corner grocer you would have noticed his technique. He kept his eyes and ears open. He chatted with customers as they came in. I used to think that he was just wasting time: "Why doesn't he spend his time out in the warehouse working, instead of making small talk with the customers?" I thought to myself.

How wrong I was! Today's successful store manager is busy in the warehouse. He runs a clean, well-stocked, impersonal store where the customer never gets to know anyone and is loyal only until the competitor's ad appears in tomorrow's newspaper.

In the next few years all successful stores will begin to return to first principles, and treat their customers as the old fashioned grocer did. They will be exploiting the circle of profits (Figure 1).

Every contact with a customer will be used as an opportunity to collect more data about the customer. This data will be used to build knowledge about the customer. The knowledge will drive strategy leading to practical, directly personal, long-term relationships which produce sales. The sales, in turn, will yield more data, which will start the process all over again.

Figure I-1   The Circle of Profits

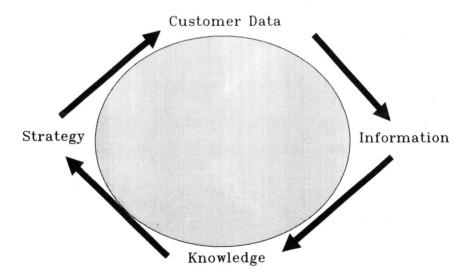

Marketing to Individuals

HOW A DATABASE AFFECTS MARKETING STRATEGY

In their stimulating book, *MaxiMarketing,* Stan Rapp and Tom Collins opened our eyes to the dramatic changes in marketing which have come about during the 1980s:

> The common wastefulness of the mass advertising of the past is giving way to the newly affordable ability to locate and communicate directly with a company's best prospects and customers. And this new-found ability can be equally rewarding to a manufacturer, a retailer, a service company, or a catalog merchant . . . Of all these changes, surely the most revolutionary is the ability to store in the computer information about your prime prospects and customers, and, in effect, create a database that becomes your private marketplace. As the cost of accumulating and accessing the data drops, the ability to talk directly to your prospects and customers—and to build one-to-one relationships with them—will continue to grow. A rising tide of technological change has brought this golden moment of opportunity.

Almost everyone in advertising has heard their message and accepted it. In every major company, every agency, in every conference and convention, marketers are discussing ways of taking advantage of this golden moment and building a functioning marketing database for their company or client.

Rapp and Collins cautioned: *"MaxiMarketing* is not a textbook or a how-to book. It is a "think" book that aims not to solve your advertising and marketing problems, but to stimulate you to think about them in a new way so that you can solve them yourself."

The book you now hold in your hands, *The Complete Database Marketer,* is a how-to book. We begin where Rapp and Collins left off in MaxiMarketing and their follow-up book, *The Great Marketing Turnaround,* to provide you with some of the background information necessary to create a functioning marketing database in your own situation.

The Complete Database Marketer is written for two audiences: the senior executive planning marketing strategy and the middle-level staffer who is actually building a database, setting up loyalty programs, developing marketing initiatives and running a customer service program.

The Complete Database Marketer is state-of-the-art. Everything that you will read in these pages is either in existence or in the active planning stage somewhere. This book is for creative people who take ideas and run with them to make profits for their companies.

Database marketing has become a buzzword. Articles and books are devoted to it and a national center has sprung up to bring professionals together. Every direct-mail agency and marketing staff in America is either looking into it or actually setting one up. If you are not sure exactly what it is, don't be embarrassed—most people still don't. (But then, they haven't yet read this book!)

Whether you are selling boots or boats, software or soap, cars or computers, pharmaceuticals or financial services, to market effectively today you will need a marketing database that links you to loyal customers who are eager to be *the first to learn* about your new offerings. You will need to be linked to active prospects whom you will transform into loyal customers. You will need to use the information in the database to understand your customers and to communicate with them one-on-one.

A marketing database is not simply an "add-on" marketing technique which can be used to supplement your existing program. That is what it may be at first. But to make maximum use of database marketing, your entire *marketing strategy* must change. Your objective is no longer just to sell the product—it is to *build a lifetime relationship* with customers who will buy your products again and again and again. These may be your dealer's customers—but they are also yours.

This book will tell you how to build a marketing database and how to use it to establish and maintain profitable lifetime relationships with your customers.

We begin with a strategic overview which addresses the questions: How will database marketing affect your marketing strategy? How will it change the way that you run your business so as to create the maximum of loyal repeat business at the lowest possible cost?

THE CUSTOMER'S NEW ROLE

Mass marketing has generated a marketplace with some notable features:

- high quality products and services at reasonable prices;
- a sophisticated delivery system;
- a highly competitive sales environment and
- affluent and informed customers.

But in the success of mass marketing, we have lost something valuable. In our drive to reach more and more people in a cost-effective way, we have lost contact with people as individuals. Instead of reaching out to them as valued repeat customers, working to maintain their loyalty, we treat them as if they were unknown masses. We barrage them with discount coupons, 15-second commercials and junk mail. As providers, we have been acting as if price, product positioning and image were the only important factors in sales.

The nature and desires of our customers are changing. These changes are having profound implications for marketing strategy. What are these changes?

- There are many more two-income families who have fewer children, more education and less time for shopping. Their needs are no longer simple. They want a wider variety of choice and more personal services.

- It is no longer useful to categorize buyers into simple groups, such as manufacturing employees, government personnel and service workers. Today customers spend their working days in thousands of occupational specialties which didn't exist twenty years ago. Many of them have very specialized needs.

- Customers are becoming skeptical and demanding. Most of them are very intelligent and knowledgeable and want more information about products than can be printed in ads or on packaging. They want a wider, more diverse group of products than they have encountered in stores as they exist today.

INDIVIDUAL MARKETING

There is a way in which the modern corporation can take advantage of these trends to develop a lifelong bond of loyalty with its customers. It is possible to develop individual marketing programs designed for each customer and prospect. We can build one-on-one relationships of recognition and service that will keep our current customers and win over users of competing brands.

The method is called database marketing. It consists of capturing quantities of information about current customers, and using that information to promote repeat sales and build an ongoing relationship. In a way, it is bringing back to us something that was lost in the development of mass marketing during the last thirty years.

In much of retailing prior to mass marketing, we had truly personal service, recognition and one-on-one relationships. In the average neighborhood, the grocer knew you and your family by sight. He knew what you wanted. He ordered things specially for you. He carried packages out to your car. He gave you credit. He talked to you as a friend. He established a two-way bond of communication that kept you as a loyal customer, made you feel appreciated and built his business.

Mass marketing ended this relationship. Stores grew larger and more impersonal. Price, not loyalty, ruled shopper's decisions. Prices went down, quality went up, competition increased. But personal service went down; individual recognition and loyalty faded away.

Through database marketing, it is today possible to recapture some of that one-on-one communication, some of that recognition and service that was lost in mass marketing.

Building Customer Relationships

The corner grocer kept his customers coming back because he knew them personally, greeted them by name, remembered their special requests and gave them personal, individual services. A modern customer database on a large mainframe computer allows a modern corporation to recreate many of these lost relationships and services.

Find out who your customers are, and build a database that contains not only their names and addresses, but also individual information vital to maintaining a close relationship, such as:

- purchasing history;
- family makeup: age, education, children, pets;
- purchasing ability: income, home value, assets, credit cards;
- occupations of all family members;
- leisure-time interests: hobbies, travel propensity, sports, what kind of car they drive;
- responsiveness to direct mail, to telemarketing, to buyer's clubs;
- media interests: magazines, TV, radio, newspapers and
- special requests, complaints, returns, refunds, mistakes.

This is basic information, the kind of data which the old corner grocer effortlessly kept in his head and recalled every time a customer walked into his store. Gathering this kind of information and storing it in a modern marketing database, through methods which are outlined in this book, is really not that difficult. Ten years ago it was too expensive to capture and use all this information effectively.

But the price of computers and software has declined dramatically, and the cost per piece of information stored is a fraction of one percent of what it cost little more than a decade ago.

The difficult feat, however, is making creative and productive use of this information in ways that will help your company to create a one-on-one dialog with customers, to build loyalty and repeat sales. This part of database marketing, the creative part, cannot be described as in a cookbook; it will vary with each business situation. What you will find in this book are hundreds of examples and suggestions to stimulate your imagination so that you can develop your own marketing strategy.

BASIC STRATEGIES

Some basic strategies are common to virtually all marketing databases:

- Develop a method for exchanging information with your customers.

- Build a comprehensive customer service system.

- Determine who your preferred customers are, and work to build their loyalty.

- Compute the lifetime value of your customers to determine the economics of your marketing system.

- Develop a customer profile, and use it to clone your best customers.

- Test and count. Make every marketing initiative an experiment to improve your understanding.

- Change roles and attitudes within your company to take maximum advantage of your new relationship with your customers.

- Set up a working team to manage your database effectively.

Let's explore these strategies.

Exchanging Information

One of the most valuable things that your company has to offer is something that is not even on your price list. It is information: information about what is available, how it works, what special features it has, how it compares with the competition, how to repair it, where to get it. In your ads, of course, you try to provide some of this data. But ads cluttered with information do not sell well—they must be kept simple.

Two groups are particularly eager for this information: your existing customers and your active prospects:

- I just bought a new Dodge *Colt Vista* 4-Wheel Drive car. It has a new kind of 4-wheel transmission. The salesmen couldn't explain it to me. The manual was uninformative. I would love to know how it works.

- Wordstar Version 6.0 has just been announced. How does it differ from Version 5.5? Is it worth it for me to upgrade?

Somewhere in your company there are people who have the answers to questions like these. Your strategy should be to find a way, inexpensively, to give your customers and prospects this kind of technical information, and make them feel good about having asked for it.

At the same time, your customers have information that you want and need for your marketing program:

- Why did they select your product?

- What features really persuaded them?

- What other products that you sell are they likely to buy this year?

Successful database marketing is a process of constantly exchanging information. Every contact with a customer (an owner registration form, a rebate coupon, an order form, a delivery receipt, a policy premium payment, a telephone call) becomes an occasion to ask a few more questions that provide more information for your database. At the same time, as you learn more and more about your customers, you will begin to appreciate what they want to find out or buy from you. Use each occasion to give them specialized and pertinent information—a fair exchange is no robbery.

Developing Relationships

Somewhere in the fine print in the instructions that come with your product you have included an 800 number. Support consists of a few pleasant but harassed operators and a telephone system which puts the customers constantly on hold listening to music. Does this sound like your company?

With database marketing, that strategy has to change. Your image has to change. Your company has to appear to your customers like an old and valued friend: someone who is always there, ready and willing to listen; ready to provide advice, help, suggestions, ideas, service, information. General Electric has pioneered with this approach. With database marketing, customer service becomes your front line. Your ads say that you are caring and helpful, but your customer service has to be caring and helpful. You must change your whole approach to customer service:

- You will need to have enough Customer Service Representatives (CSRs) so that your customers are seldom kept on hold for very long. Your Call Center has to have modern call distribution equipment as described in Chapter 17.

- CSRs must be trained to know all of your products intimately: their good and bad features, how they work, how they differ from the competition. Their functions are described in Chapter 11.

- Backing up your CSRs are scores or hundreds of people in many different departments throughout your organization who have been trained when called on by your CSRs to help build customer relationships by providing helpful information. These are people in engineering, in product design, in the warehouse, in delivery, in billing.

- Your CSRs are constantly gathering information from your customers and entering it into your database. When customers call, they get the names and addresses, and much more information—about lifestyles, reasons for buying the product, how it is used, what they want in the way of new products or new features. This information is retrieved instantly whenever the customer calls again. It is used in follow-up thank you letters, and new product announcements.

- Finally, your CSRs are always selling. Not the hard sell; the very soft sell. "Our new Version 4.0 gets around that problem. As an existing customer, you can trade up for only $179.95. I could have it sent out to you this afternoon."

Selecting Preferred Customers

Not all customers are alike. Some will buy from you again and again. Some buy once, then disappear forever. Most companies treat them all alike. With database marketing, your strategy changes: you use the database to determine who your best customers are and then you lavish your services and attention on them. At the same time, you provide minimum service to your least profitable segment. Why discriminate? Because it is more profitable to discriminate. You want your best customers to feel they are in a privileged class. You want to pamper them. You design and provide super services that you could not afford to give to all your customers.

How do you determine who your preferred customers are? RFM analysis, described in Chapter 7, provides a sophisticated analytical technique which can get you started. You will have to add your own ideas to it, based on your experience and your knowledge of your industry. The ranking system will rely on the information held in your marketing database. You will store your preference ranking in each customer's record. Then you will use that ranking to determine a whole range of benefits and services (described in Chapter 8) which will keep your best customers loyal and stimulate your second-best customers to buy more, so they also join the "preferred class."

As a part of your strategy, therefore, you must develop and install loyalty-building systems: preferred member clubs, news letters, new product announcements, sneak previews, gold cards, "loyal member nights." You will find ways to let everyone recognize your preferred customers: your employees, your dealers and the customers themselves.

Determining Lifetime Value

If it costs you $25 to acquire a new customer who buys a $50 item from you, you have probably lost money on that sale. But if that same customer, due to your marketing strategy, goes on to buy a $50 item from you several times a year for the next several years, your $25 was well spent.

Database marketing is based on the principle of lifetime value. When you acquire a customer, you try to determine what future sales you can expect from him or her. You can calculate contribution to profit and overhead for the customer's lifetime with your company. (This process is described in Chapter 10.) Once you know this, you can determine how much you can afford spend to acquire the customer, and how much you should spend on your marketing database and follow-up activities to keep him or her happy, loyal and buying.

Some executives fear that a marketing database is too expensive and doesn't pay for itself. This is a justified concern. But you needn't guess: you test, on a small scale, then you calculate lifetime value. You will soon find that it is possible to know exactly how much new business a marketing database will bring in, and whether you are making a profit or a loss from it.

Building a Customer Profile

Why do some people buy your product regularly, while others do not? This question has certainly been asked since the beginning of commerce. A marketing database can help to provide some answers.

The strategy: get them to tell you the information you need to answer this question. The answer could be a combination of several factors:

- How you have presented your product as compared with the competition.

- The perceived worth and reliability of your product compared with its price.

- The service and support you provide: the loyalty you have been able to build.

- The lifestyles, affluence, education, age, media preferences, ethnic makeup, sex and attitudes of your good customers, as compared with the people who are not buying your product.

The first three factors are within your power to change. The last factor can be investigated by *profiling your customers* (and non-customers). Profiling is a computer modeling process (described in Chapter 12) which enables you to use your database to choose, from the scores of facts known about customers and non-customers, those few attributes which seem to distinguish the buyers from the non-buyers. Once you have developed such a profile, you can use it in several ways:

- You can use it as a guide to change your marketing strategy to reach segments of the market that you have missed with your message.

- You can change your product, your pricing, your image.

- You can use it as a guide to seek out new prospects who have lifestyles that match your existing good customers. These prospects can be found reading the same media that your customers read, or you can rent their names on lists which have been coded according to the attributes you have deemed important.

Test and Count

Database strategy should always be tested. You think that something will work, but you can never be sure. The beauty of a marketing database is that you can build in response mechanisms that can prove in minute detail what happened (good and bad) to each of your marketing initiatives.

Whenever you write to your customers, you provide them with a response device coded with the source and a unique customer number, a postage paid business reply envelope, and, in most cases, a coupon, rebate offer, or some incentive which will get them to do what you want. You may also include a survey form to acquire more information.

When customers respond, the date, source code and survey data are all entered into the database. You count how many were returned, how many inquired, how many purchased. Your counts are in detail, and verify every aspect of your initiative:

- determine what type of customer responded; what type did not;

- calculate the rate of return on your investment in the initiative;

- compare customer response of those who received one inducement with the response of those who received another (or no inducement).

You should spend as much time planning how to get response, and how to measure and count response, as you do in any other aspect of marketing strategy. Testing and counting is learning. Learning produces knowledge. Knowledge helps you improve your strategy and increase your profits.

Changing Roles within Your Organization

Once you begin database marketing, nothing will stay the same. Your marketing strategy will change in many ways. Consider your dealers, for example. Most organizations operate on the assumption that they pay for national advertising, and a portion of local cooperative ads, but beyond that it is the dealer's job to find the customers, rope them in and sell them the product.

So where does the "lifetime value of a customer" fit into this scenario? Most dealers (automobile dealers, retail stores, hotels, travel agencies and so on) are too small to build a customer marketing database of their own. Most of them handle many products besides yours. So if you build the marketing database, how do the dealers fit into your strategy?

The answer is that you build them in as a part of your organization. You furnish them leads, and track their handling of the leads. You keep track of the customer: when his car is four years old, you begin to direct him to a local dealer and you direct a local dealer to him. A marketing database tends to bring the independent dealer closer to your company; he becomes a working member of your marketing team.

In a business-to-business product situation, salesforces usually operate independently of the marketing or advertising staffs. But with a database, the database telemarketers will qualify leads for the salesman, enabling him to spend more time with prospects who are ready to buy. In time, salesmen become more and more a functioning part of your marketing strategy.

Customer service reps, of course, take on a central role—they are your primary link to your customers, building relationships, providing information, extracting data, promoting loyalty, making sales. A marketing database always thrusts customer service into the forefront of marketing strategy.

Don't forget accounts receivable and delivery. Once you build a functioning marketing database, you will learn a great deal about your customers' feelings about the invoices they receive and their attitude towards the driver who comes to the door. Any service in your organization that touches the customer must be included in the database marketing system as a part of your total corporate image, as part of your one-on-one dialog with your customer.

You will soon find that the database is changing your company and its internal relationships.

Building a Database Team

A marketing database, by itself, will not bring you any of the benefits we have been discussing. It can only be profitable if it is a part of an integrated marketing strategy designed to extract data from customers, build loyalty, encourage repeat sales, include dealers and sales personnel in the loop and promote customer service. To implement this strategy, you will have to build a broad marketing team within the company, under the direction of a forceful leader with the funds and delegated authority to make the database work.

The Database Administrator (DBA) probably should be someone from marketing or sales, depending on your company. Working as active members of this team should be staff from:

- an external direct creative advertising agency,

- a telemarketing firm (or inside staff) that handles customer service and direct marketing,

- an external service bureau which manages the database (see Chapter 5 on why the database should not be built in-house), and

- your sales organization (and, if appropriate, whoever handles dealer relations).

After you organize your team, you will find that there are two types of people concerned with marketing databases:

- *Constructors*—those who are interested in putting together a functioning database, designing reports, cleaning the names and addresses, adding information to it, acquiring names and so on.

- *Creators*—those who are interested in figuring out how your company can make a profit by *using the database*. They tend to be the marketing, sales or advertising people. They will be the ones who come up with the exciting ideas for ways to cross-sell, to build continuity, to reduce attrition, to create loyalty.

Your team must be staffed with both kinds of people. If you are lacking either one, your database project will never get off the ground.

A marketing database should be operational within one year from the time that a contract with a service bureau is signed. To delay it for more than a year holds many dangers for your marketing strategy (see Chapter 5). At first, it should be tested with just a portion of your customer base. Gradually, as it proves itself, it should be expanded until it encompasses all of your repeat-business functions.

WHEN SHOULD YOU BEGIN TO BUILD A MARKETING DATABASE?

Because the learning curve and the return on investment begin after the database is operational, not during the planning phase, begin to build your database as soon as possible. You will begin to understand your customers, build loyalty and repeat sales only after the database is constructed and working to carry out your marketing strategy.

Thirty years ago, Congress voted to begin shifting the American economy gradually to the metric system. There was to be an educational and planning process, followed by a full conversion at a future date. You know the results. What has come of the thirty years of planning? How many people today know whether a room temperature of 30 degrees centigrade is hot or cold?

The lesson: planning for a marketing database will not do anything for the bottom line. Only an actual functioning database will get you the benefits you seek. (Chapter 28 contains a checklist to be used when you begin to set up a marketing database. I suggest you review this checklist now to get an overview of what lies ahead.)

Some Cautions

- A marketing database will cost money. It requires a budget and top-level support to overcome the many obstacles in its formative years.

- Marketing databases are new, charting unexplored territory. They raise issues, such as personal privacy, which, if not handled properly could bring down the wrath of consumer groups and the dead hand of federal regulation on what promises to be an innovative and useful marketing strategy.

- A marketing database requires very imaginative and creative leadership within the company if it is to succeed. Such leadership is hard to find. Unless that kind of talent can be found, all the committees and planning will come to nothing.

WHERE WE ARE GOING

Those who have caught the database marketing bug (including the author) are very excited about it and its possibilities for making America a better place to live. It is not just a better way to sell products and services; it is a way of bringing back something that we have lost during the mass-marketing fervor since the 1960s. It is a way of restoring the personal contact with customers that we all enjoyed in earlier years, when you knew your merchants and they knew you, recognized you, appreciated you and did personal favors and services for you on a regular basis.

Database marketing, when done properly, will restore loyalty and personal recognition as important aspects of the business relationships which all will come to experience and enjoy. It will be more individual, more personal, more satisfying. It should help us get the products and services we want, and should help to reduce the costs of those products and services.

Across America, the message has spread. Hundreds of marketing databases are being built. Probably your principal competitors have already started. Once their databases are up and running, they will be learning how to reduce attrition and how to win over your customers. Don't give them too much of a head start!

Part One

What Is a Marketing Database?

Chapter 1

What Marketing Databases Do

In my youth I had an Irish governess named Annie Kearney who came over from the "old country" about 1880. Whenever she encountered a silver coin—a dime, a quarter or half-dollar—she would bite it to see if it was genuine. She taught me to do this, and to this day I can tell silver from other metals by biting. It was a skill apparently needed in the Ireland of her day, and perhaps also in early 20th century America. Counterfeiters were active.

The average person has little use for this skill today. Counterfeiters seem to have gone into retirement and the government isn't making coins out of silver anymore. It is one more thing that we don't have to worry about.

In fact, there are hundreds of things that we don't have to worry about anymore:

- The products we buy in a supermarket are pure, fresh and safe (albeit laced with government-approved food additives and preservatives). This was not always so.

- If you put your money in a checking account or a savings bank, the money is safe—it won't disappear even when the bank goes belly-up due to mismanagement (although the taxpayer eventually ends up paying the bill). From 1930-1933 there were 7,763 banks that went bankrupt, and most of their depositors lost everything.

- Insurance companies, in general, can be relied upon to pay you what your policy says they will pay.

- Cars do not disintegrate as soon as you buy them (as many did in the 1950s).

- Radial tires, in general, last for 50,000 miles without ever going flat or losing air. (I spent much time in my teens and twenties changing flats and having relatively new tires recapped because they were worn smooth.)

- When you buy a dishwasher or a computer, it works. And if it doesn't, the manufacturer and the dealer will stand behind it.

- Money for many people is no longer a problem. Most households today own at least one credit card with a substantial credit limit. Almost every household has a checking account, most with overdraft protection.

What has brought about this happy state of affairs where the consumer has so few worries? Many things:

Mass advertising and mass marketing. A major company simply cannot afford to risk many millions of dollars and its market share position advertising something that has basic flaws, so they are more careful than they used to be about what they offer for sale.

Intense competition. There are three or four major producers of almost everything that a consumer or a business could possibly buy. Competition improves quality and lowers prices.

Widespread information. Through TV, newspapers, magazines, radio, yellow pages and a walk through any large supermarket or department store, the average person is exposed to much more reliable information about availability and prices than can possibly be absorbed.

Constantly advancing technology. Technology is racing ahead. Every week new products come out with surprising new features. The public has come to accept and expect this. There is little resistance to trying something new. Competitors hasten to match each innovation.

Easy credit. Almost anyone can buy almost anything on credit. This has made it immensely easier to sell and to buy.

America today is a much better place for the consumer and the business customer than it once was. Products are better, and the level of trust is higher. We now worry about much higher-level issues: stress, keeping our families together, finding time to fit in all our desired activities. We have moved several notches higher on the Maslow scale of values.

MASLOW SCALE OF VALUES

In 1950, Abraham Maslow wrote a paper which changed thinking about human values. He described a hierarchy of values for all people. At their most basic, people need air and food. They will sacrifice everything else if they cannot breathe or they are starving. When these needs are satisfied they look for shelter from the elements.

Above security needs comes love: to love and to be loved. And above love is the desire to belong: to a family, to a group, to a company.

Above love and belonging is self esteem: pride in yourself and what you do, and a confidence that you can do your work well, that you are an effective person—living your life as it should be lived. This is the level that most people are striving for, and that we hope to facilitate with our products and services. Cars are sold on the basis of pride and self esteem. The Gold American Express Card or the President's Club of a hotel chain cater to this need.

The highest level is self fulfillment, or what Maslow called "Self Actualization." In this state people feel that they are truly living a life that brings out their most creative possibilities: a musician who writes what he considers a great symphony; an author who writes what he believes is a wonderful book; a marketing professional who successfully creates a functioning and profitable marketing database. Selling Cadillacs or Mercedes to people at this level will not be enough. They already have self esteem, pride and confi-

Figure 1-1   Mankind Tries to Satisfy Higher Needs

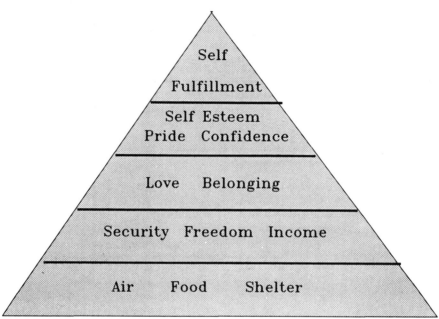

dence; you have to find a way to help them to achieve self actualization.

The interesting thing about the values that Maslow noted is that once you have attained a level, you worry about the next higher level. People rarely look down to see how far they have come. They look up to see how far they have to go. People seldom say "Well, at least I have enough air to breathe."

If we are going to reach customers, Maslow would argue, we must appeal to their current value needs. There is no point in offering love or belonging to a starving group. Nor does it help to offer basic food or shelter to someone who already has a job and a family.

WHAT CUSTOMERS WANT TODAY

What do customers want today? What are those higher levels that we have moved to?

Diversity

Our basic needs for products are satisfied; now we want something a little different. We have caught up with the Joneses, now we want to catch up with our own personal, special needs. We don't want a standard dining room table, we want a 5 foot oval glass table with brass legs that exactly fits in an area on our glass covered patio. We don't want regular dog food, we want dog food especially made for our very old dog who is getting fat and has halitosis. We can't find these things in a department store or supermarket, and it is a waste of time asking for them there.

Special Services

In the last few years, my wife and I have been working at our offices until almost eight o'clock every night. We have become like most two-income families: not enough time to shop. We are looking for plumbers and air conditioning men who will come in and fix things without our having to stay home to let them in; someone who will take care of our trees and fertilize our lawn while we are away; a delivery service that will leave things at the door. We shop by catalog and telephone.

My wife and I rent about three movies every week. I waste at least an hour and a half every week choosing them. I really want a video store that knows me and what I like, and would get a movie ready for me three times a week so I could just swing by and grab it. I haven't been able to find such a store.

Information

Despite the barrage of information coming at us from scores of sources every day, we find it difficult to acquire the information that we need in our relatively complicated lives. We have bought a slick software package for our computer, but we really can't figure out how to make it work properly. We need some expert to show us. Where can we find such an expert? The salesmen in the stores either don't know or are too busy to show us. There is probably an article in some magazine that would be very helpful, but how do we find the right article in the right magazine?

Attention

Everyone seems too busy to talk to you. Many employees in large stores either don't have the information that we need or are too busy and distracted to be of any help.

I have at last reached the point in my life where I am able to save some money every month. For several years I searched for someone who could give me some practical and helpful advice on what to put my money into: CD's? Bonds? Stocks? IRA's? Real estate? Annuities? I tried them all and, in the process, lost a lot of money in the stock market. I was looking for someone that I could talk to who would take some interest in me and my financial situation, not just in selling what he was selling. I finally found such a person. I talk to him on the phone. We have never met, but he knows me. He has my complete financial history on some marketing database, and he discusses my financial situation with me whenever I call him. He has never steered me wrong. I am saving more, paying (somewhat) lower taxes and I do not worry about losing my nest egg.

Recognition

A couple of years ago I joined the American Airlines Admiral's Club. It provides me with access to a private lounge in many major airports complete with a bar, conference rooms, telephones, clean rest rooms, free crackers and cheese, magazines and newspapers, television, Xerox and fax machines, personal computers and airline reservation service. It is only $125 per year, and everyone who has the money can join it. But belonging to it, and being greeted with special service with my reservations is really worth the money. For that $125, I have bought some recognition that makes me feel a little better when I am in a strange place thousands of miles from home. Membership has its privileges, and one of them is recognition.

DATABASE MARKETING MEETS THESE NEEDS

We can summarize the higher level needs today as:

- Diversity
- Information
- Service
- Personal Attention
- Recognition

How does database marketing help to meet these higher level needs?

A marketing database consists of a large collection of information about each customer and prospect. Most of the information is provided by the customer in orders, telephone calls and surveys. The information is arranged on a database that can be called up instantly whenever the customer is on the telephone, or has written a letter.

The telephone system can be tied to the computer in such a way that the computer learns the telephone number from which each incoming call is placed and automatically looks up that number in it's database, bringing the complete customer record effortlessly to the screen as the operator is receiving the call. The system enables Customer Service or Sales to recognize customers by name and remind them that their previous sales and interests are considered and used as guidelines in meeting their needs.

Behind the database is a huge warehouse of products, bigger in diversity than could be stocked in any single store or in all the stores in a single city. The sales staff has a product database at their fingertips which lists everything the company makes, not just the most popular items. They can get customers exactly what they want.

Also behind the database is a network that provides more information about this line of products than could be provided in any store. Does the customer want to get a replacement for the glass

Exhibit 1-2   How a Marketing Database Works

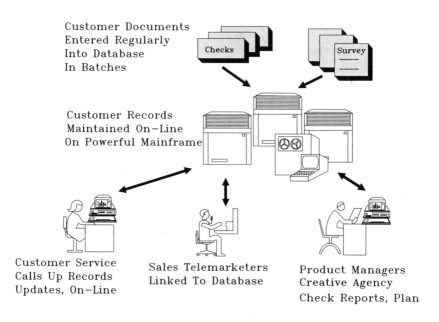

Customer Documents
Entered Regularly
Into Database
In Batches

Checks

Survey

Customer Records
Maintained On–Line
On Powerful Mainframe

Customer Service
Calls Up Records
Updates, On–Line

Sales Telemarketers
Linked To Database

Product Managers
Creative Agency
Check Reports, Plan

screen on the front? Know how to change the filter? Know what attachments come with it and what they cost? For technical questions, the customer can be routed to an expert—perhaps even the individual who designed it. He or she can find out when it was shipped, by what carrier and when it is likely to arrive.

The database permits personal services. We all have become accustomed to the super service provided today by travel agencies. They can book us on complicated tours across the country, have hotel rooms and rental cars waiting for us at each stop and deliver tickets and boarding passes to us, with a printed itinerary, the next day. All it takes is a short telephone call. It works because at the travel agent's fingertips is an airline computer database network which is linked to most airlines, hotels and car rental services.

A marketing database takes that concept one step further. A marketing database tells the travel agent that you prefer window seats, you always use a VISA® card of a certain number, you prefer American Airlines® and are an Advantage® member, you always fly economy class, you prefer Avis cars and the St. Francis in San Francisco and the Plaza in New York. The agent knows where to deliver your tickets without asking, knows your spouse's name and office phone number. You needn't repeat all these facts every time. They are on your database record.

DIVERSIFYING YOUR PRODUCT MIX

Database marketing will have a profound effect on the product and service mix of the companies that take it seriously. The general effect will be to widen the line, to diversify and add new flavors, features and sizes.

When CocaCola® decided in their executive wisdom to change the formula of their product, the public revolted. People were outraged. CocaCola had to bring back the old formula as "Classic Coke®" and, at the same time, decided to introduce Cherry Coke®, Caffeine Free Coke® and other innovations, so that CocaCola ended up with more products and shelf space in the average store than they had before. The consumers spoke, and CocaCola listened. The result was a remarkable resurgence for a company that had been perceived as being in decline.

But CocaCola was more than a household word. It was an American institution, which a mere board of directors was not meant to tamper with. When you decide to change your product, you may not be so lucky. There won't be any protest meetings. Your unhappy customers may just decide to shift to buying your competitor's product, and you won't have a clue as to why. Your first reaction may be to fire your advertising agency, on the grounds that the right words can sell anything. If you do get a new advertising agency, let us hope that the replacement suggests a marketing database, because it is one of the surest ways of really listening to the "Heartbeat of America."

All of us have said, many times, "why don't they just . . . ," completing the phrase with, "make a product that would . . . ," or "make their product easier to . . . ." How do you get through to the executives who make these decisions and tell them what you think? It is almost impossible.

I had an experience which really bothered me. In the early 1970s, I became addicted to Shape®, a dry powder food sold in supermarkets. Shape powder mixed with milk made a great breakfast drink (similar to Carnation Instant Breakfast). It was filling; it helped me to lose weight. One day, the product just disappeared from the stores. I was frantic. I went from store to store—no one had it. I called Giant Food, and was told that the manufacturer had stopped producing it. "Could I buy up some of his residual stock?" I asked. Yes, it was possible. A couple of weeks later, Giant Food delivered a special order of twelve cases to me. I was able to enjoy it for about six months until I ran out forever.

Today, of course, similar products are everywhere, but it took more than ten years—I have gone on to other things for breakfast. How many other people like me were upset at this product's disappearance? Who knows. Certainly the manufacturer didn't know, and made no attempt to find out. Why didn't he continue to make it, since there was obviously a market for this type of product? It is everywhere today. The main reason was that in the 1970s we were in the midst of mass marketing. Manufacturers were fighting for shelf space in supermarkets. If your sales did not warrant a decent display, you pulled out altogether. There were no alternate channels of distribution. Sell big or die. The same thing was happening to television shows, where Nielsen ratings doomed excellent show after excellent show because they did not have ratings as good as other shows.

Database marketing promises to change this picture. By setting up a dialog with your customers you should be able to anticipate what they want: not just what they think about what you are producing now, but what they would like to see you produce in the way of changed products and services in the future. With the knowledge that you accumulate, you will be able to make wise decisions about changing your products and services, broadening your market and finding alternate means of delivering products which may have a multi-million dollar sales potential, but are too small for supermarket shelf space.

WHAT DO COMPANIES WANT?

It would be an oversimplification to concentrate too much on the personal services side of database marketing. It is true that the main advantages *for the customer* are the recognition, personal attention, information and diversity of products which a marketing database provides. Marketing databases also provide very practical benefits for the company which maintains them. What are they?

Repeat Business

Your best prospects are your own satisfied customers. Most companies don't realize this even today. They use coupons, rebates, cashback and discounts to win over customers that they already have. A marketing database builds customer loyalty; builds repeat business. Marketing database theory studies the *lifetime value of a customer:* from this, any company can learn how much they can afford to spend on acquiring a customer because they know how much that customer will be worth to them in repeat business.

Reduced Costs

A repeat sale costs, at most, half of what the first sale cost (and possibly much less than half). Overall, a lot of repeat business can bring total costs down and profits up.

Increased Loyalty

Loyalty means more than simply repeat sales. It means that customers spread the word for you. It means that they will support you if you fail (occasionally). It means that they will buy new products that you are launching just because they are loyal to your present products.

Market Segmentation

Some companies feel that the chief advantage of a marketing database is its ability to separate out categories of users: loyalists, occasional users, switchers, competitive brand loyalists. Once you have identified these types you can design marketing strategies to win over the competitive brand loyalists while keeping your own customers satisfied.

Prospect Identification

Many companies have no clear idea of who is buying their products. They hire agencies to make up colorful ads, which seem to do the trick because their market share does not decline. But they don't really know who these customers are. Marketing databases identify them. Once you have profiled your customers, you can use lists and media surveys to locate new prospects who match that profile.

Product and Service Feedback

The world changes rapidly, particularly in a competitive, capitalistic democracy like ours. What was a perfectly good product two years ago may be outdated today. All companies must be alert to market trends: to what their customers are telling them about what they want. There is no better way to stay on top of the market than an actively functioning marketing database that maintains a two-way dialog with consumers and provides weekly reports on what they are asking for and thinking. If you don't listen to your customers every day, rest assured that your competitors will.

Other Company Benefits

Marketing databases do other things for a company:

Internal Restructuring. They can bring Marketing, Sales and Customer Service together into a single system which will reduce costs, improve sales and reduce harmful infighting.

Lead Qualification and Tracking. They can be used to set up a system to profile leads before salesmen get them, and to track action on them from inquiry to contract, thereby increasing sales and reducing the cost of sales.

Improved Internal Information. They can be used to set up a reporting system within the company which will bring everyone from top management through sales, marketing, product development, inventory management, advertising and accounts receivable into the information loop.

Better Dealer Relations. They can be used to improve relations with your dealers by giving them instant notice of leads and data on the prospects.

CONCEPTS FOR MARKETING DATABASES

Following are some examples of the ways that companies can use the marketing database concept to provide a profitable dialog with their customers.

- An electronics company packs a warranty card inside every electronic clock shipped out. The card asks the name, address and other information about the customer which will be useful later: Does he have a VCR? Does he have a CD player? Does he have a Walkman? What is his educational level? What is the household income? What is his age? His occupation? Are there young children in the house? Where did he learn about the clock? Magazine, Newspaper, TV, Radio, Direct Mail, saw it in the store?

  When these cards come in, they are keypunched and used to form a database which is used to market other products made by the manufacturer.

- A baby food company sends out coupons to every mother of newborns in America. The coupon is coded so that, when redeemed, the company knows exactly who redeemed it. The coupon also asks additional questions and promises a second, even more valuable coupon by return mail if the mother fills out the questions and checks a box on the coupon. The coupons form the beginning of a database which can follow the child through infancy to preschool, school and college; thus winning brand loyalty for the company's food and related products.

- A quick-lube company has all customers fill out a work order form. This form triggers a follow-up mailing three months later inquiring about the service and asking many other questions that will be useful later, and also enclosing a new lube coupon. The work order forms become the foundation of a database that will track these customers from car to car.

- A car sales promoter obtains a tape of all the automobile registrations in his state (about half the states in America rent these lists). Then he goes to automobile dealer showrooms throughout the state, promising to fill their showrooms on a specific Saturday morning with people wanting to test drive the latest models. He mails coupons to car owners within driving distance of the showroom, promising a free gift and a chance in a drawing for a car if they will test drive on Saturday. The owners have been selected by demographics and make, model and year of their present car. When they respond, they go into a respondent database. They will receive other mailings.

- A bank compiles a list of all its customers—which is often not as easy as it sounds. Normally in banks, each account is a separate listing with a separate name and address. Loan accounts are often on different computer files and in a different format from deposit accounts. Putting the entire Customer Information File (CIF) together by *household* is a major undertaking which most MIS departments find overwhelming. Once the database is compiled, the file is enhanced with geodemographics and lifestyle codes, and the bank begins a series of personalized mailings encouraging cross-selling of other bank products. When the customer does buy another product, his record is flagged as someone responsive to direct marketing. He will be approached again.

- American Express® is probably the most effective credit card company in the world in terms of database creation. They pioneered the concept of *membership* in which each card holder is a member of American Express and has certain privileges which are associated with the membership. They take pains to learn what kind of customer you are and use this knowledge in their marketing activities.

- A pet food manufacturer introduces a new high-end product not sold in stores. The announcement is made on TV, in print and by direct mail. Customers call an 800 number to order food shipped once a month automatically, with pre-paid home delivery (you needn't be there). As each call is received by the operators, the information goes directly into an on-line database where a record of all the customer's prior purchases are stored. The operators, thus, are knowledgeable about the customers, and can ask them for feedback on the product.

- A cosmetic manufacturer requires each customer to have a facial exam by a trained specialist before buying its products. Customers are then admitted as lifetime members with all of the pertinent data recorded in a database. All subsequent purchases are tracked by point-of-sale units triggered when the customers pass their membership cards to salesclerks in one of 400 department store outlets. In this way, very personalized customer service and follow-up can be maintained—"For as long as you own your face"—with resulting brand loyalty and increased sales.

- A cruise line has passengers fill out a comprehensive questionnaire during the cruise (there is plenty of free time). The data is used to trigger personalized follow-up mailings announcing new ships, new cruise locations and new features, and suggesting that you name some friends who might like to share your joy. These prospects are immediately sent to the travel agent who originally booked the passenger. This travel agent is a key part of the database and is a *specific target* in subsequent follow-up mailings. The travel agent has life and death power over cruise bookings: no one knows as much about the differences between various lines; the travel agent can steer customers in any direction. The database, thus, is a means of cultivating the travel agent as much as (or more than) the passenger.

- A drug company maintains a database of doctors who specialize in the ailments which their drugs alleviate. Salespeople visit these doctors, leaving samples and discussing the products. The salespeople have laptop computers which are used to plan their weekly activities and to record the results of each call. Every night they transmit the results of their activities to a central database, which thus contains details on what is happening in the field, what the doctors are thinking about the product, how the samples are moving, how well salespeople are doing their jobs. If a doctor visits one of their booths at a convention or answers a coupon in a medical publication, the information is logged in the doctor's record in the database. Direct mailings to the doctors announce new products and send monographs on existing products as they come off the press. Gifts and other emoluments go to the participating doctors. Patients are guided to the doctors by coupons reimbursed by the drug manufacturer.

- Another drug manufacturer maintains a database of 7,000,000 households in which reside persons who suffer from specific ailments remedied by their drugs. These people were discovered by household questionnaires which included a valuable premium for response. A series of newsletters about health which focus on the ailments in question go directly to the households which have responded to coupons. The sufferers may be prompted to visit specific doctors, with coupons. They may receive monographs on the products.

- A video store keeps track by category of what movies its clients rent. As new releases of interest to the clients appear (comedy, children's, sports, musicals), clients receive personalized announcements. They are invited to become members of the "sneak preview" club in which they receive notice of new movies which are not among the latest bestsellers. As club members, they learn first of these movies and they fill out an extensive evaluation of the movie, which is then averaged in with other responses to develop a "viewer's guide" available to all members. The "sneak preview" works in several ways: it helps promote the rental of older movies; it builds brand loyalty for the store; it helps the store know what movies to buy. The store also gives credit towards valuable prizes for each movie rented. Monthly mailings notify the members of the points they have accumulated, and encourage them to rent a few more in order to qualify for a valuable gift.

■ A major telephone company keeps track of all of its yellow page listings in a database. The database has the type of ad, size of ad, history of advertising, the heading and other information. Each year there is an annual season for each book in which subscribers can sign up for a new ad. The database is used to *compare and contrast* the ads taken out by (unnamed) competitors of each subscriber in the same and other books published throughout the system. In this way, an auto rental company can learn something about its competitors which would otherwise take considerable research to find out: how many other auto rental companies take out ads, and the size of those ads compared to its ads not only in the local book, *but in all other books in the system.*

■ A supermarket establishes a frequent buyers club for householders who live near the store. To join, members fill out a family history questionnaire, and are given a special card to use when shopping at the store. Before going through the checkout line, they hand in their card. As each item is run through the scanner, their purchase is recorded in their own database record. In this way, the supermarket knows exactly what everyone bought and when. Once a month householders get a check for dollar credits they have earned. But more importantly, the store learns a great deal about its patrons which it can use in planning promotions, stocking new items, giving better service. When a family starts buying diapers and baby food, a set of special marketing programs is triggered; if they start buying pet food, a different program ensues. The database earns revenue for the store through renting the names to manufacturers of baby food, pet food or other products to use in *their* databases.

REQUIREMENTS FOR MARKETING DATABASES

Any good marketing database must meet certain requirements, as described on the following page:

Custom Design. There is no such thing as a good generic marketing database—it must be custom designed for the company that is using it.

Dynamic. Constant change in the data, the software and the applications are the rule in a good marketing database. Just as you cannot maintain market share by selling a single product without change in the same way year after year, you cannot market to your customers in the same way. They will tell you things you will have to listen to. Their ideas will force you to modify your marketing plan. A revised plan means a revised database.

Huge. Any marketing database must maintain a tremendous amount of information about every customer. It will require extensive memory and a very powerful computer.

Universally available. Many parts of the company must be able to access the database at the same time. If it is available only to customer service or marketing it is not yet doing its job.

Loaded with reports. All good marketing databases provide a wide variety of reports on a regular basis for users throughout the company.

Profitable. Built into any marketing database must be an accounting system which shows clearly what the database is costing and what benefits it is providing. All good marketing databases, in addition to improving company profits, also can demonstrate how they are doing so by means of very precise systems of measurement.

Stand Alone. A properly functioning marketing database is not on the same system with other company MIS functions such as general ledger, payroll, inventory, production control or customer accounts. There must be a data link between them so that the database can keep up to date on sales and shipments. But marketing requires several features not present in normal MIS functions, among them on-line access, seven-day-a-week activity, constant software changes, addition of prospects and leads as well as customers, merge/purge, profiling involving multiple regressions and other statistical functions and matching of the file with outside data sources.

Controlled by a DBA. All functioning marketing databases are under the control of a Database Administrator (DBA). This is someone in Marketing or Product Management who has the final word on all software and data changes in the database. The DBA does not have to go through MIS or other layers to issue orders to the service bureau or others who manage the software. The DBA determines the priority of users on the system, and assures that the database improves the company bottom line through dynamic marketing and customer services.

SUMMARY

Consumers today have more confidence in the products and services they buy than consumers thirty years ago. They have fewer money worries. They have easy credit.

Customers today are seeking higher levels of satisfaction than can be met by mass marketing. They are looking for:

- Diversity in their products and services.
- Special services.
- Information.
- Personal Attention.
- Recognition.

Marketing databases meet these needs in a way that cannot be matched by mass marketing methods. The first reason for having a marketing database, therefore, is that it is the only way to meet today's customer's needs.

Companies install marketing databases because they provide several important benefits to the company:

- More repeat business.
- Reduced costs of sales.
- Increased customer loyalty.
- Ability to segment the market and treat each customer differently.
- Ability to profile customers and identify prospects.

- Ability to learn from customers how the product is being received, so that products and services can be improved.

- Marketing databases tend to bring Sales, Marketing and Customer Service into a single system which reduces costs and company infighting.

- Marketing databases disseminate information and reports throughout the company.

- Lead tracking and dealer relations can be improved.

A marketing database must meet certain requirements:

- Custom design—each company's database is different.

- Dynamic—software must be constantly changed.

- Huge—a good database requires a huge mainframe and company-wide access.

- Stand alone—separate from the MIS computer functions.

- Directed by marketing—under the control of a Database Administrator.

- Profitable—it must improve the bottom line, and prove it.

Chapter 2

The History of Database Marketing

Almost all of the techniques discussed in this book exist today. Somewhere in America, they are being tested and in many cases are working successfully. But not more than 1% of the companies in America is actively using the full potential of database marketing. Why is this so?

Database marketing is the culmination of a long chain of successful developments in marketing and selling products and services in America, beginning with the earliest advertising, through mass marketing, direct marketing, coupons, catalogs and frequent-flyer clubs, to the beginning of real database marketing today.

The position of database marketing in American business today is similar to the position of the automobile in American society in 1900. The automobile is essential to our present lifestyles, but the automobile requires a very elaborate infrastructure to make it work. In 1900, all this was in the future. A few rich people had cars. There were almost no paved roads, bridges, parking places, service stations, mechanics, laws, signals, insurance, financing. We built all this step by step as the need arose, without a real plan; without really knowing where we were going or what it was doing to our lifestyle.

The same is true of database marketing. It too will have a revolutionary impact on our lives—perhaps not as revolutionary as the automobile, but fully as widespread and pervasive. Well into the next century, database marketing will be so built into our business system and culture that it will be impossible to conceive of life without it. Every successful business will use it. It will be difficult to sustain a successful sales program for goods or services without it. Competition will insure that this is so.

Let us explore how we got to where we are today, and what is likely to happen in the future.

MEDIA DICTATES THE MARKETING METHOD

Every system for advertising, marketing, selling and delivering goods has been influenced, if not built around, the media which existed at the time. From the earliest years, print advertising existed. The newspapers which carried ads were local, with most of the advertising limited to businesses within the delivery area of the paper. There were few national brands. The birth of direct marketing came about through the Montgomery Ward catalog in 1884, the Sears Roebuck catalog in 1897 and the Spiegel catalog in 1905. Sears was only possible because the mail system, by that time, was beginning to reach most of the cities and rural communities, and the railway express was beginning to develop the capability of delivering goods to catalog recipients. By 1902, Sears had an annual business of more than $50 million from their catalog.

One of the next milestones in direct marketing was the founding of the Book-of-the-Month Club in 1926 by Harry Sherman and Maxwell Sackheim, based on their experience in direct marketing. By 1990, more than half of all hardcover books were sold by direct mail.

But for most of the twentieth century, catalog marketing was always considered a backwater, an aberration, an obscure method for unloading second-class goods on rural people. The real money was thought to be only in national advertising.

National brands became possible through national media: big city newspapers linked to national advertising agencies, magazines with national circulation, the radio and, later, television. When national advertising was born, a whole new world opened up for merchandising. The public and the business community were mesmerized by the riches, the fantastic profits that resulted from delivering the right message about soap or cigarettes through these new national media. The nation became fascinated by Madison Avenue, symbolized by the "Hucksters" and "The Man in the Gray Flannel Suit." Advertising developed its own rules, culture, systems, agencies and profits.

Successful advertising aims at creating a powerful image of a national brand in the minds of consumers. Manufacturers wanting this service were trained not to expect immediate results. The introduction of a new product required tens or hundreds of millions of dollars of advertising designed to stimulate a sequence of related events:

Awareness of the existence of the product and its name (Camay, the soap of beautiful women),

Knowledge of the product and what it could do for the consumer (softer, lovelier complexion),

Image—what life would be like if only one used the product (admiration, adoring glances, the skin you love to touch),

Preference for this product over other products (unlike cheap imitations, Camay . . .), and

Purchase—the actual sale of the product (available at fine stores everywhere).

Building this sequence of events took years. No one expected a new product to break even in less than a year; rather, it could take two years or more. But the rich benefits of creating a brand name image paid off in huge sustained sales to loyal customers for years to come. Soap and cigarette manufacturers (to mention only two) became rich. Advertising agencies became rich. Magazines and television became rich.

SUPERMARKETS

After World War II, this whole process was changed by the introduction of a new media: the supermarket. I classify a supermarket as a media because, like an advertisement, it offers the manufacturer a chance to display his product, together with a message on the package, to millions of potential buyers.

I remember when the first supermarket came to my community. I grew up in New Canaan, Connecticut during the Thirties and Forties. We always shopped for groceries at Gristedes or the First National store. These were modern shops with large overhead fans instead of air conditioning, and products stacked from the floor to the 10-foot high ceiling. To shop, you got the attention of a clerk at the main counter and asked him to get items for you. He would scurry about the store to find them, stacking them up on the counter. For items stacked high, he had a long stick with a grabber on one end and a hand-operated squeezer on the other. Customers didn't wander about the store; they were waited on.

I remember the curiosity with which we drove to Stamford to investigate the first supermarket in our area. How strange it was to push a shopping cart down the many aisles, grabbing packages out of sight of the employees. "This will never work," we said, "if you let people handle the products before they have bought them, they will steal you blind."

But, of course, it *did* work. Supermarkets sprang up everywhere, squeezing the "regular" grocery stores out of business. Perhaps the ultimate triumph of this worldwide movement appeared in 1987 in Lago Ranco, an impoverished backwater community in the south of Chile in South America: dirt roads, ruined buildings, and about ten pathetic tiny shops displayed rusting cans and distressed vegetables. But over the door of each shop was a hand-lettered sign proclaiming the establishment to be a "Super-mercado."

With the growth of supermarkets, the customer played a much bigger role in the product selection process. The appearance of the package and the shelf space devoted to it in the store became more important, almost, than what was actually in the box. An interesting case study of several years ago detailed the effort that went into designing and testing consumer response to the box of a new breakfast cereal for a national manufacturer. After they created a box that consumers really responded to, they spent a couple of months at the end of the process figuring out what to put into it.

While advertising was directed at the consumer, a good part of it was also aimed at the owners of the supermarkets. If they were going to accord shelf space to a new product, they wanted to see evidence of a huge national advertising campaign to support it. The campaign would bring customers into the supermarket looking for the product or give them awareness and knowledge of it. This awareness would tempt a purchase when they encountered it while they walked down the aisles looking for something else.

During the 1950s and 1960s, we entered the era of mass marketing through the fast-growing new supermarkets. The vast spaces in these stores permitted the stocking of three or four brands and two or more sizes of each product, and a much wider variety of new products. Advertising designed to get this lucrative shelf space really took off. Everyone was looking for an edge, a gimmick to beat the

Figure 2-1 Advertising Spending 1989 (In Billions of Dollars)

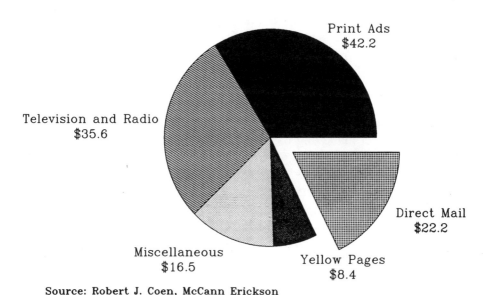

Source: Robert J. Coen, McCann Erickson

competition. For a while, people went crazy with "green stamps," which were handed out in every store with purchases—after you filled up several books with them, you could exchange them for suitcases or a set of china. They were the rage for several years, but have now died out almost completely. They were designed to stimulate loyalty to a particular supermarket chain, since each one offered different, non-exchangeable stamps.

Then came the next media: the coupon. "Twenty-five cents off" proved to be a powerful draw. Millions of people began clipping their daily papers and opening their mail to save up stacks of coupons for their weekly shopping expedition. The beauty of coupons, as compared to general advertising or stamps, was that you put something into people's hands to remind them of what they wanted when they went to the store. *And* that same coupon was left with the store manager to remind him of why you came into his store.

THE ROLE OF DIRECT MARKETING

Direct marketing is any technique designed to provoke a direct response to the advertising stimulus. Catalogs, 800 numbers and coupons are all a part of it. Direct marketing differs from general advertising in that the response is direct, immediate and measurable: you send out 100,000 letters and measure the response exactly. Usually the response can be predicted in advance. Good direct marketers are usually correct to a fraction of a percent.

But direct marketing has never had the glamour of general advertising. Direct marketing operates out of the national limelight. It is involved with catalogs, with direct mail and with free-standing coupons inserted in magazines. There is some direct response TV (DRTV) of course, and its use is growing, but it is still small compared to general advertising on TV.

One of the most important boons to direct marketing came about in the 1950s with the introduction of plastic credit cards. Diner's Club and American Express came first, followed by the "bank cards," Visa and MasterCard. These cards really permitted mail-order transactions to take off as never before.

DIRECT MAIL HAS BECOME PROFESSIONAL

The low-profile direct mail industry has attracted some big bucks. Almost $25 billion dollars was spent on direct mail during 1990, and the industry continues to grow steadily by about 10 percent per year. The telemarketing industry, both inbound at 800 numbers and outbound to homes and businesses, accounted for almost $20 billion in spending during 1990. Mail order is growing faster than retail sales.

Direct mail is really the foundation of database marketing. Probably the best book on direct mail ever written is *The Complete Direct Mail List Handbook,* by Ed Burnett. Burnett, one of the best known and most respected men in the business, has been at it for a long time.

Direct mail professionals pioneered working with lists of customers and prospects and matching them against census data. They built up national lists of households which contain amazing amounts of information about what goes on and what is spent in each one. They pioneered the Recency Frequency Monetary analytical techniques described in this book, and the concepts of demographic overlays, clustering and modeling. Above all, they created a very accountable profession where results can be measured and predicted precisely; there is a maximum of bottom-line and a minimum of mumbo-jumbo or advertising hype.

Computer Technology Leads Direct Mail to Database Marketing

In the early years, almost all direct mail lists were kept on magnetic tape. Direct mail and telemarketed response is "keypunched" and compared with output to determine the percentage return down to minute fractions. The "two percent" rule became known and accepted: in any successful direct mail campaign, you will achieve a two percent response or better. The corollary—that 98 percent of your letters will result in no response—has also been accepted as a part of the cost of doing business.

When direct mail people began working with computers, they noticed some things that were going on around them:

- The price of mainframe and micro-computers was actually going down every year, while the machines themselves were growing more and more sophisticated and powerful.

- The sophistication and usefulness of computer software was growing: merge/purge, statistical modeling, geocoding and clustering was becoming easier and cheaper.

- Relational database technology combined with full-screen access techniques made it possible to locate a wealth of information on a single household out of 85 million households and display it on the screen within seconds of access time. The data could be updated with new information, and returned to its database location at the touch of a button. All of this could be done by fifty or more operators working with the same database of 85 million households simultaneously.

Early Beginnings of Database Marketing

No one knows just who was the first person to use the term "Database Marketing" to describe their work. A lot of people in the direct marketing business were experimenting with the concepts at the time during the 1970s and early 1980s. One of the first who was successful at it was Tom Lund.

In 1969 Tom Lund founded the Customer Development Corporation in Peoria, Illinois, initially as an ad agency serving State Farm Insurance and a major consumer finance company. Both companies had the same objective: they had large customer lists, and wanted to sell more to those customers. Both had national field organizations that were at the heart of their delivery system, and both wanted to set up a system that would drive a constant flow of business into the field organization.

Mr. Lund hit on the idea of building a computer system that would mechanize the sales and service techniques employed by the best agents and managers. But he soon found out it was difficult to do—in 1969, the technology did not exist. One of the objectives was cross-selling, but the data centers couldn't even determine who had purchased more than one product. He was told that what he wanted would require ten year's work and $40 million in programming.

So Mr. Lund became a pioneer. His agency bought their own computer—a very expensive proposition in 1969. The clients wanted more research. They also wanted a direct mail program, because the field managers wanted traffic. Combined with branch variables, that meant hundreds of different lettershop lots every month. He couldn't find a lettershop willing to handle such a project. So he set up his own.

They started producing personalized computer letters. These personal letters had to be signed. In those days there was no such thing as laser imaging and digitizing so they had to go into the hand-signing business. "We ultimately were signing more than a million letters each month, making Peoria, Illinois the world capital for writer's cramp," Mr. Lund explained in his book, *The New Age of Financial Services Marketing* to be published by Financial Sourcebooks.

"The most difficult problem to solve was inventing a way to make the system interactive. The best agents and managers told us that if you asked a customer to buy something, and he did, you should recognize that fact and talk to him differently next time. Plus, the computer had to remember everything it had said to an individual customer to keep from repeating itself. There was no software available anywhere that would handle that kind of history. We had to hire programmers so that we could write our own."

To mimic the way good agents selected the best customers, Lund used RFM analysis from the mail order industry. Within a year he was generating continuous traffic for the branches, altering the product mix as the client required.

The result of this work was the creation of a new type of company with a combination of services never before put together under one roof. "In a management presentation for one of our clients, I described us as a database marketing agency,and the name stuck."

Mr. Lund took these early successes and went on to make CDC what he describes as "the largest financial services database marketing firm in America." CDC converts customer, prospect and membership information into marketing databases. These databases are then used for behavioral research, predictive modeling and strategic planning to create and inititate a selling system that includes personalized communications and other cross-selling programs to support a client's sales network.

American Express Scores a Breakthrough

Direct marketers aim at making a sale. The entire industry prides itself on the accountability of each individual mailing or campaign as a distinct entity. You invest so much money and you get so much return—period. Each campaign is self-contained.

Of course, the campaigns are related. Direct mailers, figuring out how soon after the first mailing the next mailing should be sent out, discovered the recency principle, which almost flies in the face of common sense: the customer most likely to buy from you today is the customer who bought from you last week, rather than the one who bought from you three months ago.

At the same time, the folks at American Express (and elsewhere) were looking at the customer in a different way. They didn't look at each sale, but at the lifetime value of a customer. They were able to take this longer view for several reasons:

- At the time, in 1978, they had one of the largest active lists of consumers in America.

- They also had at their disposal one of the best computer systems available to direct marketers.

- Most of the activity at American Express was financed by American Express customers and clients (the merchants who honored the cards), rather than by direct sales from American Express itself. This fact meant that American Express was able to observe and measure response to thousands of different product offers by hundreds of clients, something that few other companies in the country had the luxury of doing.

- Finally, American Express had enlightened management which employed some very sharp people and gave them the freedom and resources to experiment and learn.

The results, as they say, are history. Database marketing has now multiplied and prospered throughout this country. The database marketing concept is based on the *lifetime value* of customers. It aims not at the first sale, although that is essential, but at all the sales that come after that. Direct marketing still has the honor of the first sale. After that, you add the customers to a marketing database. You begin a dialog with them. You provide them with products and information. They provide you with sales, loyalty and more information. You listen to them and respond to their ideas and wishes. They appreciate the recognition you accord them and respond with more sales, more loyalty, more information. This goes on for a lifetime. It can make them resist the coupons, cashback, limited-time offers and discounts offered by the competition. They are your customers for life.

**Figure 2-2   Direct Mail Spending 1935-1989
(In Billions of Dollars)**

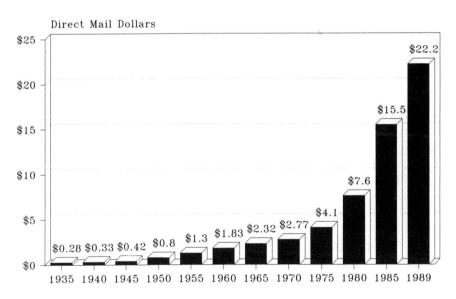

Source: Robert J. Coen, McCann Erickson

Successful Database Marketing is Difficult to Organize

Database marketing is very difficult to organize in any company. It is complicated. It involves not just the list of customers (which is usually fairly easy to come by, although not always), but the entire company in an effort to make good on the promise of recognition, response and results which constant contact with customers requires.

A marketing database connects you to your customers every day. They are writing to you, or more likely, telephoning your sales or customer service staff with inquiries, orders or requests for detailed information. "What is the status of my order?" "How do I assemble this thing that I just received?" "Don't you make one of these for left-handed people?" You get all the questions that have accumulated for thirty years while people sat out the mass marketing and catalog revolutions.

There are more than 500 ad agencies and almost as many consultants who specialize in direct response advertising. Most of them want to get involved in database marketing, although few of them really know much about it. Very few of them have yet developed the kind of creative leader who can put a database project together.

If direct marketing is complicated, and it is, database marketing is many times more complicated. There are now national organizations which recognize this profession. The first was the National Center for Database Marketing, run by Skip Andrew in Nevada City, California. They host national conferences in Orlando and Chicago, with over seventy speakers and 800 or more attendees from direct response agencies, service bureaus and marketing people from all sorts of industries from coast to coast. The enthusiasm is contagious. You can feel the excitement. It has become almost a religion to its devotees. Why?

Because you can offer something to customers that they really want, an audience, recognition and information, and get from them something that you really want, loyalty and sales. You both feel that the relationship is mutually satisfying and profitable.

This message is so exciting for its proponents that they run around inside their companies button-holing everyone trying to get *them* enthusiastic about the idea. What they find is what all other religious fanatics before them have discovered: it is easier to get excited about a concept than it is to make it a part of the society and social environment you are living in. To get a real marketing database going takes a creative genius and a substantial corporate commitment of money and resources. This commitment must be wrung from higher management who may not yet have embraced the religion, and from lower level parts of the company who, in some cases, may actually be opposed to the changes which database marketing will bring. Sales may be opposed to surrendering the names of their contacts, or to using your leads. MIS may be opposed to allowing you to set up a marketing database outside of the central computer, while also protesting that the database takes up too much space or too many in-house resources. Dealers may fight the idea of the company having direct contact with their customers.

Figure 2-3   Media Growth Rates 1980-1989
(Percentage Growth in Advertising)

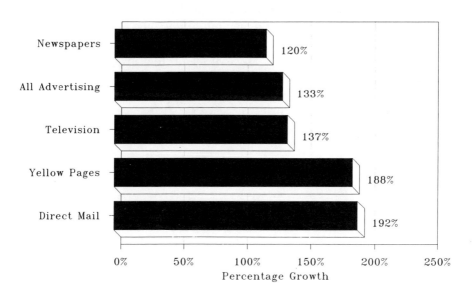

Source: Robert J. Coen, McCann Erickson

SUMMARY

Database marketing is the culmination of a long chain of developments in marketing, including:

- National advertising and brand consciousness.
- The growth of supermarkets and the mass marketing of the 1970s and 1980s.
- The success and professionalism of direct mail.
- The sophistication and reduction in cost of computers.
- The relative affluence and sophistication of modern consumers, who want more personal attention and diversity of products.

Throughout this book I have provided hundreds of examples of database marketing. Some of them are case studies; many of them are proposals which are under active consideration by major corporations. Some are only dreams which may never achieve reality. All are intended to spark your imagination, to give *you* the religion.

Database marketing is so hard to organize and carry out, and requires such a high level of creative talent, that in many industries it may never get off the ground. But from all indications, the idea has taken root across a wide spectrum of American and European business today. It is not just a passing fad. What we make of it in our businesses is up to us—the future is in our hands.

Part Two

The Technical Side of Database Marketing

Chapter 3

What the Database Marketer Needs to Know About Computer Hardware

This chapter will tell you everything that you, as a database marketing planner, will have to know about computer hardware. To make it easy for later reference, the terms defined here are also listed in the glossary at the back of the book. Computer experts will say that what is presented here is a gross oversimplification. It is, but it is all we need for database marketing.

Hardware refers to computers and the peripherals plugged into them. Software refers to the programs that make computers work. We will cover software in the next chapter.

THE IMPORTANCE OF HARDWARE

The kind of hardware you select to store your database can have a profound influence on what kind of work you can do efficiently. If you select the wrong machine, it is possible that your database will never get off the ground, will never be able to realize the benefits for your company that you are seeking.

You wouldn't choose a four-passenger sedan if you needed to transport thirty people; if you did, you would have most of the people waiting uselessly to get in the next shuttle. By the same token, you should not choose a computer that is too small to hold all of your customer records and to permit you to find them instantly and update them. Marketing databases require huge processing power; probably a bigger machine than your company uses for other applications. The computers that already exist in your company for other functions are probably not suited to a database marketing application even though they may be ideal for doing payroll, general ledger, processing customer orders or maintaining inventory. Don't make the mistake of thinking that a computer is a computer is a computer. There are big differences, and you must know the differences before you start or you will fail to reach your objective.

Another "don't": don't assume that the computer professionals in your company know anything about database marketing and are capable of advising you on what type of hardware you need. Some of them may be, but most are probably not knowledgeable in this field because it is so new and so different from other computer applications.

Your company's computer professionals in most cases have a vested interest in seeing that your marketing database is installed on the hardware already present in your company. After all, it is their hardware. Their power and influence in the company are built on their ownership of this hardware. If applications like yours are farmed out to other equipment, what will happen to their position in the hierarchy?

For this reason, these very professionals may be your biggest obstacle in your quest to establish a marketing database. They will insist that your database be installed on their hardware (whether or not the hardware is suitable) and that they control the programming of the database (since they program all applications on the computer). At first this may seem like an ideal solution, since you certainly don't want to have to hire your own programmers or to become proficient at this skill yourself.

However, putting your database on the existing hardware is probably a trap because it will undoubtedly be accorded a lower priority than the computer's other applications. You will be unable to get the programming time, the hardware attention, the clout you need to get your database going. It will take you months (or even years) longer to get your database up and running than it would if you put your database on another, better suited computer. Finally, it will probably cost your company more to install it inside than it would to set the database up on an outside service bureau computer.

Types of Computers

There are basically three types of computers: Mainframes, minicomputers and microcomputers (commonly called PCs).

Minicomputers. Minicomputers are midrange between a PC and a mainframe. For applications where you maintain a very small database (30,000 or less) they may be good. For a large marketing database they are really not powerful enough. There may be exceptions, but from what I have observed most minis, such as an IBM AS/400 or a VAX, do not have the combination of processing power, input-output capability, multi-user ability, software availability and multi-tasking flexibility that are available on mainframes. Mainframes have some telling advantages in database marketing: control, recovery, integration, high volume data access and large-scale database and network management. The factor behind all of these advantages is concentrated processing power, which most minis lack.

A large television station used an IBM AS/400 mini for their financial operations, their broadcasting operations and their membership program. About 300 staff members throughout the station were connected with the mini by terminals on their desks. This particular type of mini is very good at managing on-line operations. ("On-line" means the ability to serve many different users simultaneously.) But it was poor at batch operations; the ability to process marketing functions, like updating membership files, from external data such as mail responses or telemarketers' tapes.

Finance and broadcasting were very happy using this system. Their software had been written several years before and ran with minor modifications day in and day out. Marketing, however, was in very deep trouble. To increase membership, the marketing staff constantly came up with new initiatives, revisions of forms, special ap-

Figure 3-1   Types of Computers for Database Marketing

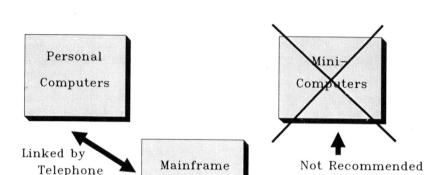

peals, special reports and selects for direct marketing and telemarketing. All of these initiatives required extensive programmer time.

These initiatives swamped the programming staff. The other computer applications (finance and broadcasting) used only one programmer each, whereas membership consumed three. The software for the mini was difficult to write, and there was not enough off-the-shelf software designed for marketing applications available for minis. The result was that membership could not get the support that it felt it needed.

Mainframe Computers. These are the big ones, like IBM's 4381, 3084, 3090 or Amdahl's V8. These large machines require special air conditioning and raised floors. Attached to them are five types of devices:

- Disks (sometimes called DASD) on which your database resides,

- Tape drives (used to get data into and out of your computer),

- Printers,

- Communications gear (used to connect the computer with the outside world by telephone lines) and

- Terminals (screens with keyboards which you use to tell the computer what to do and to learn what it has done.) You can also use a PC as a terminal in talking to a computer.

Personal Computers. PCs (or microcomputers) are just like mainframes, except they sit on a desk, don't need air-conditioning or raised floors and are less powerful. They are very sophisticated and are being improved and radically upgraded every year.

PCs also have internal disks, printers and internal communications gear. They do not normally attach to a tape drive, nor do they need a separate terminal, since the PC is its own terminal.

For database marketing as we know it today, you must have a mainframe computer which contains your database. You will want to have access to your database through a terminal or a PC on your desk which is connected to your mainframe using a telephone line.

MIPS, Chips, Bits and Bytes

Computers are rated by how fast they operate. The measurement for mainframes is *MIPS*—millions of instructions per second. A one MIP computer used to be considered fast. A 28 MIP computer is fast, but there are many new and very expensive computers that will do 100 or more MIPS. Whenever you go to a cocktail party and hear someone boast about his mainframe, ask him how many MIPS his mainframe puts out. If he says less than six, smile to yourself knowingly. For most large database marketing applications, you will need at least seven. The more the better.

For PCs the measurement is the *chip*. A computer chip is about the size and weight of your fingernail. It has thousands of printed circuits and electronics which have been shrunk by photographic wizardry to infinitesimal size. It costs tens of millions of dollars to develop one chip. To make the second copy costs only a few cents. Inside every PC there is a chip. The original IBM PC and all competing brands used an 8088 or 8086 chip, which was considered very good until the 80286 chip appeared. The '286 was about ten times as fast and powerful as the '88. It was the hottest thing for about a year, until '386 arrived. Following this was the '486, which was faster still. This improvement will continue until the outer limits of chip creativity are reached; and no one knows when that will happen.

(For your purposes, a current generation PC is just fine for anything you will read about in this book.)

Another measurement of mainframes and PCs is *memory*. Memory is a measure of how much information a computer can hold while it is working on a problem (or program). The more memory, the faster it works, and the more complex things it does. Most mainframes today have several million bytes of memory. Memory for them is not a limiting factor. PCs used to be limited to 64,000 bytes of memory. Today, PC memory is so cheap that almost any that you buy will have 640,000 or more bytes, which is plenty for any normal database marketing activity.

A *byte* is a unit of memory. It is a character or a number. The letter A is one byte. So is the number "6", or an *. Computers store information in their memory or on disks and tape reels as bytes. Normally, a byte is composed of eight *bits* or a group of 1's and 0's. The character A when written in bits is:

1100 0001   B is: 1100 0010

What is on a disk or magnetic tape, then, are groups of bits (1's and 0's), which, grouped together, form bytes, which represent letters, numbers and other characters.

Disk Memory

Disk memory is very important to database marketing because your database is stored on a disk. Disk memory is measured in *megabytes* (or millions of bytes). Disks are *direct access devices*. That means

Figure 3-2   Limiting Factors in Database Computers

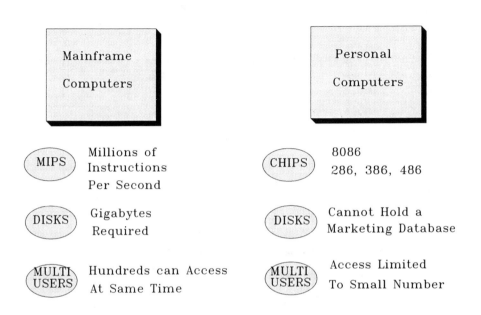

that every byte on a disk has a special disk *address*. The computer can find that byte and go directly to it if it knows the address.

Marketing databases require a lot of space on disks because they hold a great deal of information about customers and prospects. For example, in addition to names and addresses, you will want to keep records of all purchases, products bought, amounts paid, the dates and source code of the marketing activity or media that produced each sale. You may want also to record every telephone call made to you. You will also keep the results of survey questions with such information as family income, number of children, type of automobile or hundreds of other things.

On one of the databases which we are maintaining in our company we have household records on 330,000 customers. But when you total the records we are keeping on all of their purchases, we have 28 million records on these 330,000 customers. The average number of bytes in these records is about 100, so we need 6300 megabytes to hold this marketing database. But that is not all. Databases require a lot of extra space to insert *new records* which are created every day in the course of sales activity. Plan for this extra storage room. For our 330,000 customer file we actually have set aside 8 *gigabytes* (8000 megabytes) for the entire file. That is a lot of equipment and a lot of floor space in the computer room: eight large disk machines occupying 512 square feet of raised, specially air- conditioned floor space.

On-Line versus Off-Line

Catalog marketers have been keeping records on customers for more than twenty years. Most of these records have been kept on computer tape. A computer tape reel is 1/2 inch wide and holds 2,400 feet of magnetic tape. At a rated density of 6,250 bytes per inch, this tape can typically hold the records on about 300,000 customers. The big difference between tape and disk is that to find the record of any one customer on a tape, you must read through all 300,000 customers; on disk, you can go right to the customer if you know the address on the disk.

Because of the difficulty of working with tapes, catalog marketing is often done in *batch mode,* meaning that many transactions from many customers are gathered (once a week or month, for example) and then run simultaneously, making a new updated tape in the process. This is very efficient, but it doesn't work well for database marketing. Off-line batch records typically impose limits on the amount of data that you can keep on a customer; and, using tape, you can't call a customer's record to the screen when he or she calls you on the telephone.

There is no substitute for having customer records on-line on disk when doing database marketing. Every time you get a piece of information from a customer—an order, a return, a coupon, a survey response, a telephone call, a change of address—you will want to update or enter the information into the customer's record immediately, not a month later. Database marketing typically requires many different people working with customer records at the same time, and they need to be confident that they have the *latest information* about customers when they are talking to them, writing to them, or servicing their orders.

Access Time

Having a lot of MIPS in the mainframe is not the whole story. If your mainframe is busy much of the day with other company work not related to marketing (and this is usually the case), this other work will have a tendency to dominate the computer. You may find that your marketing operation is pushed onto the back burner while the computer gets out the payroll, sends out the bills, maintains the inventory or runs the factory. You will notice this most in delays in *access time*.

Consider the following scenario. Mrs. Clara Fowler calls up because her order did not arrive. She is irate. You are sitting at a computer terminal connected to your database. You enter Mrs. Fowler's name and wait for her records to appear. You wait 10, 20, 30 seconds—still no record. Meanwhile, Mrs. Fowler is steaming. You try to keep up a pleasant conversation. It may begin to occur to Mrs. Fowler that maybe the delay with her order and the fact that you can't retrieve her records are *related facts*. She may suspect not that the marketing database has a low priority, but that the *Fowler household* has a low priority.

When designing your marketing database and dealing directly with the computer systems people who will make it happen, you must set standards for access time to records. Typically, any record should come up on the screen within one second after you request it, no matter whether your computer holds 100,000 customers or 10 million. In busy times, access time could slip to three seconds, but you must get an ironclad guarantee that it will *never* be more than five seconds; if you can't you should seek some other location for your database. You simply cannot run a satisfactory marketing database with access times in excess of five seconds. Your customers will not like it, and your staff will revolt.

Communications

If you are located in the same building as your mainframe computer, communications will not be a problem for you. Your terminal will be wired directly into the mainframe. But in most database marketing applications the mainframe is in one place, and your customer service or marketing staff is somewhere else. You must set up a communications system.

Remote communication with a database is usually achieved by telephone lines. Where many people are using the database (such as on customer service), you will want a *dedicated line*. This is a private line rented from the telephone company which connects point A with point B. Using such a system, fifty or more operators can use the database at the same time over the same line. This is accomplished by an electronic marvel called a controller. All users' terminals are wired into the controller, the controller is wired into a *modem* and the modem is plugged into the dedicated telephone line. When this line gets to the mainframe, it goes through another modem and a communications unit which separates each of the eighty or more different conversations going on over the line so that the computer recognizes and deals separately with each of your service people.

You must also take line speed into consideration. Slow line speed means slow access time. Communications line speed is measured in *baud rate*. (Never mind what a baud is!) The minimum speed suggested is 9,600 baud; a good customer service operation, with lots of operators, really requires a 56,000-baud *digital* line. Digital lines have much cleaner data, less dropping of the line, better communications. What you need will vary in each case.

Nightly Backup and Down Time

One other point that should not be overlooked is the problem of down time and disaster. Computers are always going down for one reason or another: hardware problems, software problems, power problems. It is going to happen, so plan for it. Once you get deeply into database marketing, the database will dominate your business, and the computer, which is the heart of your database, can make or break you.

Insist on nightly backup on tape of all the information on all of your customers. Insist that the computer staff has written procedures on how to restore your database after a breakdown and that their staff is trained in these procedures. Your computer will need an Uninterruptable Power Supply (UPS) system with a diesel generator.

Finally, be sure that your telemarketing operators have pre-printed forms and instructions so they can keep working when the computer goes down. Train your staff to handle a one-hour downtime, a one-day downtime, a three-day downtime. Don't just assume that it won't happen.

Figure 3-3   Many Users Access Database at Once

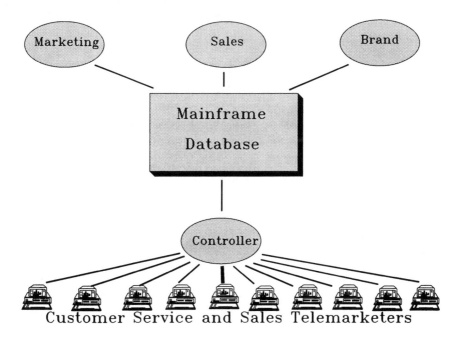

PUTTING YOUR DATABASE ON A PC

Given the growing power of PCs and the increased size and speed of their disks, why not use a PC instead of bothering with a mainframe with all the attendant problems of an unresponsive MIS staff and slow programmers? This question has occurred to hundreds of would-be marketing database planners.

The answer is that a PC has many of the attributes that we look for in a database manager, except raw power. The usefulness of concentrated processing power will not diminish as PCs get more powerful. Consider the often repeated example that a 386 PC in 1990 was as powerful as an IBM System 138 was fifteen years before. Despite its power, however, the 386 PC does not support the large-scale network and database processing that the S/138 was designed to support. In those fifteen years, as hardware advanced in speed and sophistication, it was expected to do more complex functions: functions that could not be considered fifteen years before on the hardware that existed at that time.

In other words, we expect a mainframe to handle millions of records, support hundreds of simultaneous users (telemarketers and analysts), run scores of different types of programs simultaneously (including batch and on-line), maintain a complex database system which allows direct access to millions of records on-line and, at the same time, permits batch updating, segmentation and reporting. Mainframes are not standing still. They grow as PCs grow, and they will continue to grow. Not as fast, but they were miles ahead to start with.

Of course, if you run a video store, a movie theater or a hardware store, and you want to keep a mailing list of your patrons on a PC or a mini, you may do so. It is probably the least-cost solution, and should work very well. But don't confuse such a mailing list with a marketing database. Until you are supporting on-line customer service, batch updating with transaction history, modeling, segmentation and two-way communications with your customers, you do not have a marketing database. You can call it that but it is still a mailing list.

PC TO MAINFRAME CONNECTION

Mainframes have the processing power needed for a marketing database, but they do not have, and probably will never have, the sophistication of a personal computer. This is because there are a few hundred thousand mainframes in the world, and millions upon millions of personal computers. All the great software of the future is going to be written for the personal computer, not for the mainframe. Think of the mainframe as the offensive line of a major football team. The PC represents the backfield: running, passing and coming up with new plays all the time. PCs have color, graphics, statistics, versatility, software. Because they are so impressive, some people make the mistake of thinking that they are suitable for database marketing themselves. Try putting the backfield of any major football team up on the line and see how long they last.

What you need for successful database marketing is a system which combines the power of the mainframe with the sophistication and software of the PC. Fortunately, it is not difficult to arrange this combination, through the correct computer architecture. IBM, for example, has developed System Application Architecture (SAA), which provides computer architectural standards upon which developers can build applications that simultaneously take advantage of the different strengths of mainframes and PCs.

With cooperative processing, the on-line database user begins a transaction on a PC using its local software and graphics to gather the input data. When the PC needs information from the database stored on the mainframe, it sends instructions to the mainframe (without telling the user anything about what it is doing). The mainframe receives the request, finds the needed records in the database and ships the raw information back to the PC. All of the relevant customer information is sent to the PC, which can then display it and work with it in the most effective form. The PC can then use its sophisticated software and internal versatility to provide the necessary graphics, reports, updating or statistical manipulation. If the end result of the PC activity is to modify (update) the records, the PC can ship the revised records back to the mainframe when the transaction ends.

The power of such cooperative processing is that it allows PCs to do what they do best, human interface, and it allows mainframes to do what they do best, large-scale database and network management. With this type of arrangement you can buy an off-the-shelf software package for your PC and, with suitable modifications, make it control your mainframe. For example, you can control your mainframe with a PC mouse! Mainframes, regarded by some as pitiful, helpless giants, become the offensive line of a winning database marketing team that includes the most advanced PCs, with their inexpensive but sophisticated software, directing operations from the backfield.

DIFFERING HARDWARE ROLES

Different people in your organization will have different applications for the marketing database. Your customer service people will be answering telephone calls, calling up customer records and entering data. They will need high-speed terminals to view the records, linked by high-speed telephone lines.

Your direct marketing planning staff will be using the database to do modeling and multiple regressions. They will want to have a personal computer linked to the database through cooperative processing. They probably don't need a direct line at all. They can dial up the database when they need it, which certainly will not be every day.

Your warehouse staff fulfilling orders may not need any terminals at all. They may be linked to the database by a direct mainframe to mainframe configuration, connecting the marketing database mainframe with the central company accounting and inventory control mainframe.

Top management in your company will want to have PCs which monitor the activities of the database, again through cooperative processing. Top management will need a series of daily reports which come to them in hard copy on laser printers on a regular basis. They will also want to use their PCs to access the mainframe to make simple queries to find out what is going on.

In planning your marketing database hardware, therefore, consider the needs of each unit that is likely to use the data base, and plan their hardware needs. They will not all be the same.

SUMMARY

- Your database must be stored on a mainframe which has seven MIPS or better.

- Your customer file must be on-line at all times.

- Disk space required will be much more than your data processing staff is used to.

- There must be nightly backup and good restore procedures.

- Access time should be one second; anything over five seconds is totally unacceptable.

- Remote communications should use dedicated lines with line speed sufficient to assure acceptable access time.

- You can access the mainframe using high-speed terminals or personal computers. Telemarketers probably need terminals, but your analytical staff and top management need PCs which use cooperative processing to extract data from the mainframe.

- In deciding what hardware to use for your database, consider what other functions reside on the hardware. Make sure that your application will have priority and that the people running the hardware really understand database marketing.

Chapter 4

Software for Database Marketing

When cars first appeared, people had the idea that anyone who wanted to drive one ought to learn how its motor worked: what a carburetor did, what pistons were, what a timing gear did. Nowadays we leave all that to the mechanics. The average driver never looks under the hood. If he can drive the car, and keep gas and oil in it, that is all he needs to do to be a fully functioning automobile driver and owner.

Some people today feel the same way about computer programs. They know what they want the computer to do for them. All they need to do is to tell the programmer their desires and let the programmers do the rest.

The analogy is not a good one. Automobiles have matured over the last 100 years. Computer programs have not had time to do that. Even though cars are now manufactured all over the globe by hundreds of different companies, they are all basically the same. They all have the same components. If something is wrong with the car, you don't have to explain anything to the mechanic; you just say that the brakes need adjusting.

But there is no such universal understanding about computer programs. There is no agreement on what a customer record should look like, how to store it, how to update it, how to report on it. If you travel around America looking into computer programs that deal with customer records, you will find hundreds of different ways of

75

dealing with the same fundamental situation. Some of them are brilliant. Some are terrible. Most are just variations of a barely adequate system.

To be successful at database marketing you have to come up with great creative ideas which involve manipulating your customer's records to support and expand a mutually profitable long-term relationship. The things you will ask the programmers to do will not be simple. Many of them will require the programmers to do complex things that they have never heard of before. You will be pushing the outer edges of software capability. To get the programmers to understand and create what you want, you are going to have to understand them and the media they are using: software.

A better analogy than the automobile driver and the mechanic is the analogy of the first designers of jet airplanes and the engineers who created the early models. The designers knew what they wanted aerodynamically, but they had to understand the materials and problems of the engineers if their designs were ever to result in a satisfactory jet.

For these reasons, therefore, we will cover a bit of history and database theory to explain the software that underlies successful database marketing.

Mailing List Construction

Databases began as *mailing lists*. These were, and are, flat sequential files of names and addresses and other data kept on a magnetic tape. A typical mailing list record for a household looks something like this:

Field	Size
NAME	30
ADDRESS	30
CITY	20
STATE	2
ZIPCODE	5
ID NUMBER	6
DATE	6
Total	99

Size refers to the number of bytes (characters) allowed for the information in the field. The total size of the record (in this illustration) is 99 bytes. I should emphasize that there are absolutely no standards for what the record fields and the record size should look like. Every computer center in the United States has a different format for customer records. There are no government industry standards. It is total anarchy—or free enterprise (depending on how you look at it). Typically, in a sequential file, each record is strung out on a magnetic tape immediately following the previous record:

```
     BACH     BARNES     BORK     BUSH
|_____|_____|_____|_____|
```

Each record is 99 bytes long. The bytes consist of magnetic bits on the tape. Each bit is either magnetized (on) or not magnetized (off). Eight bits make up a byte. Different combinations of on and off bits determine whether the byte is an A or a B or a C . . . or a 1, 2, 3, etc.

If you have 200,000 names recorded on your tape in alphabetical order, you will have to go through almost all of the tape to reach someone named Williams. If you want to reshuffle the names and sort them in zipcode order, you must put these names on a disk where a sorting program will do the job in a few minutes (or an hour, depending on the speed of your computer and how busy it is), and put them back on tape in the new order.

Many catalog lists are kept on a magnetic tape just like this. Nine-track 1600 or 6250 bytes per inch magnetic tape is standard in the industry. If you rent a list of names from anyone, the list will come to you on a nine-track tape. The data is written on the tape either in EBCDIC (an IBM protocol) or ASCII (everything else). Any large computer service bureau can read any EBCDIC or ASCII tape.

There are many different functions that must be performed on such a tape: sorting, selecting and updating.

Updating consists of adding new names, deleting old names and modifying (changing) existing names. Typically, as a result of an ad campaign, you may receive several thousand responses on order forms or coupons. When these are received, you send them for keypunching. In keypunching, someone sits at a typewriter-type keyboard of a small computer and enters each name and address. A program has already been written to assure that the names and addresses will end up in the correct *format*. In our case, it will be our 99 byte format. The output of our keypunching will be a magnetic tape of the new names. We will probably use this tape in a program to prepare labels so that we can mail to the respondents whatever they ordered with the coupon. After the respondent's requests have been fulfilled, we are then ready to add the names on the respondent tape to our master tape so that we can update the master. To update our master tape from this transaction tape, we will run both tapes through an update program.

Figure 4-1 Tape Updating

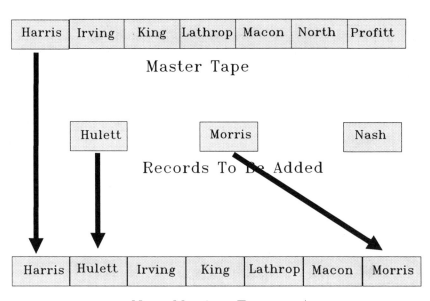

The first step in the update is to sort our transaction tape in the same order as the master tape (in our illustration it is in alphabetic order). A computer program puts our transactions on a disk attached to the computer, and reshuffles the records into alphabetic order. Then the names are put back onto tape. Now both tapes are run simultaneously.

In the update program, a new master tape is created with the combined names. Arnold goes before Bach, Benson before Bork. Suppose we add "Bush" to a file that already has that name. We have a problem: if one is George Bush and the other David Bush, we put David first and we are done, but if both Bushes are George Bush at 1600 Pennsylvania Avenue, we have a duplicate. The update program has to contain instructions for what to do in this case (delete one and mark the master to show that there was a duplicate, for instance).

This rather elemental discussion of sequential file processing illustrates a point: flat sequential files have both good and bad qualities. It is easy to run batch updates on them and to sort them. You can run simple counts on them. But if you are going to use them for complex reporting or to update one record at a time, they just are not satisfactory.

Adding Order Records

Sequential files become complicated when you want to add customer orders to them. You can increase the record size and add the orders to the format:

```
EXISTING 99 BYTES PLUS . . .
ORDER DATE              6
SKU ORDERED             8
QUANTITY                6
AMOUNT OF ORDER         8
CELL CODE               6
```

"CELL CODE" refers to the outgoing promotion which brought the order in. "SKU" refers to the number of the item purchased.

Figure 4- 2

Customer & Order Records in Separate Files

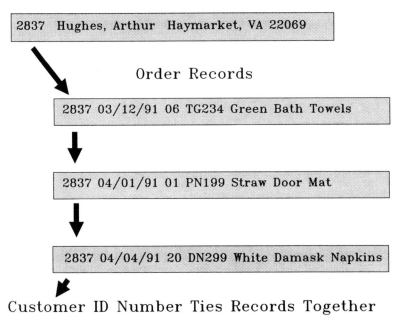

Customer ID Number Ties Records Together

Of course, this format is useless if a customer has ordered two items and you want to record the purchase of both. One solution to this problem is to make space for ten or twelve different orders after the name and address. If the customer ordered more than the maximum, you would delete the oldest order, adding a counter in the record for total number of orders.

Another method is to create variable length records with the length of the record being determined by the number of orders. The programs for sorting and updating variable length records can become complicated and costly.

A third widely-used solution is to have a separate order file not connected to the customer file at all. It would look something like this:

ID NUMBER	6
ORDER NUMBER	8
ORDER DATE	6
CELL CODE	6
SKU ORDERED	8
QUANTITY	6
ORDER AMOUNT	8

In this arrangement, "ID NUMBER" is the ID of the customer. "ORDER NUMBER" is a chronological number stamped on each outgoing order. With this system, each customer can have as many orders posted to the system as needed: some customers can have thousands of orders; most customers have only one or two. If you want to know how many orders a given customer has placed, you would have to run both the customer file and the order file in a program that matches the ID Number.

Advantages and Disadvantages of Sequential Files

Sequential files have the advantage of being the cheapest way to store data.

The disadvantages are:

- Producing marketing reports is a nightmare. For large files of millions of records, it may take two weeks or more for a data processing shop to produce the reports you need.

- Updating can only be done in batches. For this reason, it is done infrequently—probably once a month. Your files are never current.

- You cannot find any record instantly. If your customers call you on the phone, your best research tool is a thick printed book of all the customers.

- Duplicates build up and are hard to find and consolidate.

Clearly sequential files offer many disadvantages. Yet many customer files are still maintained in this way. For a marketing database, however, we need something else—a relational database.

Relational Database

Marketing databases are maintained as relational databases on disk. There are other methods, of course, but there is really no other way to have instant access to all parts of your customer file, and still do reports, counts and selects.

Instead of putting your records on a tape, a relational database stores them on a disk where they are instantly retrievable by their location. You can pull up Mr. Williams's record just as fast as Mrs. Bach's. The program tells the disk seek arm where to look. It goes there and reads the record. The program finds Mr. Williams by means on an *index*. An index is a disk file consisting of a name and a location:

Figure 4-3

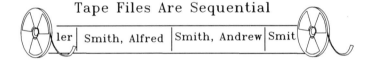

Tape Files Are Sequential

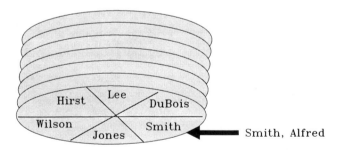

Disk Files Are Random Access

With a disk database, you can find anyone instantly

Name	Location
WILLIAMS, ARTHUR	23145
WILLIAMS, CAROL	83290
WILLIAMS, DAVID	11092
WILLIAMS, EDWARD	33325

The index is created when the record is stored. If you add a new record for Betty Williams it will be placed in any free space on the disk; you can update the index so you can find her:

Name	Location
WILLIAMS, ARTHUR	23145
WILLIAMS, BETTY	99912⇐
WILLIAMS, CAROL	83290
WILLIAMS, DAVID	11092
WILLIAMS, EDWARD	33325

Order records are stored in the same way. Every order record contains the ID number of the customer. You can have an order index that looks like this:

Order Index

Customer ID	Order Record Locations
223876	774334, 887653, 223014, 888375, 764111
223877	223145, 443526
223878	110299, 993267, 337265

Records can be indexed by more than one field. For example, you might want to find customers by their zipcode or telephone number. You would have an index for each one:

Telephone Number Index to the Customer File

Telephone Number	Customer Record Location
703 742-4470	293847
703 754-3477	983726
703 784-1234	112938
703 784-9487	887362

With a relational database, then, you build a large number of indexes. Each index permits you to access parts of your data instantly by telling your program where it is. What does this mean for your marketing database?

- Your telemarketers can instantly call up any customer record and get all the information they need on orders, telephone calls, complaints, shipments, billing problems, family relationships. They have a way of immediately knowing everything they need to know about customers.

- Your telemarketers can quickly update any record (add a new order, change a credit card number or an address, add or delete a record).

- You can create reports very rapidly on the status of your marketing program, reports that would take weeks using many other systems, (More on reports later.)

- You can do sophisticated statistical analysis or modeling with the data. You can do complex segmentation. You can quickly add data to your records (enhancement), and match your customer file to other outside data files. The sky is the limit.

However, there is a downside. There is no such thing as a free lunch:

- Your relational database will take up a lot of space on disk. Besides providing space for your existing customer records, you must provide space for new customer records and future orders. And you need lots of space for your extensive indexes.

Disk space today is dirt cheap, but many information management staffs do not yet accept that.

■ The software for your relational database is very complex and
expensive. Depending on the size of your system, you may be
spending $10,000 to $40,000 *per month* on database software.

■ Complex software *always* has built-in errors or bugs. Something is always going wrong for unknown reasons. You must
have a very alert system staff which is constantly watching the
database and patching or restoring it when it "goes down." It
may go down several times a month.

■ The more indexes you add, the slower the response. If you have
thirty indexes on your customer record, every time you try to
change any data in the file, the program will have to update
(rewrite) thirty indexes. That takes time, and you will feel it in
slower response. A batch update (where you are updating several thousand records from an outside tape in a single session)
can take many hours to complete.

■ Because you have this wonderful relational database, you will
think up scores of new functions and improvements that you
will want to add to it. You will want to add the names of the
children in the household and their ages. When you write to a
customer, you may want to suggest that you have new school
outfits which would be "just perfect for Sarah and Jonathan."
Writing letters like this can really make a marketing database
profitable, but this functionality comes at a cost of many hours
of programmer time to write the code to make it all happen. Do
you have the ability to convince the programmers to devote the
time required?

■ Finally, a relational database is often very difficult to update in
batch mode. Assume you have a large file (say 10 million) and
you have a lot of transactions from a mass mailing that you
want to use to update your large file (say a million transactions). Some relational databases can take 24 hours or more to
do the updating even on a very large and fast mainframe. Why?

Because of all the indexes that have to be updated at the same time.

Reports You Will Need

There are two types of reports that you will absolutely need to have to make a marketing database work: *ad-hoc reports* and *custom reports*.

Ad-hoc reports are reports that you create working with your database from a PC or terminal on your desk in the marketing department. You are planning a new promotion campaign for a new type of soap. You want to target users of your current brands of soap to find out information about them which will give you a clue to the new brand households. You try out one idea after another, most of them false starts:

How many households with young children, with a household income of less than $50K and two adults employed are heavy users of Brand X?

If the answer is not what you were looking for, you alter the query:

How many households with young children, with a household income of *less than $75K* and two adults employed are heavy users of Brand X?

You are working against a marketing database of 2 million households. You are spending the day on an important marketing report which is basic to your whole operation. You don't want to have to ask some programmer to give you these answers, and you want to be able to vary your question until you get the answer you need for your promotion. These are ad-hoc queries. The software that accompanies your relational database must permit you to ask these questions from your desk and get answers within a couple of minutes or so.

For ad-hocs, any indexed field is available. You cannot do good database marketing without this ad-hoc capability.

Custom Reports

The other reports you need are custom reports that you design, the programming staff sets up, and that run automatically every night, every week or every month, depending on your program and your needs. These reports will show such data as:

- Results of leads received by salesman, dealer, district: number of contacts, refusals, sales.

- Responses to most recent mailing by cell code, household income, customer recency, frequency, monetary level. Return on investment from the mailing.

- Coupon redemptions by cell, sales territory, coupon type, product type, etc.

- Calls received by Customer Service, broken down by type of call, product, hour of the day, length of call.

Every day when you come to work, these custom reports have been run the night before and are sitting on your desk, in neat laser printed forms with three-hole punch for insertion in ring binders, ready for your review and notification of top management.

If you have a good relational database and a good programming staff, these ad-hoc and custom reports will be easy to do. They are vital to your marketing operation: if for some reason you cannot get these reports, do not take no for an answer. You cannot expect to run a marketing database without them.

Changes in Your Database

Database marketing is dynamic. You are trying to reach your customers and prospects in new, exciting ways. Once you set up your database, you will discover many new uses for the data, some of which will be very successful, some of which will not work out well at all. You can only find this out by experimenting constantly, testing, trying new things. There is no such thing as the perfect marketing database.

The beauty of relational databases is that new fields can be added with little difficulty. Let us say that when you first set up the database, there was no thought of having data in the customer record like household income, educational level or number of children. You now have such data available and want to add it to the database so that you can use it in modeling. It should be possible to add this data from an outside tape in a matter of a day or two.

When you set up the database, be sure that everyone involved understands that you will be making many changes in the future. You need these changes to maintain your customer base and market share. If you cannot make changes, be assured that your competitors will.

Who makes relational database software? There are several products which you should consider. Model 204, by the Computer Corporation of America, is a well-accepted system. CCA has have developed a query language for the PC called MarketPulse which offers a lot of flexibility. ADABAS by Software AG is also a relational database system. Their programming language, Natural, is easy for programmers to learn and use. They do not have an ad-hoc capability similar to MarketPulse. DB2 by IBM is probably the most widely used relational database. It suffers from some drawbacks, principally that the query language SQL is rigid and difficult to learn and work with; but it is by far the most well-known system in use today. ACS of Reston Virginia has a query language called Market Vision which will work with any of these three systems.

Other Required Software

Relational database software is only the beginning. To support a marketing database, you will also need the following:

- *Merge/Purge Software,* to detect duplicates.

- *Zipcode, address and name correction,* to clean up your records, to make them personal and acceptable to your customers.

- *Geocoding software,* which permits you to determine the census block group of each customer and append demographic and lifestyle information to your customer records.

(All of the above software is available from Group 1 Software, whose mainframe products are probably the IBM of the direct marketing business.)

■ *Software to create ad-hoc and custom reports.* MarketVision, Market-Pulse and SQL will do this job, but there are two problems. If you have an on-line database with updates being made at all hours of the day and night, you will have a problem getting consistent reports. That is because a report created at 11:00 A.M. will be different from one run at 11:30 A.M., since many customers will have called in and placed orders or otherwise changed the database. None of your totals will agree. This will be a continual problem unless you take steps to prevent it.

The second problem is that running reports on a live database during the day can either (a) slow up the functioning of the database or (b) take a long time. Either alternative is undesirable. The only answer that I know to these two problems is to prepare an extract of your database early every morning when no one is on the machine. This extract will contain all the information you are likely to need for any report that anyone is apt to want run. This extract, then, is a sort of snapshot of your database at 4:00 A.M. You can run all your reports from this extract all day and they will all agree. Running queries or reports from an extract will not slow up your computer or impair the functioning of your database.

■ *On-line access software* to permit you and your telemarketers and others to have instant daily constant access to the database.

■ *Statistical modeling software* to permit you to perform multiple regressions and other statistical and graphics functions. We have tried many systems for this, all of which have some advantages and some drawbacks. SAS is widely used. SPSS is probably the most well-known since it has been used by many thousands of students in college.

■ *Custom software prepared for your particular application.* For example, as each customer is added to the database, you may want to assign a dealer code, sales district code, UPS district code, salesman code or other special identifier. You may want to add RFM codes or other special data of use to your company. Software to add all of this information must be written by the programmers assigned to your database. All marketing databases have thousands of lines of special code written for them, which must be kept up-to-date by your programmers.

The functions of most of this software are covered elsewhere in this book. I have listed them here merely to remind you that wherever your marketing database is housed, the computer requires a lot of expensive software available and the skilled resources of a trained staff to make it work.

The Issue of Priority

One thing that you may not know is that it is possible to set priorities for each user of a computer. Most mainframes have scores or even hundreds of jobs running at the same time. Many users are hooked up to the computer simultaneously. The mainframe works by doing a little piece of a job—for example, it asks a disk controller to go and find a customer's record on the disk—which takes several milliseconds; while it is waiting for the record to come back, the mainframe will look for something else to do. It has a long list of jobs in process, called a queue. The mainframe will run down this list and pick another job to work on. It will make this decision based on the priority assigned to each job on the queue. Once it has selected a job, it will work on that job until it gets to an interruption, such as the need to send information to a printer or tape drive. The mainframe is ready to pick another job off the queue. Eventually it will get back to the original job because the disk controller has reported back with the customer's name.

The priority assigned to each user or each job determines how likely it is that the mainframe will pick that job off the queue. When I worked at the Department of the Treasury in Washington many years ago, we used the Federal Reserve Bank of New York mainframe to do much of our processing. For some reason, the NY Fed assigned our operation a very low priority. As a result, simple jobs that I wanted to run would often take four or six hours to finish—jobs that on another machine could be completed in less than a minute. Your marketing database could be caught in the same trap unless you assure yourself of a high priority for database marketing on the machine you are using.

Insist on Excellence

Once you start serious database marketing you will discover that your marketing database *becomes your company*—at least it does to your customers.

We have all visited stores which appear dirty; trash litters the entrance and the aisles. What we are looking for is often out of stock, and no one seems to care. In fact it is hard to find anyone who seems to take any responsibility for the store at all; they are all just employees, putting in their hours to get paid. They can't or won't answer questions or be helpful. Unless there is nowhere else to shop, we try to avoid these stores if we possibly can. Why don't the owners of these stores see them from the customer's point of view, and clean up their act? Who knows?

With database marketing, you can easily fall into the same trap. Imagine a customer service operation with a telephone line that is always busy; when you do get through, the operator has never heard of you, can't find your name on the database, can't make changes in your order because it is "out of my hands:" the supervisor's approval is needed for that, but the supervisor is "unavailable."

You present an image of your company every day. If you write letters to your customers, and they receive duplicate letters addressed to A Hughes and Arthur Hughes, this is your image. If your customer billing or order records are several weeks behind, and the invoices incorrect, this is your image.

All these things *can* be fixed. You can present a first-class impression to your customers all the time, in all parts of your operation, but it will not be easy. You will need first-class software and a first-class programming staff. You will need to train all your personnel in the use of the system. You will have to monitor what is happening from the customer end, and constantly *insist on excellence*.

The essential software problem is this: because modern database marketing software is very complicated and very expensive, it is easy to get snowed by the experts. They will tell you that what you want to do cannot be done or will take a very long time or will be prohibitively expensive. In most cases, these experts are dead wrong. Today, database marketing software and hardware is so versatile that you can do virtually anything that you can imagine or visualize. Furthermore, if you let yourself get rolled by your experts, rest assured that your competition will not let that happen. *Insist on excellence.*

Programming Staff

A marketing database will not run itself. It will absolutely require one or more full-time programmers who know the database intimately. You will need a formal change order system for modifications of the database. Someone must become the Database Administrator (DBA). The DBA should be able to issue written orders to the programmer to make changes and improvements in the software for the database. The DBA must meet with the programmer or the programmer's boss on an almost daily basis to find out how things are going and to make sure that your requests are logical and reasonable.

Bear in mind that it is possible to make grave errors in writing database software which will seriously affect your customers. One line of code designed to correct one problem can cause unforeseen problems in thousands or hundreds of thousands of other customer records. The error may not show up for several days. Then your telemarketers will report strange happenings: people getting refunds for things they never ordered; sales taxes twice the order value; shipping dates canceled without authorization.

You will soon find that you need a system for testing all changes in the software before they become operational. You will probably need a *test database* in addition to your *production database*. All of your software will run on both databases. New software must be written and tested extensively on the test database before it is shifted over to the production database.

You will get to know your programmers quite well. You will need to have a good relationship with their supervisor, and you will need the capability to call on extra programming resources in a crisis.

SUMMARY

- Marketing databases must be stored on disk using relational database software. This software is expensive and will require programmer attention to keep it working properly. It will require a very large amount of disk space.

- You will want to store a vast amount of data in your database. Each new piece of data will require the addition of one or more indexes so that it is instantly retrievable and can be integrated into your reports. When the database is set up, it must be understood that you will be adding new types of data on a regular basis.

- You must be able to run ad-hoc reports from your desk in the marketing department, accessing any indexed field, and getting the output in a few minutes without any assistance from a programmer.

- You must be able to have custom reports designed and programmed so that you receive their output automatically whenever needed.

- You will need one or more programmers constantly available to make the changes, program the reports and keep your database working properly at all time. There must be a Database Administrator (DBA) who will keep tight control of what happens to the database.

- You will need a test database and a production database. All changes must be first tested thoroughly on the test database.

- You will need software for merge/purge, zipcode and address correction, name correction, statistical analysis, geocoding.

- The DBA must know and understand your software and programming staff. You must know enough about software so that you do not get snowed by the experts. You must insist on excellence.

Chapter 5

How to Build Your Marketing Database

At some point your company has to start building the database. In this chapter we take you step by step through the process.

How Long Should It Take?

Very important first question. Never start any long process without some idea of when it will be finished. I have a definite answer: while the particular database depends on the type of situation and use in your company, in general, your initial database should be up and running within *one year or less.*

How can I be so dogmatic? Won't many databases take years to design and build? Of course, but those databases may in fact never be built. They will be in the planning stage for several years, and never reach the operational phase. Why do you need to move so fast?

- Computer hardware is evolving very, very rapidly today. What is state-of-the-art today will be obsolete in three years, and not even still maintained in five. If you take too long to plan and build your database, when it emerges it will be designed around obsolete equipment. It will not be state-of-the-art and everyone will know it.

- Computer software is changing almost as rapidly as hardware. The same comments apply.

- There are powerful forces in every company which resist change, particularly the fundamental changes brought about by a marketing database. The longer the planning stage, the more opportunities the opponents have to kill your project in its cradle. You must get it up and running before this happens.

- No marketing database can be built without support at the top of the company. Someone at the top must believe in it and have acquired the money to make it happen. In any dynamic company, things change quickly. It is hard to retain your senior interest and funding over a several year planning phase. When you are ready to implement, either your backer will have been transferred or promoted or the funds will have been diverted to something else. You have to produce something and *show that it works* in a short time, or your project will wither and die.

- By waiting, you are losing money. An effective marketing database more than pays its way in increased sales and increased customer retention. The longer you wait to start, the more sales and customers you will lose. Get out a calculator figure out how much it will cost the company for each month delay in becoming operational. These opportunity costs are *real,* not hypothetical.

- By waiting, you permit your competition to surpass you. Don't assume that they are waiting for you to make the first move. If you have a leisurely three-year development plan, you may find that when your database is ready, your competition has a two-year head start and is much more proficient at it than you are. Database development plans are seldom trumpeted in headlines. They are developed quietly and tested one-on-one with customers. You may have no idea how far along your competition is until it is too late.

- Developing and making your database operational is only the start of a long learning curve that will transform the way you handle customers. The database by itself is nothing. It is the way you use it that will make the difference. Once you have it, you must train staff throughout the company: customer service, sales, billing, delivery, acquisition, telemarketers, direct-mail production. You will have to change your forms and procedures to take advantage of the increased knowledge and contact with customers. None of this can begin until you have a database. And the staff training and learning curve may take more than a year itself.

■ What if your company is too big for a one-year process? Impossible. What you must do is to begin small—start with the top five, 10 or 20 percent of your customers. Make them an elite group or club. Develop your marketing database just for them. Extend it to others only when you have a sound concept that is working well—*but you must get started.*

Recently I sat for several hours with the planning committee of a major bank which was developing a long-range marketing database plan. The committee had already decided to build the project in-house, and was heavily staffed with MIS people. They planned to use the existing terminals throughout the bank as their mechanism, so that more than a thousand different people could tap into the database at the same time once it was up and running. But when would that day come? Their subcommittees reported one by one, adding additional requirements. At first, they had planned to get up and running in three years. That was a year ago. Now they were working on a five-year program which would meet the needs of all sections of the bank. What would they do in the way of direct marketing in the meantime, we asked?

"Oh, we have a program that we developed several years ago which we will keep pursuing until our database is ready."

We nodded, saying nothing. But, as we compared notes after the meeting, we recalled that the marketing staff's perception of the failure of the current direct marketing program was the reason that we had been asked to come to the meeting in the first place. That failure was now forgotten as the group concentrated on their five-year objective. One of the first steps the group had decided upon was to "lock in" the hardware design of their terminals so that their

MIS staff could know what equipment to purchase during the next five years. We left the meeting shaking our heads.

Should the Database Be Built In-House?

There are some examples of good marketing databases built on in-house computer systems, but from my observation these are the exception. There are important and telling reasons why most companies look to an outside service bureau to build their marketing databases:

- Unless your company is very unusual, your MIS staff does not have the software and experience to mount a marketing database. As you recall from the chapter on software, you will need a very large relational database with about a dozen other major types of software including merge/purge, geocoding, statistical modeling, on-line direct access, ad-hoc reporting, custom reporting, on-line telemarketing, and so on. This software is very expensive, and takes several months to learn. The MIS staff must dedicate at least two programmers to install it and learn to operate it. This may be a difficult commitment.

- For this reason, setting up a database in-house is almost always much more expensive than an outside contract. Outside service bureaus experienced in marketing databases already have all of the necessary software and have trained their staffs to use it. Their costs are spread over several clients' accounts, so they don't have to charge you a lot of initial costs when you become a client.

- The hardware requirements are significant, and usually much more than your MIS staff and budget will normally support. From the beginning they will be telling you that your disk requirements are excessive. They will try to talk you into down-scaling your project so that it will fit on their equipment.

- The in-house priorities will usually work against you. After all, the MIS in your company exists for some very definite reasons, none of which involves marketing. They are grinding out the payroll, sending out the bills, maintaining the inventory, controlling the manufacturing process. All these projects take priority over marketing, and most of them have a long backlog of program revisions and improvements scheduled and promised. It will be six months or more before they can fit your application into their schedule. Their slow-moving schedule will wear you down.

- Even worse, the MIS culture is at variance with your marketing dynamism. Most marketing databases require almost constant testing, modification, retesting, shifts in approach. A programming staff of two or three is kept constantly busy on a full-time basis making changes in your database to support your learning curve and the dynamics of marketing. There is no such thing as a marketing database that runs itself. But your MIS staff will have difficulty reconciling that kind of resource allocation with their other applications. When they write a payroll, billing or inventory program, it is expected to run flawlessly for the next several years. MIS will expect you to draw up a firm list of software requirements in detail so that they can budget the application. The idea of changing it every week as experience dictates will be a difficult sell.

- Yours may be the first on-line operation in your company. If it is, it will be a shock to MIS. They are used to bringing the computer down any time they need to fix something. If your database has now got fifty customer service and acquisition telemarketers on-line all day and half the night including Saturday and Sunday, MIS will find that they have to make their fixes between 2:00 A.M. and 5:00 A.M. It will make them very grumpy.

- There is a more subtle reason for going outside. MIS is not your contractor. They are a sister function to marketing, with responsibilities to the entire organization. Once your database is firmly committed to inside, and funds have been expended to get it started, you are just another user. When you announce that you need some rapid changes, you may find that your changes have been shunted to a six-month queue, like everyone else's. There will be nothing you can do about it—kiss your dynamic database plans goodbye.

On the other hand, you should be able to control an outside company. Put them on a short leash. Be sure that your contract specifies that you get rapid action on your requests with rewards and penalties built in. Be sure that you are the Database Administrator, and that you call the shots on what is done, when it is done, how it is done. *You,* not your contractor, will run the database. This is the tremendous advantage you will have in building your database at an outside service bureau.

Setting Up a Database Planning Team

You will need a database planning team with someone from marketing as its clearly defined director. On the team you will need people from marketing, market research, sales, customer service, billing, dealer support, MIS and someone from your creative direct agency. As soon as you have selected your outside service bureau, add it to the team. You may also want an outside database marketing consultant and an outside telemarketer.

As you assemble the team, you will soon realize that there are two basic types of people involved with a marketing database. I call them *constructors* and *creators.* A constructor is a person who is interested in putting the pieces together to make a database work. He or she may be interested in the hardware, the software, in accumulating the names, converting them to the correct format, arranging the telemarketing system and such. Creators are people who come up with the creative ideas for using the database to provide more service to customers, to increase sales, to build loyalty, to reduce attrition, to generate repeat business.

Creators are seldom very interested in the nuts and bolts of a database which so intrigue the constructors. They are often bored by these details. But don't be misled by that boredom into thinking that you can build a working database without the creators. *Building a marketing database without creative ideas and leadership is a waste of company money*. Databases don't run themselves. They won't earn you a nickel without some very creative ideas which will serve to offset the costs and go on to generate real profits. Make sure your team includes both kinds of people.

Don't make your initial objectives too grandiose. Keep them within bounds so that you can get up and running fast. You can make long-range goals, but don't let them dominate. Remember, *the best is always the enemy of the good.* Shoot for the good now, with the best to come later.

The principal initial objective will be to compile the information for your marketing database and to make it available for several purposes:

- Determining who your best and worst customers are, and initially, developing programs to retain and support your best customers.

- Segmentation and direct mailing or telemarketing to your customers for upselling, cross-selling, retention.

- Supporting a vigorous customer service operation which has access to the database and can add information to customer records based on their contacts.

- Enhancement and augmentation of the customer information base with surveys, demographics, lifestyle.

- Analysis and profiling of your customer base.

- Using your profiles to develop useful lists of prospects and generate leads.

Developing a Standard Format

The first step in creating the database is to identify the information you will retain on each customer. Do not be overly influenced by what you already have on your customer lists. Quite often, the initial data is just barely adequate. For example, you may find that your customer list looks like this:

First Name	10
Initial	1
Last Name	12
Address	25
City	15
Slate	2
Zip	5

Fine. But what is missing here?

Title (Mr., Mrs., Rev., Rabbi, Captain)

Suffix (Jr., Sr., M.D.)

Fuller middle name (J. Richard Stokes becomes J. R. Stokes when all his friends call him "Dick")

Address and city may be truncated on the database and may look funny when used on letters—"20900 MacNaughten Pkwy. N" fills up 25 characters, with no space to put the apartment number.

You will want to create a new format that allows enough space for all the fields and adds many more: telephone, second address line, sex, spouse name, work phone and so on. Think ahead of everything that will be useful for future personalized correspondence and customer service and put those fields in.

Of course, you will want to add fields for household income, family size, educational level, home value and type, complete purchasing history with your company. You may want makes and models of automobiles age, children's names, sex and ages. You also will want fields for response to direct marketing efforts (dates, source codes, amounts) and results of correspondence and telephone calls.

Can you afford all these fields? Can you afford not to have them if your competition moves heavily into database marketing? Remember, bytes are cheap, and they are getting cheaper every year. 125 bytes of information is enough to hold the typical customer file of name, address, phone and other data.

Database Costs for Access to 125 bytes of Information

Year	$/125 bytes
1973	$7.13
1987	$0.05
1991	$0.005

The end result of your efforts should be a comprehensive format for your customer records which will serve for the initial conversion of your present lists to your new database. This initial format will last for only a few months after your database is created. You will discover many gaps which you must fill in the early months. Prepare for dynamic changes in your format. With a relational database and competent programmers, this should be no problem at all.

Determine Your Indexes

You have determined the format of your database records, and at the same time, you have to determine your indexes. An index (as already explained) is an external disk file which tells you where data in your database is located, and how many of each piece of data exist. Fields that are indexed can be retrieved much faster than other fields. Indexed fields can also be used for ad-hoc and custom reports without the need for ever calling up the customer records. What type of fields need to be indexed? Some examples:

Geocode
Age
Sex
Zipcode
Telephone Number
Telephone Area Code
Last Name
City
State
Total Purchases Since Inception

Figure 5-1   Computer Costs Are Falling
(Annual Cost in Dollars)

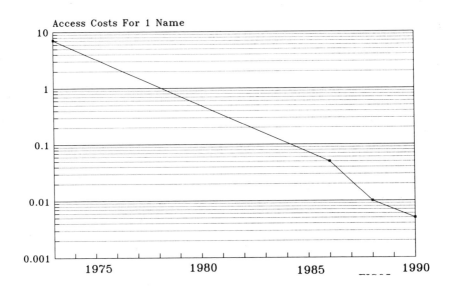

Most Recent Purchase Date
Earliest Purchase Date
Most Recent Purchase Amount
Cell Code
Highest Single Purchase Amount
Credit Limit
etc.

Designing Custom Reports

As a part of the planning process, you will have to determine what reports you expect to get from the database on a regular or periodic basis. Everyone can play a role in report design. Here, interests will diverge: market research will have one set of interests, sales another, advertising a third and marketing still another. You want special reports on customer service activity, on response by cell code, on sales by SKU, on sales by store, by salesman. You will want to know how many people have bought from you often, or recently or in large amounts.

In a marketing database, your programmers will have to write codes for each of these custom reports. Each report should be given a name or a number, and made available to everyone on a menu screen. Then, when the database is set up, individual users can access this menu screen and call for the reports to be printed for them on printers in their offices or nearby.

Custom Report Menu Screen

R01   Sales by Zipcode
R02   Sales by Month
R03   Sales by Cell Code
R04   Sales by SKU
R05   Sales by Customer Frequency Level
R06   Sales by Customer Recency Level
R07   Customers by Income level
R08   Customers Total Purchases by Occupation

Enter Rept No. ___   Begin Date __/__/__   End Date __/__/__

Customer Service versus Market Planning Databases

There really are two different types of marketing databases: those in which you will need to call up individual customer records, and those used mainly for segmenting and communicating with customers. The first type (Customer Service) is used by businesses where customer access is possible and necessary:

Banks
Frequent Flyer Programs
Computer and Software Manufacturers

Business-to-Business
Automobiles
Buyer's Clubs
Retail Stores
Non-profit fundraisers

The second type (Market Planning) is used when calling up and individual household record really makes no economic sense:

Package Goods
Prospecting Files

Examples of the Market Planning database are those maintained by Kraft General Foods, or Quaker Direct. In some companies, there is a Customer Service database for depositors or policy holders, but a separate Market Planning database for their direct programs. Examples of this are legion:

Most Banks which do direct marketing
Insurance companies
Catalog Marketers
Utilities

The fact that you will not call up and look at an individual consumer record does not mean that you do not want to capture and retain many important facts about the consumer household. The more you know, the better job you can do in providing service, and in targeting and personalizing your marketing programs.

Designing User Access

When your users want to see names on the marketing database, what will they see? Can they call up individual customer records? If so, what will they use to call them up? Names, zip codes, customer number, telephone number, company name, SIC code, contact name? These questions have to be decided.

Next you have to decide what the screen will look like. A customer service representative should have a screen that is considerably different from that needed by a researcher or someone in marketing. Screens can, of course, show anything that is stored in the database.

Besides the screens that show individual records, you will want screens that permit you to count, select and download information and records. You may want to select out a list of all customers who have purchased more than $10,000 in the past sixty days for a special mailing. When they are selected, you may want to mark their records as having been selected for mailing number SPL002 on March 24. Then when the responses come in, you can compare them with the outgoing numbers. All of this may be possible from your menu screens if you set them up that way. When these names are selected, you could arrange for a service bureau to send each selected customer a laser letter.

This is the type of advance planning you can do at this point. As a result of such planning, you may go back and revise your record format because the old format lacked some of the data needed to support your ongoing activities.

Now comes the hard part: who will have access to all of this data? Modern database software permits you to assign passwords and access codes to all users. You can have 200 or more people in your company working with your database at once or you can restrict access to only a handful of people. As Database Administrator, you are in a position to make that judgment, supported by your planning team.

You have to decide how those who will have access will gain it. If you are all in one building, the service bureau can arrange a single direct line over which as many different people can access the database at once as the line will allow. For a 9,600 baud line, that would be about sixteen different people. For a 56,000-baud line, you can have more than a hundred.

Do you want them to view the database with a PC or with a terminal? PCs are getting so inexpensive that they have become the choice means to access marketing databases since they have many advantages over terminals. With their hard disks, they can receive data from the database and load local programs such as spread sheets and graphics to display the data; with their PC printers, they can print any mainframe reports or listings or labels directly from the database.

If everyone has terminals already, you may want the marketing database to be accessed from these same terminals rather than having to equip everyone with dual screens. This can be accomplished by having the telephone line from the service bureau containing access to the database lead to a controller in your central MIS department. For any user on your system, you simply enter a command and your mainframe system will switch access from your mainframe programs to the marketing database coming in on the telephone line and controller. There are many possibilities. Your team should explore them all.

How Does a Marketing Database Relate to Existing Files?

This question comes up constantly, and has to be faced head-on. We can restate it this way: should the marketing database be a separate database, stored in a different place from the other company computer records, or should you try to modify your existing files to give them the characteristics of a marketing database?

The answer depends on the type of company and the type of records maintained.

- Suppose the company is a catalog mailer. At present you are responding to calls to an 800-number and opening envelopes filled with money and orders. You keypunch these orders, fulfill the order and add the names to the housefile of customers. Every few months you rent a million names or so, bounce them against your housefile and send out new catalogs. Here the database could be created using the housefile. The 800-number operators who now just take orders without knowing anything about the callers can look at the customer's record on the screen, with complete prior purchasing history, and add the order directly into the database. The 800-number operators can greet customers by name, ask how they liked the sweaters they bought last May and make them feel welcome, wanted and at home.

This type of database is an easy transition, but it will cost more in telemarketing time. Retrieving customer's records and looking at them will make calls last longer. Inquiring about prior purchases will consume telemarketing dollars. You must develop a creative plan to use this increased information to generate increased revenue for it to be of value.

■ What about a bank which keeps its DDA on one computer system, its loans on another, its CD's and savings accounts on a third system? It appears very successful because tellers now can look up a depositor's balance on a nearby terminal every time they cash a check, but they are a long way from knowing a customer's total balance sheet with the bank. Should they try to convert their general ledger system into a marketing database?

My answer would be a forceful "No." To understand why, we have to examine the way financial institutions maintain customer records.

In financial institutions (such as banks, savings and loans, brokerage houses, insurance companies) most marketing databases look at the *household* as a unit, rather than the individual account or individual account holder. This is partly because most individuals have more than one account and partly because the household tends to operate as a unit when it comes to financial matters.

For accounting purposes however, each account has to stand on its own. Some banks permit an automatic transfer from savings to checking and visa versa when funds run short or too high in the checking account, but few, if any, have an arrangement whereby the wife's checking account is automatically tapped when her husband's checking account runs low. The software for maintaining balances, posting interest, clearing checks and deducting fees is audited by examiners and is subject to tax laws and legal challenge. Trying to mix these complicated programs with marketing database programs could become a computer programmer's nightmare.

For this reason, financial institutions' marketing databases are normally maintained as separate files. The customer information files from each of the products sold by the bank are merged, householded and put up as a marketing database once a month. For the next four weeks, this database is used by personal bankers, calling officers, branch managers and marketing staff to support their sales and marketing efforts. To access the data, the officer enters a command from a bank terminal—the same one in which he or she views the DDA account—and gets to see the balances of all the bank products purchased by that household. It is definitely a *separate* file, not connected with the individual account information.

■ What about a cable-TV company, an electric utility, a telephone company, a water company, a cellular phone company, a gas company? Here again, to me, the arguments against converting the company's existing accounting system into a marketing database are overwhelming.

To do marketing, you will want to manipulate a customer file in unpredictable ways. You will want to add many enhancements (demographics, lifestyle, survey data). You will want to segment the file and do mailings, posting the responses by cell code. You will want to run multiple regressions, profile the data and add prospects and leads to your list. If at the same time with the same database you have to mail out monthly bills, post payments and partial payments to bills, collect utility taxes and cut off service for non-payment, your marketing activities are bound to get in the way, and, in many cases, to be shunted aside in favor of more pressing requirements.

How, then, can such companies build a marketing database? They simply spin off a copy of the customer base every month, every week or every night, for that matter, and use that copy to update and refresh the marketing database. The two functions must

---

Figure 5-2. Marketing Databases Should Be Kept Separately

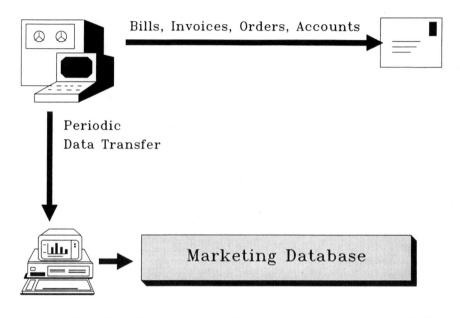

Company's Mainframe Computer System

Bills, Invoices, Orders, Accounts

Periodic
Data Transfer

Marketing Database

---

be kept separate. Marketing is a very important function: it should stand on its own and not be secondary to operational activities.

Isn't keeping two copies of a customer file more expensive than keeping just one? In most cases, the answer is no. Computer disk space is very, very cheap, and getting cheaper every year. Computer programmer's time is becoming more and more expensive. A good marketing database requires constant program changes as a result of testing, experience, retesting and dynamic new ideas. If you are working with a *live* database used for billing and accounting, your programmers will have to work twice as hard when making changes in your marketing programs because of the constant worry that some of their marketing changes would impact the billing and accounting system. In most cases keeping two separate databases is actually cheaper than combining them.

I have covered only a few of the types of businesses which should or should not convert their current customer files into marketing databases. From the discussion, however, it seems clear that, in general, you should not try to convert a customer file used for accounting and billing into a marketing database. Make a weekly or nightly copy, and use the copy to refresh the marketing database. It will be cheaper to do it this way, and more satisfactory for marketing purposes.

Where Do You Get Customer Names?

For the bank or the insurance company, the answer is easy. But what about the furniture manufacturer? Who is buying your beds and dining-room tables? If they bought dining-room furniture, what about showing them what you have for living rooms? Furniture is always sold by dealers, almost never direct. Why should you get the names of the ultimate consumers, and what can you do with them?

Of course, by now, we know the answer to these questions. Dealers are often too small to set up a database. You can help them by building a database of ultimate customers to establish brand loyalty. You work with the dealers to furnish them leads for more sales. You have to get those names, and start to cultivate them yourself. How do you do it?

Obviously, you have to pack a registration card in with each item you sell. You have to make it very worthwhile for the consumer to fill in that card. What can you offer? Cash back, low-cost accessories, a catalog, a sweepstakes? You experiment and test. Make the registration card a survey form: find out the household income, education level, house value and style, furniture style, presence of children and so on.

How do you get names if you are a retailer? It should not be difficult. Many retailers have their own credit cards. Others write down the names and addresses for deliveries. You may be able to purchase names of people who have charged their purchases of your products on their credit cards. Supermarkets have established frequent-buyer clubs. Video stores have it easy. Movie theaters have set up sweepstakes and "Sneak Preview Club" enrollments. Once you determine that you are going to have a database, you and your employees can come up with hundreds of creative ways to learn who your customers are. Reward your employees for getting the names, and reward your dealers.

One major electronic retailer Radio Shack has never failed to amaze me. I have shopped there for thirty years. They have scores of stores in cities across the country. Every time I buy anything from them, even a fifty-cent battery, I have to write down my name and address. Yet I have never received a single piece of mail from them. What do they do with all these names? Who knows? They certainly don't have a marketing database with me on it.

How to Convert Names

The names and addresses of customers you obtain to use for your marketing database will never be in the correct format which you have established for your marketing database. That is a given. But it is not really a problem. Most service bureaus have software that will convert anything from one format to another at very low cost and in a matter of minutes. I mention this simply to alert you to a step that must be taken before the database can be loaded. If you are trying to maintain your database in-house, your programmers may see this file conversion as a major exercise. If they do, try to get it done by a service bureau.

Before the names can be loaded, you must do a merge/purge to consolidate duplicates. You will want also to do an *edit check* on the data to go into your database. Check the SKU numbers for validity, the dates, cell codes, the dollar amounts. Every field should be checked by an edit program which knows what is within the correct range and what is nonsense. Records which fail the edit check will have to be corrected or, at least, the bad data should not be entered. The same edit checks should be built into the database if it is to be updated "live" by your telemarketers. The edit checks won't let them enter "Ten" in a numeric field, or AL in the state field, if the zipcode shows that the customer is in Alaska.

You may also want to enhance your data at this point. This means finding out the geocode (including zipcode, carrier route

Figure 5-3   Creating a Marketing Database

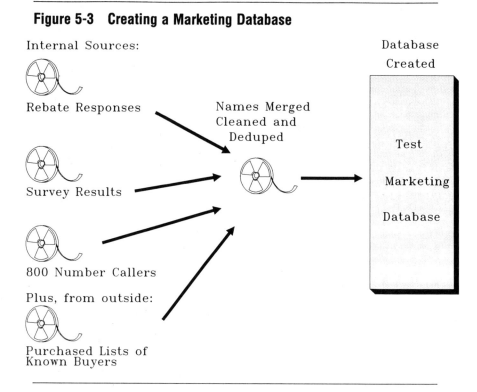

Internal Sources: Database
                                                     Created

Rebate Responses   Names Merged
                          Cleaned and
                          Deduped   Test

Survey Results   Marketing

                                                     Database

800 Number Callers

Plus, from outside:

Purchased Lists of
Known Buyers

---

number, census tract and block) using special software, and appending demographic information (assumed income, house value). You may also want to append lifestyle information which you have available, plus age, sex, motor vehicles owned and such.

Loading the Database

Now we are ready to load the database. This is a big step. All the previous steps, the conversion, the duplicate elimination, the editing, the enhancing, have been working with a *flat, sequential file.* Programs that accomplish this work very rapidly. Depending on your mainframe and how busy it is, you can usually run an edit check, for example, of a million names in a half hour or less. But when we come to load the database, the time involved increases considerably.

Figure 5-4   Loading a Database Takes Time

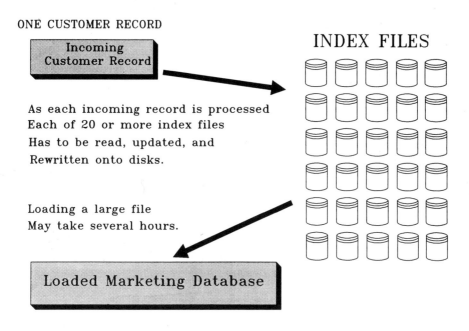

ONE CUSTOMER RECORD

Incoming
Customer Record

INDEX FILES

As each incoming record is processed
Each of 20 or more index files
Has to be read, updated, and
Rewritten onto disks.

Loading a large file
May take several hours.

Loaded Marketing Database

As we were planning our database format, we determined the indexes. Loading the database now brings these indexes into play. As each new name is added to the database, all the indexes have to be updated. This will take a long time, even on a fast computer. To add a million names to a database with thirty indexes may take all night or even longer. Fortunately, modern computers can do many things at once. Normal operations don't stop just because you are loading the database. But batch operations to load or update records in a marketing database will always be very slow.

This is not necessarily true of getting data out of a marketing database. Simple counts and reports should come back in a matter of minutes, even from a database of several million names. If you want to select a half a million names from your database, based on criteria that you have developed during previous counts and reports, the process is as follows.

Enter the select criteria from your terminal or PC, and ask the database, using a menu screen, to store the resulting names on a disk file named XXXXXX. The computer will then tackle this task, finishing up, notifying you when it has been done. At that point, you should fax to the service bureau detailed instructions on what to do with the selected names ("Make a tape and send it to XXXXX; give me a set of cheshire labels and send them to XXXXX.") Some of the software systems make heavy weather of this selection process, taking several hours or longer. There is good marketing database software that will accomplish most selects in less than a minute even from files of millions of names. Shop around and be sure you have the best.

Determining Priorities

As planning for the new database begins, you will have to consider the question of priorities for your database functions. Your DBA will play a central role in determining what the priority of each function should be.

Generally speaking, your computer will tackle the command with the highest priority (lowest priority number) before it tackles anything else. Of course, if you assign everything priority 1, then nothing has priority and everything is equally slow. You have to decide what should take precedence for "priority" to have any meaning or impact.

For database marketing, here is a rough idea of the priority you should assign, from highest priority to lowest priority:

1. Customer service screens.
2. New customer acquisition telemarketers.
3. Screens of individuals who are entering data or communicating with the database on an individual basis.
4. Regular and custom reports.
5. Ad-hoc reports.

6. Selecting records from the database.
7. Nightly batch updates and backups.
8. Market research multiple regressions and other modeling statistical functions.

Developing a Marketing Program

This is the most important part of the database building process: it is the reason that you build the database in the first place. You would think that it would be the first thing that you do, but in fact it is usually the last, and is often short-changed.

It is amazing how many companies fail to put together a functioning database marketing program in the first year. They spend all the money on putting this product together, and then when it becomes operational, they don't use it. It just sits there. One bank we knew had great plans for their database. By the time they had it set up the person in charge had left. Those who remained had no real concept of how to use the database, so it languished. The bank got little real use out of it.

Another company built a database of two and a half million customers who had bought their product. When the database was set up, no one had any real idea of what to do with the names. Almost a year was occupied in developing concepts for test mailings. Meanwhile, the names grew stale.

Why is that marketing databases get built and then not used? I have a theory:

- There are two personality types involved in this business. The type of practical hard-headed personality who can put a database together is quite different from the creative person who can visualize how to use it. The *constructors* worry about hardware, software, list acquisition, merge/purge, edit checks, user access, screens, reports and quality control. The *creators* say "OK. Great. We can deal directly with Sally Warren one-on-one, and offer her super service, recognition, diversity, information. From her we can get loyalty and repeat sales. But what do we have to *do* to get this process started?"

Figure 5-5   User Priorities Should Differ
(Database Priority by Class of User)

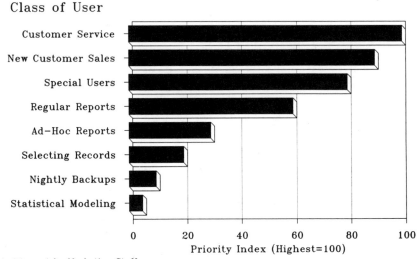

Class of User

Priorities set by Marketing Staff

That is the hard part—that is the reason this book exists.

It is pretty easy to find constructors. They are located in any good service bureau, MIS shop, and in some cases, in marketing or customer service. But finding a creative person who can dream up practical applications and sell them to management is much harder.

Of course, a database is totally worthless unless it is used. A part of your planning has to go into thinking through those first twelve months:

- When will we select our best customers and categorize them all? How will we reward loyal customers?

- What direct-mail steps have we planned? When will they go out?

- How will Customer Service be set up? How will we publicize it? How will we train employees in use of the database?

- How can we use the database to cross-sell and up-sell our customers? What practical steps will we take, and when?

- How do the salesforces and dealers fit in to the database? What will we be doing for and with them in the first twelve months?

Chapter 28 of this book contains a checklist which you should use before you begin to build your database. It is presented at the end of the book because it contains concepts that are developed in later chapters: but it is must reading before you start to build your database.

SUMMARY

Marketing databases must be dynamic instruments of change within the company. They must be used to build customer loyalty, to increase sales, to support dealers, to beat the competition. In almost every chapter of this book are hints about what you must do. Some will work in your company; many will not. Study these hints, find the right ones, add your own ideas and put them together in a plan that will work in your company.

- A marketing database should be up and running within one year from the time it is first approved.

- Waiting too long can be costly to the company and to the success of the database.

- If your company is planning on such a huge database that more than a year is required to create it, scale back your plans and build a smaller database which can get up and running fast. You learn more from your database after it is set up than you do in its construction. It is relatively easy to make changes to an established database.

- Almost all marketing databases are more efficient and cost-effective if built on a service bureau mainframe rather than on inside equipment, because few MIS staffs have the software or experience and MIS may not have the programmers needed.

- The MIS culture may find it difficult to accept a software system that requires the constant changes needed for a dynamic marketing database.

- MIS will probably assign a lower priority to the marketing database than it does to its operating functions such as payroll, inventory, billing, manufacturing. The marketing database could be strangled in red tape.

- In dealing with an outside contractor, you must have an in-house DBA who maintains tight controls.

- To plan the database you need a team consisting of marketing, market research, sales, advertising, customer service, MIS, your creative direct agency, your service bureau and an outside telemarketer.

- You must develop a format for the data you will keep on each customer. Be creative here; do not be constrained by your current format.

- Bytes are cheap. Collect as much information as you need to build a very imaginative customer database.

- Decide what fields should be indexed. Indexes make reporting and access very fast, but each additional index slows down the update and loading process.

- Designing reports will help you in the planning process. Every member of the team should design reports that are needed by his or her function in the company.

- The DBA can determine who in the company will have access to the data, and can assign access codes and passwords.

- Access can be by a PC or a terminal. If everyone in your company already has terminals, there are ways to route the marketing database to them.

- A marketing database should stand on its own and not be considered a modification or addition to existing company databases. In particular, the marketing database should not be kept as a part of customer accounting records, unless these records are created by use of the database for direct marketing.

- Keeping the marketing database separate from other company customer records may seem to be more costly, but will save money in programmer time, which is the most expensive part of any database.

- To keep the marketing database current with other customer files, a copy of the customer files should be spun off on tape periodically and used to update and refresh the marketing database.

- Getting customer names for the database is often a creative process in which everyone must come up with good ideas.

- Converting names from one format to another is very easy for any service bureau—don't make it into a major project.

- Loading a marketing database is usually a very slow process, because of the updating of the indexes. Be prepared for a full day or more.

- Your DBA will have to determine the priority of every user of the database. Customer Service screens should have the highest priority.

- As a part of the planning process, you should develop a marketing program for the first year of the database. The program will help you to be sure that the database is designed properly. It is very important that you make use of the database right away so that you can learn about your customers and how to make the database improve your bottom line.

- You will need to assemble a first-class team to run your database. It must contain both *creators* and *constructors*. Without both types, it will fail.

Chapter 6

The Personal Computer and Database Marketing

The personal computer has several important roles in the database marketing revolution: as a front-end for a mainframe, as a stand-alone display vehicle for reports, graphs and maps and as a possible mainframe replacement. We will cover all of them in this chapter.

The PC as a Front End

It used to be that when your database was stored on a main frame, it was as if it had been put into an old folk's home: you could go to visit it on Sunday afternoons, but the rest of the time it was unavailable to you. To get anything out of it, you had to call on the keepers of the institution, and they would tell you what you needed to know: how many records there were in it, the breakdown by category. But they would charge you for the information and deliver it to you two weeks after you wanted it.

As a result of the marketing database revolution, all that has changed. Marketing databases are supposed to be completely available to you, twenty-four hours a day, seven days a week. You can do your own counts, selects and reports right at your desk, even though the database is in a service bureau several states away.

Using relational database technology and computer terminals or PC's connected with controllers and modems, a few or several hundred people can work with your database simultaneously, with none of them conscious of the impact that the others are having on the system. Telemarketers taking sales and customer service calls are among those who are using these remote terminals.

Marketing professionals usually use a personal computer rather than a terminal to access their database, because they want to perform counting, selecting and reporting functions rather than looking up individual customer records. For the reporting function, the PC is far superior to a terminal.

A modern PC is ideally suited to the "front-end" role. The PC has graphics and color capability. To perform counts and selects, for

Figure 6-1   The Personal Computer as a Front End

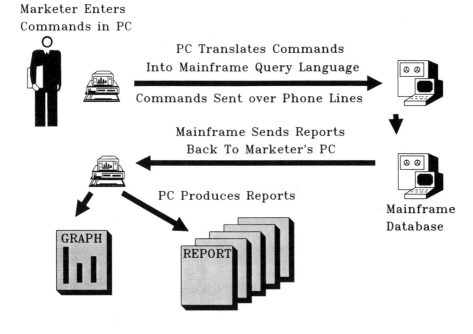

Marketer Enters
Commands in PC

PC Translates Commands
Into Mainframe Query Language

Commands Sent over Phone Lines

Mainframe Sends Reports
Back To Marketer's PC

PC Produces Reports

Mainframe
Database

GRAPH

REPORT

Figure 6-2   Windows Make Selection Easy

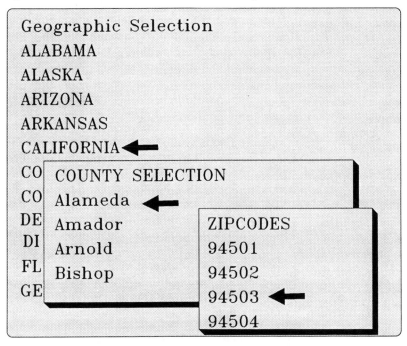

example, the PC has built-in software that presents choices in color-ful "windows" that look something like Figure 6-2.

Using a mouse or the keyboard, you slide rapidly from item to item, selecting from a wide variety of choices, indicating how you want to get information out of your database. Do you want to see the results of the last mailing, broken down by RFM categories with the percentage return on investment figured out? Just slide to the right choice lines, and hit "return." The results will appear on your screen, and, at your command, print on your PC printer.

The PC has software loaded in it which has all the possible choices, (you will help the programmers build in the choices that you want). After you have selected the information you want, the PC will (invisibly to you) reformulate your choices as a string of in-structions to the mainframe (which may work in some arcane computer selection language). These instructions go out from the PC over a telephone line to the mainframe. It uses them to query the database and produce your answers, formatted as you want them with headings, footnotes, page numbers, dates, data and totals. Then the results are transmitted back over the telephone lines to your PC, where you can view them on the screen.

If you want the results printed out, you slide to another window, choose that option, and the printer at your desk springs into action.

Suppose you want the results presented as a bar, pie or line graph. No problem. These graphs are among your possible choices. When the data comes back to the PC from the mainframe, it will automatically be loaded onto your PC hard disk. PC graphics software will take over, converting the hard disk data into a colorful graph which will show up on your screen or can be printed on your laser printer or color plotter.

If you are doing modeling and require regression analysis, you can do the major number crunching on the mainframe, and have the results appear on a PC spreadsheet where you can manipulate it into whatever form you need. If you want to single out fifty customers who have had some problem, or achieved some special status so that you can send them personal letters, the PC can help you to select them by sending your commands to the mainframe. When their names and addresses are selected, you can order laser letters with personalized information in the body of the letter:

> "I am happy to tell you, Mr. Warren, that since you have stayed with our hotels for a total of 206 nights following your trip to Seattle, you have earned the enclosed Harcourt Gold Card which will provide you with preferred service at Harcourt Hotels throughout the world. Congratulations, Mr. Warren. And, let me remind you that your gold card can also be used by Mrs. Warren when she is staying at any Harcourt Hotel, either with you, or on a trip of her own."

The PC is used as a "front end" for a mainframe because it has unique functions that are not generally available on mainframes: graphics, color, windows, spreadsheets and word processing. Mainframes can do all of these things too, but they are very clumsy at them. To use a mainframe for any of these functions would be like trying to weed the garden around your swimming pool with a bulldozer.

Not all service bureaus know how to use a PC as a front end. To find a service bureau that will do that for you will take some looking, but they are out there, and you should insist on finding the right one. Their numbers will increase as database marketing gains momentum. MarketVision is one example of software that includes the PC front end function.

Of course, the other reason for using a PC as a front end is that it is a PC. As a marketing professional, you will not spend all day playing with your marketing database. You will be writing memos and proposals, dreaming up creative copy, doing spreadsheet analysis of the latest mailing and performing other functions on your PC which do not involve access to the mainframe. Having the PC as a front end means that you don't need two keyboards on your desk, a mainframe terminal and a PC. You can do all your business with a PC, which is much more efficient for you and less expensive for the company.

Creation of Maps

Some companies have used the PC to create an almost incredible product. Claritas, Equifax and Donnelley Marketing have come out with three PC products: Compass, Infomark and Conquest, which do wonderful things with census, cluster and survey data.

Designed mainly for the financial services industry, these marketing aids will draw precise maps of your marketing areas, complete with streets and street names, census block numbers, in any area, size or shape. Data on the incomes, home values, spending habits, savings propensity and hundreds of other facts about people in any geographic area are shown on maps in living color, and presented in easy-to-read tables with labels, percentages, averages, medians and so on. They are wonderful.

For example, you can plot and label shopping centers, businesses or yours and your competitors' locations with a number, code, symbol or actual name. With the zoom feature, small areas within a market can be easily displayed. Data can be displayed in up to eight colors plus an unlimited variety of cross-hatch and fill patterns.

Figure 6-3   Market Potential Index Map

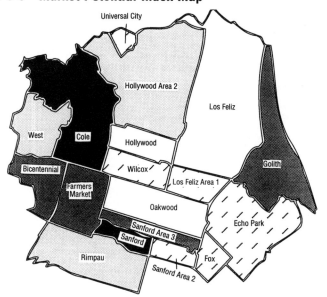

HOLLYWOOD 4 MILE RADIUS -- ZIP LEVEL

Ranked by MPI
Of Drink Rum (19.8%)

	Households			Market Potential Index		
Quintile	Count	% Comp		MPI	High	Low
▢ Quintile 1	52,169	19.16		116	122	112
▪ Quintile 2	58,354	21.43		104	110	102
▢ Quintile 3	58,353	21.43		98	99	98
▨ Quintile 4	39,161	14.38		96	96	95
▨ Quintile 5	64,256	23.60		91	94	49
Total	272,293	100.00		101	122	49

You can identify the boundaries of your own trade areas, sales territories and such using circles, polygons or zipcodes. You can map by census tract, zipcode, county, ADI, DMA, SMSA or state.

Market Potential Index Map

Used by such corporate giants as JC Penney, Aetna, McDonalds, Amoco, Southland, Pizza Hut, Sears, Mobil Oil and Citicorp, these products can be used for presenting, mapping and analyzing:

- consumer expenditure data by category
- product and media usage data
- industry specific data
- your own marketing data
- the advisability of various sites
- the coverage of alternate media
- the profile of your customers.

What's more, using large hard disks or compact laser disks, a PC can actually hold information on 85 million U.S. households or seven million businesses and industries: their financial data and geographic location for mapping and reports. It is mind-boggling to see these machines at work and to use them yourself.

At prices starting at $25,000 and going up to about $85,000 for a complete system with data on the whole United States, plus about $15,000 for a PC, laser printer and color plotter, you can turn your marketing office into a data powerhouse with maps and reports on consumers and businesses anywhere in America.

The PC data files can be programmed to accept survey data of the most detailed kind, marketing information from:

- The SRI survey of Consumer Financial Decisions
- Mediamark Research

- National Planning Data
- Dun and Bradstreet
- Equifax
- Arbitron
- SRI VALS 2 Psychographic data
- Gallup
- FDIC.

In addition to all of this survey data, you can put your own customer data into the PC. For example, banks that keep records on twenty or more customer products (checking accounts, savings accounts, consumer loans) can draw maps of each branch showing where their bank is getting its money from and *where the competition is strong*.

This software also includes TIGER, the census program that can draw maps of every road and street in America, complete with its name, latitude, longitude and census block identification.

If you want to map your market areas in detail, you must get one of these systems. They are absolutely the ultimate and they are very cheap at the price.

Do not confuse them with a marketing database, however. There is no provision in any of them for interactive input of data. Because they are on PCs they work very slowly. I tried drawing a simple map with one of the systems on a 20 MHZ 386 PC, which is a relatively fast machine. It took about eight minutes. Now that is not bad. It produced a super map.

But this is marketing research. It is not database marketing. The machines will not help you to set up a two-way dialog with your customers or to correspond with them. You cannot get their records up on the screen when you are talking to them. Because the software is mounted on a single-user PC, it is really limited to maps and reports. For marketing research, though, there is nothing better.

Stand-Alone Database Marketing

Some people are suggesting that database marketing can be done on a PC. They are not arguing in support of one of the mapping machines we have just been describing. What they propose is mounting the database on a PC equipped with database software and a large hard disk so that you can put all your customers records on it, look them up, update them and also do counts and selects.

One successful method involves restructuring the data around a household ID, with the development of indexes for each of the many factors of interest to marketers, as described in Chapter 4. Using these indexes, rather than the actual customer records, several firms have developed software that performs complex modeling functions on a personal computer. The software develops scoring equations for all desired marketing questions, and stores the results in the database.

Typically, every household has modeling scores on such items as recency, frequency, monetary amount, product purchase type, demographic and psychographic factors and so on, reduced to a numerical value (their relative decile score for each factor), and stored in the customer record. With this method, the practitioner then uses software which permits a PC to gather instantly all people who are 45 to 65, who have bought a certain product more than six times during the past year, or what have you.

This method can be used by marketers in virtually any size company, by storing the data on compact disks, accessed by rapid database software. Data on more than a million customers can be manipulated in this way by marketing researchers. When they have completed their analysis, they can select the actual customer records and use them for direct marketing.

PC Customer Database In Banking

Banc One Corporation, headquartered in Columbus, Ohio, is a holding company with fifty-two bank affiliates. A few years ago, the corporation created a central unit for Direct Marketing Services, headed by Bobbie Hagen. Every quarter, each member bank submits a tape of their customers. The seven million name customer tapes are processed by an outside service bureau and the relational database is housed on a PC in the bank's central office. Using this PC, Ms. Hagen can perform sophisticated analysis leading to about sixty different promotions every year involving mailings of about 3,500,000 plus outbound telemarketing.

Ms. Hagen has been able to learn a lot about the bank's customers from this database. They tried appending demographic information from an outside supplier. The appended data did not improve response significantly. She found that the best predictor of customer response is RFM analysis: how recently each account was opened, what the activity has been, how many products they are using, how big the balances are. Using RFM she can do predictive modeling, which helps the bank improve profitable response.

Not all of Banc One's banks participate in all of the central programs. A typical promotion will involve five to thirty banks. The bank affiliate pays for the mailing, but the Direct Marketing department handles all tracking and analyses. The bank affiliates pick the promotion that features the product they require for their bottom line.

Almost every campaign is a combination of direct mail and telemarketing, with the in-house telemarketing staff working the telephones. A customer is targeted by modeling for a particular product; if the customer does not respond as expected, he or she will get a telephone call, which helps to close the sale. In this way, Ms. Hagen has gotten responses as high as 45 percent on a credit card mailing, and lesser, but very profitable responses on scores of other promotions. Almost all products have been promoted in this way, except automobile loans. A program to promote auto loans is in the works, using data from existing loans and computing when a new car should be purchased.

Bobbie Hagen has not yet computed lifetime value for bank customers, but it is now high on her agenda. She believes that she can use the database to determine the lifetime value to the bank of each type of customer by product. In this way she will learn what the bank should spend to acquire or to promote a new product with a customer.

What Bobbie Hagen is doing is not database marketing as defined in this book. She gets responses entered into her computer only once a quarter. But the predictive modeling she is able to do has put her bank way ahead of most of the competition in terms of learning the best segment of the customer base to target, and the pitfalls to avoid. The only way to learn direct marketing is to try it. For Banc One, it has been a great success.

Many direct marketers use a statistically representative *sample* of the customer database and work with that to analyze direct mail response and do market research. This may prove to be fully as accurate as the real thing, and more rapid and cost effective.

Is This Database Marketing?

These techniques can be highly successful. Many companies are using them. But are they database marketing? There is no question that if you put all your customers on a single PC, and have someone spend full time working with the file, counting, sorting, selecting, you can learn a great deal about your customers. You can come up with very creative marketing ideas. You can do sophisticated market research, segmentation and direct marketing. You will probably be way ahead of where you were before. But this type of valuable analysis is not the same as creating a two-way dialog with your customers which, as I see it, is central to database marketing.

PCs are not powerful enough for that role. To have more than one person access the PC, you will have to set up a local area network (LAN), which is a system that links several PCs to a single hard disk where the database would be located. LAN networks are nice, but they slow down access time. Try to put three telemarketing operators on a PC database, while doing market analysis at the same time, and you will bring a fast PC to its knees in no time.

The fact is that except for very special, very small markets, database marketing cannot be done on a PC. Database marketing requires a mainframe, and will require one for the foreseeable future. Here's why:

Multiple access. A marketing database requires that many people in your company have access to the data at the same time. Sales, customer service and marketing, at a minimum. If you have any kind of a customer base, you need at least three users. Most companies will need twenty or even two hundred. If you have branches or dealers they have to be plugged into the system. Mainframes are set up for multiple access; PCs aren't. A large mainframe has forty-eight or more *channels.* A channel is an individual access route for the mainframe to talk to outside users, or internal devices such as tape drives, disks and printers.

A channel is actually a small computer. When the mainframe looks up a customer record on disk, it checks to see which channel is free. Then it asks the channel to do the work. While the channel is doing this, the mainframe goes on to the next chore, which may be

Figure 6-4   Mainframes Have Multiple Channels

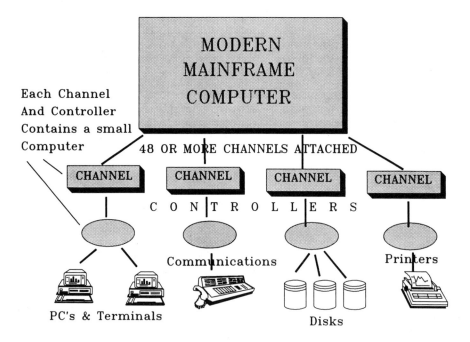

to look up another name for some other user or to perform some other program step. It seeks an appropriate channel for that function, too. After it has placed the second request, it will check back with all its channels to see if any of them have finished any of the work assigned to them. If they have, the mainframe will accept their report or data, and take action on it. All of this is happening at incredible speed—microseconds. With a mainframe, therefore, you really have the equivalent of forty or more PCs all working together in a single integrated system.

The result is rapid access time for users—far faster access than you could ever get on a PC working with a LAN.

Disk capacity. A large mainframe normally has 100 or more gigabytes of disk space in the form of twenty or more individual disk drives, complete with five or more controllers. A gigabyte is a thousand megabytes. A large PC has a few hundred megabytes of disk space. So a mainframe has the equivalent disk space of about 1000 of the largest PCs in use in normal offices. All of this disk space is available for constant use, twenty-four hours a day. Each of the mainframe disk drives is under the control of a *controller* which is actually a small computer. The controller accepts commands from the mainframe channel, and decides whether the disks under its control are free to execute the command. If not, the controller holds the command and waits until the appropriate disk is free. Then it asks the disk to get the data, or write the data requested. Meanwhile, of course, the mainframe is busy doing something entirely different for some other user, and not waiting for this controller and disk at all.

This disk space, controller and channel system means that mainframes are incredibly more efficient in handling data input and output than the fastest PCs.

Multiple CPUs. Many mainframes are really several mainframes hooked together in a single system. Each command coming in is routed to the computer which is least busy at the moment. This provides far more efficiency than is possible from a single CPU.

Backup and Service. Mainframes have round-the-clock operators and systems programmers who are always available to keep them running and fix them when they go down (which happens often). Normally, problems can be fixed in a few minutes. Every night, everything accomplished during the day is "backed up" on tape and stored offsite or onsite. If the computer has a serious mechanical malfunction in one of its disks and the marketing database is lost, it could be recreated in a few hours from the backup tape made the previous night. That is why operators are always on duty.

Of course, with a database mounted on a PC, you cannot have operators and systems programmers standing around watching the PC. You have to depend on the telemarketers or marketing staff to do their own nightly backup and restoration.

SUMMARY

PCs are improving every year, and will continue to do so. They are going to get much less expensive. They are going to get much more sophisticated. It is possible, of course, that they will eventually take on all the features of mainframes that I have just described. But then they will be mainframes!

Until then, marketing databases must be resident on mainframes, preferably in independent service bureaus under the direct control of a database administrator in the marketing department of the company. This is the only system that will work with modern hardware and software.

- Customer files used to be resident on remote off-line mainframes which did not permit constant daily access. Modern marketing databases must be accessible to users at all times. Many people in the company must be able to access the database at the same time.

- Many of these remote users will access the database with terminals working through controllers. Customer service and sales personnel can call up and update any record directly from their terminals.

- Marketing staff should use PCs rather than terminals to access the mainframe marketing database. Modern technology permits the PC to act as a *front end* to the mainframe. The PC uses window technology to set up the reports, counts and selects that the marketers want and sends instructions to the mainframe to process the request.

- When the data comes back to the PC it can be viewed on the screen, printed on a printer or converted into graphics, spreadsheets or word processing.

- The advantage of using the PC as a front end is that you gain all the sophistication of fast PC technology with the number-crunching input-output capability of the mainframe.

- PC front-end technology is new and not universal yet.

- Several companies have developed a unique combination of software and data which permits PCs to draw accurate maps of any part of the United States, down to the street level, which can visibly display data on consumer spending habits, wealth, business locations and such.

- This mapping PC software is superb. It is ideal for marketing research which is geographically oriented, such as the search for the ideal branch location, or media placement for maximum effectiveness by geographic area.

- These PC systems can also be used to show your own customer data on maps. They are not marketing databases and cannot do marketing database work.

- There is an active and useful group of companies working with special PC software which permits their clients to do effective marketing research and direct mail using a PC to hold their customer database. This is a valuable direct marketing tool, but it is not database marketing as defined in this book.

Part Three

Building Relationships
With Your Customers

Chapter 7

How to Select Your Best Customers

WHY DISCRIMINATE?

This is a chapter on how to select your best and your worst customers: how to rank them so that you can give your best service to your best customers. The obvious question is, why? Why not give super service to all your customers?

The answer is that it is much more profitable to discriminate. The old 80/20 rule is true of almost every business: 80 percent (or some other high percentage) of your business dollars comes from the top 20 percent of your customers. If you want your business to grow and become more profitable, you should lavish your attention on this top 20 percent. In addition, you should develop programs to influence the *next* 20 percent to emulate the buying habits of the top 20 percent. But if you make a major effort to serve and influence this top 40 percent group, you will not have the resources left to make a similar effort on the bottom 60 percent. Investigation may show that the absolute bottom 20 percent may be costing you more than they bring in: you may be losing money on them. So you should develop ways to spend less money on these losers.

But there are other, even more powerful reasons for discriminating:

1. It is much more costly to acquire a new customer than to retain the customers you already have.

2. Therefore, it is a mistake to concentrate on acquiring new customers without first doing everything in your power to keep your existing ones.

3. The more you know about what keeps your customers happy, and keeps them your customers, the better you will be at acquiring new ones. Studying customers and ranking them is part of the process of getting to know them.

WHO ARE YOUR BEST CUSTOMERS?

The concept is very simple: your best customers are those who:

- have bought from you most recently,
- buy from you frequently and
- spend a lot of money on your products and services.

On these three principles rest all the laws and the profits.

Let's discuss each of these factors in turn. In this chapter, for illustration, we are going to assume that you are using your customer database as a mailing file. In this way, we can measure the results of each mailing to validate the principles of Recency, Frequency, Monetary (RFM) analysis which we will explain. But don't be misled into thinking that the principles apply only to direct mail: customer segmentation is central to database marketing as well. Many people who have arrived at database marketing from some background other than direct mail (from general advertising, retailing or sales, for example) make the mistake of assuming that this RFM analysis technique is only of use in direct mail. This is not so. The examples we use for testing the RFM principles in this chapter are taken from direct mail, but the results—customer discrimination—are crucial to successful database marketing.

Recency

Recency is a very powerful factor. Obviously someone who bought from you last month is a better bet than someone whose last purchase was three years ago. But does this apply to all gradations of recency? Analysis will show that it does. Here is how you can prove it to yourself.

From your most recent offer to your *existing customers,* do a breakdown of response rates by when they bought from you last. It will look something like this:

Response Ranked by Most Recent Purchase

Most Recent Purchase	Number Mailed	Number Responding	Response Rate	Index of Response
0-3 Months	41,204	3,935	9.55	200
4-6 Months	31,012	2,409	7.77	163
7-9 Months	27,108	1,090	4.02	84
10-12 Months	19,011	539	2.84	59
13+ Months	86,502	1,817	2.10	44
Total	204,837	9,790	4.78	100

The Index of Response is computed by dividing the average response rate (4.78) into the actual response rate (9.55, 7.77, etc.) for each group and multiplying by 100. It shows that your most recent purchasers are twice as likely (200) as the average (100) to buy again. If you were to calculate the cost of the offer, assuming you mailed the same piece to everyone, it could be that you actually lost money on the 13+ Month people, while your profits from the 0-3 month customers were probably excellent.

The lesson here is obvious: lavish your attention on your most recent customers. Provide them super service. Contact them frequently. Let them know you are thinking about them. It will earn you profits, and will help you retain the most valuable group of customers that you have.

Figure 7-1 Response by Recency

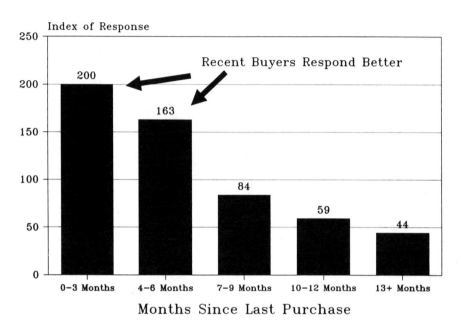

Frequency

Recency is only one part of your analysis. From the same offer you can break your customers down an entirely different way: by *frequency;* by how many times they have bought from you since they first became your customers. Look at these numbers:

Response Ranked by Frequency of Purchase

Total Number of Purchases	Number Mailed	Number Responding	Response Rate	Index of Response
5+	11,101	1,935	17.43	365
4	15,204	1,829	12.03	252
3	18,209	1,193	6.55	134
2	44,220	1,427	3.23	68

| 1 | 116,103 | 3,406 | 2.93 | 61 |
| Total | 204,837 | 9,790 | 4.78 | 100 |

Customers who buy from you many times are much more likely to buy again than those who buy seldom. Of course, some one-time buyers are folks who will be five-time buyers eventually; they haven't had a chance to make all those purchases because they just came on board. That is why your lowest quintile on a frequency rating normally does better than your lowest quintile on a recency rating. Again, remember, these frequent buyers are your best customers. You need to structure your services and benefits with this in mind.

Figure 7-2   Purchase Frequency

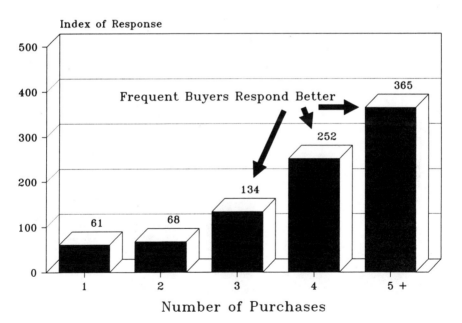

Monetary

Finally, let's rank response from customers by *monetary sales,* by the total dollar value of their purchases since they first started buying from your company.

Response Ranked by Total Lifetime Purchases

Lifetime Purchases	Number Mailed	Number Responding	Response Rate	Index of Response
$500+	4,151	788	18.98	397
$300-499	12,254	1,829	14.93	312
$200-299	15,277	1,493	9.77	204
$100-199	34,220	1,735	5.07	106
$1-99	138,935	3,945	2.84	59
Total	204,837	9,790	4.78	100

Figure 7-3   Response By Lifetime $

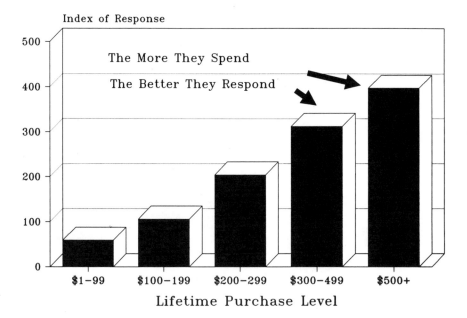

Monetary amount can be calculated in several ways, each of which has benefits. You can measure:

- amount of last purchase,
- amount of total purchases (as shown above),
- amount of average purchase and
- amount of purchases last twelve months.

A PREFERENCE PLAN

From the above three lists, it is possible to develop a preference plan for your customer file. These customers can be grouped into a "preference cube" which looks like Figure 7-4.

Figure 7-4   Preference Cube for Mailing Selection

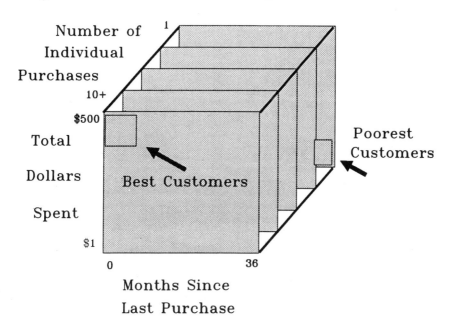

Using the five divisions developed in the previous three examples, you can isolate 125 classes of customer (5 x 5 x 5). The best are those with high-dollar, frequent and very recent purchases. The least desirable are those with low-dollar, low-frequency purchases and a very long time since they last bought.

You can assign a letter codes for each of your classes, and develop a strategy for each group of customers:

- *Top Twenty-Five:* your best customers. Let them know you are thinking about them. Give them preferences that they understand.

- *Next Twenty-Five:* your hope for the future. Put them in a special cultivation program designed to encourage them to move to a higher status. Most of your creative energy should go into this group.

- *Middle Twenty-Five:* your average customer. Hang on to them. Give them good service. Retain them. Try to get them to upgrade.

- *Next-to-Bottom Twenty-Five:* below average, but still profitable. Offer them minimum, but stable and satisfactory service.

- *Bottom Twenty-Five:* these may be losers. Don't waste resources on them. Scrutinize every offer to make sure that you will more than break even with this group, otherwise don't mail.

Recency, Frequency, Monetary (RFM) analysis is standard procedure in the direct marketing business, and has been for a long time. You don't need to stop there, though. You can add other factors which you know about your present customers which may help to discriminate between your best and your worst. You can include such factors as:

- Do they have your own house credit card, or have they established a charge account with you?

- Do they have a good credit rating which is relevant to their buying your products?

- Do you know their telephone numbers, and have they responded positively to telemarketing?

- Have they referred neighbors, friends or family members to your company (getting recognition or rebates for having done so)?

- Have they redeemed a coupon or rebate check with you?

Adding these factors to your information base will somewhat complicate your preference cube. Instead of having three dimensions, it may have five or six. You cannot draw such a cube, but the computer can imagine it and produce reports based on it.

A practical example of the use of RFM analysis follows, to demonstrate how you can use it to improve profits. Then we will take you behind the scenes to see how the analysis is actually constructed on a computer database.

The example used here is simplified. Instead of RFM, we are using only Recency and Monetary. Instead of five quintiles of each, we are using only three measures. The Preference Cube becomes a two-dimensional Preference Square with Recency on one side and Monetary on the other. Much simpler, but it will help to introduce some new concepts, including profit calculations.

A RECENCY—MONETARY EXERCISE

This example was suggested by Jack Lloyd, Vice President of Direct Marketing Technology, Inc. Let us rank customers in a mailing by segments based on their previous purchase date and previous purchase amount (RM), with three breakdowns of each.

- Recency: 0-6 Mo. 7-12 Mo. 13+ Mo.

- Monetary: $0-49 $50-99 $100+

An actual mailing might result in the following results:

Mailing Job Listed by Previous Purchase Amount

Recency Months	Previous Purchase	Pieces Mailed	Number Sold	Dollar Sales	Sales/ Piece	Sales Index	Rank
0-6	0-49	20,000	600	$ 60,000	$3.00	117	4
7-12	0-49	20,000	300	$ 30,000	$1.50	58	7
13+	0-49	20,000	100	$ 10,000	$0.50	19	9
0-6	50-99	20,000	800	$ 80,000	$4.00	156	2
7-12	50-99	20,000	500	$ 50,000	$2.50	98	5
13+	50-99	20,000	200	$ 20,000	$1.00	39	8
0-6	100+	20,000	1000	$100,000	$5.00	196	1
7-12	100+	20,000	700	$ 70,000	$3.50	137	3
13+	100+	20,000	400	$ 40,000	$2.00	78	6
Total		180,000	4600	$460,000	$2.56	100	

We mailed out 180,000 pieces to former customers, broken down into nine different segments based on their previous buying record. We are selling something for $100. The number of items sold in this present mailing is shown, along with the total amount spent (quantity times $100). "Sales/Piece" is a measure of how much we received in sales from that segment divided by the number of pieces mailed (20,000). The index is the average sales per piece ($2.56) divided into the sales per piece of each segment ($3.00, $1.50, etc.) times 100. Finally, the ranking is the rank order of sales per piece, with the highest rank (1) going to that segment of customers who had bought from us previously within the last six months and whose last purchase was more than $100.

Figure 7-5   Mailing Profits By Recency-Monetery

Mailing Segment

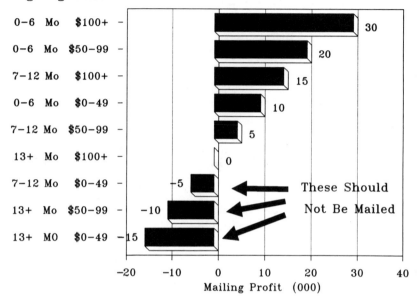

Mailing Profit (000)

Let's rearrange this chart in order of rank. To do this we add the costs of the mailing and the products sold, and substitute profits for sales. Let us assume these prices:

Cost of each direct mail piece	$	1.00	
Total cost of mailing	$	180,000.00	(180,000 x $1)
Number of items sold		4,600	
Cost of mailing per item sold	$	39.13	($180,000/4600)
Selling price of each item sold	$	100.00	
Cost of each item sold (50%)	$	50.00	
Less cost of mailing	$	39.13	
Average profit on each item sold	$	10.87	
Total profit	$	50,000.00	(4600 x $10.87)

Mailing Job Ranked by Successful Sales

Recency Months	Previous Purchase	Pieces Mailed	Number Sold	Dollar Sales	Sales/ Piece	Sales Index	Rank
0-6	100+	20,000	1000	$ 30,000	$5.00	196	1
0-6	50-99	20,000	800	$ 20,000	$4.00	156	2
7-12	100+	20,000	700	$ 15,000	$3.50	137	3
0-6	0-49	20,000	600	$ 10,000	$3.00	117	4
7-12	50-99	20,000	500	$ 5,000	$2.50	98	5
13+	100+	20,000	400	$ 0	$2.00	78	6
7-12	0-49	20,000	300	$ -5,000	$1.50	58	7
13+	50-99	20,000	200	$-10,000	$1.00	39	8
13+	0-49	20,000	100	$-15,000	$0.50	19	9
Total		180,000	4600	$ 50,000	$2.56	100	

Figure 7-6   Profit from Mailing
Total Sales $460,000

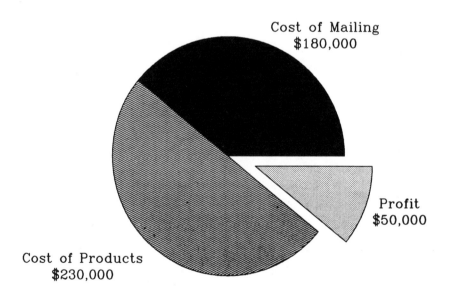

Cost of Mailing
$180,000

Profit
$50,000

Cost of Products
$230,000

Dollar profits are computed by number sold x $50 (gross profit on each item) less $20,000 (cost of the mailing to that segment).

From the above, it is obvious that the lower ranking segments 6, 7, 8 and 9 yielded no profit or a loss. It would have been much better if these segments had not been mailed to at all. If only the first five segments had been mailed, the total profit on the job would have been $80,000 instead of $50,000.

This shows, numerically, why it is better to discriminate among your customers, providing special services to those who are very profitable and less costly services to those who do not yield much net return.

CODING CUSTOMER RECORDS

It all looks very simple and straightforward on these charts. It is a wonder why anyone would mail to these losing segments in the first place. But if you look at the typical customer file, you will discover that the actual records are far more complicated than our neat nine segment analysis. The purpose of this book is to put some practical tools into the hands of marketing database practitioners, let's examine some actual computer programs and show how customer records are coded for RFM.

The first step is to develop a good scheme for natural gradations of recency, frequency and monetary. For example, in recency, should you be looking at the last three months, last six months or some other period entirely? There is a simple answer to this question, which I have found very useful:

Find all the values which exist, arrange them in order and divide them up into five equal parts. These will determine your natural breakdown.

For example, when dealing with recency, tell your programmer to compute for every customer the number of months (or weeks) since his most recent purchase, and put that number into his database record. Then do a computer count of all these numbers, arranging them in order. It will look something like this:

Number of Months Since Last Buy	Number of Customers With this Number
0	2,130
1	4,141
2	3,120
3	2,224
4	2,431
5	4,400
6	1,234
7	5,233
8	2,555
9	7,788
10	5,531
11	3,344
12	4,201
13+	9,803
Total	58,135
Divided by 5	11,627

These numbers then can be broken down into five quintiles with approximately 11,627 customers each, as follows:

Quintile	Date Range	Number of Customers
A	0-3	11,615
B	4-7	13,298
C	8-9	10,343
D	10-12	13,076
E	13+	9,803

Notice, some quintiles are over the average of 11,627, some are under. That does not matter. You have five working groups of approximately equal size which can be used in your analysis.

What happens to the letters ABCDE which we have used to name each of the five quintiles? You put them into each person's record. They take up one byte (character) in the record. Specifically, I mean that you add an additional field to each person's database record called "RFM" which has three spaces for letters in it. The first space is used for Recency. You insert in it either an A or a B or a C, etc. depending on how recently the customer has purchased from you.

Next, do the same thing with Frequency, assigning five quintiles, called ABCDE, and put that code *right next* to the Recency code in each person's record. Finally you put an ABCDE code for Monetary, again breaking the dollar amounts into five approximately equal portions. Since this is often difficult for programmers to visualize, let me explain how it is done.

When you look at many customers' purchase histories, they are often a mess of numbers:

$$\$ \ 34.76$$
$$\$118.22$$
$$\$ \ 12.39$$
$$\$155.00$$
$$\$ \ 70.75$$

These are not clean numbers like 3 months, 4 months, 5 months. How do you handle the breakdown?

The easiest rule is to ignore the dollars and cents, and concentrate on rounding to even $10 increments. For larger customers, it could be even $100; for business clients it might be even $1,000, $10,000 or $100,000.

Actual Purchase	Rounded Group
$ 34.76	$30
$118.22	$120
$ 12.39	$10
$155.00	$160
$ 70.75	$70

From here, it is easy to create the five quintiles. Again, put the ABCDE code *right next to* the other codes in each person's record. If you have other codes for credit or other factors, put them next to the previous ABCDE codes also.

What you have now is each customer's record with three letter codes (at least), each of which has five possible values: A, B, C, D or E. Each person, then, can be segmented by code into one of 125 different segments: (5 x 5 x 5). You are either an:

AAA or AAB or AAC or AAD or AAE or ABA or ABB or ABC, etc.

You should arrange the values of the letters so that their expected purchase behavior is represented by the letters. An AAA is the most recent buyer, with the largest frequency of repeat purchases and the largest quintile dollar purchase. EEE people are the lowest

Figure 7-7   Treat Your Best Customers Better!

Excellent	Top Customers - Treat Them Well
Very Good	Your Hope for the Future
Good	Average Customers - Retain Them
Fair	Offer Standard Service
Poor	Losers: Do Not Waste Resources Here

in all three categories, and probably should be dropped from your database. They bought very little, and only once, and that was long ago.

Classifications change from month to month as people buy more and as time goes by. An AAA can slip to a BAA, and ultimately to an EAA if he or she stops buying. An EEE can rise to being an AAA by simply making many large purchases.

Every time you make an offer or provide special services for your customers, categorize your customer recipients by their RFM (ABC) code beforehand to determine how you think they will respond. Then check the response afterwards to see how close you were to being correct. You will soon learn to save your money by not wasting resources on the EEEs, although you may always want to try a small test just to be sure. (Hope springs eternal in the human breast!)

SUMMARY

The first thing that you should do with your customer data base is to use it to discriminate among your customers: use Recency, Frequency and Monetary (RFM) analysis to pick out your best customers, and your least desirable customers. This is very important. It is the beginning of knowledge. Your database will be much more profitable if you use it correctly to pre-screen your lists. It is also the beginning of a relationship building process with your customers that will help you to modify your behavior and their response in the future, giving better service to them and more profits to you.

- Recent buyers respond better than older buyers. This general law applies to all periods of time.
- Frequent buyers respond better than infrequent buyers.
- High-dollar buyers respond better than low-dollar buyers on almost any kind of offer.

- All databases should be categorized by RFM and the codes for their level should be inserted in their database records so that you can use the codes to discriminate in how you treat them.

- Other information which you know about customers can also be coded into the database.

- Whenever you do mailing, telemarketing or other promotions, the RFM codes should form a part of your selection methods. You should estimate your response by RFM group. After the promotion ends, check your results against your predictions. As time goes by, you will get better and better at predicting results. You will learn to concentrate on the winners and ignore the losers. As a result, you will become more profitable.

- The easiest way to code RFM is by quintile: dividing your customers into five approximately equal groups. The highest groups are the most responsive, and the lowest are the least.

- RFM coding, predicting, testing and counting are the beginnings of being able to understand your customer. It is part of the science that underlies database marketing.

Chapter 8

Maintaining Loyalty

We have already determined who our best customers are through RFM analysis. How do we "lavish attention" on them?

To approach this question, let's go back to the old corner grocer. When we last saw him, he was standing in the front of his store meeting his customers as they came in to shop. He calls them by name, and asks about their families, vacations, houses, jobs. He doesn't say, "What are you going to buy from me today?"

Perhaps the customer has a request or a complaint. He listens; he agrees with her. It *is* too bad that they were out of rosemary last week, and that she had to go over to that horrible supermarket to buy it. "We have your rosemary today, a little late, of course. We won't run out of that again soon, I can tell you that. We also have some fresh salmon, and I know that Dan loves our salmon."

"Can we get some coconut extract? I'll have it for you Tuesday morning. When do you need it? . . . Oh, oh. I'll run over to the warehouse myself after lunch, and have some for you this afternoon."

What is he doing? He's wrapping that customer in a cocoon of loyal services, kindnesses and understandings that will keep her buying at his store forever. How can he make any money driving to a warehouse for an 85-cent bottle of coconut extract? He can't. What he is doing is maintaining the loyalty of a customer whose lifetime value to him is several thousand dollars. He thinks long-term. He isn't thinking about the sale. He is thinking about the loyalty of Sally Warren and her family, and what that means to his business.

Can we hope to duplicate the activities of this caring man with our marketing database? Never. But we can try to come close, and that is the focus of this chapter.

If you look at what the grocer is doing, you can break it down into specific actions and reactions by the customer. When you walk into his store:

You are recognized and greeted by name.

Your family and prior history are remembered.

Your prior transactions are remembered.

Your special preferences are remembered.

Your special requests and complaints are listened to, and *something is done about them.*

We can do many of these things on our marketing database. Let's first visualize the telemarketing situation. We have a telemarketer who is responding to calls on an 800 number. As soon as the call comes in, we have to decide whether this is an old customer or a new one. How do we do that?

One possibility is to equip our telemarketing terminals with ANI, the equipment that tells us instantly the telephone number of the calling party. ANI gives us the area code and number. As soon as we enter that into our system, our computer can do an automatic search of a telephone number index and determine that the person calling is customer number 1234567. Her record comes up on the screen. We have her name, address, credit card number, prior history and so on—everything needed to make the call. Instead of "Hello," we could say, "Mrs. Warren! Good to hear from you again."

Knowing the number of the calling party as you receive the call provides the following advantages:

- Allows you to treat incoming calls from non-customers differently depending on where the call comes from. Even though they are all calling the same 800 number, the call can be taken by different sales personnel based on territory.

- Lets you tell the caller who the nearest dealer is, since you know the geographic area.

- Flags your loyal customers so you can greet them personally by name and give them expedited service.

- Enables your computer to call up the customer's entire record on the screen so that the operator can speak knowledgeably at the very outset of the call.

What Telemarketers Do

Imagine Mrs. Warren's reaction. Instant recognition. She is pleased, flattered, surprised. She feels at home with your telemarketer *even though this particular operator has never spoken to her before.*

If you recall the old fashioned telemarketer, you can hear the traditional exchange: "May I have the catalog number of the first item, please." But that is not what our marketing database operator is going to say at all.

"How was your trip to Spain? Did you stay at one of the Paradores?" (What does this have to do with selling luggage? Nothing. It has to do with the lifetime value of Sally Warren.) "How did your overnight suitcases work out on the Spanish Railway system?"

Our operator is compensated on two things: sales (as at present) and *recorded information.* As Sally Warren and the operator chat about life, the operator is entering important information into the database. The information: "Lock forced on suitcase on Spanish railroad. Camera stolen. Dan promoted to head of engineering department. She is buying leather briefcase for him." This information is converted by the operator and the software into some simple codes that can be used later to provide better service to the customer.

"You have a lifetime guarantee on that suitcase. If anything happens to it, we replace it at 50 percent of its original cost. Shall I send out a replacement for the one that had the lock smashed? . . . Oh, sure, I know the number. It is the green carry-on bag with the red satin interior. We will send one out next week. Now here is what we have in briefcases . . . ."

But Sally doesn't want to buy this briefcase over the telephone. This is too important. It is for a party to celebrate Dan's promotion. She wants to learn what is available and then go and see the ones she is interested in at a local store. A briefcase with a built-in calculator, a holder for business cards and such, in maroon leather strikes her fancy. We give her the telephone number of the luggage departments of several local stores that stock this briefcase. And we give her a code number over the telephone. If she buys at any of these stores, she gives the clerk the code number and receives a $5 credit on her Master Card account.

Why the $5 credit? She is in the market for the briefcase. Isn't this just a waste of money? Perhaps. There are two good reasons for this credit. The first is that, when she gets to the store, she may see a competing brand that looks better. But she won't have a $5 credit on that brand. The real reason for the $5 is to get her to *use the code number*. This code number will assure that her purchase of this briefcase will get into the database. We now have tied two things together: Sally Warren's desire for a briefcase for Dan's promotion, and the fact that she bought one of our briefcases. We have the model, color, style, date recorded. One more strand in the cocoon of knowledge and relationships which will bind the Warren family to our company.

Another feature of the code number is that we will know which dealer sold her the briefcase. As far as we are concerned, dealers are customers too: very important customers. We are keeping track of the fact that we steered Sally Warren to Fisher's. And a whole new story opens up from that.

Enter the Dealer

Just as we want to keep the Warren family loyal and buying, we want to keep Fisher's and the other dealers loyal, stocking our merchandise, cooperating with our programs. We will never make a direct sale without also suggesting that customers call a local dealer, giving the names and telephone numbers of these local dealers. We sell at list price. The dealers discount. We tell everyone that. We deliver by UPS. The dealers also deliver.

The dealers have come to understand the value of our data base. Every month we give them a printed record of the business we have supplied to them through the database. And what's more, we give each dealer a direct access to our database through a terminal at their store!

This is modern database marketing. Many dealers will be equipped with a small PC or terminal (which costs only a few hundred dollars) and an automatic dialer which puts them in direct contact with the marketing database. When a customer walks in to buy a name-brand product made by a firm with a marketing database, it will be automatic to dial up that database during the sale process. Not only can the sale be entered, and the customer given a rebate (if any), but the dealer can also have access to valuable information about customers which permit the dealer to understand them, talk with them knowledgeably about their former purchases and lifestyles, and, in the process, offer them better service: possibly cross-selling or up-selling based on prior history.

The dangers of untrained personnel in the dealer's store messing up the database with their entries is significant enough that safeguards must be built in. The dealer's access must be essentially "read only" meaning that his staff can access and read data from the database, but not update or change it. This protects the database from being accidentally destroyed. The software *does* permit the dealer to enter some new data: the current purchase, the code number and so on. As this data goes in, it is checked by an edit program to insure accuracy. If the dealer tries to enter an SKU which does not exist, he will get an error message. The same thing happens with the code or other data. The date and time of purchase and the dealer ID is entered automatically by the system.

The customer may be a member of a special "gold card," preferred customer class based on prior sales history with a particular manufacturer, or with the dealer. If so, this fact can automatically be triggered by the sale—even if the customer did not present a "gold" card at the point of purchase. The Visa, MasterCard or American Express card number will be automatically registered by the dealer at the time the card is presented. If the customer is on the "gold" list, the store record or manufacturer's database record will be called up and displayed. At the same time, of course, if he or she is a customer with a bad credit history, presentation of the card will also trigger appropriate action at the point of sale. No more looking up

information in a thick pamphlet. The credit card verification process
will turn up the good and bad information, and bring up the appropriate database.

But we are getting ahead of the story. Let us return to the corner grocer for a moment, and explain this "gold card" concept.

Preferred Customers

Not all customers are equal, as we have already seen. Some must be
courted. Some are not worth bothering with. Some are new, and we
must be very nice to them until we can learn more about them.

The corner grocer knows this. He knows that if he is too chatty
with his preferred customers, he may "turn off" new people who
have just come in and who are beginning to feel that one must have
a long prior history to buy anything in this store. The preferred
customers are aware of this, too. They realize that he cannot spend
all day with them. He gives them a knowing wink as he leaves them
to turn to the newcomers to say in a loud voice, "Well, what can I
do for you folks?" Such gestures convey to preferred customers that
they are "in" and that these newcomers are not yet; to the newcomers, he is warm and welcoming.

How do you let database customers know that they are "in?"
There are many ways, and still more will be developed as time goes
on. This process lies at the heart of the loyalty program. What is
loyalty?

Essentially, it is a two-way relationship. The seller makes you
feel that you are known, appreciated, welcome and *better than most.*
You are conscious that he does things and will continue to do things
for you that he probably wouldn't do for everybody. You trust him
to look out for your welfare, and you impart to him information
about yourself which you would tell only to a friend.

How can you show a customer that he or she is special? The
answer depends on your business and your creative ideas. Here are
some ideas:

Offer a Special Card. Gold, platinum, silver. Be sure it reads
"Loyal member since XXXX." The software to put this on the card
takes four lines of code. The benefits to you can be worth millions

of dollars. I have had many such cards for years. I feel that somehow the company is going to give me better service because I have been with them for twenty years. Of course, that isn't true of many stores or companies today, but it will be increasingly true in the future.

The card may have a special 800 number on it different from your regular 800 number that puts the customer directly through to a special operator for loyal customers.

The special card represents a special status. The experts at this are companies in the travel business. Some hotels have different classes of business customers. Special cardholders who are frequent guests get extra-special service. The hotels train their employees to recognize these guests and to treat them in a special way to emphasize the hotel's responsibility to maintain the loyalty bond. This is also true of many airlines and car rental agencies. These institutions are pioneers in the marketing database industry, and have much to teach everyone else.

Create a club. The Bank of Boston did an analysis of their depositors to isolate the high-income segment. They inducted these depositors into a luxury service club. Elaborate and elegant direct mail was sent to the club members, encouraging them to mix their investing with living with the arts, music and social events. The direct mail contained invitations to prestigious events such as polo matches, exclusive art auctions and concerts. This successful club produced valuable leads which resulted in millions in additional deposits and investments.

Give "Points" to Frequent Flyers. This is a controversial issue. Do frequent flyer credits really build loyalty? Many experts say no. They say that programs that award points or miles don't really build loyalty at all. What they do is provide incentives for doing business with one company over another. They help maintain market share in a hotly competitive environment—especially where the competing products are seen as being similar.

Have these incentives really created loyalty? The acid test is whether market share changes if the program is cancelled. Just how long would that loyalty last if all your competitors in your category were to continue their programs after you stopped yours?

In a true 'loyalty' program, there has to be something more; something that appeals to another personal need in the consumer. Some component of your program has to make your customer feel special and appreciated: that you recognize his or her importance to you. For true success, there must be *recognition.*

You must be able to tie some tangible level of special service to the amount of business you get from a customer. Many airlines have figured out a way to pick their most frequent travelers out of a coach seat and plunk them into an empty first class seat, thereby developing an emotional sense of loyalty.

The future will see loyalty marketing mature beyond its status as a direct marketing tool. The databases we create and the technological tools we've developed, perfected and continue to enhance will completely reshape the way business is transacted.

By using today's technology—and tomorrow's—we can place in the hands of the customer interface personnel, valuable personalized information that helps them treat customers in a prescribed manner based upon their value to the marketer.

The more we can link marketing databases to operational systems, the better we can serve the customer. And it will be this higher degree of personalized service, combined with effective incentives, that will develop true, long-term loyalty.

Communicate Often. Not to sell, but to ask opinions. "Is the new service/product well-received? Do you have suggestions?" And, if they do, take some action and *let them know* what you have done. Encourage their calls. Listen to them; make them feel appreciated.

Several years ago I spent $100 and became a member of a think-tank institute in Washington. It was everything I wanted: they showered me with newsletters and policy papers on important public issues and invited me to seminars. I went to one seminar, a week long live-in sojourn at Dartmouth University with outstanding speakers from all over the country. On the strength of that seminar, at which I got to meet all the members of the staff, I increased my voluntary annual payment to $250. Here was the kind of institution that was interesting, and, I thought, was interested in me.

That was my big mistake. After a long overseas trip to a politically hot country, I sent the president of the institute a twelve-page analysis of the political and economic situation in the country, asking for his views. He never answered. I sent a follow-up letter a month later. Still no answer. Two months later I sent another follow-up letter. I finally received a letter after three months from a low-level staffer who said that he disagreed with my analysis. He didn't thank me for preparing it. I got the impression that he thought that my letter was a nuisance and a waste of his time.

My mistake was thinking that they had me on a marketing database. Actually, they had me on a mailing list. It was intended to be a one-way communication. They sent out the policy papers, I sent in the money. My attempt to write a policy analysis paper just did not fit into the mailing list system that they had going. I cut my annual contribution back to $100.

My lifetime value to this institute went from about $2,500 to about $1,000 due to one unanswered letter. I would have been happy with a one paragraph letter from the president (drafted by his secretary or someone else) saying, "Thank you for your very interesting letter on xxxxxx. I am passing it on to our foreign policy group as input to their thinking on this very important country. I appreciate your taking your time to write to me."

There is a point here: marketing databases permit any organization to maintain one-on-one communications with their customers or members in a *mutually profitable* relationship. They create the *illusion* of a close relationship. It lies in your hands to determine whether this illusion is to be maintained and supported, or shattered by your responses to customer input.

Once you have set up a database, many of your customers would like to feel that the flow of information and products from you to them and the orders and payments from them to you has created a friendly, close, mutual relationship between them and your company. But if in setting up your database you do not provide for two-way communication, customers will eventually realize that they are corresponding with a computer, not a person. The illusion of mutual interest will be shattered, and you will lose loyalty and sales or contributions as a result.

Total Organizational Commitment. Customers see your company as an organic whole. What you do as a marketer can be completely destroyed by what happens in customer service, sales, billing, delivery or technical support. You may be building loyalty like mad, while your billing department is treating these same people as deadbeats and your delivery department is dropping off damaged packages two days late. For loyalty programs to work, you need:

- strong support at the top of the organization;
- the ability to communicate to everyone in the company who the preferred customers are;
- an agreed upon method of treating these customers by all departments who have any direct contact with customers,
- promulgation of your loyalty goals throughout the organization, and an employee training program to support them;
- active support by your retailing arms, whether they be stores, hotels, agencies, dealers; and
- a marketing database accessible throughout your organization, which is constantly updated with accurate information about the activities of your preferred customers.

Loyalty Maintenance Case Study— a Hotel Program

An interesting case study of loyalty maintenance is this story of a frequent guest program in a major hotel chain.

A direct response agency was recruited to develop a program to help the guests of the hotel chain identify themselves with the chain, instead of just with the particular hotel they were staying in at the time. The chain was anxious to build a system-wide loyalty in their guests so they would seek out the chain's hotels in every city.

To make the program work, the agency realized, they had to assure that guests received the same high quality of personal recognition at any any of the chain's hotels, whether in New York or in Hawaii.

The objectives of the program were:

- To identify the chain's most frequent guests;

- To figure out a way to facilitate consistent, superlative service worldwide;

- To provide special recognition to the best customers;

- To generate incremental revenue, because the program had to pay its own freight and deliver substantial return on the investment; and

- To provide a strategic marketing tool for the chain.

They started with an existing customer base, but the records available were skimpy. The chain had been a participating member in United Airlines' Mileage Plus Program, which provided the names and addresses of the hotel guests who received Mileage Plus credit. United Airlines let them append additional travel history regarding origin and destination cities, frequency and class of travel and average nights away from home.

Some of the hotels did maintain guest data. All the data available was merged into the rapidly building database. Some of the gaps were plugged by information from a major credit card company. The chain was able to find otherwise unidentified frequent customers by their credit card history. Most credit card companies keep a very detailed file.

To segment the database, the direct agency developed a Preference Profile, which requested information from each hotel guest. They combined the information they wanted to know from both operational as well as marketing perspectives, with the information research had shown that customers were willing to provide. They were surprised at the willingness of customers to supply information useful for the database.

Once the information was stored in the central database, they set up a system that made it available throughout the hotel chain, everywhere the customer was likely to interact with the company. By electronically linking it with the reservation system, they were able to send preference data along with reservation data down the line to each hotel. The information included special instructions for each individual. The information was put on-line for both the reservations center and the customer service center.

To be sure that all customers are properly recognized, each active member of the chain's frequent guest club received a personalized plastic card, color-keyed to the amount of business they had given the chain. Royal Blue indicated a moderate level of activity; gold signified the very highest.

To know whether they were generating more revenue through the system, they had to know what revenue was coming in. So the database was updated constantly. Letters of appreciation went out automatically, including gold cards when that level of activity was reached.

The database also measured the results from special offers extended to individual members. The hotel could monitor the effectiveness of offers and efficiency of packages on a one-to-one basis. The database was also used to help individual hotels in the chain test and validate their own individual promotion programs.

Some of the information for the database was provided by a sweepstakes. People were asked to select their desired resort vacation. The sweepstakes generated interest and activity on its own, but also enabled the chain to construct specifically targeted offers to members based upon their stated interests in specific types of vacations.

The loyalty program was a great success. The hotel was able to prove that the incremental revenue produced far exceeded the projections for the program. And the increased utility of the database exceeded nearly everybody's expectations.

The key to the success of this loyalty program was linking the marketing database information to operational systems throughout the hotel chain so that everyone knew who the preferred customers were and could give them super service. This helped to build a profitable long-term relationship with the best customers.

Figure 8-1 Building Customer Loyalty Through Dialogues

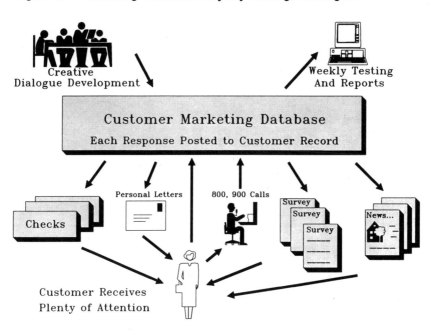

Missed Opportunity: The Automobile Industry

At the time of writing this book, the papers were full of articles in which leaders of the American automobile industry predicted slack sales in the future, and wondered how to maintain their market shares. It was another reminder that many industries have yet to explore the tremendous possibilities which exist in database marketing.

Several years ago, my wife and I both purchased identical Dodge Colt Vista's with four-wheel drive. These were really wonderful cars: very roomy, plenty of power and with the traction needed to get up to our house on top of a mountain in Virginia. We bought the cars brand new from a Virginia dealer for about $14,000 each. But in the four years we owned them, we never received a single letter from the salesman, from the dealer or from the Chrysler

Corporation, thanking us for the purchase or making any suggestions for the future.

When the cars were four years old, we began to think about trading them in. Do they still make Colt Vistas, we wondered? Have they added any new features? Or should we go back to Subarus? It was obvious that all the automobile companies were spending a fortune on general advertising, but we saw no ads relating to the type of car we were interested in. General Motors, to mention one, spent more than a billion dollars on general advertising, but practically nothing to reach out and communicate with its current customers. It is obvious that some of the automobile companies, at least, have forgotten one of the oldest rules in marketing:

Your own customers are your best prospects for future sales!

Everyone accepts this in principle, but very few companies act on it.

How difficult would it be for the automobile companies to divert a small percentage of their general advertising budgets to establishing a loyalty link with their existing customers, and what would be the results? Consider the facts:

- Automobile ownership, second only to home and telephone ownership, is one of the best-documented and publicly available sources of information available today. In more than half the states, motor vehicle registration information is provided for a nominal cost by public agencies. Everyone with a new car has to go to the dealer periodically for scheduled maintenance. It would be a simple matter for dealers to forward to a central source the fact that vehicle #1234567890H678 was still being driven by Arthur Hughes of Haymarket, Virginia.

- Automobiles are probably more expressive of the lifestyle and personality of their owners than anything else purchased today. Many people are in love with their cars: the car says who they are and what they like. Most people are far more loyal to their cars than they are to their brand of soap, shoes or shirts. The loyalty on the consumer side is there, but it is not being reciprocated by actions on the part of the manufacturers.

- The time when the average person is ready for a new car can be pretty well determined from reliable statistical sources. There is very little guesswork involved. No one knows when the average person is going to fly on American Airlines again, but AA maintains a very accurate marketing database trying to insure that when we do go it will be with them. Yet all automobile companies know almost exactly when their customers are going to need a new car, *and they are doing almost nothing about it.*

- There are frequent stories appearing about particular car salesmen and car dealerships that have had phenomenal success with direct marketing to their current customers. Some salesmen send hand-written notes to their customers on their birthdays and anniversaries. They have proved that it works, and works very well. Buick, Ford and Volvo have launched very promising loyalty building programs. They have built marketing databases which are used to send letters periodically offering discounts on accessories and tips on maintenance. But most of the major manufacturers have done little or nothing to pick up and build on this experience.

The Catalyst Project

Austin Rover, the biggest British-owned car manufacturer, has had a marketing database program in operation since 1980, as reported by Chris Richards in *Direct Marketing* magazine. The strategy is a series of time-related communications throughout the life of a car. Once the customer is in the database, he or she receives a welcome letter, warranty and service reminders, special offers and a sequence of sales propositions once the car has reached a certain age.

The system works well, but it rests on two shaky assumptions: that the customer's replacement timing coincides with the computer program and that the customer wants to buy the model chosen by the database. Systems Market Link (SML), a London direct agency that set up the Austin Rover program, decided that they needed more information and that the information could come directly from the car owner.

They developed a glossy, high-calibre magazine called *Catalyst* designed to maintain a dialog with existing customers and to warm potential customers to Austin Rover. To obtain a subscription to the magazine, a car owner fills out a questionnaire about the customer's current car, replacement plans and the type of car he or she wants next. In addition, the customer indicates his special interests from six choices: sports, dining, home and garden, entertainment, female interests and travel. As an added inducement to complete the questionnaire, they offered a sweepstakes.

The magazine is produced by split runs so that every reader gets a personalized magazine, with the features he or she has requested. The response rate to the first issue was close to 40 percent.

Questionnaire data is entered into the database and kicks off a multimedia campaign including direct mail and telemarketing. Each dealership is connected with the database so that they know what the consumer wants to buy and when.

Once the day for car replacement comes near, the prospect is qualified by the dealership through a telemarketing program, and sent a VIP pack (Vehicle Information Portfolio) specific to the model range interest indicated on the database. Personalized and designed to be retained for reference, the VIP is accompanied by an invitation for a test drive and purchase incentives targeted for the lifestyle of the recipient.

Once the buyer has made a purchase, a customer retention program takes over. It uses the database to issue a sequence of essential letters that maintain a caring dialog between customer and dealer about the manufacturer's warranty, servicing and government safety checks, as well as strategically timed dealer phone calls until six months before the next purchase is due.

Central to the program is the Catalyst Collection, a selection of high-quality products and services offered exclusively to purchasers of new cars. The catalog offers armchair shopping at its best, with a choice of activities which can range from wine-tasting weekends to a session on a DC-10 flight simulator.

Participating dealers must have their staff trained by SML in telemarketing technique, or contract the telemarketing work out to a SML marketing agency. The Catalyst program has created a stir in marketing circles in Britain, with the potential for being modified to serve other industries.

Prediction

I will make a prediction. Database marketing in the American automobile industry will be one of the major success stories in the 1990's. They have tried everything else: cashback, TV specials, four-page spreads in major magazines, quotas on imported cars. Now they are going to try to market cars to their own loyal customers through marketing databases. They are going to experiment with loyalty marketing. Once one does it, they will all do it; this has been the history of the auto industry.

Figure 8-2   Everyone Helps to Build Loyalty

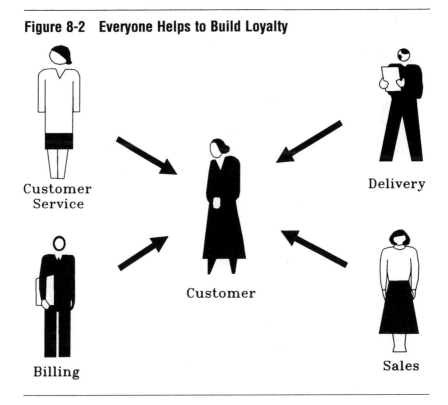

Customer
Service

Delivery

Billing

Customer

Sales

SUMMARY

Once you have identified your best customers, you must work very hard to maintain their loyalty.

- Loyalty is not maintained by money or points or anything that you can count. It is maintained by *recognition*. You must find a way to use the database to recognize your best customers and to *let them know* that you recognize them.

- You must provide them special services. You must listen to them when they say something, remember it and *act on it*. Then you must tell them what you have done.

- You must work very hard to get everyone in your organization—sales, customer service, billing, delivery—to participate in your loyalty-building program.

- You must have an accurate and constantly updated marketing database which is accessible to everyone who deals with customers, so they will recognize them and know their preferences, and respond appropriately. There must be a way that these individuals can *input data* into the database as they learn of customer needs and requests.

- Some of the things that you can do to maintain the loyalty of your best customers include:

  - Equip your telemarketers with ANI, which can provide the name and customer record of each caller while he or she is calling you on the telephone.
  - Encourage telemarketers to take down customer information which can be used to build a bond between your company and the customer.
  - Include the dealer in the loyalty loop: encourage customers to visit the dealers with inducements, telephone numbers, etc. Let the dealer know that you are doing this.
  - Give customers special cards which identify their customer buying status.

- ➤ Create your own buyer's clubs.
- ➤ Communicate with your loyal customers often. Be sure that your communication is two-way: that you listen as well as speak.

■ Hotels, airlines and car rental companies are masters at loyalty building today. We can learn much from them.

■ Most American automobile manufacturers are far behind every-one in loyalty building. They sell a big ticket item which is easy to follow, yet they manage to lose track of their customers and ignore them as soon as the sale is over.

■ A successful loyalty program requires total organizational com-mitment by your company. It can pay rich dividends

Chapter 9

How to Maintain a Dialog with Your Customers

Pop quiz: What is the difference between a mailing list and a marketing database?

Answer: There are many differences, but the principal difference is that a mailing list is designed for one-way communications: products and literature out, orders and money in. A marketing database is designed for two-way communications: either party can initiate communications. Each party thinks about what the other has said, remembers it and modifies his or her behavior based on the knowledge and understanding of what the other party wants.

This tells us that a vital part of the design and functioning of any marketing database is the development and use of creative response mechanisms whereby you can get feedback from your customers on what they are thinking and *what they want*. A marketing database is not just a list of customers which you use for segmentation and mailings. The database should be designed as a computer simulation of the mind of the old corner grocer: a thinking machine that stores up information received from the customer, retains it and *modifies its behavior* based on that information.

Whenever you design a marketing database, then, you have to think: How are we going to get customer feedback? What are the methods whereby we can get data about how our programs are being received? How can we store this data? How can we modify our future communications to show that we have remembered what we learned, and are acting differently because of it? In short, we have to plan for customer response.

There is one fundamental rule: make every contact with your customers a learning experience for you. Find out more information from your customers about them and their lives, their desires, their opinions, so that you can be more helpful, more understanding, a better friend in the future.

Coupons

In some ways, direct marketers seem like a herd of sheep. Somewhere they got the idea that coupons help to increase sales (as they clearly do), so they are investing hundreds of millions of dollars in them. Two hundred billion of them are sent out every year. Many customers look for them in their newspapers, magazines and mailboxes. They save them and use them in their shopping. Although there is some cheating, most people actually buy the products listed on the coupon, and, in many cases, buy some product that *they might not otherwise have bought* because of the coupon. What could possibly be wrong with that?

Nothing. Except that the same money might have been spent in other ways which would have produced more sales and more profits. Direct marketers have learned the coupon lesson so well, and they see their competitors using coupons so constantly, that it has become a vast and expensive game which no one can afford not to play: if you don't send out coupons, your competitors will grab your market share. If you experiment with some other technique, and it does not work, you will lose market share. Most direct marketers thus are set on coupons: they won't listen to any other possibility, even though they know all of the faults of the coupon system.

What are these faults?

- Ninety-six percent are thrown away unused (no real loss).

- There is a non-negligible percentage of cheating: people who take your forty cents but buy some other product.

- A high percentage are used by your own customers, who would have bought your product anyway.

- Coupons encourage the public to concentrate on price and rebate as the only reason for choosing one brand over another.

- Coupons do not build brand loyalty, they tend to destroy it.

- The coupon redemption system is so cumbersome and slow that it is sometimes a year from the time they are sent out until you receive reports on how many were redeemed, and to which offer the public responded best.

Figure 9-1   What Happens to Coupons

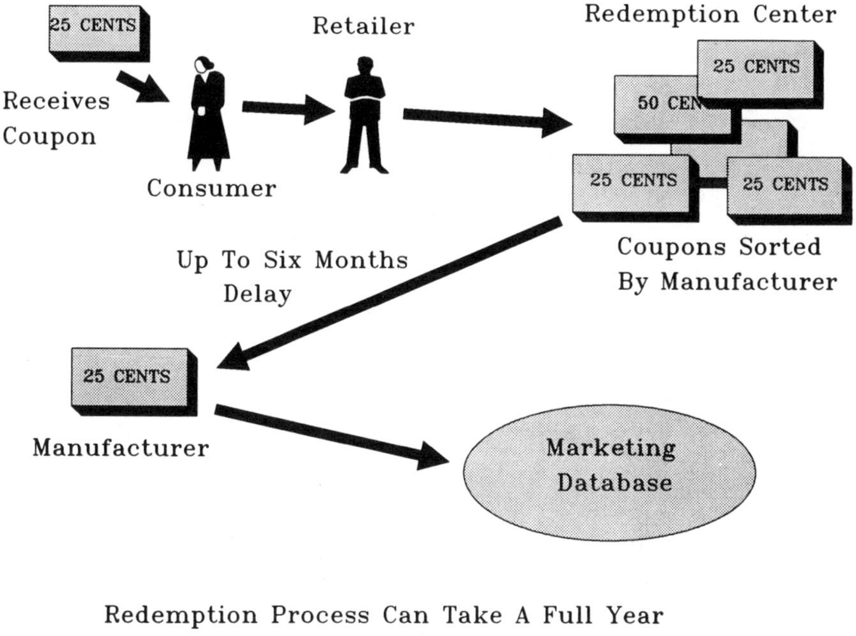

Redemption Process Can Take A Full Year

- As a result, you seldom learn anything about your customers from these coupons. You can hold in your hand coupons which your customers held in their hands several months ago. But from that piece of paper you can tell nothing about who they are, why they bought your product (if they did), what their purchasing habits are, what they were thinking about. You have missed a golden opportunity for getting responses and building a database.

What are the alternatives to the coupon treadmill?

Instantly Redeemable Checks

Several companies, including Unique Marketing of Omaha and Moore Response Marketing, have developed a substitute for coupons in the form of a check (which we will call the INSTA-CHECK) that offers you an opportunity to find out exactly who is redeeming your coupons within days after your promotion is started. The INSTA-CHECK is an actual check, processed through the normal U.S. banking system back to your bank within the federally prescribed one-week clearing process. But the INSTA-CHECK is also a survey form which can be used to capture information.

The INSTA-CHECK looks like a coupon. On the back, however, it has space for the endorser's name, address, city, state, zipcode, phone number and signature (required by the bank). The remaining space can also be used for a few survey questions.

The INSTA-CHECK has the bank's code number printed in magnetic ink characters which are read by the bank clearing system's machinery. Because this magnetic ink has metal particles in it, you cannot produce a Xerox copy of the check. Without the metal particles, the bank's system will reject it.

The clearing process is entirely different from the coupon redemption route. When coupons are redeemed they are bundled and given to the store manager. Eventually, the coupons are sent to a regional redemption center where they are painstakingly sorted by hand by product and company, and counted so that the stores can get paid and the companies can be billed. As a by-product of the

Figure 9-2   Insta-Checks Come Back Fast

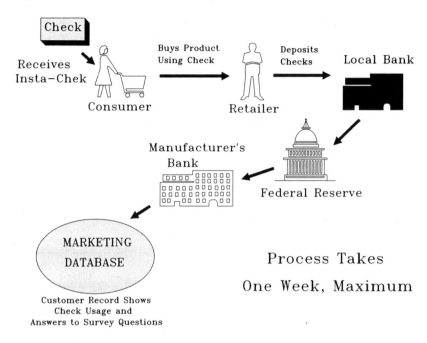

payment process, reports are generated which will tell the manufacturer (months later) how many coupons were redeemed, and for what.

INSTA-CHECKs are handled entirely differently. The customer must endorse the check and hand it to the checkout clerk. The clerk then puts the INSTA-CHECK in *with the other checks,* not with the coupons.

When the store presents the INSTA-CHECKs with their regular checks at the bank every day, they receive immediate reimbursement (weeks ahead of the coupon reimbursement). Within a short period (an average of three days) the check is processed through the Federal Reserve clearing system, and arrives back at the manufacturer's bank. The bank charges about eight cents for processing. As soon as the checks arrive at the bank, the manufacturer can have them keypunched. Voila: here are the names and addresses of customers, two to four weeks after they bought the product (depending on key-punching time), together with whatever survey data was included on the check. These names can be used to build and to update the marketing database.

General Mills used the checks in Honey Nut Cheerios. Their offer resulted in a 30 percent response. This was extremely high in comparison with coupon redemption rates. Direct mail coupon redemptions vary from 5 to 14 percent. Freestanding inserts are redeemed at a rate of 4 percent. Newspaper redemption is about 2 percent. Yoplait Yogurt did a promotion with INSTA-CHECKs in a freestanding insert. The INSTA-CHECKs included a survey of the customer's most frequently purchased brand. In this case, some customers redeemed so many that they suspected fraud. Their follow-up mailing to these customers included a survey of customer satisfaction with an additional check.

Pillsbury used INSTA-CHECKs to introduce a new brand of pizza. They were very pleased with the results. Eighty percent of those cashing the INSTA-CHECKs filled out all of the survey questions on the reverse side. Pillsbury built a marketing database with the survey results which told them what competitive brands were used in the household, which family members liked the pizza and so on.

Rebates

"$1 rebate coupon enclosed!" You buy the product, and inside is a coupon you send in to get $1, or $2 or $5 or more. You have to use the coupon, and you usually have to include an IPC seal, or proof of purchase or something else. By the time you have met all the requirements, found envelope and affixed a 25-cent stamp, you may have used up the rebate in energy and frustration. But millions do send these rebate coupons in. They can be a wonderful way to start a database.

Unfortunately, very few manufacturers who offer these rebates are using them to construct a marketing database. I find it hard to understand why they offered the rebate in the first place, unless it was just another sales gimmick. Here they have the name and address of a purchaser. A golden opportunity. Yet if you go from company to company, you will find that somewhere in a back room they have a tape of 200,000 customers who have received a rebate or responded to an offer of a premium. No one has any idea what to do with these names; so they just sit there and get out-of-date. Twenty percent of Americans move every year. After two years, forty percent of your file has moved somewhere else. As for the rest, after two years, they have forgotten that they ever sent in the rebate coupon, and probably have forgotten about you and your product. There seems to be a great deal of push in creative departments thinking up these sales ideas, and practically no long-range planning involving the question of what do to with the results.

I think the reasoning goes this way: "The customer sees $1 off on the package. He likes what he sees and buys it. When he gets home and realizes what a nuisance it is to get the $1, he gives up. Fine. No need to give him a rebate, and *he has bought the product!* So what if some clowns send in for the $1? Punch their names, send them a buck and forget it."

With this kind of reasoning in your company or your advertising agency, you will have an uphill battle trying to get a marketing database started. If you can turn it around, however, you may find that the rebate respondents represent a place to start building your database.

Orders With Surveys

The easiest way to begin a two-way dialog is often over looked. It is the order form. Here is a piece of paper which comes from your customer to you. She is writing down her name and address and the products she wants. Why not also get some other information that you need and can use later?

How many children under the age of 10 in the home?
What magazines do you read?
Do you have a compact disc player?
Do you live in a house or an apartment?
Do you have a child in college?
Are you planning an addition to your home?

Does anyone in your family suffer from diabetes?
Are you planning a trip overseas?
How did you find our catalog? [ ] clear and informative
                                              [ ] hard to read
                                              [ ] thin on descriptions

You create questions that will have some relevance to your business. They should be asked in a non-threatening, voluntary way, which makes it clear that you can buy the product without answering the questions. You will be amazed at the response. In a well-crafted database environment, the answers to these questions can be the start of a real dialog with customers.

Of course, the process of creating a dialog is a new one for most companies. Design of the order form is usually left to the creative agency. Processing of the orders is handled by a different department. No one will know just what to do with the responses. As the marketing database planner, you will have to get everyone together to plan your strategy. Once the responses are safely in the database, you will have to plan how to use them as a part of an intelligent dialog. This calls for creative marketing strategy of a high order. You will have to be not only an imaginative marketer, but also an effective coordinator of several parts of your organization for these survey questions to do you any good. Customer service personnel will have to be trained to work the questions into their talks with customers. Outgoing letters will have to have paragraphs derived from the survey responses. Your company may not be ready for intelligent use of survey data, but you will have to start sometime, because your competitors are thinking about it right now.

In-Product Money

A household products manufacturer sought a way to build a marketing database of his customers. He was sending out 800 million coupons per year, and using them to maintain his competitive market share. But he wasn't learning anything from his coupons — they were just being scattered to the four winds. He was scared of using INSTA-CHECKs because he felt that forcing the customer to put their name and address on the check would reduce response. He could not afford

Figure 9-3 In-Product Money Builds Loyalty

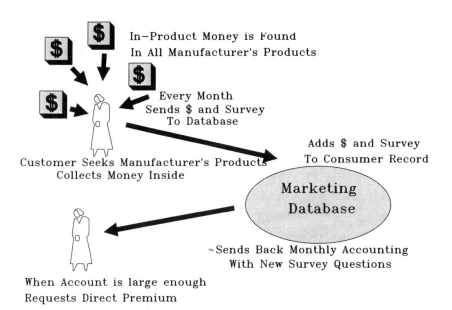

In-Product Money is Found
In All Manufacturer's Products

Every Month
Sends $ and Survey
To Database

Adds $ and Survey
To Consumer Record

Customer Seeks Manufacturer's Products
Collects Money Inside

Marketing
Database

Sends Back Monthly Accounting
With New Survey Questions

When Account is large enough
Requests Direct Premium

---

to have that happen in his highly competitive situation. A consultant suggested an idea which we will call In-product Money.

The basic problem was that most of the company's products sold for about $1 in grocery stores. They tried rebates: send in a wrapper, and receive $X or a premium in exchange for your name and address. But the customers had to put a 25-cent stamp on the envelope, and the company had to do the same with their response, so the economics of providing a rebate for a $1 product just weren't there.

In-product money was a compromise concept. The idea was to include in-product money inside the wrapper of all the company's products. The money would be bar coded on both sides, and of different denominations depending on the product it was wrapped into. The money would have an expiration date. The idea was that the householder collected the money from every product that the company sold. Since the company was a major household goods manufacturer, they had more than twenty different items in the average supermarket. It would not take a household long to accumulate $20 or more worth of the money.

To use the money, you have to join the club. Membership would be free—you just send in your name and address. The membership application would be really a survey form which lists household members, age, income, lifestyle questions and a large number of product preference responses of interest to product managers. With the receipt of your membership application, you begin with a membership in-product money balance of $5.

Every few weeks, you send in all the in-product money you have accumulated, together with a required survey form that you received with your welcome kit. This survey form, which varies from month to month, would include data which is scanned and entered into the member's marketing database record. The in-product money would be added to the member's account. Every quarter, club members would receive a quarterly statement showing their current balance in the club. The quarterly statement would include more survey forms and envelopes used to send in more in-product money. It also would include a catalog showing all the premiums that you could buy with in-product money. They would include such items as TVs, microwaves, VCRs, cameras and many other items. What to offer in the catalog would be part of the data gathered in the survey forms. The catalog also lets you know just what products on your supermarket shelves contain in-product money.

There would be an expiration date on the money because the company wanted to maintain a constant flow of information from the customer to the database. By scanning this flow of data, they could learn more about customer response and behavior than could be gleaned by all the other sources of information available.

What would in-product money do for brand loyalty? Theory suggests that it should do wonders. Unlike coupons, which destroy brand loyalty, in-product money would make the householder look on the shelves for one particular brand. Prior to the use of in-product money, customers had no real idea of which products were made by the company; afterward, they would be very aware of this. The result could be an increasing cross-product loyalty which should increase: the greater the balance in your in-product club account, the nearer you are to having enough to get the new television set for the family room.

On the company end, the process should be automated. Every household enrolled in the club should have a club membership number which ties the household to the database. The quarterly mailings could include peel-off bar code labels with the club membership number. To receive the credit for the survey forms and the money, the envelope containing them must have one of the peel-off bar code labels affixed.

When the envelope arrives, the bar code label would be scanned, and the money dumped into the hopper of a money counter. It reads the bar codes on the money, rejecting money which has expired, rejecting counterfeit (it can tell), adding up the denominations to get a total and counting the number of different products represented (the bar code on the money varies with the product it was wrapped in). After this thirty-second process, the database would be updated with the family money balance and the products purchased since the last response.

The survey forms can also be automated. Scanning devices like the TARTAN X-80 from Recognition Equipment Incorporated read regular letter-sized survey forms *filled out in pencil or pen* by a householder. These devices have an accuracy rate in the high ninety's. All letters and numbers that it cannot read are shunted to human operators who view the survey forms on their terminals and determine what the writer was trying to say. A survey form asking twenty or more questions can be scanned and entered into the database at a rate of about ten per minute.

Once the survey data is in the database, it can be available to the company for market research, for modeling, for new product introductions, for further loyalty-building programs. The one group it doesn't reach are the users of competing brands. Unless they buy one of the company's products, they will never hold in-product money in their hands. For these people, the company must continue their coupon programs. But, because of the data in the database, they will better be able to target non-users and send their coupons to *them,* not to their own loyal customers.

A final advantage is the secrecy of the program. Unlike massive advertising promotions and coupon offers, the world will know little about how in-product money is doing. How many people are members? How many are sending in money every month? How has their loyalty shifted due to the availability of money in all of those different packages? Only the company will know, and they are unlikely to say. At last reading, the company is still considering the plan.

Point of Sale Response

A cosmetic and skin-care company which we shall call Eugenia had a different problem. Women came to them for total facial care. They had skin-care specialists trained to study a customer's face and to make recommendations on a series of creams and treatments which would bring out the best. Customers were typically given a lifetime membership, and expected to buy about $700 worth of products every year, following the recommendations of the specialists.

Eugenia has more than 400 outlets across the country, most of them located inside large department stores. When the specialist is not on duty, a regular sales clerk from the store makes the sales. Sales are good. They have a database of members. Members had plastic membership cards with a membership number and the number of the program that was appropriate for their face. The problem was, Eugenia didn't have any response data. They didn't know what their customers were buying. Store clerks were supposed to send in one copy of the sales slip with the member number written on it, to be keypunched centrally, but the system was spotty and had fallen into disuse.

The system they finally decided to adopt was suggested to them by a database consultant. It was based on the little credit card verification (Datacomm) units found all over America. Eugenia plans to buy these units, and put one in each outlet. They will add a magnetic stripe to the back of the member's cards. The stripe will hold the member's name and number. The Datacomm units contain an automatic dialing device, a modem and a small computer. When a

Figure 9-4 Tracking Customer Sales Automatically

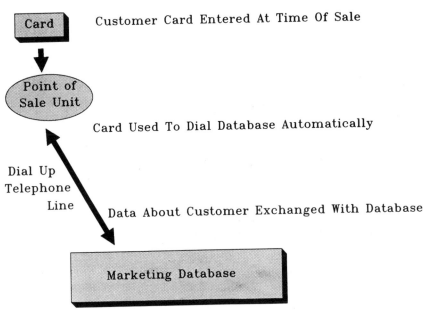

Card — Customer Card Entered At Time Of Sale

Point of Sale Unit

Card Used To Dial Database Automatically

Dial Up Telephone Line

Data About Customer Exchanged With Database

Marketing Database

member's card is passed through the slot, the datacomm unit automatically dials up the Eugenia database, going though an 800 number. The Datacomm sends across the telephone line the customer number, the date and time, the store number. In response to prompts on the screen of the Datacomm, the clerk enters her number, the SKU numbers of the products purchased and a code for any special promotion that the customer may have mentioned which prompted her to visit the booth. That is all. The process takes less than a minute, and the database now knows who is shopping where, at what time of day, what they bought and, in many cases, why.

The beauty of this system can be demonstrated when they begin test promotions in various cities. By studying the responses, they can tell store-by-store and hour-by-hour how many respond to a particular promotion, versus those who just wandered by the outlet.

It will be easy to identify customers who fail to buy products when they should, which was impossible previously. When the database detects someone who has clearly run out of product, the software can initiate a friendly reminder letter. If this does not do the trick, telemarketing follow-up is appropriate.

Data from Diskettes

A major manufacturer of microcomputers has been one of the leaders in database building. From the moment of their inception, they packed with every computer they sold, a comprehensive registration card with more than twenty different questions in addition to the name and address. They inquired about the type of computer purchased, from whom, whether it was bought by an individual or a company, the occupation, income and age of the user, the principal application, whether it replaced a current computer, and if so what make and model, whether the purchaser had considered other brands and what they were, and many questions about the configuration of the computer, the peripheral equipment and software purchased, the type of company the user worked at, the size of the company and much more.

All of this data was keypunched into the company's owner registration database. The company developed a unique series of cross-tab reports displaying all of the above data. The information was used by product planning, by advertising, by market research, by direct marketing, by dealer relation. But they wanted more.

They had two problems: they felt they weren't getting a high enough percentage of completed cards, and they weren't getting the answers to as many questions as they wanted. At the suggestion of database marketing service bureau, they switched to using a registration diskette. They created a colorful interactive diskette which they packed with every new computer. This type of diskette is one of the products of CompuDoc of Edison, New Jersey. The program welcomed the customer, then put them through a query session which enabled purchasers quickly to provide the company the numerous data elements needed for its database. Most of the data was furnished to the owner on pop-up menus; he or she had only to choose from several choices offered. The choices were hierarchical:

"Did you purchase a printer?" [If no, it would automatically skip the next series of questions.]

"Was it thermal, daisy wheel, laser, dot matrix, ink jet?" [Laser]

"Which brand of laser printer (choices shown)?" [Hewlett Packard]

"Which model Hewlett Packard Laser Printer (choices shown)?"

At first, of course, the diskette was tested on a single product. They were ready to can it if the response was poor. What happened? They doubled their response rate. They were getting double the number of customers. They introduced one innovation which tipped the odds in their favor: they automatically entered everyone who sent in a diskette in a quarterly sweepstakes to win a computer. Now, as new computers are added to the line, a diskette is packed inside rather than a card.

One feature of the diskette response that is interesting is the open-ended, free-response question. There are eight questions which ask such things as "Why did you choose our computer?" "Did you get good service from your dealer?" "How do you like your new computer?" They did several things with such free-form data. First, they coded the responses into the database, so they could count them on their reports: X percent did not like the new diskette unit; y percent felt that the dealer should have had more training; and so on. But they went beyond this. The free-form responses were printed out separately and sent to the appropriate department: Customer Service, Dealer Relations, Product Design. These departments studied the responses. That is using your response—that is database marketing!

The company sells its computers heavily in Europe and elsewhere in the world. They are packing their diskettes into computers going to Europe, with responses coming back in French, German and other languages. They have trained the organization to read and code these responses, and to provide the proper response to the purchasers.

Citicorp Customer Buying Cards

One of the best ways of knowing what your retail customers are doing is the Ukrop's Valued Customer card. Ukrop's, a twenty-one store supermarket chain in Virginia, provides its customers with cards with a unique bar code in a system which they purchased from Citicorp. Each customer's card is read at the checkout scanner. Everything the customer buys is then scanned, as usual, but the results go into a special database in the store that keeps track of everything that the Hughes family bought.

Why do the customers participate? They get automatic discounts. What does Ukrop's get out of it? A way of building a relationship with their customers. They can communicate with them and build customer loyalty. they have had the original scanners in place

---

Figure 9-5   Supermarket Buyer's Cards Build Loyalty

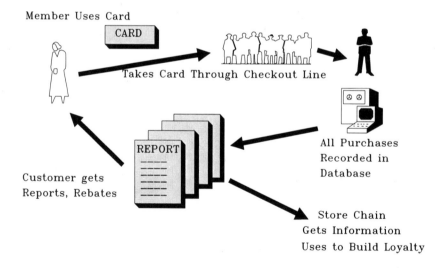

in stores since 1979, but with the Valued Customer Cards, they now have movement data pertaining to households, or zip code areas or areas around a new store—information that they didn't have before they introduced the cards. If a customer stops buying, Ukrop's can, and does, write and call. If Ukrop's has done something wrong, they can attempt to rectify it.

Ukrop's uses their marketing database to mail out over 200,000 newsletters every month: *Ukrop's Valued Customer News*. The newsletter reports on new food products coming out, new store openings, news about pesticides or prices. "Before we had the val-ued-customer program, we didn't really know who our customers were. Today we do," said Carol Beth Spivey, Ukrop's manager of advertising and marketing. "If a competitor opens a store in the area, we can see which customers are dropping us. Then we can write to them and invite them back."

Early returns suggest that the card program increased sales for Ukrop's by 10 percent. But what about the big picture? What happens when every store chain has a similar card program? Won't that wipe out the advantages? As Gary Arlen, publisher of *Electronic Shopping News* said, "Retailing is a me-too focus. When someone finds the formula, they'll all do it."

Of course, he is correct. But looking at such card programs strictly as a means of increasing sales misses the point entirely. To make adequate use of such a card, a retailer has to establish a marketing database. "It is not easy or cheap to set up a program like this," according to Carol Beth Spivey. The very act of establishing this database forces the company to begin to know their customers, to understand their purchasing behavior, to build better loyalty programs, to improve service, to change the behavior and policies of the store. The response derived from such a system provides information of tremendous value to retailers, if only they can organize properly to take advantage of it. Clearly, stores like Ukrop's which do pioneer with this system will have the jump on all the others who do so later.

To argue that such cards will be of no value when all stores have them is like arguing that automobile service garages should not install engine diagnostic machines because all other garages have them. The fact is that a diagnostic machine permits the garage to do a much better job of servicing a customer's engine rapidly and correctly. They are essential to providing good service. That is why the Citicorp customer card system, or something like it, will be adopted by most large chains, I predict, in the years ahead.

Expansion Plans

These programs are expanding rapidly. By 1990 there were twenty-five chains enrolled, accounting for 1,400 stores. Ultimately, there may be data on 40 million households. Keeping data on the transactions of these households means databases holding tens of billions of records, according to DM News.

The inducements to consumers to participate in the programs include:

- *Coupon Bank,* an electronic couponing program that provides automatic discounts to cardholders without the bother of clipping or saving paper coupons.

- *Preferred Customer,* which is customized to each retailer and includes cash rebates, straight discounts, tiered coupons and multi-level point systems.

Catalina Marketing Systems in Anaheim, California has developed a similar competing system with 3,300 stores signed up by 1990. Others are entering the field.

What Can They Do with the Data?

Market Research Information. Product manufacturers, of course, are anxious to purchase names of their customers. They can use these names for direct marketing and for targeting their ad messages to the correct audiences.

Coop Mailings. Most coop mailings of coupons are addressed to "household," rather than to an individual family. Armed with the data from their household purchase history, a retailer or manufacturer using their data can mail coded coupons and checks to households, *based on their known buying habits*. The results should be a vast improvement in effectiveness per dollar spent.

Retail Loyalty Programs. This is what Ukrop's is doing. It should be noted that Ukrop's has refused to sell its customers' names to others. If other retailers follow Ukrop's leads, the central databanks may become significant.

Retailers currently experimenting with this type of point-of-sale membership program include Kroger, American Stores, A & P, Winn-Dixie, and Holiday.

Manufacturers, however, have been slow to invest in this type of program, just as they have been hesitant about building marketing databases. Not until these programs have successfully signed up 20 percent of more of the market will the package goods manufacturers begin to make significant purchases of their data. But when that happens, the rush is likely to be overwhelming. To get from here to there, these programs may have to invest several hundreds of millions of dollars in technology and promotion.

A Weight-Loss Program

The manufacturer of a weight-loss powder to be mixed with milk was quite successful in his primary sales. People were responding to the advertising and making a first purchase, a two-week supply for fifty dollars. But repeat purchases were running about five percent. Clearly, a marketing database was needed. After several false starts, the company finally hit on a solution which promised to turn things around.

They developed a concept whereby they stopped describing their product as a product, and started describing it as a program. Purchasers were to be called members, and each was expected to sign on to reach a specified goal: a loss of so many pounds, a reduction of cholesterol of so many points, a reduction of blood pressure or a slimmer waist. With the first purchase, each member fills out a fitness statement with personal goals. The statement is forwarded to the company, where it is entered into the database. In addition, members are given weekly report cards which they return, listing the amount of exercise, their eating habits and their progress towards the goals.

Meanwhile, back at the database, there would be much activity. After the first fitness statement is received, the database generates a personalized letter from the fitness director congratulating the member on his or her selection of a goal; in some cases, warning the member against such a drastic change in eating habits or too rapid a shift to strenuous exercise. The personalized comments are built up from an analysis of many data elements in the fitness statement: age, weight, height, previous exercise level, blood pressure, cholesterol level and so on.

Figure 9-6   Members Report on Weight Loss

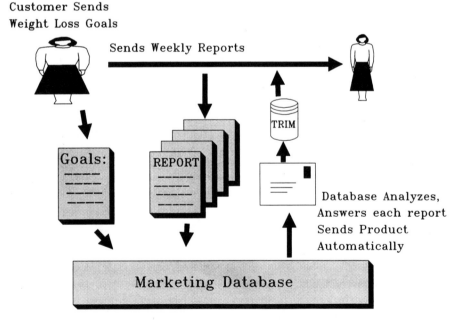

Customer Sends
Weight Loss Goals

Sends Weekly Reports

TRIM

Goals:

REPORT

Database Analyzes,
Answers each report
Sends Product
Automatically

Marketing Database

As each weekly report is received, the database generates a personalized analysis, again in the form of a laser letter, congratulating members on their progress, sympathizing with them on problems reported, making helpful suggestions on exercise, eating, relaxing.

Telemarketers are to be trained as "Fitness Specialists." Customer service will have the entire database available to them on their terminals so they can see the customers' records as they consult with them. The most important single element in the package, however, is the weekly report returned by members to the database. This initiates the two-way communication which is essential to successful database marketing.

THE 800 NUMBER

Of course, the best response device ever invented is the 800 number. Invented by AT&T in 1961, it really took off in popularity in the 1980's. In 1984, AT&T registered 1.9 billion calls made to 800 numbers. Five years later, the total calls had skyrocketed to 7.0 billion calls, and the service is continuing to expand. Originally, many companies saw the 800 number as an order-taking opportunity and a method for customers to let off steam. Today, it is viewed as an essential customer response device: a marketing tool that feeds information into a marketing database.

Companies which have invested heavily in their 800 number operation have found that it pays off. Answering the telephone is much cheaper than writing a letter, and the ability to service customers and thereby build loyalty is unparalleled.

The GE Information Service Center receives more than three million calls a year. Some calls prevent the return of an appliance by allowing a representative the opportunity to explain to customers how to operate appliances that they don't understand. The system also supports dealers who are featuring GE products by providing those dealer's names first to callers who want to know where to buy it.

When people call an 800 number, they are usually trying to tell you something or to ask questions. Fine. Answer the questions. Then listen to what they are saying and make a note of it. Tell them what you are going to do with their ideas. Be sure that something *does* happen: put customers' ideas into the database, code them, and make sure they get follow-up letters or phone calls afterwards. Then, ask them some questions. Get information which you can use. All customer service reps should have a list of questions that the company is interested in asking, in general and about this particular customer.

Kraft General Foods is using their hot line to get consumer opinions on packaging colors, product tastes, annoying advertisements and hot microwave containers. Kraft acted: they redesigned Kool-Aid boxes due to consumer complaints, rearranged the vents on packaged microwave meals to avoid burning customer fingers. Con-Agra, Inc., rewrote instructions for its Healthy Choice frozen dinners to clarify how to cover them before microwaving.

Customers calling Warner-Lambert told them that Efferdent, which is designed to clean dentures, works wonders on toilet bowl stains. The calls gave them an idea for a new product. One company modified their advertisement of a child unrolling toilet paper after parents called to say that the ad set a horrible example for children.

Coding Responses

Your database design must include a plan for coding responses. That means developing a series of alphabetic or numeric codes that summarize what the customer is trying to say to you. For example:

BE	Billing error
PD	Product damage
DP	Delivery problem
DE	Product design problem
AD	Problem with the advertisement
HP	Happy with the product or service
SV	Problems with service or response

Operators can be trained to enter these codes. Pop-up windows on their screens can be used to jog their memories. Your system must be flexible, so that you can add codes.

Some codes do not require any action; some codes do. Your software should be designed to distinguish these, and to call up screens for action by the proper people. Your codes should also be used for reports, so you can monitor on a regular basis how many people are calling with delivery problems or what have you.

Keeping Track of and Fielding Responses

Responding to your customers will keep your database planners and programmers busy all the time. If you have an active program, the diagram of the response activities can get very complicated. In brief, here is what has to happen:

- Every outgoing message from you has to have a source code assigned to it. The table of source codes is stored in a promotion history file. Also in the file is the cost of the outgoing message, the date, the number sent out and a trigger to a series of program steps telling the computer what to do when someone responds or doesn't respond.

- When a response comes in, it could be in the form of a letter or card, a telephone call, an order, a visit by the customer to one of your showrooms or a non-response—no customer activity after a certain number of days.

- The response itself can have many gradations:

  - Send literature
  - Call me
  - Answer to survey questions
  - Here is a check or credit card, send product
  - Send product and bill me
  - Send a salesperson to visit me
  - Get lost-not interested
  - I don't live here any more, wrong address
  - Nothing . . .
  - And many more

Each of these responses should call forth a specific action from you which has to be planned out in advance. First you diagram the activities, and then you have your programmer write into your database software the steps to be taken in response. Figure 9-7 is a sample diagram of just a few of the steps you will need to take in response to one simple mailing.

"Why," you may ask, "do you go to the bother of diagramming these activities? The diagram makes the activities seem more complicated than they really are. Don't you just put the "Yes's" into one pile, and the "No's" into another, and get to work?"

Good old-fashion thinking. It works fine with a simple direct-mail campaign, but not with database marketing. You have to draw diagrams and write programs because any active database will be developing scores of different initiatives in a single year. You need

Figure 9-7   How to Handle Customer Response

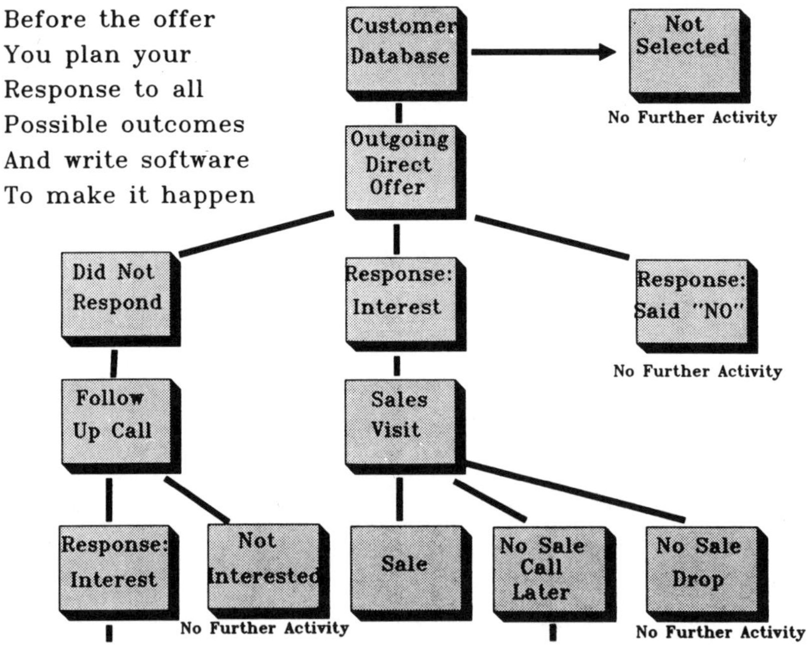

Before the offer
You plan your
Response to all
Possible outcomes
And write software
To make it happen

Customer Database → Not Selected
No Further Activity

Outgoing Direct Offer

Did Not Respond

Response: Interest

Response: Said "NO"
No Further Activity

Follow Up Call

Sales Visit

Response: Interest

Not Interested
No Further Activity

Sale

No Sale Call Later

No Sale Drop
No Further Activity

to be sure that each one is a *test*. You need to produce reports that show you, for each initiative:

- How many went out, how many were responded to, week by week until the responses die out. What was your percentage response?

- How much each one cost to send out, and how much revenue was generated. What was your return on investment?

- How many people responded in each of the possible ways.

- How many answered the survey questions, versus those who ordered product or took some other action. There should *always* be some survey questions.

- How many bad addresses were there?

- How many people didn't respond at all, and why?

- What type of person responded, versus the type that did not respond. What type made a purchase, versus those that just asked for literature?

- Which of the packages (envelopes, texts, offers) got the best response, and which got the worst?

- How many people responded in unexpected ways: by writing an unexpected question or comment on the card, or asking an unforeseen question in the telephone call. You must tabulate these unexpected responses. They can be very important.

How do you get all of this information into your reports? In the first place, your telemarketers need special screens which permit them to call up the customer's record (or create a new record in the case of a response from a prospect), and enter these responses into fields already pre-programmed into your database. If the responses are in writing, you will have them keypunched, off-line, by outside keypunchers. The tape they generate will be run against the master database to insert the responses into the customer records, just as if you were getting the responses by telephone.

Don't count on the programmers to design your reports. You will have to do that. It takes time and is very demanding work. It is easier to create a report than it is to think it up. Be sure the report provides *relevant information* which you can use to take other steps to improve your program.

ACTING ON THE RESPONSES

Reporting on the responses is just the beginning. How often have we heard the phrase "Allow six to eight weeks for delivery." That is fine for direct marketing, but it isn't database marketing. You can't maintain much of a two-way dialog if you take six to eight weeks to respond. "Next-Day Service" should be your goal, even if you cannot move quite that fast.

The way you fulfill the response is usually by means of some sort of computer generated-action:

- The computer will generate labels to be affixed to the literature or the product ordered, and it can be shipped out the next day.

- The computer will produce a thank-you letter with personal references throughout the body of the letter, based on data in the customer's database record. "Thank you for calling us on October 12. We sent out the replacement motor housing by UPS the next day. Please call us again if you have future needs.

"The XR50 has been one of our most successful products. Many customers like you, Mr. Soule, have been using them for years. Others have traded up to our new XR100, released last year, which does the job in half the time. For your information, I am enclosing a brochure on the XR100 which is available at hardware stores everywhere. If you decide to step up to the XR100, you should use the rebate coupon which I have included with the brochure. This coupon gives you a special discount *because you are a loyal customer who is trading up from an earlier model.* And, if you have a moment, you might fill in the enclosed service questionnaire. We would like to hear from you what you thought about our customer service operation. It takes just a couple of minutes to fill out the questionnaire. It will help us to give you better service in the future."

■ The computer will generate lead cards which will be assigned to a salesperson or dealer automatically, printed on a printer in the dealer's office, and will trigger an automatic lead tracking sequence.

■ The survey response will be planned in advance to put the customers into a special category:
  ➤ if they make more than ten business trips a year, you will code them for a different sequence of follow-up letters than those who make less;
  ➤ if they have over 60 years old, it puts them in a special class;
  ➤ if she has children under 12 in the house, you need to react properly;
  ➤ if they took a trip abroad in the past twelve months, they are going to be invited to take another.

■ *Bounce Back* is a concept invented by catalog mailers. It works this way: when someone buys an item from one of the small catalogs sent by direct mail, they "bounce back" with another copy of the *same catalog*. Why? Because these small catalogs are usually tossed out once used. If your customers found one thing they liked in your catalog, there is probably something else in the same catalog which would appeal to them. With each sale, there is usually a "rush" of brand loyalty for that particular catalog, which is soon dissipated because the catalog is no longer around. You have a tiny window of time to build brand loyalty. Bounce back helps to widen that window.

Sears Roebuck has refined bounce back to a fine degree. When you buy a farm product from their general catalog, they bounce back with a specialized farm catalog. It requires computer programming to be sure that that happens automatically.

All of this requires advance planning, diagramming and elaborate computer programming. Remember what you are doing: you are trying to recreate the thinking that goes on in the brain of the old corner grocer. What would he do with each of these pieces of information? He would turn each one to his advantage, making appropriate suggestions on purchases, advising his customers on particular specials *of presumed interest to them.*

That is what you will have to do. But you will be handling several hundred thousand customers, not just a few hundred. There is no time to make little stacks of responses.

Your systems planner makes up a diagram of the sequence of events. You check it. Then the programmer translates the diagram into a series of computer program instructions. Then these instructions are tested with dummy data, in every possible combination of response, to be sure that you are not skipping something.

For example, you may be sending out the literature promptly but not also acting on the information that the customer is a senior citizen, and receives a special offer *in the same envelope.* You may be wasting postage on a second senior-citizen mailing.

Testing is one of the most difficult parts of response tracking, and one of the most neglected. Quality control: without it, database marketing falls apart.

SUMMARY

In the design of any marketing database, you must plan on effective ways for the consumer to contact you, to respond to you, to tell you things: unexpected things, important things, trivial things. A marketing database is a mechanism for two-way communication.

- You provide a way for consumers to contact you with their ideas, thoughts, complaints, compliments, suggestions.

- You store these things in the database so that you can remember them, quantify them, act on them.

- You design your database software so you can poll the database constantly for unresolved issues, new ideas, gripes, types of questions being raised.

- You act on what you learn from your customers.

- You reach out and tell your customers that you have listened, remembered and acted. Give them credit for their ideas or for pointing out flaws in your product, delivery, advertising.

- You remind them of how much you appreciate their business.

- While you are telling them what you have accomplished with their ideas, you ask for more.

  Result: true two-way communication.

Chapter 10

The Lifetime Value of a Customer

How do you know how much to spend to get your customers to buy your products? This vital question has been asked over and over again in every business for years. Mass marketing provided one answer. Direct marketing provided another. Database marketing provides still a third way of doing the computation.

MASS MARKETING ACCOUNTING

In mass marketing, the idea is this: generate brand awareness through massive advertising in print, TV and radio. We spend many millions of dollars to become a household word. Our spending is aimed at two markets: the customers and the retailers. The retailers have to give our product shelf space. They will give us this space only if they think that enough customers will recognize or ask for our brand due to the advertising. How long does it take to build up this brand awareness? Perhaps it takes two years before you make a profit. It may be three or four years before you pay back all your early costs and are truly profitable. But once you are over the hump, and everyone knows about your product and is buying it, you should have a mass market and clear, profitable sailing for years ahead.

Mass marketing works. Many companies have made millions doing it, and are still doing so. Many have fallen by the wayside: unable to convince enough customers or retailers that their product really is as good as the competition, or is something that they need or want in their home. Only about five percent of all products that are introduced in this way still exist five years after inception. Mass marketing is only really successful if you can persuade millions of people to think about a single brand or product. You calculate your profit by adding up all your sales since the beginning, subtract your costs since the beginning and see if you have come out ahead. When you begin with a new product, there is no way of being sure whether you will win or lose. Since expenses often far exceed sales for two or more years, you cannot relate the cost of a single advertisement to any specific sale, and no one tries to. You measure success by whether the average person in the street can remember your ad or your product. "Awareness" is what you are trying to create, and that is hard to put into a profit and loss statement.

DIRECT MARKETING ACCOUNTING

The accounting for direct marketing is quite different. In direct marketing you are not trying to build up a massive awareness of your presence or your product. You are trying to sell a specific product or service *right now* based on *this particular advertisement*. For this reason, direct marketing ads are coded with a *cell code*. This is a four- or six-letter code which identifies the magazine, the issue, the offer (in the case of a print ad); or the list, the package, the message (in the case of a direct mail piece). When your mailing is over, you prepare an account that resembles the table below.

Results of a Direct Marketing Program

Cell	Cost of Effort	Revenue	Profit	Return on Investment
QRW123	$82,345	$ 74,100	–$ 8,245	–10.01%
WGE200	$94,020	$170,200	$76,180	81.03%
DDD100	$55,200	$ 65,120	$ 9,920	17.97%
Total	$231,565	$309,420	$77,855	33.62%

Find out what went wrong with QRW123, and don't repeat that mistake. Perhaps it was the wrong magazine, list or offer. Find out what was so great about WGE200, and try to repeat it.

Direct marketing stands on its own. You can prove that it works (or has failed) by charts such as the one above. But it works only in the present. Tomorrow is another day, and it must start with another promotion. It cannot rely on national awareness to provide effortless sales.

My wife, Helena, is a great catalog shopper. Our mailbox is always stuffed with very slick expensive catalogs. She buys dresses, blouses, Christmas presents, birthday presents. She must spend a couple of hundred dollars a month shopping by mail. The list owners must be going crazy over her. They trade her name back and

Figure 10-1 Return on Investment
(Direct Marketing Program)

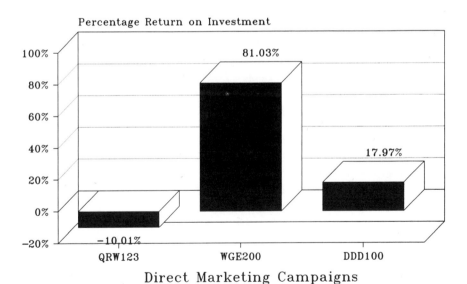

Direct Marketing Campaigns

forth, so she is now on more than 200 different lists—and with good reason.

But with Helena, each sale is a single sale. She saw a dress that she liked, spent $170 on it and took it with us to a wedding in South America. She remembers that she bought it from Knights, Ltd., and she likes that catalog. But her next purchase will not necessarily be from Knights. She threw that catalog away as soon as she ordered the dress, and Knights failed to "bounce back" with another copy of the same catalog (as they should have—see Chapter 9). In this situation, direct marketing is probably the best and only method. Database marketing would not work.

DATABASE MARKETING ACCOUNTING

Database marketing is designed for the situation in which a customer is going to come back and buy from you again and again. What are some examples:

> grocery products
> automobile sales and service
> insurance
> video rentals
> gardening supplies
> airlines, hotels, rental cars, travel agencies
> clothing, luggage
> medical, dental care
> restaurants, dinner theaters, movie theaters
> cable TV, telephone
> health centers, country clubs, diet centers
> . . . and thousands of others.

With database marketing, you are not aiming at a sale, but a series of sales. Your focus, then, is not on a transaction but on a customer. Suppose it costs you $25 to find someone who will buy a $40 item from you. Direct marketing would count this as a loss. But if this customer is entered into your database, and as a result you sell him her $25 a month for the next two years, the $25 was well spent.

THE MEANING OF LIFETIME VALUE

This is where the idea of lifetime value comes in. It is really the core of database marketing. If you look on each customer as someone valuable to you, someone who will come back again and again, then your whole approach to marketing changes radically. You need a different type of accounting. Let's take a specific example.

A major package goods company set up a program whereby their customers could receive automatic delivery of their product every month without requiring a repeat order. The customer just has to call to cancel or modify the order. After the program is successfully launched, they discover that it is costing them a great deal in advertising and other costs to obtain the customer in the first place. They wonder how much they are justified in spending to attract customers. They stop their promotions to attract new customers and

Figure 10-2 Lifetime Value
(Customers Who Dropped Out)

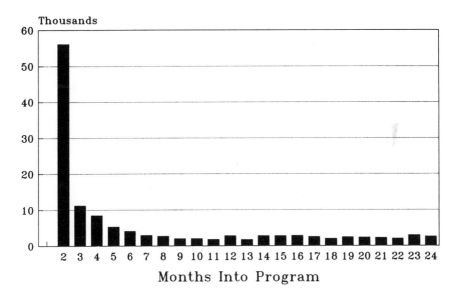

Months Into Program

switch to maintenance of current customers until they can answer this question (see Figure 10-2).

Based on two year's experience in the program, they had gathered figures on people's behavior dating from the first month they were enrolled in the program, as shown in the next table.

Households buying and households dropping out of the program (by month since each began buying)

End of Month	Dropped in Month	Still Buying	Percent Remaining	Average Lifetime in Months
1	492,404	274,400	35.8	1.0
2	56,102	218,298	28.5	1.4
3	11,200	207,098	27.2	1.6
4	8,488	198,610	25.9	1.9
5	5,302	193,308	25.2	2.2
6	4,100	189,208	24.7	2.4
7	2,930	186,278	24.3	2.7
8	2,670	183,608	23.9	2.9
9	2,003	181,605	23.7	3.2
10	1,987	179,618	23.4	3.4
11	1,764	177,854	23.2	3.6
12	2,790	175,064	22.8	3.9
13	1,722	173,342	22.6	4.1
14	2,801	170,541	22.2	4.3
15	2,755	167,786	21.9	4.5
16	2,810	164,976	21.5	4.8
17	2,533	162,443	21.2	5.0
18	1,977	160,466	20.9	5.2
19	2,402	158,064	20.6	5.4
20	2,320	155,744	20.3	5.6
21	2,191	153,553	20.0	5.8
22	2,008	151,545	19.8	6.0
23	2,940	148,605	19.4	6.2
24	2,588	146,017	19.0	6.4
Total	620,787	4,278,031	19.0	6.4

What they learned from this data was that two thirds of their customers dropped out in the first month. Of the balance, about half were gone after two years. How long did the average customer stay with the program? After two years, the average customer stayed with the program for 6.4 months. But at that point, 19 percent of the original customers were still in the program. Since there was insufficient time to tell when these customers would drop out, it was decided to project the drop-out rate at its current level. In addition, an allowance had to be made for the new people who had joined the program recently despite the absence of promotions, and had not yet dropped out. After all these calculations were completed, it was decided that the average customer would stay with the program for about 8.6 months.

Figure 10-3 Lifetime Value II
(Customers Still Buying Product)

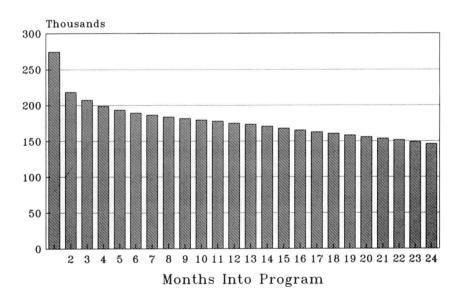

Months Into Program

Records showed that the average monthly purchase of product was $27.44, so that the average customer spent $235.98 before dropping out. After deducting the cost of the product, administrative costs, customer service and database management, the net profit out of the $27.44 was found to be about $3.71. That meant that the lifetime value of a customer was $3.71 x 8.6.

Next, they had to compute the acquisition cost of a new customer. Adding up all the direct mail expenses, advertising and telemarketing plus database costs, and dividing that by the total number of customers, they came up with an average figure of $17.88. Their final conclusion was that the lifetime value of a customer, $31.90, was in excess of the cost of acquiring the customer, $17.88. The program was considered a success.

Figure 10-4 Lifetime Value III
(Average Lifetime in Months)

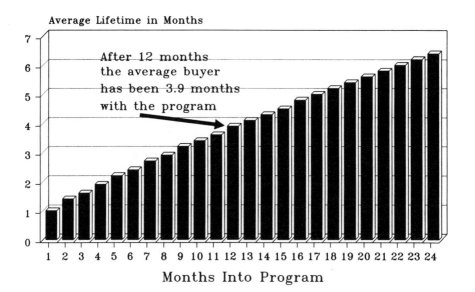

Average Lifetime in Months

After 12 months the average buyer has been 3.9 months with the program

Months Into Program

Figure 10-5 Lifetime Value IV
   (Average Customer Profit $38.82)

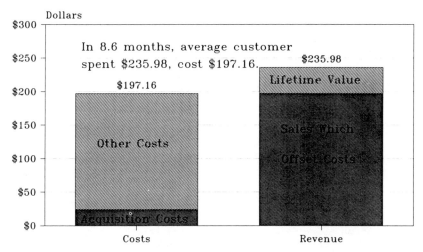

Acquisition Cost VS Lifetime Value

Average Customer Buys for 8.6 Months

When Lifetime Is Really Lifetime

Lifetime in this program was defined as: "How long did customers continue to buy this product?" There is obviously another meaning to lifetime: "How long does a customer live?" This number is of great interest to the insurance companies, which are just beginning to apply the concept of lifetime value to marketing programs.

Life insurance companies traditionally spend a lot of money acquiring customers. Very few people will buy a substantial life insurance policy by mail. Life insurance, after all, requires a lifetime commitment, sending in the premiums every month or every quarter without fail, for a payment somewhere in the future after your death. Salesmen are needed to explain the benefits and the payment method. Vast sums are spent acquiring names, doing telemarketing to qualify leads and then arranging home visits to promote family

participation. Even then, a substantial percentage of people drop out
shortly after starting a policy. For these reasons, life insurance companies keep a sharp eye on the cost of acquisition as compared to
the return.

Donald R. Jackson is a direct marketing consultant with twenty-
five years of experience in the industry. His practice focuses on financial services with a specialization in insurance direct marketing.
In his book *Secrets of Insurance Direct Marketing Practices Revealed,* he has refined the concept of a "Policyholder Lifetime
Value":

> Policyholder Lifetime Value is the present value of a future
> stream of net contributions to overhead and profit expected from
> the policyholder. Profitability, in the long term, will be the result
> of two factors. First, the difference between the acquisition al-
> lowance developed *using Policyholder Lifetime Value,* and Poli-
> cyholder acquisition cost. Second, the number of policyholders
> that can be acquired at an acceptable investment cost determined
> by their Lifetime Value expands your Policyholder base. More
> policyholders mean more policyholder sales. More sales mean
> more net contribution to overhead and profit collected.

> "Because, policyholder acquisition is less a function of a single
> solicitation event . . . than it is a function of a related string of
> solicitation events, all of which taken together produce long-
> term profit at an acceptable return-on-investment . . .

> "Policyholder LTV provides a financial foundation for key man-
> agement decisions:

> 1. Developing rates for insurance products.
> 2. Assigning acquisition allowances for policyholder acquisition.
> 3. Setting selection criteria for policyholder marketing.
> 4. Choosing media for initial policyholder acquisition.
> 5. Investing in reactivation of old policyholders.
> 6. Assigning an asset value to your policyholder base.

> "Policyholder Lifetime Value is determined by examining the
> income and expense streams you can expect from your policy-

holders. The sale of a single insurance product produces income over a long period of time—this concept is called persistency.

"In insurance, this is done by creating a profit study. A profit study examines what happens to the income and expense streams over a period of time, usually ten years. It results in a 'profit' figure over that period of time, as well as a return on investment measure.

"The first step to determine Policyholder LTV is to generate a profit study for your base product—the first one you intend to sell. The next step is to create a profit study for every additional product you intend to sell to your policyholders over a period of time, perhaps three years: every rider, and every cross-load product.

"Finally, you summarize the results of each profit study in a model format. And you calculate Lifetime Value. Using the Life time Value of the customer, you can then determine how much money you can afford to spend to acquire the policyholder, all the while maintaining a *target customer profit* and *return on investment.*"

In many cases, you will discover that the amount which you can afford to spend to acquire a new name is greater than the amount that is currently being spent.

Each group of customers, of course, has a different lifetime value. You cannot treat them all alike. To become proficient at LTV analysis, you have to develop formulae so that you can predict the LTV of groups of customers at acquisition time. Based on your experience, and ranking customers by source, by demographic profiles and type of initial sales activity, you can get a clear projection of subsequent sales, profitability and name flow. The more experience you have, and the better job you do in ranking and classifying your customers, the better you will get at determining the LTV of each newcomer; the better job you will do of knowing how much to spend on acquisition.

Database Builds Bank Business

The Meridian Bank in Reading, Pennsylvania, began to experiment with database marketing to their existing customers when they realized that their general advertising was by itself not producing the results that they projected. By creating a comprehensive customer database they were able to target particular segments. They looked for the right demographic makeup, age, financial status and combination of current use of bank products to identify the ideal prospects for expanded product usage. Their senior's package, called Club 50, had a wide variety of inducements. A coupon in their direct-mail package encouraged senior customers to visit their branch to sign up. Eighteen percent of those mailed did just that. The total advertising and marketing program produced in their first wave 60,000 new accounts, according to Harvey Corbett, Vice President for Marketing. Later follow-up efforts increased the total to more than 100,000.

The Meridian Bank also pioneered using their customer base to increase their home equity customers. A study of the database convinced Harvey Corbett that the average life of such a loan is about seven years. Within the first year after approval, the average customer had run up about half the total authorized borrowing limit, and kept that balance until the house was sold. This fine estimation of customer lifetime value enabled the bank to know how much it could afford to invest in a home equity promotion, and still be profitable. "We have made our share of mistakes," Mr. Corbett admits, "but having a database at our fingertips has helped us to monitor what we are doing and make each test mailing a learning experience. Overall, we now feel that we really understand our customer base much better than we did when we started. We have profited by the experience."

USING LIFETIME VALUE KNOWLEDGE

When you have calculated the lifetime value of your customers, you have a powerful tool. Not only can you determine how much you should spend to acquire a customer, you also have a basis for knowing the value of a marketing database and of customer service. 800 numbers, once perceived as a necessary but losing proposition for public relations value, now can be looked on as an extension of your lifetime customer contact. It also helps you rethink your customer service function as a supplementary sales function. You can put a dollar value on your database.

But the knowledge goes beyond aggregate amounts. Some customers have a higher lifetime value than others. Which ones are they? Using your database, you should begin doing some careful analysis. If yours is a business-to-business selling situation, do you find that most of your long-term sales come from large businesses or small businesses? Which SIC codes provide the best customers? In consumer databases, you may be able to classify customers by demographics, clusters or psychographics to identify the ones with the highest lifetime value.

What do you do with this valuable information? You discriminate, of course. If you have a pretty good idea of who the most valuable customers are, it will help your bottom line to see that they are encouraged to remain loyal to you, are given super service, are enrolled in a prestigious buyer's club with special benefits and recognition.

SUMMARY

- The lifetime value of a customer is defined as the contribution to overhead and profit which each customer provides you during his or her purchasing days with your company.

- In a business that counts on repeat sales, it is important to calculate how long people will remain your customers, how much they buy each year and how much profit and overhead is represented in their purchases. This is their lifetime value.

- Once you know lifetime value, you can use it to decide how much to spend to acquire a customer in the first place. In many cases, companies are not spending enough on acquisition, because they don't look beyond the first sale.

- You can use lifetime value to segment your customers. Determine which ones have the greatest lifetime value potential based on your experience, and cultivate these people. Give them special recognition.

- General advertising accounting figures the cost of establishing *awareness* of the product in the public's mind.

- Direct marketing accounting figures the cost of making a single sale.

- Database marketing accounting figures the lifetime value of a repeat customer and balances that off against the cost of acquiring the customer and servicing his or her needs during the years to come.

- Figuring lifetime value is complicated because customers come and go, and do not stay with you for defined periods of time.

- Lifetime value considers repeat sales, upgrades, cross-selling, interest on investment.

Chapter 11

Providing Services to Your Customers

If Nancy sells a book to Dan for $10, what is the book worth? If you said $10 you would be wrong. If it were worth exactly $10 there would have been no trade, no transaction. Would you go to town with a $10 bill, take it to the bank, exchange it for an identical $10 bill, and drive home satisfied? Of course not.

To Nancy, the book is clearly worth much less than $10. After all, she had to bring the book to their place of exchange, wait while Dan examined it, run the risk that he would decide against buying it and waste her time. Nancy wants the $10 much more than the book. The book is probably worth $9 or perhaps even $5 to her.

To Dan, the book is clearly worth much more than $10. After all, he is exchanging a $10 bill which can be used to buy a meal, a haircut or transportation, for a book which probably has very little liquid exchange value. He had to believe that the book would provide him with information or entertainment worth far in excess of $10—perhaps $11 or even $15—to be willing to give up his $10. Just try going to a restaurant and offering the book in exchange for a meal, or giving the book to a cab driver in exchange for a ride to the airport!

This example shows that in a free exchange, there is profit, sometimes a lot of profit, to both parties. If the book was worth only $5 to Nancy, she has walked away with $5 profit. If it was worth $15 to Dan, he too has a $5 profit.

This is the core reasoning behind customer service. Companies trade something that does not cost them much, information and helpfulness, for something that is worth a lot to them—customer loyalty and continued sales. Customers trade something that does not cost them much, loyalty, for something they really value a great deal: information about the product, and helpful service in using it, understanding it or getting it repaired.

If the database is the trunk of the tree, customer service is the fruit. In the past, companies thought of customer service as a losing proposition. They spend a lot of money on an 800 number and operators to man it—but where are the sales that would justify this expense? Better to print up clear instructions, paste them to the outside of the box and forget it!

But, of course, all that is now in the past. Most companies have gotten the message that contact with customers can and should be a mutually profitable experience. They have learned that one of the most important commodities that they have to sell is information. Prospects and customers want information:

- about what is available, and how much it costs;
- about where to get it, and how to get it;
- about how it works, how you put it together;
- about what to do if you can't get it to work;
- about upgrades: things that go with it, plug into it, make it more useful and attractive; and
- about spare parts.

MAINTAINING CUSTOMER CONTACT

With this as a background, it is easy to see how a marketing database can be used to maintain a one-on-one relationship with each customer. Every time a customer writes a letter or makes a telephone call, one of your customer service reps can get your customer's record instantly up on the screen. Visible will be all the contacts, all the purchases, all the data about this customer. "Yes,

Mrs. Warren, did the baby car seat arrive in time? Was your daughter happy with it?"

This time Mrs. Warren may be calling to order something else, or she may be calling with an inquiry or a complaint. No matter what it is, the substance of the call should be recorded in her file for later reference. (This is what the corner grocer did. He remembered that you asked when peaches would be in stock. When the peaches came in, he reminded you of it, and you thanked him for remembering.)

How do you keep track of such telephone calls in a marketing database? In two ways: coded records and free-form records. The free-form records are made while Mrs. Warren is on the phone. They might read like this: "UPS man left car seat at wrong house. OK now. Invited to wedding on May 14. Can suggest luggage gift at $50? Can bride exchange for credit if wants other?" The free-form record will have the date, the customer ID and the free-form ID.

When the call has ended, the customer rep will review the free-form record, and enter suitable codes into a coded record. There will be a code to send a gift catalog and gift coupon to Mrs. Warren, an exchange certificate letter, a wedding gift reminder code for May 14, a UPS delivery error code. These codes will trigger mailings and reminders for outbound telemarketing. For example, there could be a telephone call late in May. How was the wedding, and what did she end up by buying as a gift? (If it was not luggage, maybe it was something that we should have in our catalog.)

The coded record will be used to prepare reports: problems with UPS, coupons sent, catalogs sent, customer events and such. Every time Mrs. Warren calls, her free-form records will show on the screen. After a year, they will be automatically purged, to be replaced by the coded records only.

Disk Space

"Keeping all this information is going to require a tremendous amount of disk space," I can imagine you thinking. "Hughes has really gone overboard if he thinks that we can keep all that information in our file of 6,000,000 customers. We will go broke."

Old-fashioned thinking. As detailed earlier, new advances in computer technology has caused the cost of maintaining data on disk to drop every year. It will continue to drop.

Your competitors have already realized this and are developing marketing databases which will hold this data. And what's more, *you won't be able to find out about it* because marketing databases are private, one-on-one affairs. Mrs. Warren will think that it is because their customer rep remembers their many phone calls (even though the rep is not always the same person). As time goes on computer disk space will be dirt cheap, and no longer a worry.

Figure 11-1 Customer Service Knows the Whole Story

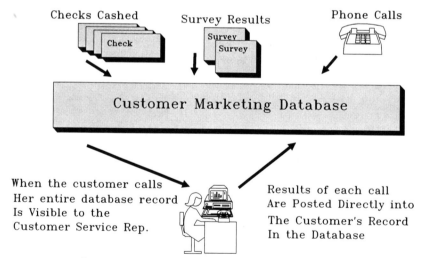

Customer Service Reps Have Complete Prior History Available

Checks Cashed   Survey Results   Phone Calls

Customer Marketing Database

When the customer calls
Her entire database record
Is Visible to the
Customer Service Rep.

Results of each call
Are Posted Directly into
The Customer's Record
In the Database

Customer Service Info Desk on 800 or 900 number

Total Company Involvement

When you get your database set up, your company's entire operations will change in ways that will be dictated by your database. Customers will ask for service, and expect it the next day (not in "six to eight weeks"). If you offer the old service, they will go elsewhere. You will be able to do a much better job of predicting sales and consequently predicting needs for inventory replenishment.

Product design will rely more and more on the intelligence provided by the database. As we move from the mass marketing of the past, it has become obvious that customers want more products and services in ever-increasing varieties. What these varieties are can be learned from the database.

CUSTOMER SERVICE FUNCTIONS AND ATTRIBUTES

What do you expect of customer service? Let's make a list:

Cheerful, helpful, interested. A fun person to talk to. A sense of humor. Someone who is really interested in people.

Intelligent and knowledgeable. Customer service reps must know not only your products but your *business.* It is not enough to know that you have fourteen different computer models available; they have to know what each one does, and why someone would buy one over another. They have to have at their fingertips (not necessarily in their heads) the answer to any question that could be asked. They have to know how to use their fingertips to get that information. They have to be smart enough to figure out what customers are trying to find out so that they can supply it.

Linked to technical resources. No one customer service representative can know everything. But somewhere in your company there is someone who knows what the customer is asking about. Your telephone system has to be such that reps can quickly send callers to the right place for an answer. Ideally, however, they should be able to talk to the resource on the intercom first:

"Roger Harris is on the line. He has a scanner which produces a bit-map. He wants to know if our product can read the bit map. He has version 2.0. I think that he may need an upgrade to 2.2, but I am not sure. Can you talk to him and be sure that that is what he needs. If so, give him back to me, and I will place an order for him."

The technical link requires something more than a good customer service rep and an excellent telephone system. It requires that almost *everyone* in the company understand and be prepared to play a role in customer service. The whole company has to become *dedicated* to thinking that providing information to customers is an *important part of their jobs.*

When someone asked the old corner grocer how big a turkey was needed to feed fourteen people, he didn't say, "Don't bother me. I have a delivery truck broken down and ten orders to get out." Somehow he found a moment to tell you, "A pound and a half per person, and sometimes a little extra. We will have some fresh ones coming in on Wednesday morning. Can I save one for you?"

In the same fashion, when customer calls come in, your technical personnel, billing clerks and shipping staff have to realize that responding to this call right now is as important as whatever they were doing when the call came in. The message of customer service has to permeate the whole company, or your reps will have a hard time projecting a helpful image.

Delegated real authority. There comes a time when someone has to say to a customer: "That is too bad, Mrs. Michaelson. You know that we stand behind our products 100 percent. No one should have to put up with what you have gone through. I am going to send you a replacement today, right this minute. It should get there in two days, three at the outside. There is no charge. Please call me and tell me when it arrives, and if it is working OK. I want to be sure that you are happy with us and our products."

Figure out what decisions you can delegate to your experienced customer service reps, and *delegate them.* This delegation will have important benefits for you. Customers will get better, more responsive, speedier service, and your reps will begin to feel that they are important in the company. They will take a greater interest in their work, do a better job, represent you better. They will become "old corner grocers."

Of course, when they do give away replacement products, or refunds, they have to record this information in the database—that is how the replacements and refunds get to the customer. The database triggers an order or a refund check.

The fact that the decision is in the database means something else: there will be reports generated. You can see how much each rep has given away each month. The authority you have delegated carries responsibility with it, and accountability. You know, and the reps know, that there will be a printed report every month on refunds and exchanges. If there is a question, they have a complete database record on every transaction. They can document what they did, and why they did it.

Thus, your database makes it easier for you to delegate responsibility. And this delegation enables you to provide quicker and more responsive services to your customers.

Motivated to sell. People used to think that customer service was an information function, and not in the business of selling. That was old-fashioned thinking. Today we know that customers are busy people. Both the customer and his or her spouse are working. They don't have time to fool around. If a product or service that they need, want, or would be beneficial to them, is available, they want to know about it and be able to place an order for it right then and there.

That is the whole point of this chapter: a successful sale means that both parties walk away with a profit. Your customer service reps have to understand this, and use this understanding in selling upgrades and new products.

Willing to fish for and record information. In the modern supermarket, when you ask a clerk where you can find canned Polish ham, the clerk says "Against the wall, near Aisle 8." That is all— there is no more to the exchange. But when your caller says, "Do you have cruise ships that go to Jamaica?," this should open up a whole line of information-gathering. Not only do you tell the caller that, in fact, you do not go to Jamaica, but you do go to Aruba, the Virgin Islands and a dozen other nearby places. And you also try to get other facts:

Who is the customer?
How many people might be going?
Has the caller been on a cruise ship before?

What was good or bad about the previous cruise?
Where else have they been on vacation?
What travel agent they usually use?
What occasion prompted the call
   —a birthday, an anniversary, a retirement party?
What does the caller's spouse do for a living?
Do they know someone else who has cruised?
Would they like to receive literature, video?
When was the caller thinking of going?

Is this information relevant? You bet it is.

Can your customer service rep record it? It depends on how good your database system is.

Can you put the information to profitable use? Again, that depends on you and the resourcefulness of your company and your marketing database system. The result of this call should be a phone call or a letter to the customer's travel agent or one of your preferred agents, with some very hot information.

TRAINING CUSTOMER SERVICE REPRESENTATIVES

Equipped with screens that show a customer's entire history and potential, the customer service representative becomes one of the most important sales forces that your company has. You will have to completely revamp their training, not just to know how to work the database, but in the techniques of selling, cross selling and upgrading. They will have to know everything about the products that you sell, but also about the competitor's products and "competitive advantage." They must be trained to lead the conversation in certain directions. The menu screens available will help to profile the customer against available products and services. The rep can suggest the correct additional product or service through using the right questions at the right time.

Customer service reps must be trained in responsiveness. If your company culture says they should not sell, you will have to change your culture. Professionals in this field often need training in sales techniques: initiating the right questions, asking for the sale, following up. You will need a high-powered planning staff to design the training and support the effort.

At first, you may want to use an external telemarketing company to provide your customer service staff. A good service bureau can get you started immediately with experienced telemarketing staff. The costs of outside start-up are usually much lower. And the outside staff can handle the staffing problems of evenings and weekends which are typical of 800 number respondents.

Customer service reps receive their compensation not only in the number of customers that they handle, but also in the number of sales that they can make. They have the entire product line with quantities and prices available on pull-down screens. If the product is insurance, they will be prompted for about twenty questions that they should ask to qualify the customer for the product, as well as information they should provide to whet the customer's appetite for the upcoming appointment with the salesperson. The selling script is contained on each screen, so the rep does not need to look elsewhere to figure out the right question to ask or answer to provide.

Besides training your customer service reps, you will want to train a hundred or more other people in the company on their roles in customer service. You want them to know how they should react when they get a call: what they can say, how important the function is and *what to do with the caller when they have finished providing the information*. They must learn not to drop the ball. Keep it in play, and pass the ball back to customer service for the score. Customer service is everybody's job. You may also want to be sure that whatever your technical people discuss with the customer is entered into the customer record. Either they can do it themselves, through their direct access to the database, or they may call the customer service rep to do it. Either way, the database should have that information.

SUMMARY

All calls and contacts with a customer should be logged into a marketing database. These calls and contacts should be instantly recov-

erable when the customer calls again so that your rep can knowledgeably discuss the customer's purchasing history and life. The
database should permit your rep to continue an interrupted dialog
with your customers whenever they call and talk with a complete
knowledge of the past, *even though the last company rep who spoke
with this customer was someone else.*

- There is plenty of inexpensive disk space available on which to
  store all this customer information. The disk space is much
  cheaper than the value of the information to you.

- Everyone in the company will have to play a role in customer
  service, once the database is set up.

- Customer service reps have to be:
  - cheerful, helpful, interested
  - intelligent and knowledgeable
  - linked to technical resources
  - delegated real authority
  - motivated to sell
  - willing to fish for and record information.

- Training of customer service reps is a very important function.
  In addition, many other people in the company will need the
  same training.

Part Four

Reaching Out
to Prospects

Chapter 12

Building a Profile of Your Best Customers

Our database contains the information that we need to analyze our current customers. Their responses and purchase histories will tell us what we need to know about them to select our best and our worst, and to develop programs to keep the best happy and buying.

But companies do not live and grow by current customers alone; new customers are needed to grow, and to balance the inevitable attrition. What kind of new customers do we want? The answer must be: ones similar to our best current customers. That is the challenge discussed in the next chapters: how to find people who resemble in their purchasing habits the best customers that already exist on the file.

This is not an easy task. At this point, all we really know about these customers is their purchasing history. They buy often and in large amounts, and they have purchased from us recently. But if we go to any external source of possible customers, whether it be a rented list, convention attendees, responders to an advertisement or people who walk into our store and apply for a credit card, we may not be able to get information about them which would classify them for us in this useful way. Are there ways, in advance, in which we can select people who will have purchasing behaviors which meet our expectations?

Perhaps. There are now a score of well explored methods for finding new customers, none of which is foolproof, but most of which offer an improved chance of finding the type of people that we want. All of them are expensive. Some will cost more than they are worth. But in a some cases they will be exactly what we need, and will pay us rich dividends.

Modeling, which we are going to explore now, works under a single premise: the desirable behavior of our best customers can be traced back to some combination of measurable qualities in their lives or lifestyles. Other people who share these lifestyles will exhibit similar behavior.

On the surface, this seems a weak premise. You and your next door neighbor may have identical homes, identical jobs, incomes and families, but you are as different as night and day. He likes sports, drinks heavily and dresses badly. His children are a wild bunch. You read books (thank goodness for that), have well behaved children, like classical music and dinner theater. You buy excellent clothes and keep them neat and clean. Your purchasing habits are probably very different from those of your neighbor. Yet, compared to people in other subdivisions in other parts of town, the two of you look very much alike. Neither of you resemble the family on welfare only three blocks away, nor the owner of the water works who owns half the town. You are different from the farmers who bring produce to the market every morning, and the science teacher in the high school who is saving up to buy a cross-country skiing outfit.

Here are some similarities: you and your neighbor both have identical mortgages. You have to buy outfits for two school children. You have the same doctor and dentist bills. You get three weeks vacation a year which you spend somewhere else. You have lawns to mow, TVs and VCRs that break down and two college educations to save up for.

So for some vendors selling certain products, you and your neighbor may exhibit similar behavior. Our job, with our data base, is to find those qualities which work *for our situation* and use them to select future customers.

The method we will use is to add to (or append to) our customer file as many known qualities about these customers as we can discover. We will use computers to help us know whether these qualities serve to separate our good customers from our poor customers. When we find some group of qualities that seem to work for us, we apply them to some group of unknown new prospects to see if these prospects are worth pursuing. The qualities we are seeking are those which:

1. Can be found out and recorded about our customers.
2. Serve as a significant discriminating factor between good customers and poor customers.
3. Can be found out and recorded about prospects who are otherwise unknown to us.
4. Help us to pick the good prospects from the poor ones.

Figure 12-1 Developing a Customer Profile

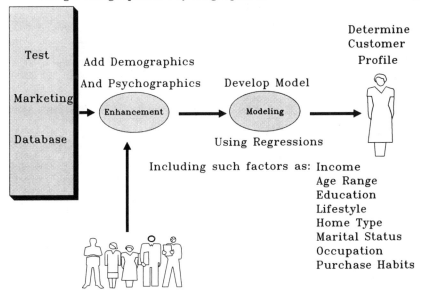

Using Demographics, Psychographics, and Statistical Modeling

There are many sources of such new information. In this chapter we are going to explore only one of them—demographics. Subsequent chapters will cover other enhancements, such as clustering, psychographics and lifestyle information.

DEMOGRAPHICS

The technique of using demographics is built and based on the U.S. Census. In the latest version of this massive exercise undertaken every ten years, the government have broken the country into 7.5 million or more blocks for which it obtains and supplies data. A block has a small number of families, such as twelve or fourteen. In most cases all of the houses in a block contain households which are similar in terms of income, home value, age of head of household, presence of children, educational level, ethnic background, occupation of head of household and so on. This is not, of course, universally true. Of necessity some blocks are very heterogeneous in makeup. But, across the country, the vast percentage of blocks are made up of similar households.

A certain percentage of the households in each block are asked fill out the "long form" in the census. This long form asks more than a hundred questions about the background and lifestyle of the household members. When the forms are tabulated, the census staff determines the set of lifestyle factors which are dominant in the block. So, for each block, it is possible to assign to all fourteen families the same average income, home value and such. This is mere chance, of course. By chance, the census may select the richest family on the block or the poorest to represent the entire block. As a result, some block data may be quite unrepresentative. But overall, with 7.5 million blocks surveyed, the chances are that the data on most blocks is fairly representative of all families on the block.

As part of the census, the computer has been supplied with all of the streets and house numbers included in each block. These are preserved on magnetic tape. So a mailer with a tape of customers or prospects can match their addresses with the census files to determine the "geocode" of each household, the geocode being nothing other than the number of the relevant block.

To assign demographics to a household, therefore, a mailer runs a tape of prospects against a census tape and geocodes it. Then he or she transfers (appends) to each household from census data the income, home value and other attributes of the block to which that household belongs.

Qualifications

This method is fraught with error. In the first place, the dominant household income in the block—even if it is representative—may not be the household income of the particular household we are studying at all. But, statistically speaking, it is as close to the real truth as we are likely to get.

The second qualification is that census figures will become more and more out of date as the years go by. How do we adjust for the changes that will take place each year?

There are several important commercial firms that do projections. They use national, state and county aggregate data on income changes to adjust block income levels by appropriate percentages. They use information on housing starts at the county level to apply back to home construction in particular blocks. They use information which may have come to them about ethnic shifts in neighborhoods to adjust the ethnic percentages in blocks. They apply home value increases in particular areas to recompute home values in each block. This attempt by individual companies to do this job accurately in a nation of 250,000,000 people broken down into 7.5 million blocks will obviously yield only approximately correct results. In some blocks, the resulting numbers will be just plain wrong.

In 1989, I did a presentation to the senior staff of a large bank. We had provided them with statistics on the population surrounding several areas where they planned to locate new branches. The executive vice president of the bank was livid: "Your figures showed that there were only 400 people living in that area, but I drove out there myself and saw four huge brand new high-rises there with hundreds of families in each one. Your figures are nuts!"

Of course, all we had to go on were commercial projections of the 1980 census. When that census was taken, nine years previously, the area in question was largely desert. We explained that our numbers were projections based on state and county data, and could not be accurate for every intersection in the state.

"I don't want projections, damnit, I just want to know how many people are living there now. You people don't seem to know."

Needless to say, we did not add this vice president to our list of satisfied customers.

But, when looking at hundreds of thousands of households on a prospect list, the numbers available from commercial firms are all we have to go on, and in most cases will yield helpful results, so we use them. No private company has the resources to research every intersection in America every year to see what has been happening so that they can update their statistics. Take all this information with a grain of salt.

DEMOGRAPHIC INFORMATION AVAILABLE

The type of information we can determine from demographic overlays is staggering:

Household and family income
Source of income
Per capita income
Poverty level percentage
Percent households with children
Marital status of heads of households
Median age
White-black percentages
Home value
Percent professional, technical, managerial, clerical
Percent sales, craftsmen, operatives, blue collar, service
Percent farmers, laborers
Schooling of adults
Persons per household
Type of housing unit; number of rooms
Length of residence
Age of construction of units
Energy source for heating, cooking

Number of bedrooms, bathrooms, telephone, air conditioning
Public water supply, sewer
Rental versus home ownership
Date moved in to residence
Rental value
Percent married, widowed, divorced
Motor vehicle ownership
Ethnic makeup
Principal type of employment
Male and female employment
Mortgage information
College and school attendance
Social Security and welfare recipients
Ancestry
Travel time to work
Military service
Language spoken
Urbanization

The headings presented here represent only an introduction to the information available. Under ancestry, for example, there are twenty-one different pieces of data, from Dutch to Ukrainian.

How do you get this information applied to your database? The simplest method is to make a tape of your names and addresses and send it to one of the hundreds of firms which will add updated demographic information to clients' tapes. For a fee, which is probably about $30 per thousand names, or three cents per name, they will add (append) as much (or all) of the above information to every name in your file for which you have a correct street address. We must make space in our database for this additional information, and it will become a part of our marketing program for the foreseeable future. We have vastly expanded our data base and its possible uses.

A few cautions are in order. New streets are being created every day. Many of your customers may live on new streets which have not yet found their way into the commercial compiler's list of geocodable streets. In other cases, the address may be use less for geocoding. Route 1, Box 378, will deliver a letter fine, but may not be sufficient for determining the block. In some cases, the geocoder cannot match more than 60 percent of the households on your list with a valid geocode.

What do you do when you cannot geocode a particular address? The answer is that you use the zipcode to assign to the household the demographic information at the zipcode level. There are 7.5 million blocks, but only 36,000 zipcodes. Clearly information at the block level is much more pin-pointed and accurate than zipcode level data. Paradoxically for this valid reasoning, some studies show that demographic analysis performed at the zipcode level works just about as well in predicting behavior as block group level data. Zipcode analysis is much cheaper since it is quicker and easier to do. In some cases you can save money and not sacrifice accuracy by doing your demographic appending at the zipcode level. Experiment and see what works best for your company.

The other caution has been already mentioned: what is true of the block may or may not be true of your customer's household. Don't get into the habit of thinking that appended demographic information is true data. It is *approximate* data.

Is Appended Data Correct?

Before you invest a lot of money with a vendor doing enhancement, do a small test to convince yourself that the vendor's methods and his data are correct. Take a file of a few thousand names where you already know the actual age and income. Mix this file with other names, and ask the vendor to enhance the file with age and income. Check the results. You will probably find a soberingly high percentage of error. Glenn Hausfater of Precision Marketing Corp., Northbrook, Illinois, did just that with two vendors. As he reported in an article in *Direct* magazine in June 1990, he found that each of them appended totally incorrect information to his test names about half the time.

True Age Versus Appended Age

True Age	Names Classified as "Under 25"		Names Classified as "Over 25"	
	Vendor 1	Vendor 2	Vendor 1	Vendor 2
Under 25	12.5%	6.4%	3.6%	3.9%
25-34	6.3	26.9	13.4	14.2
35-44	18.8	20.5	12.9	11.9
45-54	12.5	10.3	11.1	10.6
55-64	6.3	10.9	13.4	14.3
65+	43.8	25.0	45.7	45.0
Total	100.0	100.0	100.0	100.0

In this test, more than 40 percent of the names overlayed as being "under 25" by Vendor 1 properly belong in the "over 65" category. For both vendors, more than half of all names tagged as "over 65" actually belong to a younger category.

In short, beware: you may be paying good money for erroneous information—and what's worse, you may be basing a multi-million dollar marketing campaign on these errors. It is easy to assume that because a vendor is a large corporation with a good reputation and a massive mainframe, you will be furnished with reliable and correct information. That is not necessarily so. You must check everything.

Tiger System

Even more interesting than the block breakdown is the new TIGER mapping system upon which the 1990 census was based. TIGER (Topographically Integrated Geographic Encoding and Referencing) is a computerized map of the entire United States that can be directly related to census data. TIGER mapping displays every street, road, railroad and river in the country. This mapping system permits marketers to create accurate maps of their market areas. These maps can show clearly the location of all their customers. From surveys they can also learn the spending, wealth and income of their non-customers, which can also be accurately mapped.

Figure 12-2 Errors in Appended Data
(True Ages Versus Appended Age)

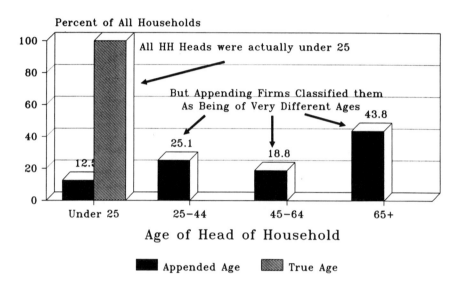

Source: Precision Marketing Corporation

Determining Which Factors Relate to Behavior

The next step is a difficult one: difficult to accomplish and difficult to justify by the laws of common sense. Out of the hundreds of facts that we have appended to our customer file, we must find those few which best "explain" the differences in behavior between our customers. We have already coded our customer file using RFM analysis so we know our good customers and our poor customers. Can we use a simple factor, such as income or home value, to pick the good ones from the poor ones? Let's use a simple example as a model.

Analysis of 2000 Customers by Value of Home

Type of Customer		Value of Home			
	Total	$200K+	$100-199K	$50-99K	Below $50K
Good Customers	1000	200	600	150	50
Poor Customers	1000	50	400	300	250

This chart is typical of the disappointing results you get from demography. It is clear that people in $200K-plus houses make better customers, but common sense might have told you that. If the world were made up only of people with homes of this value, our marketing job would be a lot easier than it is. Unfortunately, we

Figure 12-3 Customers by Home Value
(Comparing 1000 Good and 1000 Poor)

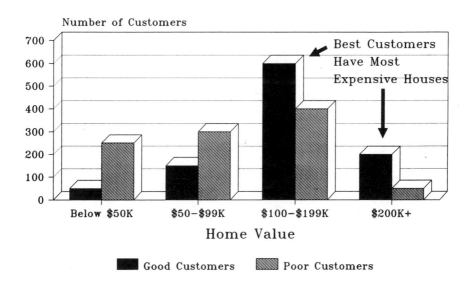

must make our sales in the world as it is, not as we would like it to be. As for the rest of the chart, home value is only a weak discriminating feature.

Let's try another feature: own versus rent.

Analysis of 2000 Customers by Own versus Rent

Type of Customer		Home Ownership	
	Total	Own Home	Rent Home
Good Customers	1000	700	300
Poor Customers	1000	300	700

Here is what appears to be a much more powerful discriminating factor.

You can run counts by each of 100 different demographic factors to try to pick the ones that work best for your product or service.

MULTIPLE REGRESSIONS

Instead of the painstaking work of running tables for each separate factor, you can use a technique called a multiple regression. This technique permits you to merge together the data from a few or many different demographic factors like the above to pick the one or ones which taken together do the best job of separating the better customers from the poorer customers.

Regression analysis is a statistical model-building process that analyzes the relationships between a dependent variable (behavior) and a set of independent variables (demographic data). Regression analysis assumes a straight-line relationship between the independent variable and the dependent variable.

Ideally, the results of multiple regressions should tell you that your good customers have attributes A, B, C and D, whereas your poor customers have attributes M, N, O and P. It is seldom a clean and clear-cut process, however. Many of your good customers will have M, N and O, and many of the bad ones will have A, B and C.

Figure 12-4 Customers by Own VS Rent
(1000 Good VS 1000 Poor)

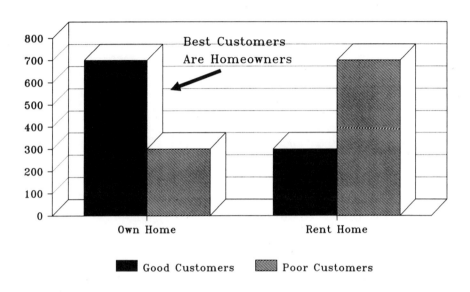

Best Customers Are Homeowners

Good Customers   Poor Customers

A multiple regression takes into account a couple of dozen factors and, when run successively, helps to determine which of the factors are useful in explaining the dependent variable (behavior of the customer) and which are not useful.

To prove the validity of your predictor, apply your formula to your entire database. Then sort the file by your predicted response. Break the sorted file into ten groups (deciles) from highest to lowest predicted behavior and the predicted behavior compared with the actual known behavior. If the formula has worked correctly, the differences between actual and predicted behavior should be small.

Why is it that multiple regressions are not more widely used in direct marketing? Clearly it is because in many cases the modeling is not helpful. The fact is that the reasons for consumers' behavior are usually much more complex than the data that we have available to us about them.

Why someone buys a product can seldom be explained by income, education, age, marital status and ethnic background alone. Most of the important factors cannot be derived from external sources: they can only be learned from direct surveys of our customers, and sometimes not even then.

If you are serious about profiling, you should secure the services of a consultant who knows the field. For reference consult *The New Direct Marketing,* by David Shepard Associates (Dow Jones-Irwin 1990). This valuable book has more advanced information on modeling and its use in direct marketing than you could possibly use. The book covers not only modeling but the economics of direct marketing and much about the building of a database marketing system. It should be on your office bookshelf.

Figiure 12-5 Profiling Your Customers

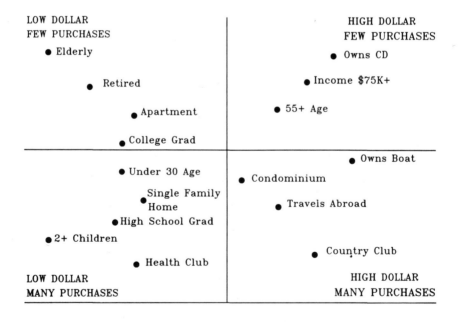

PREDICTING RESPONSE

The most common use for model development from demographic data is to predict response to a mailing. Every time you mail to a group, you record the date and source code of your outgoing mailing in their database record. When the responses come in, the date, source code and amount received is also stored. Once the mailing is over, you can determine the response rate.

As we know, the average response to a well-designed mailing to prospects is often about two percent, with 98 percent non-responders. The object of the modeling is to predict which of the 100 percent mailed will fall in the two percent responders and which will be in the 98% non-responders, based on their demographics. Once you have this formula developed to your satisfaction, you use it to select names from prospect lists before your next mailing. You mail to those prospects with demographic factors shown by your formula as most likely to respond, and you suppress mailing to those least likely to respond. The result should give you a much higher response rate per piece mailed. The difference between the average response rate expected (two percent) and the actual response of a segment achieved using the results of the regression formula (4.6 percent?) is called the *lift*. Lift is figured by dividing the response rate for a segment (4.6) by the overall response rate (2) and subtracting 1 (4.6/2 = 2.3 − 1 = 1.3) and multiplying by 100 (1.3 x 100 = 130). The lift for this segment is then 130.

To illustrate the lift, suppose we had a mailing of 1,000,000 with a two percent response rate. From this database a sample is used to develop a regression segmentation model. The formula is applied to the entire file, which is then sorted and ranked by predicted response from highest to lowest. This file is then broken down into 10 equal segments of 100,000 each.

Figure 12-6 MailingResponse
(Showing the Lift due to Segmenting)

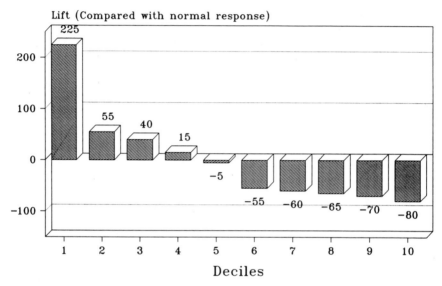

Lift (Compared with normal response)

Deciles

Lift = compared with non—segmented mail

1,000,000 Mailing in Deciles Ranked by Response Rate

Decile	Mailed	Response Rate	Lift	Cumulative Response
1	100,000	6.5	225	6.5
2	100,000	3.1	55	4.8
3	100,000	2.8	40	4.1
4	100,000	2.3	15	3.7
5	100,000	1.9	-5	3.3
6	100,000	0.9	-55	2.9
7	100,000	0.8	-60	2.6
8	100,000	0.7	-65	2.4
9	100,000	0.6	-70	2.2
10	100,000	0.4	-80	2.0
Total	100,000	2.0	0	2.0

Clearly the mailing to the top four deciles was far more profitable than the mailing to the bottom six deciles. It could be that the bottom deciles should not have been mailed to at all.

Requirements

You can do regression analysis using demographics and other factors on any well designed marketing database. Most mainframes have the statistical software needed. You must have at least one marketing research analyst who is skilled at using regression analysis. These days, any person with a college background in econometrics, statistics, marketing research or mathematics should know these tech-

Figure 12-7 Mailing Response Rate
(By Decile)

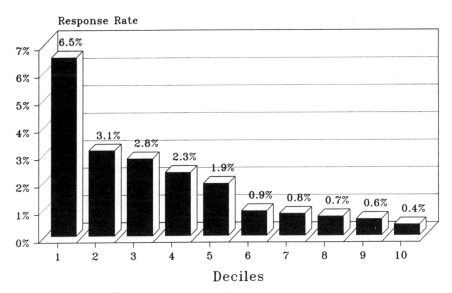

Response rate = % mailed who responded

niques. You can also send your data somewhere else to have the analysis done, but, as you know from the philosophy of this book, you will want the analysis done by yourself or someone on your staff. Why? Because you will get it wrong the first time, and will want to do it again and again until you learn how to do it correctly and start to make a profit from your database. If you are paying someone else to have it done for you, you must pay money for every false start. You may do *less experimentation* rather than more to save money, which is exactly the wrong philosophy for successful database marketing.

Using Demographics and Regressions in Lead Generation

Let's suppose that you are selling a big-ticket item. You have just laid on a national campaign to generate leads for your business. You have 100,000 leads which you are going to follow up with additional mailings and ultimately telemarketing to close the sales. How can demographics and regression analysis reduce the cost of converting these leads to sales? One method involves the selection of certain names for repeat mailings.

Suppose you regularly schedule a series of four repeat mailings to convert your leads to customers. Actually, demographic analysis may show that some names merit only two mailings, while others should receive six. Using your past experience at conversion, as charted against demographic factors, you may decide to mail your top three deciles six times, your next four times and your last three only twice. The number of mailings will be identical, your costs the same, but your return much greater. Let us assume the response to successive mailings is as shown in the following table.

Response Rate to Successive Sales Mailings To Leads by Decile Group Ranked by Demographic Propensity to Respond

Mailing	Top 3	Middle 4	Bottom 3	Average
1	7.1	4.1	2.2	4.5
2	6.2	3.4	1.9	3.8
3	5.4	2.9	1.5	3.3
4	4.6	2.4	1.2	2.7
5	3.9	1.6	0.9	2.1
6	2.6	1.4	0.6	1.5
Cumulative	29.8	15.8	9.8	17.9

Let us assume that under the old system, you mailed four mailings to the entire file of 100,000, 400,000 pieces in all. Under the new system, you will mail six times to the top three, four times to

Figure 12-8 Successive Mailing Resuts
(By Demographic Propensity)

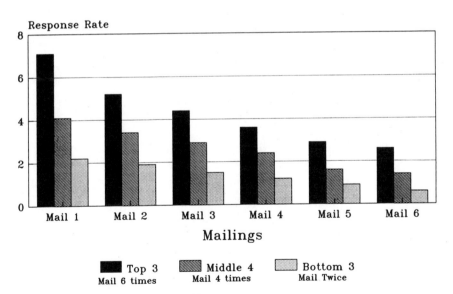

Idea: Mail more to the most receptive

the middle four and two times to the bottom three, for a total of the same 400,000 mailings. But the results will be somewhat better, as shown below.

Old System—New System
Mailings Keyed to Demographic Decile

	4 Mailings Old System	Response Rate	Sales	Varied Mailings	Response Rate	Sales
Top 3 Dec.	120,000	5.8	6960	180,000	5.0	9000
Next 4 Dec.	160,000	3.2	5120	160,000	3.2	5120
Bottom 3 Dec.	120,000	1.7	2040	60,000	2.1	1260
Total	400,000	3.5	14120	400,000	3.9	15380

By varying your mailings, you produced 1,260 more sales without spending any additional money. If you average $30 per sale, you have made $37,800 in additional sales with no increase in outlay other than the manipulation of your marketing database to vary the number of mailings by demographic decile.

$37,800 is not a fortune. It represents an increased return of only 9 percent. If you had to geocode your mailing file, enhance it and perform regressions to determine the best performing deciles, you would probably use up much of the $37,800 in the process. But *once you have your file geocoded* and have done the necessary enhancements and regression analysis, the $37,800 is but one of the many benefits you can derive from this kind of painstaking analytical work.

Should you do demographic enhancement on a consumer file, and perform regression analysis to improve your response rate? Of course. Until you have tried it, you will never know whether you are missing an effective way to improve your response, save money on mailings and increase your profits. Whether it will save you more money than it costs can only be learned from experience. For some types of products in certain industries, it may be almost useless; for others, it will prove essential. This is the art of database marketing:

Figure 12-8 Increased Sales
(Through Demographic Segmentation)

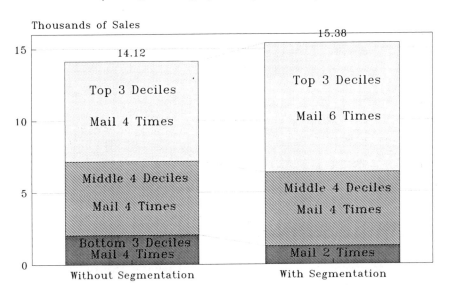

Thousands of Sales

14.12	15.38
Top 3 Deciles Mail 4 Times	Top 3 Deciles Mail 6 Times
Middle 4 Deciles Mail 4 Times	Middle 4 Deciles Mail 4 Times
Bottom 3 Deciles Mail 4 Times	Mail 2 Times
Without Segmentation	With Segmentation

Mailing more to top 3 improves sales

experimenting, testing, trying new things, exploring new horizons, being creative.

USING NON-RESPONDER DATA

In most direct marketing, a two percent response is considered a success. That means that for 100 letters sent out, if two people use your coupon, telephone you or write to you, you have a success. These are your customers. But what do you do with the names and addresses of the ninety-eight people who did not respond? Of what value are they?

A few years ago, many direct marketers threw these names away. No more. Non-respondents are the key to improving your marketing strategy. You must find out *why* they did not respond.

Non-response can be due to an endless list of possible factors:

- bad address
- envelope looked uninteresting
- message did not strike a responsive chord
- product or service too expensive or not wanted
- wrong audience

There are ways of measuring and correcting each of these factors—check and test.

SUMMARY

- Your marketing database file can be *geocoded* to identify the census block in which it is located.

- Private companies can help you to *append* hundreds of items of demographic data to your marketing database records. This data tells you the median household income, education, home value, ethnic makeup and other attributes of the average family in each block.

- The appended information may be correct, or it may be wrong. In any case, it is not information about *your customer,* only about his or her other *average neighbor.*

- This information is most useful in selecting prospects for new business. You must rent lists of people who have demographic profiles that match those of your best customers.

- It may be that the demography really has nothing to do with predicting behavior in your case. The decision to buy your product may result from some factor in the customer's mind or background which cannot be classified by demographic variables. But demographics have been shown to work in some cases with some types of products.

- One commonly used method of relating demographic variables to purchase behavior is multiple regressions. The result of such "modeling" will be the statement: "People who have demographic characteristics A, B and C are more likely to buy your product than people which characteristics D, E and F."

- Since it is easy to rent lists of prospects by demographic characteristics, you can go out into the market and obtain names of prospects that match the demographic characteristics that your modeling has shown to be best for you. The result should be more successful direct marketing than mere chance, and enough of a "lift" to more than pay the cost of your appending and modeling.

- Geocoding and appending demographic data may not work for your product. You will never know, however, until you experiment and test. It is clearly an area that you should look into once you have established your marketing database. If nothing else, you will learn a little more about your customers than you did before, and this is all to the good.

Chapter 13

Clustering: Short-Cut Modeling

Demographic enhancement of a marketing database and the use of these demographics in modeling is a big leap forward in developing a profile to better understand your customers. To the demographics, you can add lifestyle information, media interests and even psychological characteristics. Once this information is coded into your customer file, the real modeling can begin. But modeling is difficult and often expensive.

For many database marketers, there is a useful shortcut called clustering. I call it a shortcut because clustering is a technique for classifying your customer file by coding it with external data in which the modeling is already done. Clustering companies have already taken the entire United States population, coded it by hundreds of demographic and lifestyle characteristics, and broken it down into approximately forty separate types or clusters. You can have your customer file coded to tell to which cluster each customer belongs. With the cluster comes a wealth of prepackaged information on what type of media the customer responds to, his or her product purchasing behavior and so on.

Some would argue that clustering is not appropriate for database marketing. Robert Smith, President of Targeted Communications, points out that once you have a customer database, you can learn much more information directly from each customer than you could possibly get from a prepackaged clustering system. He favors individual marketing with a marketing plan developed for each customer. Myles Megdall of Advanced Information Marketing, Inc., argues that cluster analysis is done for the general case, and almost never with the problem of selling your product in mind. It is no substitute, says Myles, for the hard work of case-by-case modeling.

Nevertheless, hundreds of companies have found cluster analysis a useful tool to understanding their customer database and finding clones of their best customers in the outside world. Let's examine how it works.

RESPONSE TO ADVERTISING MESSAGES

For years, direct marketers have pondered the age old question, "Why do some people react to a message, while others do not?"

Part of the answer is mere chance:

- they didn't read the paper or magazine that day;
- they were out of the room while the message was on;
- they were more interested in something else that day.

Part of the answer is psychological:

- some people are psychologically immune to ads;
- some people resent direct mail.

But part of the answer is lifestyle. Research has shown that:

- People in some neighborhoods react better to a certain ad or product than people in other neighborhoods.

- People with certain income levels are more influenced by certain types of appeals (coupons, free samples, better quality, lower prices) than people with other higher or lower incomes.

- Some people's educational level has a direct bearing on their response to certain messages.

- Some people's age bracket (new homeowners, middle age, retirement years) influences their response profile.

- Whether or not they have young children in the home can be a factor with some people.

- In fact, there are dozens of measurable factors which can be used reliably to predict response to advertising messages.

CAN THE RESPONSE BE IMPROVED?

It has long been known that the "country club set" responds differently to certain advertising than blue collar workers or urban ghetto dwellers. These classifications of people are called social groupings or lifestyle descriptors. For many years, using US Census data, subscription lists, catalog response information, and hundreds of other factors, market researchers have been able to identify at least forty distinct lifestyle clusters which can be used to predict response to advertising.

The central concept in clustering is that "birds of a feather flock together." The country club set lives together in a subdivision out near the country club; blue collar workers live in a moderately priced subdivision on the south side of town.

The US census has divided the whole population into 7.5 million blocks: areas containing an average of about 14 households. Several commercial statistical analysis firms have classified each of these 7.5 million blocks into one of 40 different lifestyle clusters, each of which has common identifiable characteristics.

CLUSTERING

There are several companies which do a good job of clustering, among them Claritas, Donnelly, Equifax and CACI. The clusters listed in this section are taken from Claritas. The others have very similar systems.

Table 13-1

Social Group	Clusters	Households
S1 Educated Affluent Executives and Professionals in Elite Metro Suburbs	Blue Blood Estates	1,023,102
	Money and Brains	870,363
	Furs and Station Wagons	3,090,554
S2 Pre- and Post-Child Families and Singles in Upscale, White Collar Suburbs.	Pools and Patios	3,172,075
	Two More Rungs	654,303
	Young Influentials	2,684,868
S3 Upper Middle, Child-Raising Families in Outlying, Owner-Occupied Suburbs	Young Suburbia	5,073,624
	Blue Chip Blues	5,551,127
U1 Educated, White Collar Singles and Ethnics in Upscale, Urban Areas	Urban Gold Coast	437,231
	Bohemian Mix	1,009,642
	Black Enterprise	673,211
	New Beginnings	3,934,913
T1 Educated, Young, Mobile Families in Exurban Satellites and Boom Towns	God's Country	2,560,446
	New Homesteaders	3,980,107
	Towns and Gowns	1,419,614
S4 Middle-Class, Post-Child Families in Aging Suburbs and Retirement Areas	Levittown, USA	2,724,640
	Gray Power	2,777,323
	Rank and File	1,261,156
T2 Mid-Scale, Child-Raising Blue Collar Families in Remote Suburbs and Towns	Blue-Collar Nursery	1,999,178
	Middle America	2,962,345
	Coalburg and Corntown	1,778,768
U2 Mid-Scale Families, Singles and Elders in Dense, Urban Row and High-Rise Areas	New Melting Pot	820,438
	Old Tankee Rows	1,407,860
	Emergent Minorities	1,526,890
	Single City Blues	3,121,180
R1 Rural Towns and Villages Admist Farms and Ranches Across Agrarian Mid-America	Shotguns & Pickups	1,661,675
	Agri-Business	1,916,950
	Grain Belt	1,114,044
T3 Mixed Gentry and Blue Collar Labor in Low-Mid Rustic, Mill and Factory Towns	Golden Ponds	4,639,065
	Mines and Mills	2,747,560
	Norma Rae-Ville	2,168,340
	Smalltown Dontown	2,239,020
R2 Land owners, Migrants and Rustics in Poor Rural Towns Farms and Uplands	Back-Country Folks	3,122,838
	Share Croppers	3,668,104
	Tobacco Roads	1,120,273
	Hard Scrabble	1,366,641

Table 13-1 (Continued)

Social Group	Clusters	Households
U3 Mixed, Unskilled Service	Heavy Industry	2,422,975
and Labor in Aging, Urban	Downtown Dixie-Style	3,126,084
Rows and High-Rise Areas	Hispanic Mix	1,699,999
	Public Assistance	2,795,577
Total Households in US in 1989 (from 1980 Census)		92,324,103

Source: Claritas Corporation (Copyright 1989).

Claritas breaks all the millions of blocks listed in the census into forty cluster groups. These, in turn, are grouped into twelve social groups. The social groups are further classified as (U) Urban, (S) Suburban, (T) Town or (R) Rural.

Years of research have gone into classifying the lifestyle of each of these forty clusters. Here are summary descriptions of two of the clusters, as examples:

Blue Blood Estates. These are America's wealthiest socioeconomic neighborhoods populated by super-upper established managers, professionals and heirs to "old money," accustomed to privilege and living in luxurious surroundings. One in ten millionaires can be found in Blue Blood Estates, and there is a considerable drop from these heights to the next level of affluence.

God's Country. Contains the highest socioeconomic, white collar neighborhoods, primarily located outside major metros. These are well educated frontier types who have opted to live away from the big metros in some of America's most beautiful mountain and coastal areas. They are highly mobile and are among the nation's fastest growing neighborhoods. They are outstanding consumers of both products and media.

How the Cluster Indexes Work

Over the years the clusters have been run against a host of lifestyle indicators to further sharpen the image of what the people who live in them like, want, buy, prefer, dislike, vote for and so on. To represent these lifestyle preferences, statisticians use an index.

An index shows whether the cluster is more likely or less likely than the average to have the characteristic. One hundred is average, so an index of 200 shows that the cluster is twice as likely to have the characteristic as the average. An index of 50 is half as likely.

How Can Clustering Be Used to Improve Response?

The concept is simple. For direct mail, you cluster code your outgoing mail and your response. You find that certain clusters respond better than others (see Table 13-2).

The index is computed by dividing the response percentage by the mailed percentage and multiplying by 100.

Your greatest number of respondents was in cluster D, which brought you 20 percent of your buyers. But mailing to this cluster was very inefficient as compared with mailing to A or B, where the response per mailed piece was much better.

Once you know which clusters respond well and which respond poorly, you can use this information to change your mailing patterns:

■ mail more often to good clusters, less often or not at all to poor clusters;

Table 13-2 Response to a Mailing By Clusters

Cluster	% of Mailing	% Response	Index
A	8%	16%	200
B	2%	3%	150
C	10%	12%	120
D	25%	20%	80
E	10%	1%	10
Others	50%	48%	96
Total	100%	100%	100

Figure 13-1 Response vs Response Index
(Picking Out the Best Cluster)

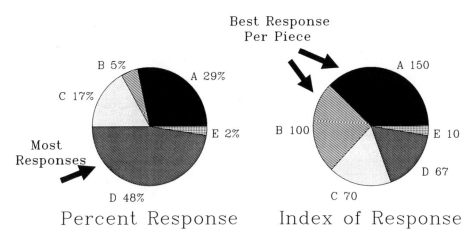

Best Response
Per Piece

Percent Response   Index of Response

Most responses came from Cluster D.
But most response per piece mailed came from A and B.

- change your message to poor response clusters to try to get their attention.

How Can Clustering Be Used in Direct Mail?

Once the outgoing and incoming direct mail has been coded for life-style cluster, here is what can be done:

- For clusters that appear to respond well, try a second or third mailing to all those within the cluster that did not respond.

- To prove your analysis is correct, mail also to a control group from clusters that did not respond well.

- Seek out new prospect lists already coded for clusters responding well. Do not rent names or mail to names from clusters that show a poor response.

- Conduct focus groups from poorly responding clusters that you think should do well: for example, affluent people. Your message to these folks could be wrong. By varying and targeting your message by cluster, you may be able, at low cost, to raise your number of buyers.

- Some people just sample and don't ever buy. Could it be that these samplers-only can be identified in advance by cluster? If so, you can either stop mailing to these people, or make them a different offer.

- There are actually scores of different things that you can do to raise response at low cost once you have the information about the lifestyle cluster of your buyers, samplers and non-responders.

How Can Clustering Be Used to Increase Response to Print Ads?

For each identified cluster, you can examine hundreds of different variables that are true of the cluster. You learn not only about their income, age, education, house value, children, automobiles, occupation and family employment situation; you learn what magazines they read, what type of radio and television programs they tune in to, what hours of the day they are likely to be home. How can you use this in the selection of print ads?

- Suppose you have placed advertising in general circulation publications such as *TV Guide* or *Parade*. From the response to these publications, you can learn what clusters respond. But this will also tell you something else very interesting (see Table 13-3).

This table tells you that cluster B is a sleeper—not many of them read *Parade*, but of those that do the response was phenomenal. Here are folks just waiting to be reached, but probably *Parade*

Table 13-3 Response to *Parade* Ads

Cluster	% Readers	% Responses	Index
A	30%	15%	5
B	5%	10%	200
C	35%	2%	6

Figure 13-2 Response to *Parade* Ad
(Response vs. Index)

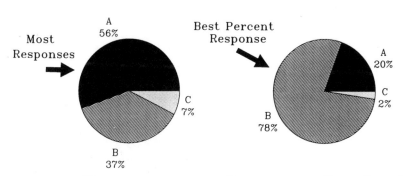

Most responses came from Cluster A people.
But Cluster B people's response per reader was higher

Table 13-4   Reading Habits of Cluster B People

Publication	Percent of Readers Who Are Cluster B
Parade	5%
Publication X	10%
Publication Y	42%
Publication Z	18%

is not the correct vehicle to reach them. What would be a better way?

This would suggest that you might try an ad in Publication Y targeted directly at cluster B people. Perhaps try a focus group to design the perfect ad. In any case, you may be able to reach these

Figure 13-3   What Does Cluster B Read?
   (% Readers in Cluster B)

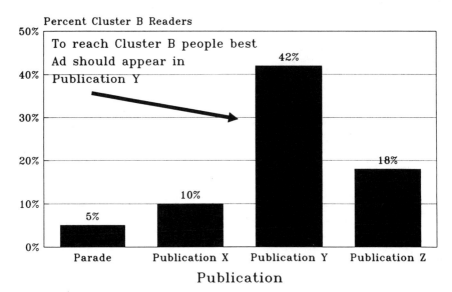

% Readers of Each Pub. who are Cluster B

cluster B people less expensively in Publication Y than you can by scattering your shot in Parade.

How Can Clustering Help with Television Advertising?

What station, what hour of the day, what market, what message, how many viewers, how much does the ad cost? These are the factors that go into a normal TV ad selection.

Clustering allows you to add some other important factors. Based on response to TV ads thus far, we can get a good idea of what clusters are responding. From national media surveys we also know what clusters are watching those programs at those times. You know who you want to reach. This can help to:

- Design your message

- Pick your market areas

- Pick your stations

- Pick your hours

Clustering requires a leap of faith on the part of the direct marketer: the assumption that the people in Sacramento who live in a cluster called "Furs and Station Wagons" will react the same way to your message as people in Milwaukee and New Haven who also live in clusters called "Furs and Station Wagons." In some cases this may be true; in other cases it will not be true. The direct marketer has to experiment and test mail to be sure that things are working properly.

Target Grouping

Clustering works because forty (clusters) is a much easier number to work with than 7.5 million blocks. But often even forty are too many different variables to work with for direct marketing. For this reason, most marketers group the forty clusters into six or eight primary groups which, after analysis, break down into:

- those six or seven clusters who respond best to your product or message;

- the next lower group of six or seven clusters;

- the next lower group, and so on.
- You will normally avoid the bottom groups and concentrate your attention on the top groups.

Each of these groups of clusters is assigned a descriptive name, such as:

- Greenbelt Families
- Affluentials
- Post-Child Middle Class
- Exurban Families
- Middle America and Rustic Towns
- All Other

Attributing Lifestyle Characteristics

Clustering companies have spent years matching their clusters against scores of national surveys and purchase data. They do this to determine true, or mostly true, statements that can be made about each cluster. As a result of this process, they can determine the likelihood of a particular person having done some of the following things:

- Bought a new imported car
- Bought classical music
- Received a passport
- Took a cruise
- Went in downhill skiing
- Played tennis ten times or more in the past year
- Contributed to public TV
- Joined a country club
- Used chewing tobacco

- Owned a pickup truck
- Watched professional wrestling
- Ridden a motorcycle
- Spent $10 or more at a Tupperware® party
- Attended a rodeo
- Went bowling twenty-five times or more in the past year

In terms of media interest, they can attribute likelihood of this behavior to a person:

- Reads the business section of a newspaper
- Reads science or technology magazines
- Reads the editorial sections
- Reads the sports section
- Reads the *Smithsonian*
- Watches C-SPAN
- Reads *Hot Rod*
- Reads the *National Enquirer*
- Reads *Ebony*
- Has a satellite dish
- Watches daytime TV dramas
- Watches college basketball on TV

How Will Clustering Help in Database Marketing?

In theory, clustering is really most useful for direct marketing situations where not much is known about your customers, and you are trying to make sense out of direct response data. But companies properly using marketing databases probably know a great deal more about their customers than they can ever learn from clustering.

While doing business, you can ask questions directly and get direct answers that you could only infer indirectly from cluster data. Thus, you may find that clustering is not worth the extra expense in your marketing database.

Where clustering will help you is in prospecting. If you are trying to rent a list of prospects, or to advertise in a magazine, radio or television station to reach new prospects, clustering can be a great help in making the correct choices. By coding your existing customer database with cluster codes and comparing these codes with the results of your RFM analysis, you can learn in which clusters your best customers live and therefore in which clusters new prospects are likely to live. Armed with this information, you can rent lists loaded with people living in the correct clusters, or advertise in media which people in these clusters read, watch or listen to. You should markedly improve your response over less sophisticated media selection methods.

Clustering will be more useful for some products than for others. If you have a database of diabetes sufferers, or cat owners, or music lovers, or gamblers, you will find that they don't seem to live in any recognized cluster. Clustering is seldom useful for business-to-business marketing, since the clusters are based on residential households. One company, which was marketing ethical products through pediatricians to the general public, tried to use clustering to categorize the practice base of the physicians in their database. The results were gibberish, since the patients of physicians seldom live within walking distance of their doctors. The cluster code of the block group or zip code of the doctor, therefore, reveals little about the cluster code of the patients.

All that glitters is not gold.

Financial Clustering

For businesses in financial services, such as banks, insurance companies and stock brokers, clustering has taken one step beyond the simple forty groups, into lifecycle clusters that include the age of the head of the household in the equation. It makes for a much more interesting targeted segmentation which often works very well for these industries.

Lifecycle clustering is based on annual surveys done by SRI, Equifax, Accountline and other companies. SRI, for example, has a national mail panel study of more than 3,000 households representing consumers of all demographic and financial product use categories. The selected families are paid $10 for their completion of the survey. A 70 percent response is achieved in most cases.

The questionnaire is extremely detailed, including such questions as "What was your family income last year? Consult your Federal Income Tax Form in answering this question."

"Think of all the securities your household bought in the last year. What was the approximate amount of securities you purchased from each type of firm?"

"How often does your household borrow on margin?"

The responses are tracked by cluster *and by age of head of household.* This is because, for financial services, age is one of the most important predictors of purchase behavior. Vision Financial Marketing, from Equifax Marketing Decision Systems, a leading target marketing and marketing information company in Encinitas, California, divides the households in the country into ten financial groups with details of their predicted financial behavior based on the SRI survey. To illustrate what these groups are designed to predict, descriptions of two of them follow.

Well-Heeled Achievers. This group represents those households at the peak of the financial world. They have the highest incomes and the highest net worth of any financial group. Typically families with heads of households between 40 and 55, the households are heavy users of financial products and services, but also hold high balances.

They are five times as likely as the average household to have an asset management account with average balances of $150,000 (they make up 38 percent of all balances).

They are six times as likely to participate in a limited partnership with average values over $70,000 (37 percent of all balances).

They are the lowest users of renter's insurance of all the financial groups.

They are twice as likely as the average household to own in-vestment or vacation real estate with an average value of over $560,000.

Well-Heeled Achievers represent over 3.3 million households and are projected to grow by 55 percent over the next ten years (four times the U.S. growth rate).

Bank Traditionalists. This group is made up mostly of upper middle class families. These are generally larger than average fami-lies, with very young or school age children. Mostly homeowners, the heads of household are above average in education and income, and often employed in white collar occupations. The group has the potential for growth, but not all of the households will move into the upper financial groups.

They are less likely than average to participate in a mutual fund.

They are one and a half times as likely as the average house-hold to have a first mortgage with an average balance of $35,000 (22 percent of all balances).

The most likely of all groups to have a retail loan (15 percent of all balances).

They are likely to have life insurance (23 percent of all premi-ums for universal life).

Bank traditionalists represent almost 12 million households and are projected to grow 32 percent (2.5 times the US rate) over the next ten years.

Using this lifecycle technique, which combines age with demo-graphics and lifestyle, Equifax Marketing Decision Systems, Claritas and others are able to make what they believe to be far better predic-tions of purchase behavior for financial services than clusters alone can provide.

This information can be coded to a mainframe file and stored in your marketing database, or it can be provided in a PC format on a stand-alone system with mapping capabilities (see the chapter on PC databases).

Keeping Hospital Beds Full

An interesting example of the practical use of clustering with a marketing database was provided by Anthony Agresta of INFORUM, a healthcare target marketing company based in Nashville, Tennessee. One of INFORUM's targeting techniques is to use patient databases to analyze payor mix. Many hospitals have too many empty beds, and not enough patients with adequate medical insurance.

The technique is to set up a database of all past patients, and geocode and cluster code them using their home addresses. The database records show the type of hospital stay, the method of payment and the amount of revenue. Analysis clearly shows which patients were profitable and which were not. By studying the cluster codes of the profitable and unprofitable patients, the hospital can get a pretty good idea of which neighborhoods within the hospital's service area are providing its principal revenue-producing customers. Once this is known, the hospital can mount an aggressive campaign of direct mail to those profitable areas.

Further use of the media preference data linked to the cluster codes can tell the hospital which print media is read by residents of preferred areas. This helps target the advertising to the correct audience.

In 1988, a hospital in Dayton, Ohio, had 2,277 inpatients admitted for Major Diagnostic Category 01. They stayed a total of 16,975 days, spending $12,984,477, or $765 per day. But who pays for these days? While 92.2 percent of all households carry health insurance, the percentage insured varies considerably by cluster as shown by INFORUM's Pulse annual survey of 100,000 households nationwide. One of the clusters with the highest percentage of health insurance is Furs and Station Wagons at 97.1 percent. One of the lowest is Public Assistance with only 81 percent insured.

Clearly, Dayton hospitals seeking to improve their bottom line can and do concentrate on attracting patients from heavily insured segments. How is that done?

One way is direct mail and advertising. Another is to reach out to physicians, who are usually the ones to designate the hospital where patients will stay. The INFORUM software can locate

---

Figure 13-4 Health Insurance Coverage for Various Residential Clusters

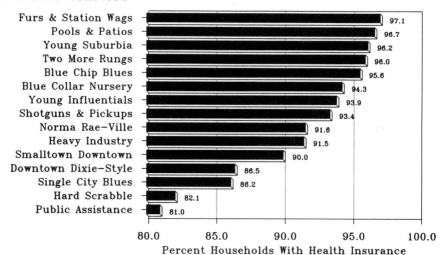

Selected Clusters

Copyright 1989 Inforum, Inc.

---

physician's offices on computer maps, and can calculate which physicians serve patients who are likely to be insured. A direct approach to these physicians can be very fruitful.

Summary

- Clustering is a way of categorizing the 7.5 million blocks in America into forty useful types of households based on common neighborhood characteristics such as housing type, demographic similarities and socioeconomic characteristics which can, in certain cases, make it easier to understand the response to direct marketing efforts.

- Clustering can help you find new prospects by looking for people who live in clusters similar to those in which your best customers live.

- Clustering will not be cost effective in all cases with all products. You should test clustering on a small scale before putting major resources into it.

- For financial services, age of head of household is a very powerful predictor of purchasing behavior. Several companies, such as EMDS, have combined annual financial services questionnaires, such as those prepared by SRI International, with clustering and age to create a very useful and accurate tool for use by database marketers.

Chapter 14

The Psychology of Your Customer

You have built a customer marketing database. You have more than a million names, and their purchase histories. You have geocoded it so you know where they live, and you know the demographics and lifestyle of their block group. But what are they really like? What motivates them? What do they want? How can you appeal to them to buy more of your products and services than they do now?

There are many answers, of course. The problem is complex. No one has the complete and final answer, because the American consumer is constantly changing. But you, as a provider of products and services, must make some decisions. You must reach some conclusions.

SURVEY QUESTIONS

The best single method is to survey your customers. This is what two-way communication is all about. You use every opportunity to converse with them to ask them a few more questions and tabulate a few more answers. People like to answer questions, particularly if they think that someone is listening to what they are saying.

I have been a member of a Public Radio station for more than ten years. I donate about $300 per year. The station calls me twice a year to participate in a "challenge grant." They announce on one evening during their fundraising week that Arthur Hughes has agreed to contribute an extra $100 if the number of calls between 9:00 P.M. and 10:00 P.M. exceeds 50, or the dollars pledged in the period exceeds $1000 or some such gimmick. It is flattering to be called, and I always agree. I suppose that the audience always meets the challenge, since they always want my $100. I am sure that they tuck this information about my participation away in some database ready for the next drive, since they always call me again. This is excellent loyalty marketing.

But they have never asked me any questions. They know nothing about me, and have no idea why I listen to the station, what I want to hear or why I agree to the challenge grant. They have someone call me twice a year and spend time with me on the telephone, but they ask for, and receive, absolutely no information from me at all except my credit card number. They just want the money.

I used to listen to, and contribute to, another Public Radio station in Washington. But this one began to play bluegrass music for more than half of every day, and consumed much of the rest of their programming time with ultra left-wing talk shows. I found little that interested me, and I stopped contributing. They don't know why, and they never asked.

Both stations have missed an opportunity to understand more about their audience, and to use this information in designing their product and sharpening their fundraising message. This missed opportunity can mean missing out on several million dollars of contributions which they might otherwise get.

Surveys are often easy to organize, if you have set up a database and have some mechanism for a two-way dialog built in, as these stations do. The limiting factor is the creativity of the marketing staff. You have to figure out *what questions to ask* and *what to do with the answers*. One of the biggest problems with survey data is being able to understand, quantify and apply the results to your particular marketing situation. Some companies are stuck with scores of facts in a database without a useful technique for turning the data into sales. Because this type of research is difficult, many companies are trying shortcuts to understanding their customers, such as using general surveys done by others and psychographics.

PSYCHOGRAPHICS

VALS 2, a product of SRI International, of Menlo Park, California, is the most outstanding example of the psychographic technique. SRI conducts surveys of customers of products or audiences of radio stations. The forty-three questions ask people to agree or disagree with statements such as, "My idea of fun at a national park would be to stay at an expensive lodge and dress up for dinner," or "I could stand to skin a dead animal."

Depending on the answers to these questions, they categorize the respondents into one of eight different psychographic groups with catchy names such as Achievers, Believers, Strugglers. They arrange the eight groups into a hierarchy in terms of resources (income or wealth). From left to right the groups are divided into three classifications: Principle Oriented, Status Oriented and Action Oriented.

Figure 14-1

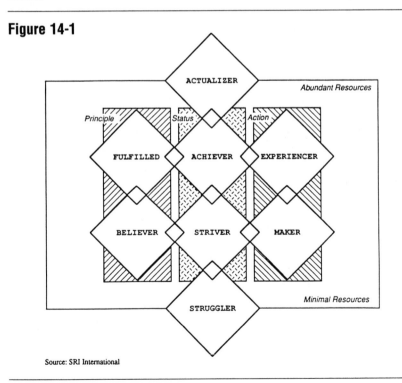

Source: SRI International

To illustrate the VALS 2 system, consider the description of three of the groups:

Achievers are successful, work-oriented people who get their satisfaction from their jobs and families. They are politically conservative and respect authority and the status quo. They favor established products and services that show off their success to their peers.

Fulfilleds are mature, responsible, well-educated professionals. Their leisure activities center on their homes. They are well informed about what goes on in the world, and they are open to new ideas and social change. They have high incomes. They are practical, value-oriented consumers.

Makers are practical people who value self-sufficiency. They are focused on the family, work and physical recreation. They have little interest in the broader world. They are unimpressed by material possessions other than those with a practical or functional purpose.

Each group is roughly equal in size in the American market, varying from 8 to 16 percent of the population.

How can you relate VALS 2 to other data? If you are doing market research and are a subscriber to the SRI service, you can include VALS questions in your survey questions, and SRI will analyze the data and type your respondents according to the VALS classifications. Once you have done that, you can compare your customers to the many surveys that SRI has done on consumer attitudes and purchasing behavior which are keyed to the VALS types. Simmons Market Research Bureau and Mediamark Research, Inc., have tabulated their consumer databases by VALS. This opens up their research data to companies with VALS-typed customers.

In addition, VALS 2 is linked to the major lifestyle cluster systems: Claritas, Donnelley Marketing, Equifax and CACI. If you are a subscriber to one of these systems and to SRI, you can find out which VALS 2 types dominate in each of the forty clusters. You can learn the percentage of Strivers and Achievers in "Shotguns and Pickups."

Most companies who subscribe to VALS 2 are using it to position their advertising message to appeal to groups that VALS 2 shows will be responsive to the message and buy the product. The proof of the effectiveness of VALS 2 has to be measured with each situation. It is generally considered that psychographics works best for big-ticket status items such as automobiles, boats, vacation cruises. But there are increasing numbers of companies looking into the possibility of using VALS 2 to target marketing for products such as hand soap and toilet paper. If VALS 2 helps to design advertising and improve sales, use it.

Psychographics of the Elderly

An interesting example of the psychographic idea was developed by SRI for the National Association for Senior Living Industries (NASLI). The survey was called "Lifestyles and Values of Older Adults" (LAVOA). It studied 3,600 representative people 55 years old and older. The study grouped these people into six VALS-type segments with similar catchy names: Attainers, Martyrs and Preservers.

Each of the six types was ranked by five psychological factors: independence, extroversion, self-indulgence, openness to change and health. To illustrate the way this is done, consider two examples: Explorers and Martyrs.

Explorers do things their own way. They are self-reliant. They feel that children do not have an obligation to help their parents. They are in good health and are fairly introverted. They don't rely on others. They are likely to sell their homes for cash. In a retirement home environment, they do not look for cultural and recreational services, maid and laundry services or health care, relying instead on their own resources.

Martyrs fight change. They think that children should help their parents. They are poor, poorly educated and in poor health. Like the Explorers, they are introverted. They tend to live with their children or relatives. They want to move away from their home and into an adult community. They seek closeness to medical care, shopping and religious facilities.

What can be done with this information? NASLI has used this survey to help to explain some current trends: there are many more older adults today than there were twenty years ago, but they are not flocking to retirement housing as one might have expected. NASLI

Figure 14-2 Older American Psychographic Profile

Pop. Percent Age 55+	Median Age		Median Income	Education Level
9	60	ATTAINERS	$35,500	2 Yr. College
11	74	ADAPTERS	20,500	2 Yr. College
22	65	EXPLORERS	9,500	High School
21	76	PRAGMATISTS	8,500	Grade 11
26	63	MARTYRS	6,000	Grade 9
11	78	PRESERVERS	4,500	Grade 8

companies had previously specialized in congregate-care housing and retirement communities such as Leisure World. These have been a "seller's market" with long waiting lists.

What has been happening today is that the lifestyles and values of the new entrants to the over-55 group are different from those of the previous decades. They are wealthier and more independent. The competition for their dollars has increased with hotels, hospitals, nursing homes and insurance companies moving into the retirement housing markets. The needs and interests of these older adults are far more diverse. To compete effectively, you have to offer specialized products for a specialized group of consumers.

USING PSYCHOGRAPHICS WITH YOUR DATABASE

How do you relate these techniques to your marketing database? It seems to me that the most useful method of using psychographics is to open your eyes to possibilities. You have one million customers on your database, and you want to create a dialog. You want to collect information, to segregate your customers and offer them new opportunities in terms of products and services. You should be constantly trying to figure out what your customers are thinking about, what they want. In many cases, consumers do not know what they want until you give them a choice. Psychographics can give you an idea about how to structure your surveys and questions so that customers will respond.

The key contribution which SRI has made to the industry is the concept of developing meaningful groupings out of what might otherwise be a mass of unintelligible data. You cannot manage a million separate dialogs and make any sense out of them. You must segment your customers in some way, and offer each segment something that appeals particularly to them. The fact that NASLI found one set of groups when measuring the population as a whole, and another when looking at the over-55 market, illustrates the point. You as a database marketer should work to create meaningful segmentation of your own customer file and prospect market, based on what they seem to want. Vary your product and service mix for each segment.

NICHE MARKETING

Mediamark Research, Inc., is one of the leaders in using segmentation to break down a market into meaningful groups for product targeting. They published a small booklet called *Niche Marketing* in 1988 which provides an excellent introduction to this technique. The idea is that by seeking out specialized market niches, a marketer can find an area where the competition is less intense and where it is easier to acquire dominance. You identify a narrow and specialized group of consumers with particular needs or desires. You find out just the product or service that appeals to them. You design a product or service for that market alone. Then you find a way to target that segment and tell them about what you have for them.

Mediamark has developed a database of 20,000 consumers who are representative of the U.S. market, which they survey extensively once a year. A personal interview is conducted with each respondent in which demographic information and data about exposure to print, radio, broadcast television and cable media are collected. Data about the use of products, services and brands are collected in a self-administered questionnaire which the interviewer leaves with the respondent and returns to pick up at a later date. Approximately 450 product categories, 1,900 product types and 5,700 individual brands are studied and reported.

What they have been able to accomplish with their system can be very useful to marketers. For example, in looking at what female housekeepers buy, they have broken this market down into Working Moms, Full-Time Workers, Part-Time Workers and Not Employed. When you index items like toaster products, Working Moms buy far more than the others.

As an example of creative segmentation, they did a detailed study of the affluent, defined as the 10 percent of the population with the highest income. Their studies showed that this group can be broken down into five lifestyle segments:

1. *Well-Feathered Nests*: households with at least one high-income earner and children present.

2. *No Strings Attached*: at least one high-income earner and no children.

3. *Nanny's in Charge:* two or more income earners, none high-income, and children present.

4. *Two Careers:* two or more income earners, none high-income, no children.

5. *The Good Life:* high affluence with no one employed, or head of household unemployed.

They back up this segmentation by showing that the spending habits of each of the five groups is very different.

Mediamark publishes *Upper Deck Report*, which offers data on purchases by these affluent segments of over 400 categories of consumer products. As they point out, "a good imagination is critical to creating a marketing breakthrough, but only in conjunction with reliable market data. Find out what's really going on in the marketplace and be prepared. Your hunches may be off-base—or brilliant."

Regional Differences

Despite the McDonaldization of America, there are still significant regional differences which you will have to take into account in your marketing, and which, of course, can represent profitable niches for your company if you can recognize them and exploit them. Consider

Figure 14-3 Convenience Foods
(Who buys the most?)

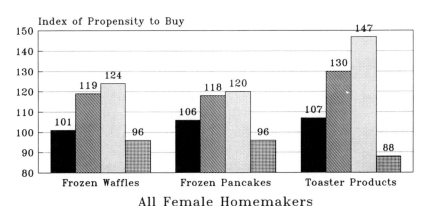

Source: Mediamark Research

Figure 14-4 Regional Preferences
(In Salad Dressings)

All Female Homemakers

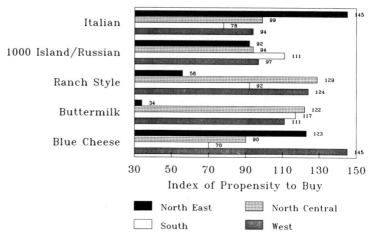

Index of Propensity to Buy

Northeast Hates Buttermilk; West Loves Blue Cheese

Source: Mediamark Research

---

the different sales of salad dressings in the four regions of the U.S. as researched by Mediamark (Figure 14-4).

To take advantage of these differences, you can vary your promotional efforts and product offerings by region. Some food manufacturers, for example, have increased the spiciness of their products in some areas of the country and toned it down in others. To do this, however, you have to know what you are doing. You can get some clues from surveys such as those of Mediamark.

Heavy Versus Light Users

It is not enough to know who buys a certain product. Everyone buys soap and electricity. Better to find out who buys a lot of your product, and concentrate on them. Forget the light users. As one example

Figure 14-5 Ground Coffee Consumption
(In Average Day)

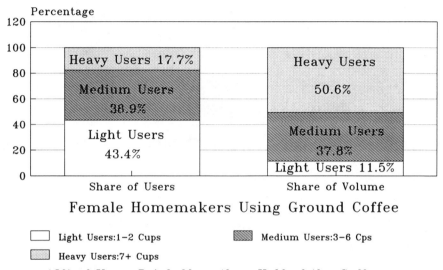

Female Homemakers Using Ground Coffee

☐ Light Users:1–2 Cups   ▨ Medium Users:3–6 Cps

▨ Heavy Users:7+ Cups

18% of Users Drink More than Half of the Coffee

Source: Mediamark Research

of this type of concentration, consider Mediamark's study of consumers of Ground Coffee (Figure 14-5). They found that half of all ground coffee bought by female homemakers is bought by only 17.7 percent of the women.

The next step was to identify the characteristics of the ground coffee consumer so she can be differentiated from the ordinary female homemaker. Doing modeling analysis, they were able to develop a profile of ground coffee users (Figure 14-6).

This tells you that one of the best places to sell ground coffee is in the West Central region, to female householders from 35-54 with a household income between $25,000 and $35,000 and three or more people in the home—very pinpointed and targeted. This type of analysis can also tell you why you are not succeeding in a market that you think you should be doing better in. Maybe the market just

Figure 14-6 Demographics of Coffee Drinkers

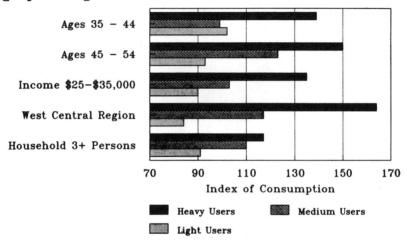

Demographic Segment

Source: Mediamark Research

isn't there. There may be many people, but they may be the wrong kind.

Charting Market Growth

Surveys such as Mediamark's can also tell you something about what is happening to your market from year to year. Looking back at their annual survey results from prior years can be very instructive in telling you whether your market is growing or that you may be missing a trend (see the following table).

Table 14-1

	1984	1986	1988
Bought Video Tapes in last twelve months	8.4%	25.5%	38.5%
Bought Microwave Cookware in last twelve months	5.8%	10.4%	10.1%
Bought Chocolate Chip Cookies in last six months	39.9%	37.4%	37.3%
Have Mastercard	17.5%	26.7%	28.5%
Have Visa Card	28.2%	34.1%	37.3%

If you have a consumer product, chances are good that Mediamark surveys cover your area. The data can be broken down by geographic area, by cluster or by psychographics. You may be wondering why business is bad; it may help to know that it is bad all over and that the fault is not yours alone.

COMBINING PSYCHOGRAPHICS, MARKET RESEARCH AND DATABASE MARKETING

Suppose we are selling a particular brand of luxury automobile. We want to know how big the market is for our type of car and how to target the right customers. How can we figure that out?

From the R. L. Polk Company you can learn how many of each type of automobile is owned in each area of the United States, together with the age of the cars. You can find out how long the average person keeps a particular make of new car before he or she turns it in for a new one. This varies, of course, by lifestyle and by region. Mediamark can help you determine the figure for your region and the purchasing habits of each type of psychographic or lifestyle group.

You can learn, for example, that:

Group A gets a new car every three years
Group B waits until four years

Group C waits five years
Group D waits longer.

Let's say you decided to target a message to Group A. From psychographics combined with clustering, you can identify Group A people by their block. From R. L. Polk you can get the actual names and addresses of everyone in your geographic region who is in Group A and who owns a two-and-a-half year old model of one of the cars you are targeting. Most of these people will certainly buy some car in the next few months. You can quantify that, and target direct mail to these people.

It is really very simple, yet, even today, few dealers are using this technique. This is because most automobile dealers are really too small to have a marketing staff which is in a position to know these things and to use these techniques. Instead, they have salesmen who sit in the showroom and wait for people to come in in response to classified ads.

What is the answer? Clearly the answer lies in database marketing on a large scale. Since even the big dealers are too small to have marketing staffs, the automobile manufacturer or distributor should have the database and furnish leads to dealers. A perfect example of the combining of all of these techniques, plus dealer-manufacturer combination. Although it is obvious, there are very few such arrangements in existence today. Targeted direct marketing using a database plus psychographics and clustering is very rare. Those companies which successfully exploit these techniques could become very profitable.

SUMMARY

- Surveys of your customers are the best way to find out about them. Most companies have simple ways of getting data from their customers.

- The problem with survey data, however, is understanding it, quantifying it and applying it to your marketing situation. Psychographics and external survey data can help.

- Psychographics attempts to break consumers down into a small number of segments with similar attitudes towards life and similar buying habits. This technique is often used to design and target advertising.

- Psychographics can be combined with clustering and market survey research such as that of Mediamark to identify special market niches of great use to the database marketer.

- Psychographics helps the database marketer break down a million consumers into a few manageable segments which you can understand, relate to market trends and target with a meaningful message, or a special niche product or service.

- VALS 2 segments your market by resources into eight types based on three psychological orientations. These eight types have been found to be predictors of buying behavior for certain products.

- The psychographic principle can be used in other ways. SRI used it to segment the over-55 market into six groups which help explain their attitude towards moving into retirement communities. The same idea can be used for your customer base.

- Mediamark has developed a database of 20,000 consumers which are surveyed annually concerning their purchase habits covering 1,900 product types and 5,700 individual brands. This data is available to subscribers, and can be used in connection with your database.

- Survey results can show regional differences in purchasing behavior for certain products. Perhaps you should not treat customers in Arizona the same as those in Connecticut; they may have very different tastes. Survey results can teach you this.

- Surveys can also help you to pinpoint the heavy users of your product. Normally only 20 percent of your customers account for 80 percent of your sales. Knowing who those 20 percent are *while they are still prospects* can be immensely valuable.

- Many opportunities to exploit these techniques are missed today because the units, such as dealers, are too small to have marketing staffs which understand and make use of the techniques. Manufacturers and distributors are beginning to realize that they must provide assistance if their business is going to grow.

- Psychographics is one of the valuable tools of database marketing. Every database marketer should know about it, and some should be making active use of it.

Chapter 15

Getting the Names Right

"Yes, Mr. Hughes" has a nice ring to it, doesn't it? For some strange reason, everyone likes to hear their own name or to see it in print. But the magic doesn't work if you get the name wrong. "Yes, Mr. Higgs" just doesn't do much for me. Getting the name right is crucial to successful database marketing. If you are the manager of a marketing database, you must be sure that every name on your database is:

1. *Correct*—correctly spelled and punctuated, with the correct address. If getting someone's name right is a compliment, what is getting the name wrong?

2. *Unique*—not duplicated somewhere else in the file. If you have duplicates in your database, you cannot develop a valid lifetime relationship with your customers. You will be sending duplicate letters to them, and posting their responses in different records in the database; thus you will never get the whole story when you call up a customer record.

Let us see what the science of direct mail merge/purge can offer to database marketers as we attempt to maintain a clean file of customers and add to it leads that are developed from the outside world.

Figure 15-1 Direct Mail Costs
(Data Processing Least Costly Segment)

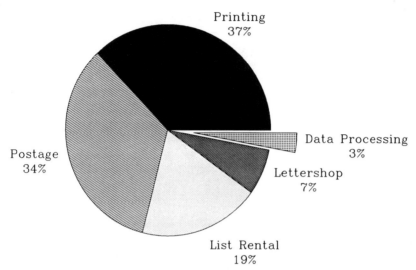

Address Correction Costs Little

Source: John H. Sutton, Creative Automation Company

Name Processing Is the Least Costly
Part of Direct Marketing

John H. Sutton of the Creative Automation Company conducted a small survey of direct mail customers to get an idea of the normal cost distribution of a third-class direct mail package. The results are typical of what seems to be the current trend:

    37 percent of the in-the-mail cost was spent on printing
    34 percent was spent on postage
    19.5 percent was list rental
    7 percent was lettershop costs
    2.5 percent was computer processing of the names.

This book has emphasized that the correct use of computer technology is one of the most important factors in marketing success. The fact that it is so cheap in relation to other costs makes it practical, and it is imperative to insist that the very best techniques be used.

What techniques can be used today to assure that a mailing database is correctly processed? We will list them here, and then explain some of them in detail. As a marketer you will not be able to do these things yourself, but you must know what they are and see that they are accomplished.

- *Zip Code Correction.* If the zipcode is wrong, a third class letter will be *thrown away* by the post office without a word said to the sender. Some modern service bureaus have elaborate software which will compare the city, state and street address, and correct the zipcode, even when the post office has made mass changes to the zipcode areas, as they frequently do. You should not pay more than two dollars per thousand for this, and probably much less. If you do not insist on zipcode correction, the step may be omitted.

- *Address Correction.* NCOA stands for *National Change of Address*, a system which has been licensed by the Post Office to many large service bureaus throughout the country. They have tapes of address changes registered with the Post Office by people who move. If your correspondent has moved, the service bureaus can automatically update your outgoing mail to the correct new address. When you rent names, you should insist that this be performed before you receive the names. If it is your house file, you will have to do it periodically. Again, you should not pay a service bureau more than about two dollars per thousand for NCOA; and while they are doing this, they should do the zipcode correction free of charge.

- *Nixie Elimination.* When you mail specifying *address correction requested* on the envelope, mail that doesn't reach the sender is returned to you. This returned mail (and any other undeliverable mail) is called *nixies*. It has a very important purpose. It should be keypunched and dropped from your database so you don't waste money on a second mailing. On rented lists, the company who rents the lists is supposed to do this. If you get many nixies from a rented list, go back to the list source and ask for a substantial rebate. After all, you have paid postage and probably spent considerable sums on the outgoing piece. If it is a new list that you are unsure of, mail a certain randomly selected group first class as a test. If a high percentage come back as nixies, don't mail the rest.

A second use for nixies is to review the actual appearance of the mail as it looks to the recipient. Study the addresses. Are they correctly spelled and punctuated? Are the names neatly typed? Is the package inside exactly the way you requested it? Did it drop at the post office on the day you were told that it dropped? You should always include "seed names" in any mailing. These are your own names, mixed in with the prospect file. Normally, seed names are your own employees at their homes with disguised names, used to check on the package and delivery. Seed names are useful, but can easily be "fixed up" by the mailshop, while the balance of the job is not done correctly. Nixies tell the real story of what went out and *why it didn't get there.* Insist on studying these things yourself; don't delegate it to someone. And, before you start on any job, ask the list owner what he or she expects in the way of nixies. If the owner is wrong, you may have grounds for a rebate.

■ *Special Address Elimination.* Do you want your mail to go to government offices? To overseas military? To federal prisons? To apartment buildings? If you are mailing to consumers, do you want your mail to go to office buildings in downtown areas? Do you want to eliminate people who have specifically asked that they not receive unsolicited "junk mail"? You can have the service bureau find and eliminate all such addresses before you mail for a very modest cost (not over $1 per thousand). Remember, you are running this mailing. Don't just assume that these things will happen without your asking for them—they won't.

WHAT IS MERGE/PURGE?

We come now to the core of this chapter: merge/purge. Duplicate detection and consolidation. A make-or-break process for any marketing database.

We have come a long way in this process in the last twenty years. Service bureaus who are specialists in this business can do wonderful things in finding duplicates from otherwise clean files. Look at some examples:

Mrs. Elizabeth Holbard	Betty Holbard	EA Halbert
4144 Howard Avenue	RT 1 Box 378	4144 Howard
Kensington, MD 20895	Kensington, MD 20895	Kens MD 20859

All are obviously the same person. Zip correction will fix the 20859. But will your software catch the Route 1? Will it find that Halbert is really Holbard? These things are being done every day with sophisticated merge/purge software.

Modern software looks for similarity of names, for misplaced digits, for different types of addresses. Look at this example:

Richard Van Dorn	Dick Vondorn	R Vandarn
Ridge Road	RT 3	2008 Ridge
Haymarket, VA	Haymarket, VA	Haymarket, VA
22069	22069	

Again, duplicates, and one without a zipcode.

Why do these differences exist? Mailing lists are typed by hundreds of different keypunchers from a variety of sources: magazine subscriptions, catalog orders, post office changes of address, membership lists, voter and motor vehicle registrations, coupons, application blanks. There is no similarity in computer record style. Some use separate first name last name fields. Some have free-form name fields. Some have separate space for titles (Mr. Mrs.) and suffixes (Jr. Sr. MD, PhD); many do not. Some have room for only a middle initial, so Mary Jane becomes Mary J. Many lists are typed overseas by foreigners with only a rudimentary grasp of English, so Mac

Laughlin becomes M. Laughlin. In direct mail, you have to take the world as you find it, and make do. This is why merge/purge is so difficult to do correctly.

For a typically large merge/purge job you will have up to forty different input tapes, all in a different format. For some the names will look like this: RITTER/PHILLIP/MARGOLES/III. To do the merge/purge, you first have to translate all forty different tapes into a single format. This can take days, involving the study of the peculiarity of each format. Some (including the Post Office), for example, will put the street number in one field, the street direction in another, the apartment number in a third, the street name in a fourth and the street type in a fifth:

AV   MAPLE   00003125   E   21B

Which is actually 3125 East Maple Avenue, Apartment 21B.

When all records are in a single format, the various processes begin, including zip and address correction. To find the duplicates, several different approaches are required. First, the file is sorted by zipcode, and all similar names within a zipcode are compared. Phonetic spelling is often required, with MORE MOORE MOOR MOHR MURE MOUR MUIR all included for comparison. Often it is necessary to compare all names within a state on the ground that zipcodes are often wrong, and some escape zip correction.

If software identifies two people:

Ralph Smith   R A Smyth
2235 Willow   235 Willow

The same guy, or two different people? And which is correct: 235 or 2235? And is it Smith or Smyth?

Numerous decisions are required, most made by the software, of necessity. Ideally, you should compare every record with every other record to see if you have a duplicate. If you have a million records, this would require more than four hundred billion comparisons. Computers can take on this job readily. It all depends on how much time and money you are willing to spend on the process. One thing to keep in mind: *because of the decisions required, it is absolutely impossible to eliminate all duplicates in a large (100,000+) file.* How can you check whether duplicate elimination has been done correctly?

I have one fairly foolproof method. Tell the service bureau to give you one state: New York, California or Texas. Sort all records by last name. Then pick a name at random: Jones, Murphy or Simmons. Ask that the next 200 names and addresses be printed out for you. Study the list. If you can't find a single duplicate in 200 alphabeticised names, the job probably has been done correctly. Don't rely on the service bureau to do this final checking. Do it yourself. Duplicate elimination is vital to successful database marketing.

Why Duplicates Must Be Consolidated

Database marketing is really individual, one-on-one relationship marketing. What kind of a corner grocer would keep getting Mrs. Klein mixed up with Mrs. Keene and addressing them both as Miss? There are several vital reasons why this process must be done absolutely correctly:

- If more than one identical letter arrives at a household on the same day, both letters will be thrown in the trash unopened. You will have wasted not only your mailing cost, but your chances of a sale.

- Worse still, your company reputation in the household will suffer. They will realize that when they see something from your company, they are dealing with a computer. The illusion of communication will be shattered before it even has a chance to begin.

- Relationship marketing involves keeping track of what the other person said to you, as well as what you said to them. If you have sent duplicate communications to a household, it means that you have duplicate database records. Responses are unlikely to be posted to the correct names, and gradually confidence within your company in the whole database system will become eroded.

When in doubt, it is better to send no letter at all than to send a duplicate to the same address.

Why Duplicates Are Good

In merge/purge, duplicates are usually a very good sign. If you are merging many different lists, and one household shows up on several different lists, you have an ideal correspondent. Here is someone who responds to direct mail. Duplicates should not be *eliminated*, they should be *consolidated*. Leave a space in your record to indicate how many different lists the name appears on. These multi-buyers (as they are called) should receive a second and a third mailing if they don't respond to the first. These are response-prone people. Keep ringing their bell. Eventually they will answer.

Even if the duplicates are already on your house database as a customers, knowing those customers are on many other lists is a useful fact to add to your knowledge of who they are and how to approach them.

Good and Bad Merge/Purge

Look closely into the methods to be used by the service bureau or in-house computer staff when merge/purge is being planned. The fact is that most merge/purge today is badly done. Several inferior methods are widely practiced.

The first is the match-code or keyline process. In this process name and address are combined into a collection of fourteen or sixteen digits, and the resulting match code compared.

Keyline:

Arthur M. Hughes
3014 Ridge Road   22069HGH2A3014R9
Haymarket, VA 22069

Anne Hoghey   22069HGH2A3014R9
3014 Round Robin Road
Haymarket, VA 22069

These are clearly not duplicates, but will show up as such with a match code. The more common error with match codes is that they will identify many duplicates as uniques. As a first cut, match codes are useful, but more sophisticated methods are needed.

It goes without saying that no system is acceptable that looks only for exact duplicates. Because of the many ways that names and streets can be spelled and keypunched, the chance of eliminating many duplicates with an exact match is very remote.

George A. Weller   G Weller
Dr. George Waller   George Weller MD

Four duplicates. How many systems will spot this?

Good software for duplicate elimination is sold by Group 1 software for mainframes. But just buying this software (for about $25,000) does not assure good duplicate elimination—it requires many months and several million names worth of experience before a programming group can really master this art.

An in-house staff will find that it takes specialized manpower, increased disk space and a very large mainframe to do the job. The process of converting the many unusual tapes you will receive will often require writing ad-hoc software. Unless your staff does this kind of work every day, it will take up to three times as long to do the job in-house (meaning three weeks in-house, versus a week in a service bureau).

Even if you are trying to maintain your marketing database in-house, you should probably insist on the merge/purge being sent to professionals on the outside. What does outside merge/purge cost? For a large job you should expect to spend $2 per thousand records.

How Many Duplicates Will You Find?

As already noted, no large file is ever free of all duplicates. A good individual house file will probably have 2-4 percent duplicates. When you combine many different lists, you should expect to find about one third duplicates (depending on where the lists come from). In many cases, you can buy names from suppliers on a *net name* basis, paying only for the unique new names that they contribute to the job.

HOUSEHOLDING

In most cases in prospecting, and in many cases in a database, you will want to group people by household, so that only one name or telephone call is devoted to a single household. The process is called *householding*.

| Mrs. Carol Braemer | Roger Braemer | Julie Braemer |
| 221 Old Post Drive | 221 Old Post | 221 Old Post Dr. |

You clearly want to send only one letter to 221 Old Post Drive, but to whom do you address the letter? If you are like most novice marketers, have never thought about this question. Think about it now. The possibilities:

The Braemer Family	The Braemer Household
Roger Braemer & Family	Roger and Carol Braemer
Roger & Carol & Julie Braemer	Braemer or Current Occupant
Roger Braemer	The Braemer's
Mr. & Mrs. Roger Braemer	Mr. Roger Braemer

I am not going to give you a pat solution. The answer may depend on the file you are using, the product you are selling, the image you want to project. It is preferable that you think this through and discuss it with your service bureau *before* you send the job over. If you don't the service bureau will pick their own solution, which may be the worst one as far as you are concerned.

Remember, anything is possible. With modern software and a few lines of code, the service bureau can produce any result you are looking for, but you have to know what you want. Remember, this is your mailing. You have paid for the names, the postage and the mailing piece. Why spoil it all by messing up the householding process?

AUTOSEXING

Insist on sexing a file. The response to:

Mr. Archibald Foster   beats: Archibald Foster

Dear Mr. Foster: Dear Friend:

Dear Friend is such a weak salutation it is a wonder that anyone uses it. But without knowing that Archibald is a man's name, what else can you say?

Most service bureaus will be able to autosex your file. Some names, of course, cannot be autosexed: Pat, Robin, Chris and Dana are examples. Also, people who use only their initials cannot be sexed. But it is well worth the extra money to pay for autosexing. Many companies throw in sexing free when you do the mailing in their shop—ask about it.

While you do the autosexing, you must consider what to use as a default salutation. Consider the possibilities, when you do not know the sex:

Dear Chris Winger: Dear Chris: Dear Winger:

Dear Friend: Dear Nature Lover: Dear Winger
                                            Household:

Again, there is no really good answer. You must decide what works best. With a large file, test several approaches to see which works best.

THE APPEARANCE OF THE ADDRESS

It should go without saying that all your outgoing correspondence should be properly punctuated and presented. It is so easy to do correctly, yet how much of our mail is sloppily addressed? Consider these names:

WM A MADDOX JR   Mr. William A. Maddox, Jr.
100 MAYFLD BLVD   100 Mayfield Boulevard
W HAMPTON MA 04123   West Hampton, Massachusetts
                                     04123

DEAR WM MADDOX JR: Dear Mr. Maddox:

Notice that:

WM A	becomes	Mr. William A.
JR	becomes	Jr.
MAYFLD BLVD	becomes	Mayfield Boulevard
W	becomes	West
MA	becomes	Massachusetts

Not all service bureaus can do this. Catalog mailers never bother with it. They are sticking labels onto catalogs. Few people look at the label. But if you are sending a letter or a self mailer, the appearance will often determine whether it gets opened or tossed in the trash. It is worth shopping around for a service bureau that can make your output look first class.

Do not accept the excuse that "the keypunching was poor" as the reason why your database records look poor. Modern software can correct almost anything, and you should insist that the service bureau make a flawless presentation.

LASER VERSUS LABEL

The cheapest method of sending anything is to use a cheshire label. Cheshire labels are plain paper, printed four across, which are automatically cut and glued to your letter, catalog or self mailer in the mailshop. You should probably spend about $1.50 per thousand for labels and another $1 to have them cut and affixed.

But there are times when you want something better. When you have a marketing database and are corresponding with your customers, there are plenty of occasions when a label just won't do. This is the time for a laser letter.

Laser letters can be printed on one side or both sides. They can be letter size, legal size, almost any size that you want. You can have cut sheet lasers (using preprinted stationary or forms) or continuous form lasers (which work with quite complicated and sophisticated forms and letters, such as a four-page personalized letter.)

One of the problems with the way direct marketing agencies are organized is that *production* is a separate function from *creative*. Production people deal with the letter shops and arrange for the labels or the laser letters. They may have become worlds removed from the rest of their organizations. Creative people and database marketers design a nice mailing, oversee the selection of the list, look at the merge/purge and then assume that production will do the rest.

Big mistake. If you, as a database marketer, are in charge of and worried about customer contact, then production is very much your concern. You want the finished product, as it arrives at your customer's mailbox, to look absolutely stunning. Your whole company image is at stake in every communication—don't blow it.

For example, consider the content of the letter. If you have a laser letter, it should be fully personalized. By that I mean not just the name, address and salutation; I mean the paragraphs and personal references throughout the body of the letter.

"I know that Mauser has been used to dry dog food. It is easy to prepare, easy to store and keeps him in top condition. But every once in a while, a dog likes to get a special treat. Last month, we introduced Adult Dog Treats, which have already proved very popular.

"On your next order, which is due there on February 12, may I suggest that we include a one-pound bag of Adult Dog Treats, along with your regular bag of dry formula, Mrs. Warren? If you just give a few of these treats to Mauser whenever he is especially good, you will make him very happy. This bag should last you for a month or more. These treats are scientifically . . ."

This is individualized selling. You recognize the dog's name and sex. You recognize what Mrs. Warren normally buys. Mrs. Warren can easily see that this letter is directed personally to her, is not general mass-marketing hype.

Of course, the laser letter can go on to get more information from Mrs. Warren. And why not?

"I know that we had a delivery mixup last October. I want to be sure that everything you are receiving now is getting there on time and in good condition. Could you take the time to fill out the little questionnaire at the bottom of the order form to let me know how we are doing in our service to you, Mrs. Warren? It is by helpful comments and suggestions from our best customers, like you, Mrs. Warren, that we can correct whatever is not right, and bring you the kind of responsive service that you want and deserve. Your comments are very valuable to me. Please feel free to call me directly if there is anything that you do not want to write on the form. I am anxious to hear from you.

"Sincerely yours,

"Myron Fuller, Nutrition Specialist."

Why do I introduce this concept in a chapter on getting the names right? Because it is at the service bureau and mailshop level where this type of personalization gets carried out—and gets mixed up. Many service bureaus cannot do a decent job of producing a personalized letter. They may charge you a lot extra. They will say that it will delay the job. They will point out all the problems with the exceptions (no dog name in the record; dog sex not in record; customer's name is S WARREN, so sex is unknown) and try to talk you out of this kind of personalization. If this happens, perhaps it is time to get a new service bureau.

Of course, your database record has gaps in it. For this reason you must prepare defaults. It is complicated, but it is what the corner grocer did which kept him in business. He took an active interest in the lives of his customers. As a database marketer you must take an active interest in the appearance and quality of every communication with every customer. Laser letters are an important example of what you must do to improve communications and maintain a lifetime relationship with your customers.

Merge/Purge Reports

Most service bureaus can now produce for you, as a standard service at no extra cost, a set of very valuable reports on your merge/purge which will tell you:

- How many names were used from each incoming list. Each list should have its own source code.

- How many bad addresses there were on each list. In general, you should not use lists that are "dirty."

- How many duplicates you had on each incoming list, and how many inter-list duplicates you had. These "multi-buyers" should be specially flagged.

- How your file is broken down by state, by SCF, by zip code, by sex and by other factors on the file.

Business-to-Business Merge/Purge

When your list is not a consumer list, you have a much bigger problem. Business addresses are very different:

- Whereas 20 percent of all Americans move their residence once a year, about 40 percent of businessmen change their business addresses every year. People are transferred, promoted, fired

and they change jobs. The companies they work for are always
changing their locations, internal structure and even names.

■ Decisions need to be made: do you want to mail to a company,
or a specific title within the company, or a specific named individual? For a marketing database, the last is clearly the best.
But it is the hardest to get.

a.   Arthur Hughes, Exec. VP
     ACS, Inc.
     1807 Michael Faraday Ct.
     Reston, VA 22090

b.   Jim Nathan, Research Div.
     ACS, Inc.
     4011 Sunset Hills Drive
     Reston, VA 22090

c.   Chris Ogden
     ACS, Inc.
     Michael Faraday Court
     Reston, VA 22090

d.   R & D Division
     ACS, Inc.
     1807 Michael Faraday Ct.
     Reston, VA 22090

e.   Director of Research, ACS
     Room 117
     Sunset Hills Drive
     Reston, VA 22090

f.   ACS
     1807 Michael Faraday Ct.
     Reston, VA 22090

These are all different people. Or are they? Do you want to saturate the company with mail in the hopes of getting to the one person who is interested in your offer, or are you sure you can pinpoint Chris Ogden as your man, even though you are unsure of his title and division?

- In your reformatting of the input names, you should allow separate spaces in your record for specialized business-to-business fields such as:

Last Name
First Name
Title (Mr. Mrs.)
Suffix
Position (Vice President)
Division (Personnel)
Branch (Recruitment and Training)
Company (Denver BioLab Company)
Parent Company (XYZ Drug Industries)
Internal address
Street Address (2 lines)
City, State, ZIP

And you will want to add such fields as:

SIC Code
Position Code
Division Code (04=Personnel)

- Any software designed for consumer merge/purge *will not work properly* with business-to-business files. Be sure that the software used is specialized for your purpose.

- You must set up some sort of internal coding system which categorizes the types of industries, divisions and positions you are seeking in your job. A purchasing agent is one code, an end-user is another. A little advance planning and ingenuity here is absolutely essential if the final product is to reach the correct people.

■ Be sure that your merge/purge programmers are clear as to who you are seeking and who are duplicates. Are the Vice President for Engineering and the Assistant Vice President for Engineering duplicates or not? If you have the name of the Assistant VP, but no name for the VP, do you drop the VP?

The best solution is to have a couple of hundred sorted names printed out, study them, and mark who you want in and who out. Then write some rules which explain your decision so that a computer can use these rules to include and exclude names.

Figure 15-2 Steps in List Processing for Mailing

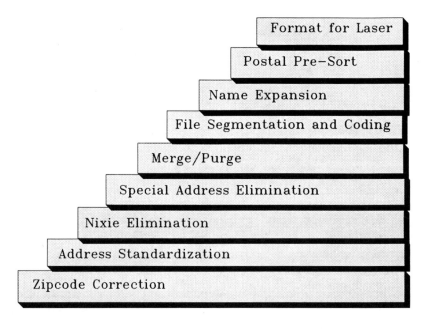

Format for Laser

Postal Pre-Sort

Name Expansion

File Segmentation and Coding

Merge/Purge

Special Address Elimination

Nixie Elimination

Address Standardization

Zipcode Correction

SUMMARY

- Computer processing and correction of names is the least expensive part of any mailing job, but can have a major impact on deliverability and response. Correct processing is very important.

- Service bureaus can correct zipcodes and correct the addresses.

- Nixies are non-deliverable returns from previous mailings. They should be studied closely for what they tell you about a mailing.

- All large files contain duplicates. It is hard to find them, but you must do so: duplicate names in a mailing cost money and reduce response.

- Duplicate names in your marketing database will reduce confidence in the database and weaken its impact on the customer.

- Duplicate identification is a specialized art which should be done by professionals with professional software. Don't try it in-house unless you do it on a regular basis.

- Duplicate names occurring on several lists can be very valuable: they are multi-buyers. Mail to them more often.

- You should check for duplicates yourself before any job goes out. It is better to drop some non-duplicates than to mail in a questionable case.

- Householding means mailing only one letter per household. You should get a plan for how to address a household which is consistent with the image of your product.

- Insist on autosexing—determining the sex of your prospect, so you can use a title: Mr. Spaulding, Ms. Rothrock.

- In many cases, the appearance of the address can sour your prospect before the envelope is opened. Service bureaus can do much to make an address look attractive.

- Laser letters look better than labels, and may not cost much more.

- All laser letters can contain many personalized paragraphs and references for little or no additional cost. These can help sell your product.

- Business-to-business merge/purge is specialized and different. Household software does not work. Be sure the correct software is used.

Chapter 16

Cloning Your Best Customers

Most marketing databases contain two types of people: customers and leads. A *lead* is someone who has responded to one of your offers but has not yet purchased anything. Leads may come to you from many sources: general advertising, direct response advertising, direct mail. One of the best sources of leads is a direct offer to a likely prospect. A *prospect* is a person who you believe should be buying your product because he has qualities which resemble those of your best customers. He is a "clone" of your best customers. How do you get the names of prospects to use for your direct marketing effort?

Let us assume that you have already profiled your current customers. You have determined some characteristics that distinguish your best customers from your worst, and from non-customers. Once you know that, then you can screen names from outside lists to get people who look like your best current customers. These are your best prospects.

PICKING THE CORRECT AUDIENCE

We are now down to the heart of profiling: finding characteristics of your customers and your non-respondents which will help you to determine which names on an unknown rented list will respond to your next direct marketing program. You want to *predict* your results. For the purpose of this chapter, we will be drawing examples from direct mail, since it is easily the most quantifiable for illustrative purposes. But the principles apply to any type of direct marketing.

It used to be that profiling would consist of finding the characteristics of your customers:

Age: 25-35
Income: $35,000–$70,000
Education: College Graduate

These seem like good criteria, until you profile your non-respondents. Their average profile might be:

Age: 25-35
Income: $35,000–$70,000
Education: College Graduate

In other words, your non-respondents look just like your respondents. This could be because most of the people you mailed to looked like that. More likely, it is because in your profiling, you have not hit on the criteria that separates the sheep from the goats.

You must do more research, more modeling. That is why modern database marketers include a vast array of data in their marketing databases. After further research, you may find that the chief difference between your respondents and your non-respondents was something else:

Respondents:

Housing: High-rise and condominiums
Children: Low percentage
Clusters: Pools and Patios, Young Influentials

Non Respondents:

Housing: Single-family homes
Children: Medium percentage
Clusters: Young Suburbia, Blue Chip Blues

Now that you see the difference, it is much easier to pick the good prospects from the poor prospects. But to get from ignorance to knowledge takes trial and error. Profiling is a hands-on activity in which your marketing staff should participate actively. Profiling is too important to be left to some data processing staff. As a professional database marketer you will want to have database software that permits you to do exhaustive research yourself, with a cost structure in which you don't have to worry how much each iteration of the model will cost. You will also want to have some professional help with what is at all times a complicated process.

LIST SELECTION

Your marketing database has now provided you with a profile which will help you to separate good prospects from the general public. The profile can be used to screen lists for rental, to pick the right publication for advertising, to pick the correct radio or TV show, or even to pick the right time of day. The profile will certainly help you frame your offer by knowing what your preferred respondent looks like. But demography and lifestyle are not enough. They can be outweighed by additional facts that you can discover.

You cannot sell pet food to people without pets. You cannot sell software to someone who has no computer. A list taken from subscribers to a pet magazine or a computer magazine should obviously outweigh any results from modeling if your product falls into one of these or similar specialized niches.

Do not automatically assume that there does not exist a list of just the type of prospects that you are looking for. Nowadays if you work with a good list broker there is almost no limit to what can be done. But you yourself must be resourceful.

Let us assume that you have done a good job of profiling. The characteristics you have selected are those which are likely to be coded and selectable in outside lists. Thus armed, you venture forth to seek good lists.

Selection of the correct names is probably the single most important factor in any mailing. Ed Burnett developed the following rough statistics on the importance of various factors in the success of a mailing:

Category	Potential Variation in Response
Lists	300% – 1000%
Offer	50% – 200%
Package	10%
Timing	10% (Except at Christmas)
Copy	10%

In most cases, your creative people are involved in designing an attractive piece, and in some cases you might have a modeler who is working on multiple regressions. No one is giving adequate attention to list selection, yet the list is the most important single ingredient in any mailing. We must set about correcting this situation right now.

OBTAINING PROSPECT NAMES

The United States is a direct marketer's dream. Nowhere else on earth is there such a profusion of available lists of names of prospective buyers and donors. When you first go forth to find the names of people to add to your prospect list, if you are not experienced, you will be overwhelmed by the numbers and seeming quality of the lists available.

There are books available which cover this subject in great detail. The best is *The Complete Direct Mail List Handbook*, by Ed Burnett, one of the most knowledgeable and experienced professionals in the field. Much of what I am outlining here is derived from this excellent book, but my brief extract is no substitute for obtaining a copy of this valuable work for your office bookshelf.

Inside Names

Before you spend money to go outside to find prospect names, you should canvas your internal resources. There are often more names available than you might think.

You can start by getting a list of your customers which may be obtained from a variety of sources: warranty registrations, sales slips, credit card charges, checks, order forms. If your system does not provide these names today, perhaps some minor changes in the systems in your company or at the dealer will yield you hundreds or thousands of names at little cost.

The next step is to get your customers to furnish you names. Every time they buy a gift for someone else, you have a very valuable linked pair of names. You should keep both names, and retain the linkage in your database. You can reward customers for recommending your product to others and for supplying you with their names. Again, keep the linkage to use in later correspondence.

The telephone is ringing all day at your 800 number with people calling to inquire about something. Never, never tell anyone anything without first getting their name and address and their phone number. Keep your telemarketers equipped with a list of standard questions they must ask. Are the callers customers? What product did they buy and when? What caused them to buy it? Where did they hear about you? How many other people in the household use the product, or ought to use it?

In most companies, if you scratch around enough, you will find a dozen prospect or customer lists being kept by special groups unknown to one another. You may find rebate respondents, sweepstakes entrants, membership lists, upgrade respondents, sales leads and prospects and so on. Don't forget lists of employees, stockholders, suppliers and newsletter readers. You may be able to assemble quite a large group of names without spending a cent. If you turn all of these lists over to a service bureau, they can quickly merge them into a single list, eliminating the duplicates and retaining codes that show where each name came from. Don't let them make a major project of it. If the names are on magnetic tape to start with, you shouldn't have to spend a fortune nor wait more than two weeks to get the job done.

Looking Outside

Once you have exhausted your inside resources, you can begin to explore outside lists for prospects that match your ideal profile.

Figure 16-1 Mailing Response
(List Selection is Key Factor)

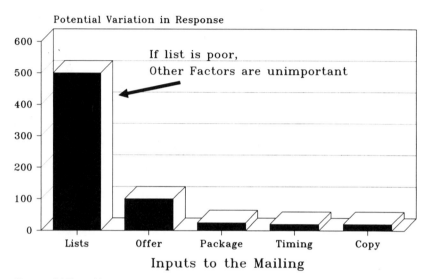

Potential Variation in Response

If list is poor,
Other Factors are unimportant

Inputs to the Mailing

Source: Ed Burnett

There are about a million mailing lists, of which about 20,000 are commercally available. Many of them are kept in good order with correct addresses (by frequent application of NCOA), and a great many are enhanced with demographics or lifestyle information so that you can select names by criteria that match your preferred customer makeup. New lists are being created every month which list new households, businesses, professionals, graduates, institutions, babies, marriages, credit card holders, automobile registrants.

There are twelve major list brokers and hundreds of minor ones. There are six major list compilers who have lists covering almost every household in America, plus most of the businesses.

If you are a newcomer, you should begin by selecting a professional list broker to help you. Unlike real estate, where a broker may know only about property in his immediate neighborhood, any large list broker will be able to find out about and obtain for you names from almost any list in the country.

What the List Broker Can Do for You

If you take the list broker into your confidence, he can be very helpful. Tell him the type of customer that you have now, and the type of prospect that you are seeking to attract. Explain your product and your offer, how you plan to go about lining up new customers. He has experience. He can help to keep you from making costly mistakes. He may not only find you the right names, he may also help you to structure your offer, to design your tests, to segment your list and to evaluate your success. For free—just the cost of the names that you rent through him—your list broker may provide you tens of thousands of dollars worth of valuable consultation. I have seen several clients who did not put their list broker on their marketing team, and lost big money because of it.

The list broker works for you, not for the list owner. He has no vested interest in which list is used. He usually makes very little money on a test. His real return comes on the "continuation" (the large repeat mailing to a list after a successful test). So he is very anxious to find lists that work for you. Here are some of the things that your list broker will insist that you do to craft a successful test by mail or by telemarketing:

- *Use several lists for your test.* You will learn twice as much by mailing to two lists, ten times as much if you select from ten lists. Often the list you thought would not be too useful proves to be the best of the lot.

- *Test different packages, offers and copy.* While you are testing, test everything. Test your price, your premiums, your envelopes, your sales arguments. While you are doing this, be sure that every variation is tested equally on each list so that you can have a real test. This means *nth* name segmentation of each list for each test package.

Let's take an example. Suppose you have four lists of 30,000 names each. You have three different offers and two different types of envelopes. That makes twenty-four different segments, six for each of your four lists.

You will have to do a *nth name split* on each of your four lists to split them into six statistically equal parts. Then each of these six parts gets a different offer and envelope.

Put source codes on the response device in your promotion. A source code is simply a unique combination of letters or numbers that identifies each of the segments that you mailed. The segment source code tells you what list the name came from, what offer and what envelope (in our present example). In a real life example, we might have many more than twenty-four segments if we were testing more aspects of the promotion.

Be sure that the source codes are captured when the prospects respond to your offer. I have seen mailings where the client developed some excellent source codes, but the letter shop printed them in such a way that they were cut in half when the customer clipped them out to put them in the BRE (business reply envelope). The result was tests with no final scores: wasted effort.

Analyze your results. Again, I have participated in tests where the client developed a grand plan, but didn't take the time to find out what went wrong or right with the final mailing. Back-end Analysis is important not just to prove a single mailing, but to prove an entire marketing theory. Let me explain what I mean:

- Most successful test mailings to prospect lists produce a given (and relatively small) percentage response. Depending on your offer, that given percent may make money for you or it may lose money. But either way, you now have the names of customers who have responded and paid money for your product (or provided an inquiry which you later convert to a sale via catalog, telemarketing or salesman visit).

- Your next step is a *second offer* to those initial respondents. This second offer, if successful, may result in a substantially larger response. You follow that up, right away, with a *third offer* which also should net you a goodly response. We are now getting into "lifetime value."

- However, this is where the ball is usually dropped. How do you determine whether your initial test was successful? By the responses to the first promotion, or to the first plus the second, or to a whole chain of promotions stretching over several months or years? In one project I worked on, we found that TV ads produced excellent responses, but that in the long run people who responded to direct mail bought more (in follow up promotions) than TV respondents. We finally determined that the direct mail respondents were more valuable, even though they were *initially more expensive to acquire.*

- To develop this kind of knowledge requires that you keep track of the initial source codes and all subsequent source codes in a customer's database record. Some companies just keep the *latest* source code, discarding all previous codes. What a mistake! Without these earlier source codes, we would have decided that TV was a better recruiting source than direct mail, whereas the opposite was the case.

Avoid false theories. Mailing list selection is fraught with "old wives' tales" which usually surface as dogmatic statements which may, in fact, be right sometimes and dead wrong other times. A good list broker will help you avoid being mesmerized by these false theories. Let's list a few of them:

- *Direct mail is easy to enter; anyone can make a go of it.* Dead wrong. This is a business for professionals. You can lose your shirt (or your company's shirt) if you are not careful.

- *All lists are pretty much the same.* Completely wrong. The variation on a single large job from best to worst list may be as much as ten to one.

- *For my special situation, there is only one source for my prospect names.* It may be true today, but there is such constant movement in the list business, with new lists coming on the market every month, that you may be missing some very good bets by not constantly testing.

Figure 16-2 Mailings Assure All Aspects Are Tested
(So That Rollout Dollars Are Spent Most Efficiently)

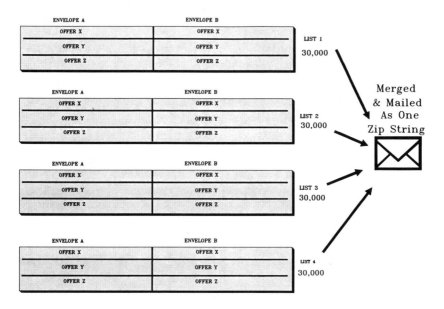

■ *All list brokers are the same.* Despite the fact that any list broker can theoretically find for you names from any rental list in
the country, the fact is that most brokers specialize in a few of
the hundreds of possible areas and are weak in their knowledge
of the other areas. A broker who has been finding good names
for a non-profit mailer may strike out when seeking customers
for a bank or an encyclopedia.

■ *Good lists should not be mailed too often.* If the list is working
for you, it means that you have developed some synergy with
the people on that list. They like what you are selling. If that is
so, why would they stop liking it just because you mail to them
once a quarter or once a month? This is as true of your customer file as it is of your rented lists. Constant, familiar, friendly,
profitable contact is what database marketing is all about.

■ *Large lists are better than small lists.* This theory is based on the idea that if a test is successful, but the list is very small, there will be no rollout potential (i.e., the test will have used up all the names). The trouble with this idea is that by selecting only large lists, you may be (and probably are) overlooking gold in a lot of small specialized lists which may give you phenomenal response.

Selecting by Profiled Criteria

How do you, and your broker, decide which will be the best lists for your promotion? Let's assume that you have profiled your best customers, and have arrived at some notion of what makes for a good customer for your particular product or service. You want to find more prospects who match this profile of the good customer. There are several ways you can go:

Find people who are known to need or like your product. Here you can ask for specialized lists:

■ A Buick dealer can get a list of owners of three-year-old Buicks.

■ A pet food company can get a list of cat or dog owners.

■ A bank selling CD's can get a list of affluent older people.

■ A cruise line can rent a list of people who have said that they would like to take a cruise (in a national survey).

■ An environmental organization can rent a list of people who have responded to some other environmental cause.

■ A baby food manufacturer can rent a list of new mothers.

■ A furniture company can rent a list of people who have just moved.

Find people with the correct demography. If you are selling a non-specialized product, such as a credit card, a general interest magazine or lawn care, you may not have any specialized list sources available. For these products, your analysis of your existing customer base might tell you that the ideal customer for your product:

- lives in a single family home;

- has a family income of $40K to $60K;

- has two wage earners in the family;

- has no children;

- is between ages 40 and 60.

Can you rent a list consisting only of people who fit this description? Absolutely.

Figure 16-3 Conduct Series of Test Mailings
(To determine the best lists, offer, package, response.)

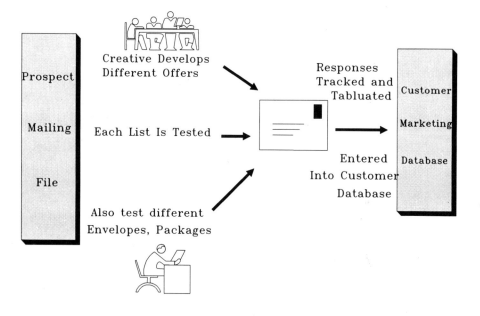

Find people with the correct lifestyle. At least four large companies specialize in compiling lists of people who have answered survey questions about their lifestyles. "The Lifestyle Selector" has compiled a long list of questions on surveys which are packed into millions of warranty cards of products bought at retail by consumers. About 18 percent of those who "register" their warranty by mailing it in furnish data as to hobbies, interests, reading, mail order purchase and demographic information. Another service, "The Behavior Bank," asks consumers to indicate their brand usage in coffee, pet food, cereals, milk, coffee creamer, saltines, floor wax, pantyhose, denture cleanser, laxatives, cigarettes, detergents and so on. In addition, they ask about credit cards, mail order buying habits, hobbies and occupations.

Find people who have bought by mail (or telephone) recently. In many cases, your broker may be able to identify lists of people who have purchased something by mail which is similar to your offering (for instance, in price or in type of product) within a specified period. Recency here is very important. Frequency can also be requested as a discriminant factor. The dollar amount is also a key. If you are selling something that costs $89, a list of proven buyers of some product for $15 may not be very useful.

Find people who live in the right place. Sometimes you want only people who live in your state or city or congressional district. That is very easy to arrange. All lists can be selected by zipcode. In most cases, you can also get an overlay for political districts.

In some cases, you want *everyone* who lives in a certain area (for cable TV, for example). One of the "big four" list compilers can fix you up with all of the people in Pocatello, Idaho, even including the households ("Current Occupant") where the name of the person living there is as yet unknown.

LIST REFORMATTING

You have selected your lists, and the tapes are beginning to arrive. The first thing you will notice is that some of the tapes are late. It is almost always true that if you order nine different tapes, three will come on time, three will be a week late and three will be two weeks late. This may delay your drop date, unless you plan in advance. Ask your list broker when the tapes will arrive, and then add two weeks. The merge/purge process cannot really begin until the last tape has arrived, so the early tapes will just sit.

Long before the tapes arrive, you should have made up a list of source codes for your test. On a typical test, you may have 160 different source codes:

Four different offers
Four different packages
Ten different lists

$4 \times 4 \times 10 = 160$.

Assign a different code to each which will help you find out what was working after the test: for example, AA01 AA02, where the first letter is the offer, the second is the package and the next two digits are the list number. Write these codes down in a book or on a PC, and make sure that everyone involved knows what they are and what they mean.

At this point you also will want to give your service bureau a list of seed names. These are names of employees of your company or the creative agency, usually at their home addresses, so that they can receive the package and monitor the mailing to be sure that it has been done correctly and arrives on time. The seeds should be inserted into every package and every offer.

After your service bureau reformats your tapes to a common format, be sure that the job has been done correctly. There are several features to consider.

Appearance. Do the names and addresses look correct and attractive after the reformat? Insist on a dump (legible printout) of at least 300 names, including all lists. To be sure you are getting a random sample, ask for all the names beginning at a certain zipcode which you specify. Here is what to look for:

1.   File in upper/lower case, punctuated correctly.

2.   Address correct and standardized.

3.   Names include titles.

Freedom from Duplicates. Read the Chapter 15, and follow it.

Complete Statistics. Get the whole story of what happened to every incoming name. How many bad addresses there were; how many were corrected; how many could not be corrected; how many duplicates were found in each list; and how many duplicates there were found against your house file. All new duplicates (appearing on two or more lists, but *not* on your house file) should be set aside in a special file for a follow-up mailing. These are multi-buyers, very powerful names, and should be used in any repeat mailing.

Check the Segmentation. After the list has been corrected and deduped, it should be segmented by package and offer. The tapes already have the original list code in them. They will now get the package and offer letter added. This segmentation should be done on an nth name basis across the file from a zipcode standpoint, so that each package and offer will get a proportional number of names, randomly distributed across the entire mailing. The best way to check this is to get a report showing zipcodes by package and zipcodes by offer, with the zipcode being only the first digit of the zip on a large list, or more digits on a smaller list.

PKG/Offer	0	1	2	3	4	5	6	7	8	9
AA	213	423	651	142	91	86	73	76	34	1076
AB	212	420	650	142	92	87	74	77	35	1075
AC, etc.										

Bad Addresses. Some rented lists are loaded with old and incorrect addresses. You can check on this by marking the envelope *ADDRESS CORRECTION REQUESTED*, which alerts the Post Office to return to you all the undelivered mail. These "nixies" cost you money, but it may be well worth it, depending on your program. (Read Chapter 15)

Improving your Message. There are thousands of different envelopes and millions of different messages and inserts. Something that worked last year may not work this year. The public is fickle, tiring easily of something that once excited it. *Every mailing* should be considered as an experiment. Always try something new: different shape envelope, different stamps, varying message. Assign a different source code to each different test, and get prompt reports from your database on which test package pulled the best.

You should also be constantly testing price. It is not necessarily true that lower prices will improve sales. With some products, in certain circumstances, a price increase with appropriate message may position the product in a different "quality niche" which will have it perceived as being better than the other brands, and thus result in increased sales. The only way to know this is to test constantly and produce and study reports. This is a tremendous feature of database marketing: each message stands on its own. If you are selling in a department store, you cannot very well offer an item at one price to one group of shoppers and at another price to others. But in the privacy of one-on-one mailings, every letter you send offers an opportunity for a test, an opportunity which you can exploit.

Proper report design and careful study, plus creative imagination in designing test packages, will enable you to get better and better results, and eliminate the envelope and message as a negative factor in your direct mail.

RENTING YOUR OWN LIST

As a direct marketer, you may dread the idea of renting the names of your customers to others. After all, you spent a lot of money acquiring these names; they are *your customers*. They may resent being *shopped around* to every vendor in the country.

But consider what we have been saying in this chapter. We have been advising you on how to find prospects by renting names from other companies. If they all felt the way you feel about renting, then why are they renting names? Do they know something that you don't know?

Probably. Let's consider some of the advantages of renting out your names.

Lists get stale. Twenty percent of Americans move every year. If you sit on a list for two or three years without using it, it will become almost worthless. If you have a valuable list, consider it as a rapidly depreciating asset. Get value out of it before it is too late.

Renting can rejuvenate a list. If you develop a cooperative relationship with another company that is using your list, you can agree jointly that they will share with you the results of their mailing: the nixies, the changes of address, the households that responded and how much they bought. After all, you are in the driver's seat. You can insist on anything you want. When they give you their results, you enter the data into your database. You have a better list after each mailing.

Some people like receiving mail. My wife Helena is a confirmed catalog shopper. She gets an average of about five catalogs *a day* all year round. She buys most of our Christmas presents and a good amount of her wardrobe by mail. She looks forward to seeing new catalogs. She scans every page eagerly for new ideas. She is aware that, because of her activity, her name is being actively traded. She is a multi-buyer. She loves it.

Renting the names of people like Helena is a favor to them. There are millions like her.

Database marketing permits "No Rental" flags. If you are worried that some of your customers will be turned off by having their names shopped around, ask them. They won't mind at all telling you their preference. When they do, code their answer in a "No Rental" flag in the database, and don't rent names that don't want to be rented. Many of your customers will appreciate your surveying them on this question, no matter what their preference, and this survey is just one more little dialog which helps maintain the relationship with them.

Renting names is profitable. Depending on the value of your list, you should be able to realize from 20 cents to one dollar per name per year after all expenses and broker's fees are paid. This means that if you have a customer database of 500,000 names, you should be taking in $100,000 or more in list rental fees. This revenue could be enough to pay a lot of the expenses of your marketing database. This is not insignificant revenue for most marketing staffs. It should permit you to do a lot more experimentation, enhancement, modeling, surveys, NCOA and other activities which you otherwise might not be able to afford.

Exchanges can be even more profitable. Here is a chance for you to become a creative database marketer. Who has a list that you could use in your business? Who would like to use the list that you have? If you sell nuts and bolts by mail, wouldn't the Black and Decker mailing list be ideal for you? And wouldn't your list be ideal for them?

Two possibilities open up: you can exchange lists, or you can go in for a cooperative mailing and share the costs. You will not only share the costs, you will share the benefits. Even if the other company makes more sales than you do, you should still come out ahead: your database will be bigger, your customer names will be refreshed, another chance for dialog with your customers has occurred.

Remember, the fact that you have a marketing database has made this all possible.

SUMMARY

- Picking the correct names is the most important single factor in the success of any direct mail effort.

- Before you look outside to rent prospects, explore your own company. There may be, and probably are, many useful lists of customers or prospects resident in different branches of your organization. Consider in particular people who are calling in on your customer service hotline.

- If you decide to go outside, the first step is to find a good list broker and take him fully into your confidence.

- Always test several lists at once. At the same time, test variations of your offer, price, package, premiums and copy. Test these variations equally across all lists.

- Use a different source code for every different offer, package, or what have you, in each list so you can do sophisticated back-end analysis of your success.

- Be sure that your source codes are captured when the responses come in.

- Keep track of source codes for the life of the customer, not just during the response period. The success of a list may be finally known only after several repeat promotions, not just after the first response.

- Avoid false theories or rules of thumb, such as "Good lists should not be mailed too often," or "Large lists are better than small lists."

- In finding people who match your customer profile, you may find a list that is tailor-made for your situation (such as a list of new mothers for a diaper manufacturer).

- You can also find lists that match your sought-after demographic factors.

- There are four major compilers who specialize in "Lifestyle Selection," including information on what brands of hundreds of products they currently buy.

- Allow enough time for proper reformatting and merge/purge of your list. Oversee the process yourself.

- Test different envelopes, packages, offers. Test, test, test. Count, and learn.

- Rent your own list to others. Work out intelligent exchanges and profitable cooperative arrangements.

Chapter 17

Telephone Technology

On Monday nights a large section of the American public is glued to television watching "Monday Night Football." Beginning in 1989, during halftime, viewers were given a chance to participate in an innovative audience opinion poll which takes place before their eyes. They watch a series of the best plays in the twenty-year history of the series in different categories: running, passing, tackling. Viewers vote to select the winners by calling a 900 telephone number. When they call, the hear the digitally recorded voice of commentator Frank Gifford greeting them and explaining how to vote for their favorite plays. ABC Sports then tells the viewers how the vote is going throughout the second half of the game.

The product of *Call Interactive*, a joint venture of AT&T and American Express Information Services Corporation, the technology makes the event possible because it can process 10,000 calls in ninety seconds, 450,000 calls in one hour. In the ABC broadcast of the Sugar Bowl using this system, ABC received 110,000 calls during the broadcast.

Before this venture began, it was not possible to receive this many calls in 90 seconds in any place in the world. The automatic machinery which they used to handle the calls, therefore, was in fact the only way that the calls could have been handled. The interactive poll would have been impossible without the machines.

This is an illustration of one of the principles of database marketing: modern technology is not only making it easier for us to keep up with customer demand at lower and lower cost, but it is creating new customer demand by providing new services that could not exist without the technology.

Why did the promoters decide on such a football poll? Let's analyze some of the possible reasons:

- Since calls came in on a 900 number, they undoubtedly made a profit on the poll itself, while costing each caller only a nominal sum.

- ABC Sports management can use the results of this poll to demonstrate to advertisers how many people were really watching, from what parts of the country, and how responsive they were to the right message. The poll will help to sell other advertising.

- The service is tailor-made for automatic order entry. To facilitate this, *Call Interactive* is tied to a fulfillment operation which can verify credit cards, prepare mailing lists and labels, print shipping instructions and invoices, and deliver a product.

Organizing the equipment to put on such an event is no small feat. But it is only a little more complicated than what the average company must go through to set up a modern telephone call center. Without a functioning telephone call center, you cannot conduct effective database marketing today. That is what this chapter is about—what telephone technology is needed to support effective database marketing, and what new marketing opportunities are presented by modern telephone technology.

THE GROWTH IN TELEPHONE TECHNOLOGY

We have all seen amazing changes in telephones in our lifetimes. I grew up in New Canaan, Connecticut, a bedroom community for New York City. All during the Thirties, our telephone number was 87 Ring 5, which meant that we were on a party line. All the families on our line had to count the rings to know if the call was for them or for someone else. When you picked up the telephone, you didn't get a dial tone, you got an operator who said "Number please." It wasn't until the eve of World War II that we got a dial telephone. Of course, that was followed 30 years later by touch tone phones, and 10 years after that by modems that enable us to connect our PCs by phone, and by the ubiquitous FAX which has made it so easy to exchange contracts and data across the country. The real advances in telephone technology are still to come. They will greatly affect database marketing.

There is hardly any company today which does not expect to do some portion of its sales and a large portion of its customer service by telephone. But many of them do not yet realize how to organize around the new technology to get the most out of their new system. Consider the cost of acquiring a new customer.

Every year McGraw-Hill reports the cost of acquiring a new customer by direct sales visits. Business-to-business direct sales calls averaged $291.10 in 1987. Using the telephone, acquisition of a residential customer often is computed at between $15 and $25 for each new customer. A breakdown of that $25 (Figure 17-1) is provided by Andrew J. Waite, Publisher of *Inbound Outbound* and author of *The Inbound Telephone Call Center,* published by the Telecom Library.

Figure 17-1 Cost of Aquiring a Customer

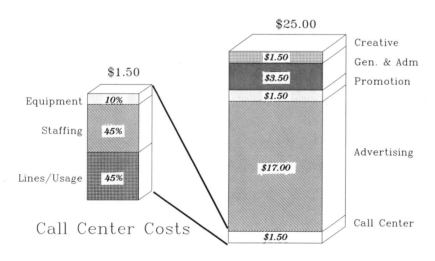

Source: Andrew J. Waite

Andrew Waite is the source for much of the information in this chapter, as well as being a leader in the telephone marketing industry.

This shows that a call center costs only $1.50 of the total of $25 to acquire a customer. Yet, if the call center does not have proper equipment or properly trained staff, their mismanagement of the incoming call can defeat the rest of the marketing effort and expense. In fact, the more effective a campaign is (unanticipated huge volume of calls), the greater the potential of the incoming call center to destroy it by failure to react promptly and effectively.

Good marketing and good products put heavy inbound call volume demand on your lines, your equipment and your people. Your callers get busy signals. They get put on "Eternity Hold." They are forced to listen to boring music (often on your expensive INWATS lines), and they hang up ("Call Abandonment"). At this point they may never call back. They become lost as a prospective customer, despite your elegant, expensive marketing and your beautiful new product.

Waite, in his book, quotes a nice example of a failure of communication between a marketing staff and the call center. The case involved the call center at a bus line. One morning, the center was swamped with inbound calls. Not until the morning break, when an employee got a chance to read the morning paper, was it discovered that the company had run a huge advertisement pushing a new, low fare. The call center was totally unaware of the promotion and of the anticipated increase in customer calls. It was understaffed to meet the demand. It dulled a potentially good ad campaign, not to mention wasting valuable advertising dollars.

SUPPORTING EXISTING CUSTOMERS

Any call from a prospect or a customer usually involves more than the business at hand, which may be a simple inquiry or a service request. The call may be to buy a ticket, to request help for a complex piece of software leading to the purchase of the latest release, an emergency call for help or an inquiry about an invoice discrepancy. Whatever it is, it can be and should be a part of a larger business transaction which concerns the lifetime value of this customer to your company. The call center can determine, in one short interaction, whether this customer will be with you for years buying again and again, or leave you forever in disgust and anger. Figure 17-2 shows all the ways in which a call center is used in companies today.

Most of these uses are obvious. A few need amplification:

Reservation sales and service are not only common telephone applications, they are the reason for the current technology. Most of the existing call equipment was designed first for the travel industry, and has spread from there to other uses.

Catalog Sales. More and more companies are discovering that catalog sales cannot only supplement their retail business, but can

Figure 17-2 Call Center Application Matrix

	Customer Service	Order Entry	Credit Authorization	Information	Reservations	Catalog Sales	Dispatch	Claims	Shareholder Service	Technical Services	Help Desks	Appointment Centers	Registration	Circulation	Classified Ads
Banking	▲		▲	▲					▲						
Travel Agents	▲	▲			▲					▲					
Airlines	▲			▲	▲		▲	▲							
Public Utilities	▲	▲		▲		▲				▲	▲	▲			
Newspapers		▲				▲								▲	▲
Hospitals	▲			▲		▲				▲		▲	▲		
Air Freight	▲	▲		▲			▲	▲							
Insurance Companies	▲			▲				▲			▲	▲			
Cable TV Companies	▲	▲		▲		▲				▲	▲	▲			
Public Transit				▲	▲										
Gov't. Info. Agencies	▲			▲	▲	▲	▲	▲		▲	▲	▲			
Ticket Offices		▲	▲	▲	▲										
Railroads	▲			▲	▲		▲	▲							
Universities				▲	▲	▲						▲	▲		
Hotels					▲										
Telemarketing Companies		▲	▲	▲		▲									
Credit Approval Companies			▲	▲											
Distribution Companies	▲	▲	▲	▲			▲	▲	▲		▲				
Manufacturers	▲	▲				▲		▲		▲	▲				
Department Stores	▲	▲	▲	▲			▲	▲			▲				

actually result in *bringing more people into their stores.* A major computer company started an experiment to see if selling small items and supplies by catalog and telephone was a viable business. Five years later, its two call centers were responsible for 10 percent of its total revenue.

Dispatch of taxis, delivery service, police, ambulances, fire departments and repair crews.

Claims processing by telephone is growing in the insurance industry. It speeds up service, reduces cost for the company and helps to serve an aging population which cannot get around very well. The Social Security Administration now does a significant portion of their application and claims work by telephone without the need for senior citizens to stir outside of their homes. Contrast that with the long waiting lines usually associated with any governmental service office. The beauty of the Social Security system is that the government service worker has the senior citizen's entire contribution and claims history available on a terminal connected to the SSA database, and can thus talk knowledgeably with the applicant about eligibility. In earlier days, a clerk at a window would merely receive paper application forms which would have to be checked weeks later against the claimant's paper dossier in a subsequent, labor intensive operation—the outcome of which might be a letter to the applicant informing him or her of ineligibility because of an improperly completed form.

Stockholder Relations. The junk bond raiders of the '80s have led management in many companies to realize that cultivation of the stockholder can be as vital to survival as the retention of the customer. American Transtech, a call center service agency, is an AT&T unit that began life in the early '80s, consoling widows and orphans who held stock in the about-to-be dismembered AT&T. Transtech was so successful that they have continued as a profitable strategic unit within AT&T.

Technical Services and Software Support, otherwise known as Help Desks. Effective management of calls in this type of service is particularly important because the personnel involved are, of necessity, highly trained and expensive. Every unnecessary minute they spend on the telephone is quite costly.

Registration by telephone is growing in community colleges, hospitals, motor vehicle agencies. Volume in such cases is often concentrated in a few days every quarter or year. The equipment has to be efficient.

HOW A CALL CENTER IS ORGANIZED

A modern call center is designed to efficiently handle a large volume of calls with minimum personnel. There are many different aspects of the center which we will consider here. They include:

- the Automatic Call Distributor (ACD);
- Interactive Voice Response Units (IVR);
- DNIS and ANI telephone features which detect the number dialed (DNIS) and the calling number (ANI);
- the agents (your operators who talk in the telephone);
- the economics of the center.

The Automatic Call Distributor (ACD)

This vital device does several important things:

- It manages the incoming calls automatically, taking the one that has been waiting longest first.
- It places the call automatically with an agent who is free to talk. If there is more than one free, it gives the call to the one who has been idle longest.
- It gives calls to those agents designated to handle the calls. In busy times, it can give calls to overflow agents or supervisors, or route them over to entirely different departments, depending on your instructions.
- Using Automatic Number Identification (ANI), it can tell who is calling you, and automatically signal your marketing

database to retrieve the customer record of the agent with whom it has placed the call.

■ Also using ANI, if the caller is not on your database, it can trigger Donnelley FastData to display the name and address of the caller automatically on the agent's screen. The agent does not need to waste valuable telephone time typing in a name and address. The agent can get right down to taking the sales call and providing service.

■ Also using ANI, it can automatically route the call to the dealer who handles the incoming caller's area code, rather than wasting the caller's time while the agent asks the address. Your dealers can be located in every state of the union, but they can all be reached by calling a single 800 number.

■ Using Dialed Number Identification (DNIS), the ACD can know what incoming number was dialed. Depending on your setup, this number could trigger a different routing. For example, one number could be for encyclopedia sales, another for country-western records, another for health insurance. All these calls might be fielded by the same call center with many incoming lines. The ACD can alert your agent to the type of call to expect. The computer screen will already be displaying health insurance questions when the caller comes on the line.

■ Of crucial importance, the ACD contains a computer with extensive memory. It uses this computer to monitor what is happening in your call center all day long, providing up-to-the-minute reports to your call center supervision and post-call printed reports to your management. The ACD permits you to manage your agent resources effectively.

Interactive Voice Response Units (IVR)

Interactive Voice Response Units permit the incoming caller to determine his or her own routing within the company. "Thank you for calling Wearever Windows. For Sales, push '1'; for Service, push '2'; for Information or an operator, push '3'." This unit can save you

you the cost of one or several operators, and get the customer connected to the right party faster than most other methods. Why faster? Because often with human operators, what you get is, "All Wearever Windows agents are currently busy. Please stay on the line and your call will be answered in turn." When you finally do get to talk to an operator, he or she will just switch you to Service, where your wait starts all over again.

Another feature of voice response units is that you can ask the customer to enter some meaningful number such as a personal ID, social security or account number, or telephone number. This number, rather than ΛNI, can be the trigger to bring the customer's database record up on the screen. Using such a number eliminates the "privacy" issues surrounding ANI.

Figure 17-3 The Automatic Call Distributor

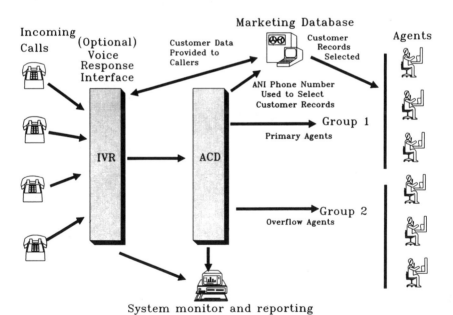

Available Agents

It is not easy to find enough people to handle your telephone calls.

If you visit a large mail order catalog company, you will often see rows upon rows of empty telephone representative positions, ready to be used at the slightest uptick in business. Expensive telephone lines and switching facilities lie idle waiting for the next catalog mailing drop or the onset of the Christmas buying season. This idleness and under-utilization is the way of life of the call center manager. No call center can ever afford to be equipped to handle the *average* capacity; it must be equipped for the *peak.*

Call centers typically grow beyond reasonable expectations at unanticipated rates. Once your customers know that they can get you on the telephone whenever they want, and that you will provide helpful service, they will call you constantly. Your business may grow at frightening speed.

Where will you find all the agents you will need to meet peak loads? This will normally be your biggest problem. You can buy equipment and have it installed anywhere, but agents must be found where they live. For this reason, call centers are not necessarily located where your company is. You may find it more economical and practical to locate your call center in Nebraska or Utah or Colorado, when your company is in Chicago or New York, simply because you will be unable to find the full-time and part-time agents needed in the area where your company is located.

For that reason also, you may find that it is more practical to contract out your call center function to a telemarketing firm. Let them have the problem of finding agents, training them, laying them off in slow periods and motivating them to come in on Saturday and Sunday when you have peak calling times.

When you have over 150 agent positions, a call center becomes unwieldy to manage. It is very hard to maintain a full complement of staff. Industry sources have estimated that during the '90s, 8,000,000 new jobs will be created in telemarketing and call centers. Many call centers in the Northeast have experienced high abandonment rates (incoming callers hanging up because of too long waiting on hold) due to lack of staff. One solution has been to establish a secondary center in other parts of the country.

Part-time employees are a vital resource for any call center, but it is not economical for most of them to drive for an hour to reach a three- or four-hour part-time job. A partial solution to this problem is to build decentralized call centers, close to the workers, with calls switched easily and transparently from the central ACD unit.

There are many communities dependent on some seasonal business, such as fishing or winter or summer tourists. Many of these communities have a steady core of well educated labor looking for the steady schedule offered by a call center. Today's technology make the promise of this decentralized siting a viable alternative.

How Much Do Call Centers Cost?

A telephone center with thirty telephone representatives will cost you approximately $1,500,000 per year. Here is the breakdown:

Thirty Representatives @ $7 per hour plus benefits......$550,000
Two Supervisors @ $9 per hour plus benefits................$ 50,000
192 hours per day of WATS service @ $16 per hour...$775,000
Telephone equipment @ $3,500 per position................$100,000
Total cost for one year...$1,475,000

How many calls can a thirty-agent system handle in a year? I can answer that with a question: "What are you trying to accomplish with your calls?"

Telephone directory service calls average fifteen seconds per call. A "Help Desk" information service may average twenty minutes per call. But most sales and support transactions average about three to four minutes per call. Depending on the time of day, you can expect your agents to be talking on the telephone about forty minutes out of the average hour.

If your call center is working a normal business day, forty hours a week, your thirty agents will be taking about 2,400 four minute calls a day. Using our figure of $1,500,000 per year, your typical day will cost you $6,000. Your 2400 calls, thus, will average you about $2.50 each. This price includes everything: WATS charges, labor, supervision and equipment.

WHEN TO ANSWER THE TELEPHONE

In normal telephone work, the call begins when you answer it. But with ACD, your equipment can sense a call even before it has started ringing and begin to process it *before the call is answered.* The standard North American ring cycle is two seconds of ringing and four seconds of silence, for a total of six seconds. A caller, calling a business, will typically accept hearing a ring tone from two to seven times, or twelve to forty-two seconds. An intelligent inbound call phone system can use this time to its advantage in busy times. A careful management of delay and abandoned call statistics will allow a call center manager to determine the actual "threshold of pain" that callers are willing to accept. The logic is that it's cheaper to let the phone ring than to answer it and put the caller on hold on your expensive 800 number circuit.

In non-busy times, the ACD could pick up the incoming call at electronic speeds, before it has even had a chance to ring. But experience shows that this does not really save the time per call that you might think. The reason is that our phone conditioning causes us to expect some amount of ringing when we make a call. By eliminating all ringing, the inbound caller becomes disoriented and uses up more than six seconds trying to figure out what happened. Any saving is thus offset.

The delay before answering can serve even more useful purposes for a call center. Using ANI, the ACD system can determine who is calling you before the call is answered. That means that if your system involves switching certain incoming calls to certain agents or dealers or salesmen, depending on the location or identity of the caller, all this decision making and switching can take place before the call is actually answered.

For example, let us suppose that you have determined who your best customers are by RFM analysis. You want to give these customers "gold card" treatment with special agents. When any call comes in, your ACD determines from ANI what the caller's number is. This number is checked against a table of "gold card" customer numbers. If it is there, the call is automatically switched to the "gold card" agents *before the telephone is answered.* This is more efficient for you and much more satisfying to your callers, who don't have to wait to be rerouted after they first reach an agent.

When to Hang Up

In most telephone service, the caller controls the length of the call. Your call center is thus at the mercy of your customers. If they take a while hanging up after their call, your call center is still connected. You may lose several seconds at the end of each call while your equipment is waiting for your callers to disconnect. This wait is billed at 800 number rates, and ties up your call center which could be using the time to talk to someone else. Modern ACD equipment will cut the circuit as soon as the agent has disconnected, not waiting for the caller. Over a year, this feature could save you a hundred times its cost.

Delay Announcements

You place a call and the Voice Response Unit tells you that all available agents are busy. You have to wait. Experience shows that people wait longer if they have something to listen to. What will it be? What are the options?

- Music.
- Silence, broken by constant repeat announcements: "All available agents are still busy. Stay on the line and your call will be answered in turn."
- An intelligent speaker providing useful information about your company, products, and services.

Clearly the last option is the best. Whoever is calling you is interested in your company, or they wouldn't have called. Movie theatres have learned this. They know that 99 percent of all calls are from people who want to know what's playing and when, so they tell you that in a recorded announcement up front. The best announcements also tell you that there are long lines for "Dick Tracy," so you had better get there early.

Despite the last option being the best, few companies are doing it yet. Why? Because it is a lot of work figuring out what to say and getting someone to record it. Customer service is not yet an important enough function in most companies to command the resources necessary to create and present an imaginative and helpful recorded message. As database marketers we know how important this is. We will see that something is done about it.

HOW DO CALL CENTERS HELP BUSINESS?

Twenty-eight million grapefruits are processed annually by the Crest Fruit Company of Alamo, Texas. In 1987, they spent $6.62 to process each telephone order. Three years later, after installation of ACD equipment, their cost was down to 75 cents per order. Crest employs twenty-eight order takers and two customer inquiry reps in four user groups. Crest operates a grapefruit club that ships produce to its members each month. Keeping track on their database of who buys seasonally helps them target customers who might be interested in buying year round. Since Crest installed its ACD system, its operations have grown by 30 percent.

Rogers Cable TV Ltd, Canada's largest cable provider with 1,580,000 subscribers, created a regional call center to improve subscriber service. The first result of the new center was to cut the call abandonment rate from 16 percent during peak periods to two to five percent. After the center was operating, they were able to answer 95 percent of their calls within 15 seconds with an average wait time of seven seconds. The modern ACD equipment helped not only customers but also the staff. Turnover is down among the 125 customer service reps from an attrition rate of 60 per year before to 15 or less per year.

Carnival Cruise Lines maintained 142 reservation agents in their call center handling calls from travel agencies. Shortening the time a caller spends waiting is essential. The average time that a travel agent spends waiting before a disconnect is just 15 seconds. There are a lot of cruise lines out there.

Carnival installed an ACD called Infoswitch by Teknekron, in Fort Worth, Texas. Carnival organized their agents into groups of twelve, each with a supervisor. The ACD gives each of these supervisors a color-coded real-time display console showing what each agent is doing at any given moment. A supervisor can easily find out how much time agents spend on calls, how much time they spend working after each call and how many calls each agent handles in a period. The support to supervisors is revolutionary. The colored screen takes on an overall hue based on the various levels of business. A roving supervisor can see this overall color from a distance and react if critical thresholds are reached.

Howard Savings Bank in Livingstone, New Jersey, installed an ACD with 78 incoming lines to process calls from its 350,000 customers. Previously, the calls had gone to 75 different branches. With the new call center, call volume has gone up by 14 percent per year. The number of call abandonments had declined dramatically. On one typical busy day, more than 2,500 calls came in and only two were abandoned.

SUMMARY

- Database marketing means a lot of customer contact. One of the most effective means of contact is the telephone. Customer contact by telephone is growing faster than any other method. For successful database marketing, the telephone call center must be state-of-the-art. Why?

  - Telephone calls are expensive. You should be as efficient at handling them as possible to reduce your costs.
  - Your call center, to your customer, is your company. What your agents say and do on the telephone will determine whether the customer stays with you for a lifetime or abandons you in disgust.
  - Proper, modern equipment can help you to process more calls per hour, make your customers happier and boost your sales and service.

- You will need an Automatic Call Distributor (ACD) which unclogs the telephone lifelines that stand between you and your

customers. It distributes incoming calls among available telephone agents, and provides efficient reporting systems so that
you can manage your agents and calls effectively.

■ You will probably need Automatic Number Identification
(ANI) and Dialed Number Identification (DNIS). You will also
probably need automatic attendants that ask your callers to select the department they want to speak to by pushing buttons.

■ Finding good agents is always a problem. There are three solutions: 1) Locate your call center where the agents are, rather
than where you are. This may mean Utah or Nebraska. 2) You
may try splitting your call center up into several decentralized
centers linked by switching equipment. 3) You may find it
more practical to contract with a telemarketing firm to staff and
manage a call center for you.

■ Call centers will cost you about a half a million dollars per year
for every ten agents. Depending on what you are selling and
how you manage, that translates into about $2.50 per incoming
call.

■ ACD units should be used to route your calls, even before answering them. Using ANI and DNIS you can figure out who
the caller should be talking to, and put the call through directly
to the salesman, dealer, service unit or Gold Card Response
Unit, rather than making the caller tell you that after you have
answered.

Chapter 18

"In Six to Eight Weeks"

The ultimate test of the usefulness of any marketing database from the customer's point of view is the fulfillment system. How fast can you respond to a telephone call or letter with the catalog, the sample or the product that is ordered? In your customers' eyes, all your computers, software, soft-talking sales representatives and personalized direct mail are worthless if you cannot deliver what they want when they want it.

General Electric is one of the leaders in this field. In 1980, they decided to set up a customer service operation that would be second to none. They tackled a field which is one of the most difficult to deal with in any industry: spare parts for appliances. You know how tough this is. Something breaks on your refrigerator, washing machine or dryer. You need a part. You cannot describe it properly, and you have no idea of where to go for it. The dealer you bought it from is probably a discount house which no longer stocks the model you bought, and doesn't keep spare parts anyway—that is why he can afford to discount. You are on your own.

If you look in the yellow pages and are lucky enough to live in a major metropolitan area, you will probably find an appliance parts warehouse on the other side of town. Their hours are from 7:00 A.M. to 3:30 P.M. Monday through Friday. They don't deliver and they don't take phone orders. You take a day off from work, travel across town, wait in line, work with an employee who peers at a dozen

microfiche transparencies, and finally tells you that the part you
want is probably a GGH223-033YY-3310, which costs $26.30 and
will have to be special-ordered. You can pick it up here in six to
eight weeks; you'll get a post card when it arrives.

The alternative is to take a couple of days off from work to
wait at home for a repairman who, when he comes, has to special-
order the same part for you with the same six- to eight-week delay,
charging you $26.30 plus $120 for his two visits.

How did GE tackle this seemingly impossible problem? With a
parts database and a super customer service attitude. They built the
GE Answer Center at Louisville, Kentucky, where a well-trained
staff of 250 answer three million telephone calls a year from people
who are considering buying a GE product, or who have already
bought one and need a part or information. When you call their nationwide 800 number, you get an intelligent sounding operator who
has at hand the diagrams and parts lists of everything that GE has
ever made. The part number and price is quickly determined. the
operator takes your name and address and credit card number, then
tells you that your part will be delivered to you by UPS within three
days. The operator is electronically connected with four GE parts
warehouses throughout the country.

To make such service effective, GE has unusually good software and unusually well-trained employees. Each of their candidates
has to memorize 120 product lines and over 8,500 models. A college
degree is mandatory. After five weeks of training, they begin work.
They receive 100 hours of additional refresher training every year.
Turnover is very low, and GE Answer Center employees stay in 'the
family' for many years.

The GE Answer Center is the brainchild of N. Powell Taylor,
who has managed it since its doors opened. He figures that each call
costs an average of $4, but that the center generates multiple times
that in sales, profits and savings, since the calls help the company
avoid service calls for products under warranty. Their trained employees can often explain to people over the telephone how to operate their new appliances and how to make simple repairs.

Pre-purchase inquiries represent 25 percent of the calls. The center knows the complete GE line with colors, sizes and specifications. They can also direct the caller to the nearest GE dealers.

You may be wondering what they do with these three million names per year. In 10 years, they could have built up a tremendous database of people owning or interested in GE products. Actually, there is no database. Names are retained only long enough to assure that the parts are delivered on time, or that the complaint is resolved. N. Powell Taylor says that GE is interested in using the center only to provide information, parts and service to customers and would-be customers. "We don't believe in sending junk mail to the people who call us," he explains. So callers do not receive anything beyond what they have requested—no catalogs, no promotional literature. And the names are not turned over to GE dealers. Whether this is sound marketing policy, I will let the reader judge. There is no question, however, that GE is providing probably the best customer service provided by any major corporation in America.

HOW DO THEY DO IT?

Rapid fullfillment of orders which may seem from the outside like a fairly simple and straightforward process is really quiet complicated. The secret of success is tight system integration. In any database operation, there are at least a dozen separate functions that have to be closely linked together electronically to make things happen fast. The following diagram, prepared by MCRB, a leading fulfillment house with warehouses on both coasts, illustrates the complexity of the operation.

MCRB guarantees 48 hours order processing, or the order is free. At the top of the diagram, customer orders are received either by mail, by the client's 800 customer service, by MRCB's telemarketers or by an outside telemarketing company. Orders have to be processed electronically: the items are called up on the screen and orders are entered directly into the computer along with the customer's name, address and credit card number. All these services must be linked electronically with MCRB.

In the event of mail orders which may include cash, checks or money orders, MCRB has to check the order, collect and deposit the remittance, and enter the order into the computer within a matter of hours after opening the mail each day.

Credit cards are verified and automatic deposits made to the client's accounts by an outside credit card authorization company in another state, with the action taking place at electronic speed. Several quality control steps take place during the first day to assure that the customer is actually getting what he or she ordered, and that the amount remitted or charged is the correct amount.

All during this process there are decision branches (not enough remittance, incorrect item number, incorrect quantity, bad credit card). These errors are flagged to customer service for prompt follow-up with the customer to explain why the order cannot be filled as promised.

Day Two: Processing the Qualified Orders

At the end of the first twenty-four hours, the order has been qualified. That means that the payment has been assured, the item number is correct, the ship-to address is confirmed. The second day is equally hectic.

MCRB has two fulfillment centers, one in California, one in Maryland. Each must be stocked with inventory from the client. The computer will decide which center ships the item: the one closest to the customer, unless that center is out of stock.

Shipping labels and packing slips are automatically generated. The inventory system must be posted to show the drawdown of items. And even at that stage the customer could call up and cancel the order, or ask for a change in the quantity or color. The system has to be responsive up to the last minute. The warehouse must stock both client's products and packing materials. The labeling system, therefore, must be so designed to tell the packers what type of carton or bag or envelope to ship the item in—and this brings up a whole new database function: multi-pack.

Figure 18-1 MCRB Diagram

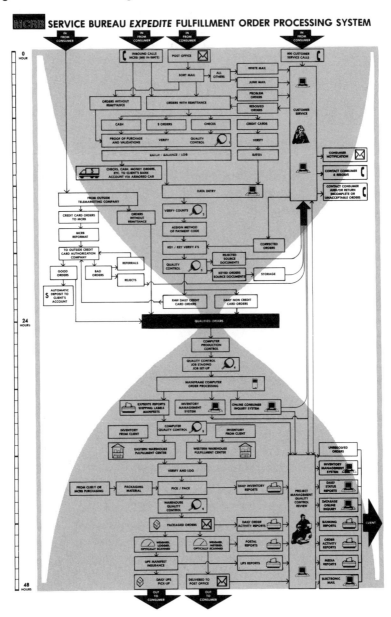

Packing Several Items to a Box

You can order one item or a dozen. They can be the same, or all different shapes, sizes and weights. No matter what you order, to save shipping costs, they should all go out in the same UPS box, if possible. To assure that this happens, the computer should store the dimensions and weights of all products in the warehouse, plus the capacities of all containers. The computer determines which container to use, and what goes in it. A label is generated for each container. If what you ordered won't fit in one box, the computer will select two appropriately sized boxes, and generate labels and packing slips for each.

The last step is the UPS manifest. This is a computer-generated report that tells UPS every day all the items that they are to pick up, where they are to go, how much they weigh and what UPS zone the customers lie in, in relation to the warehouse.

Once or twice or several times a day, UPS trucks back up to the loading ramp and take on hundreds or thousands of packages. Some items go by U.S. mail. Others go by Federal Express. The customers, the client or the product may determine the routing.

But shipment is not the end of the process. Daily reports must be run: back order reports, inventory reports, status reports, banking reports (credit cards, checks, returns, bad checks and so on), order activity reports and source code reports (which media ad or type of customer call produced which orders). These daily reports are vital to let both the client and the fulfillment house know exactly what is happening: where things need improvement, where the problems are, where the profit is.

How Things Are Usually Done

Most fulfillment operations are not like GE or MCRB. Most of them are really pretty sloppy, and heedless of their impact on customers. We did business with one fulfillment house that was supposed to send out samples to people calling an 800 number. Two months after the program started, we visited their warehouse to fix a printer connection. We noticed stacks of labels that had been Federal Expressed to them every day since the program began. There were thousands of them. Some were covered with a little layer of dust.

"What are all those labels doing there?" we asked.

"Those are just for samples. We thought that the priority was to get out the paid orders. so we have concentrated on that. Paid orders go out within a couple of days."

Eye-balling the samples, we could see that there were about 100,000 sample orders sitting there. A part of our direct marketing test program was designed to determine how many people who received samples converted to paid products and how long it took. Of course, our statistics were worthless since most people ordering samples either never got them or got them two to three months late. We fired the fulfillment house, but the test was ruined.

How common is this experience? Consider these statistics (collected by Ray O'Brien for Inquiry Systems and Analysis, a Boston fulfillment bureau, and reported in *Inbound Outbound*):

20 % of inquirers never receive information
40 % of inquirers receive information too late to use it.
70 % of inquirers are never contacted by a sales representative.

Why is this so? Part of the answer is sloppy fulfillment. The rest is due to the attitude of the sales staff towards DM-generated sales leads: they don't think that most leads are worth the effort. But consider these further statistics (from Ray O'Brien):

60 % of all inquirers purchase something within a year
20 % of inquirers have an immediate need
10 % are hot leads
60 % of inquirers also contact your competitors
50 % of all new business starts as an inquiry.
Conclusion: If you don't react immediately, you will lose sales.

When we recently needed an exhibition booth for a convention, I replied to two ads from an in-flight magazine, both of which advertised the type of booth required. One company contacted me within a week. A saleswoman from the company visited us very soon thereafter. Three weeks later we bought her booth. The week after we had signed a contract I got a catalog from the second company. We filed it. A month after that, an executive from the second company called me on the phone to learn of my reaction to their catalog. I told the executive that I had already bought from a competitor, and that he was much too late with his response. He had wasted the money he spent on the in-flight advertisement and had the wrong fulfillment house.

What Should You Do?

Fulfillment is often the weak link in your database marketing system. If you can't fulfill a customer's request rapidly, all the rest of your database system is really wasted effort. To make database marketing a reality, you must set standards for fulfillment and live up to them. What should those standards be? As far as I can see, you should have your response (product, sample, catalog, letter) out the door in 48 hours or less. This is an achievable goal. Many companies are living up to it today. In our program for fulfillment of pet food, we achieved a 24-hour out-the-door record on a sustained basis, so I know it can be done. Yet most companies still advertise shipment in six to eight weeks, and are content with it.

What does it take to assure 48-hour out-the-door fulfillment?

1. *Set the standard.* Let everyone in your organization know what your standard is. Get daily reports and circulate them. Give awards for timesaving ideas. Make everyone time conscious.

2. *Get a rapid data-entry system.* Study your data capture methods. Most of them can be improved.

Some companies send their inquiries to Jamaica or India for keypunching, thus cutting the data entry costs by fifty percent or more. Of course, the time consumed may be more than a month. To decide whether the delay is significant, you should analyze how much business is generated from these inquiries and how much business is lost through late fulfillment. It could be that the dollars saved through offshore data entry are dwarfed by the cost to you of lost sales.

Some companies have developed creative solutions to the data entry problem. A major software house uses order forms designed for the Tartan X-80, a scanning machine created by Recognition Equipment, Inc. of Dallas, Texas. The order forms are printed on 8 1/2 by 11 inch paper with light colored blue squares for the customer to fill in name, address and other information. The Tartan X-80 has the capability of reading handwriting in pen or pencil. The mailshop opens envelopes and feeds forms into the hopper of the X-80, which reads at a constant rate of sixty forms a minute. It takes an electronic picture of the form as is reads it. If there is any letter or number on the input form that the machine cannot read, it flashes an alert to the two or three data entry clerks located in offices adjacent to the machine. The clerk sees the photograph of the form which the machine could not read, together with a little arrow pointing to the blue square with the questionable letter. The clerk enters the correct number, and the machine speeds on.

Delays by the data entry clerks do not slow down the X-80: it keeps reading at a constant speed. The errors accumulate on a disk, waiting for the clerks to correct them.

Why this system? Because it is a very cost effective way of getting product out the door in twenty-four hours. And twenty-four hours service is vital to maintaining the validity of database marketing.

If you study data entry techniques needed to achieve forty-eight hour fulfillment, you will probably conclude that you will be successful only with an outside service bureau or telemarketer who can handle your peak loads, has a lower wage scale and has the experience to move as fast as you need to move.

3. *Tie your data entry to your payment system electronically.* There are several services nationwide that will give you instant turnaround on credit card authorization and posting. All you have to do is write the software to link up with them, and make the link an automatic part of your ordering system.

Handling checks is more difficult. There is no instant way to learn if a check is good. You will have to decide whether to accept small value checks without waiting for clearance, and to hold orders over a certain value until the check clears.

4. *Use an outside fulfillment bureau.* There are two reasons why you should go outside rather than use your own company warehouse: time and money.

If you are a large package goods company, most of your current business comes from servicing large distributors and retail stores. Your warehouse operates in carloads or skids. The minimum order is a carton. Your employees are well paid.

But database marketing involves, typically, sending single orders to individual customers. The whole pace of the operation is different. You will need a different type of employee with a different concept of the job. You will soon find that the pay scale and incentive wage for your warehouse employees do not jibe with the system you need to set up to service your direct customers. You may find that the best way to assure twenty-four hour turnaround is to have a super-sophisticated computer system with automatically generated packing lists, labels and manifests, combined with a large group of minimum wage employees working long hours and chattering away in a language that you can't understand.

Trying to introduce this type of operation into your company warehouse may be difficult and costly. Better to go to one of the hundreds of professional fulfillment houses that are used to single orders, fast service and low-wage employees. You will get the orders out faster and keep your costs down.

5. *Spend the money on good computer software.* Fast turnaround is the result of streamlined operations where computers do most of the thinking and most of the work. Diagram out your ideal system just as MCRB has done. Try

to keep paper flow to an absolute minimum. Use an outside
service bureau to write the software, and run your system
on their equipment.

6. *Keep your eye on the ball.* Getting literature, samples or
products out the door in 24 hours is only one objective of
fulfillment. The other objective is sales: converting samples
and literature into orders, and converting product shipments
into repeat business. In many cases, the "Constructors" who
are busy setting up a super fulfillment operation lose sight
of the objective of the operation: to make a profit.

Making a profit requires closing the loop: every outgoing communication has to have a planned incoming response, preferably an
order. How is this accomplished?

- Make sure that every outgoing product or sample package contains literature and an order form. Put source codes on the order
forms so that you know which orders resulted from "bounce
backs."

- Build in an automatic follow-up system for all outgoing goods
and messages which invites customers to tell you how they
liked the service, and asks them for additional orders. Your
computer must be programmed to know when to drop that follow-up message. Again, code the order forms.

- Spot-check your system with telemarketing follow-up in such a
way that you can find out what you do well, and what you do
poorly.

We set up a fulfillment system for one client which did result
in 24-hour turnaround. But for the first six months, he didn't get
around to designing any order forms to accompany his outgoing
products and samples. By the time the order forms were printed, the
client's management was ready to scrap the program because of the
failure of repeat orders. Only by pointing out that repeat business
had not yet really been given a chance were we able to keep the
program going long enough for it to prove itself (which it did).

SUMMARY

- Fulfillment is the most important part of database marketing from the customer's point of view. To be successful, you must get catalogs, literature, samples and products out the door in 48 hours or less.

- To accomplish this, you must set up an integrated system that links electronically:
  - cashiering (opening envelopes and extracting orders and re-mittances)
  - telemarketing sales and customer service calls
  - data entry of orders, names, addresses, credit card numbers
  - authorization and deposit of credit card accounts
  - verifying and posting inventory
  - creating packing slips, labels, shipping manifests
  - determining what type of packing materials to use
  - warehouse fulfillment operations
  - daily reports on your operations.

- To achieve 48-hour fulfillment you will need to:
  - set high standards and stick to them
  - get a rapid data-entry system, probably at a service bureau
  - get automatic credit card verification
  - use an outside fulfillment bureau
  - use an outside database management service bureau.

- To make your operation profitable, you need to close the loop: make every fulfillment action the beginning of another order cycle by including literature and order forms in with the outgoing fulfillment. Keep track of source codes, and report on every action that you take.

Part Five

Operating a Marketing Database: Two Case Studies

Chapter 19

A Direct Marketing Database: A Case Study

In this chapter we are going to try something different. We will go behind the scenes and recount the construction and operation of a marketing database from scratch. We will try to tell it all, the good and the bad, so you can see what actually happened.

The marketing database I am describing is a real one, but to protect the source I have made changes in some of the locations and the description of the product. Everything described really happened.

The goal was to introduce a health food for adults direct to the consumer. The competition was selling this food in major stores. Selling direct would bypass the huge expenses needed to advertise and establish the health food throughout the store distribution network. For the customer, it had two advantages: home delivery and automatic shipment every month without having to call in orders.

The San Francisco-based company worked on the concept with their direct advertising agency for almost a year before the launch. Sufficient budget was set aside for the two years needed to get started. They knew that they needed a database, but it took them some time to find someone to create the database. When they did, it was almost too late.

The plan was to begin direct mail and print advertising in certain limited regions in January. The product had been designed, packaging was arranged, creative copy for the ads and the direct mail were being designed. In September they selected a company to set up the database.

The job was a very significant one for the service bureau selected. By the time they got the contract, there were only ninety days left to create the design, write the software, buy and install the equipment and train everyone on it. Fortunately, the service bureau had sufficient resources to devote about six systems designers and programmers to the project full time.

As the program developed, it involved a number of different customer service operations in states from coast to coast. The computer which held the database was in Texas. Directly connected with the computer by leased lines were the telemarketing operators in Colorado. The credit card verification was done by a bank in New Jersey. The warehouse was located in Chicago. A central accounting unit and product management were located in San Francisco as well as the creative agency. All of these units were to be on-line every day entering and receiving data from the database.

TELEMARKETER'S SOFTWARE

The first step was writing the software for the telemarketers who would be taking the incoming calls on an 800 number. This was a new experience for the telemarketers. A large, well established company, the telemarketers had been using their own proprietary software system for several years. They were taking calls for dozens of different clients. As the calls would come in, the operators on duty could tell by the number called which product the customer was interested in: encyclopedias, bibles, clothing. Their software presented each operator with screens to take the name, address, phone number and credit card information; then pop-up windows would prompt the telemarketer to ask the customer to select the color, style, size and so on of the product desired, plus showing the costs involved. Each day, all the orders taken for each client were put on tape and sent to the client companies for fulfillment. The computer

Figure 19-1 Database Links Many Organizations

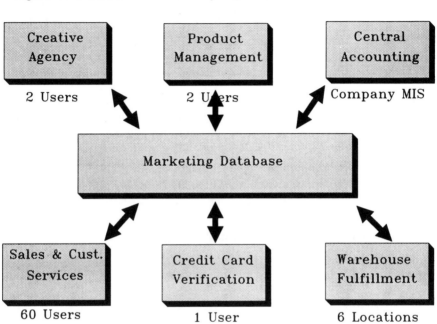

used was owned by the telemarketing company and operated from their headquarters. It was a highly efficient, cost-effective marketing system—but it was not the system chosen for the new product.

For the health food, the database was set up on a very large relational database in Texas. The database was designed not only to take order information, but also to serve as a complete marketing database once the orders were received. Telemarketers therefore would be able to retrieve and view the complete purchase history of all callers: when they had called last, what they ordered, the names of the adults in the family that were consuming the health food, any problems they had and so on.

It was a completely new experience for the telemarketers. Special training was arranged for more than 100 of them in the nutritional needs of young, middle-aged and elderly adults, with special attention to the thin and the overweight. They had to know about side effects of overconsumption of the product and a host of other important facts about nutrition in the home. The telemarketers became "Nutrition Advisors."

LONG PHONE CALLS

Whereas the main concern for the telemarketers handling other products had been to get the order and get off as fast as possible, the new system was designed to build up a long-term relationship with the customer *right from the start*. That meant that telemarketers were encouraged to talk longer on the telephone and to extract a lot of information from the customer which was to be entered permanently into the database. They tried to build bonds between the customers

Figure 19-2 Database Users Span the Continent

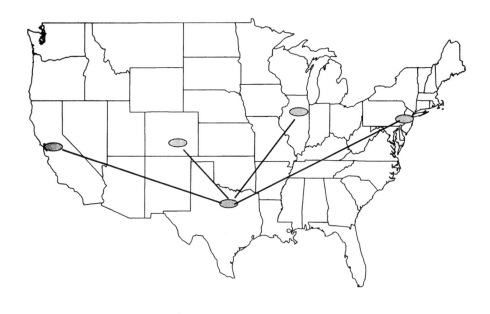

Figure 19-3 Products Shipped Next Day

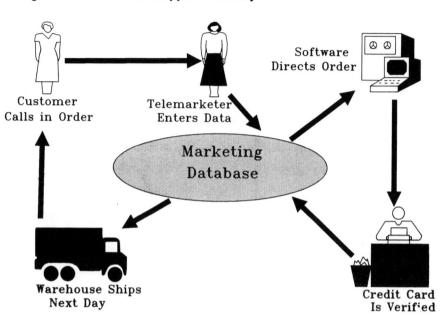

Customer
Calls in Order

Telemarketer
Enters Data

Software
Directs Order

Marketing
Database

Warehouse Ships
Next Day

Credit Card
Is Verif'ed

and the Nutrition Advisors by having the customers know their Advisors and ask for them on repeat calls. This led to the development of several different schemes for compensating telemarketers, which they continued to experiment with for many months.

The other difficulty for the telemarketers was working with the new database software. The fact was that at first, the software designed by the service bureau did not permit the telemarketers to work fast enough. It delayed them in their calls. There was a learning curve for the software developers in this process.

The original software was built around a system which is used in leading hospitals for entry of patients. It showed a customer entry screen with blocks to be filled in:

FIRST NAME_____ LAST NAME_____

STREET ADDRESS_____

CITY_____ STATE_____ ZIP_____

TELEPHONE_____CARD TYPE _____ CARD #_____

The software was set up so the telemarketers could tab quickly from field to field using the tab key. Additional screens for taking orders worked in the same way, with pop-up windows for the product list and such. At the top of the screen was the *script*: the words that the telemarketer would say to customers when they called.

THE FAST PATH

It probably works wonderfully for hospitals, but it wasn't fast enough for telemarketing. After six months, the screens were entirely revamped. They developed what they called "the fast path." In this system, the operator worked with a "command line" at the bottom of the screen. Everything was entered there in a random order, which could be changed by entering "slash commands." The new system was set up so that the operators could type as fast as the information came to them on the call: there was no waiting for screens to come up. The command line looked something like this:

Cmd>_____

To enter a new customer, the operator typed something like this:

Cmd>CT/MR./CF/ARTHUR/CL/HUGHES/CS/3014 RIDGE ROAD/CC/HAYMARKET

One return code could properly place all of that information in the database and free up the command line for the next group of data. The operators had to remember that CT/ meant customer title; CF/ meant customer first name; and so on. Pop-up windows were used to refresh the operator's memory of the "slash commands," which were easy to memorize and greatly speeded up the entry of data. If the customer began talking along a different line than expected (such as by giving a credit card number) the slash commands made it very easy—the operator just entered CA/VISA/CN/ 1234567812345678.

Meanwhile the script, at the top of the screen, had to keep up with what was going on at the bottom of the screen (rather than the other way around) so that the operator didn't forget to record the family members' names, the expiration date of the credit card or other information.

Health clubs and spas were targeted by a special database, and encouraged to recommend the product to their clients. This meant additional software and special mailings and telemarketing to these institutions. Commissions were provided to them for sales made to customers to whom they recommended the health food. That required having the code for the club in the customer's database record, so that when the customer made a purchase the club would get the credit. Also required were quarterly reports to the participating clubs on their customers' activity.

NEIGHBOR REFERRALS

Customers were encouraged to recommend the product to their neighbors. They received a credit on their own orders if the people they recommended purchased the product. All this had to be entered into the database, and software written to show the credit automatically whenever a customer ordered new product.

Whenever there was telephone contact with the customer, the date, time of day and nature of the call were recorded in the database so that the advisor could know about and refer back to previous problems or comments in subsequent calls. As much as possible the goal was to use the information in the system to strengthen the bond between the nutrition advisor and the individual customer. The database contained complete information on all orders, whether called in or generated automatically by the system.

The advisor could see the exact time that each order was shipped and any problems that may have come up.

If you called the 800 number, they would take your order and credit card number. That night, the database automatically sent all credit card orders generated that day to the New Jersey bank where the cards were automatically verified. One hour later all the orders came back, and the database made up delivery labels for the next day. At 5:00 each morning the warehouse received a set of labels for the products to be shipped, together with UPS manifests covering the shipment. As a result, anything ordered the day before was on a UPS truck for delivery the day after.

Demand Exceeded Expectations

Of course, as soon as the program was launched demand exceeded supply, so that the warehouse ran out of some of the products. Back to the drawing board to develop software to handle selective back-ordering: a portion of an order is shipped, and the balance sent automatically when it arrives.

Even after the system was going well, problems continued to crop up. Media placed ads, in some cases, without adequate warning in advance to the telemarketers. As a result they were swamped with thousands more calls than they expected; some people got a busy signal and were probably lost.

At first, the system was programmed for one label per order. Too much money was being spent on UPS costs, so they developed multi-pack software: software which knew all the sizes and weights of all the 40+ products and the sizes of the available standard packages. Complicated mathematics went into determining which product to pack into which box to minimize UPS charges while still keeping the health food well-packed.

Every morning the database cranked out accounting data which was automatically posted to the proper accounts in the central accounting system in San Francisco. In addition, the database produced about forty pages of detailed reports which were printed out by product management and creative in their offices.

Report Happy

Reports, of course, are one of the key outputs of a marketing database. From the start, the system produced reports by source code: which direct mail piece, which print ad, which television ad, which referral process generated this particular customer. To determine this, each different advertisement listed a different extension to request; the extension was the source code. As you can imagine, not all the telemarketers were able to enter all the source codes in the rush of getting all the data about the customer and the order. Some customers could not remember their source codes.

Reports were developed on nutrition advisors to determine how much business each one was bringing in. They also kept track in the database of how long each advisor was on the telephone. An advisor who talked for a long time on each call might actually be doing a very good job, if his or her sales were greater than average.

One important report measured customers by entry day. This report was used to determine the lifetime value of a customer. How long did this customer stay with the program? How much product did he or she buy per month?

There were reports on average order size, average order weight, orders by product, orders by warehouse. There were reports on bad credit cards, returns, canceled orders. But the most closely watched reports were those on buyers, samplers and converters.

Samplers Rarely Buy

At first, the program was designed around a concept: people called up and ordered a free sample. As a result of the success of the sample, the customer would place an initial order of product. Eventually, the customer would get tired of calling every month and would ask for automatic delivery, with the product charged to their credit card without a call.

Wonderful theory, but it didn't work out that way. In the first place, it became clear after a few months from the reports that samplers rarely bought and buyers rarely sampled. There were two kinds of people in the world, apparently: people who were interested in buying a health food and people who were interested in getting something for nothing. They were mutually exclusive.

The reports disclosed this, and permitted the company to make a major shift in their creative strategy away from samples and onto premiums with first order. The other problem with samples was that, from the start, they were not geared up to ship the samples fast enough. So much attention was focused on getting the warehouse to ship product *the next day* after the order that everyone assumed the samples (which were sent out by an independent fulfillment house) would also be sent quickly. Unfortunately, the fulfillment house had worked too long in the television environment ("allow six to eight weeks for delivery"); they delayed delivery of the samples by several months, so that many of the statistics on behavior of samplers were flawed, since most of the samples came very late or never arrived at all.

Conversion to Automatic Delivery

The biggest problem disclosed by the reports was that people were not converting to automatic shipments as the planners assumed that they would. Many did convert, but many others continued to buy from month to month, using up valuable telemarketing dollars with each order. Still others dropped out, and went back to buying food at their supermarket. Clearly, if the program was to be a success, there would have to be more automatic purchasers.

The program designers tried many techniques to encourage automatic ordering before they finally hit on the right one. From the start, they offered a dollar credit for going on the automatic plan. This helped, but not enough. They used outbound direct mail to encourage the shift, plus outbound telemarketing. They gave telemarketers themselves a bonus for conversions. This proved to be the most effective strategy, and gave the marketers the clue to the real answer, which when they tried it, proved to be so simple that they felt a little foolish for not having thought of it in the first place.

The planners finally decided to continue the ads exactly as before, offering a health food with home delivery, but when the caller reached the nutrition advisor on the telephone the script was altered in a way that created an underlying, unstated but pervasive impression that this was strictly an automatic program. Your family could not get much long-term benefit out of a couple of meals of this wonderful product: to do any lasting good, your family had to consume it with some regularity over a period of many months or years.

The nutrition advisors were suitably rewarded for each customer signed to the automatic program, with much lesser rewards bestowed for signing up a single order buyer. The effect was dramatic. Whereas for the first year the manufacturer was lucky to get a couple of automatic customers out of a hundred initial buyers (with some of them converting in subsequent months), with the new system, most days a *majority* of the initial buyers signed up for automatic delivery, *and stayed with it.*

This is an important lesson for database marketers. You are alone on the telephone with the customer, one-on-one. You know what you want to say. You have a script and experience. The customer is making up conversation as you go along. If you have a good product or service, and you believe in it, it is pretty easy to convince most people to accept your offer right then and there. Waiting for people to sit at home and decide to convert to automatic delivery all on their own without help flies in the face of all the theories of human behavior.

The marketing database enabled the company to make the customer the center of attention. In addition to inbound telemarketers, there were customer service advisors with access to the database and outbound telemarketers. The outbound advisors called any customer who had canceled automatic service and had not renewed after a certain period of time. The customer's number was provided automatically by the database, which displayed the complete customer history. Creative software was needed to decide when a customer should be called, and to produce reports on the outbound process to be sure that the effort was paying off. The critical question, of course, was to decide when to call. Wait until 45 days had gone by since the last order? Compute when the current order will be used up, and call then? You don't want to call too early (waste money) or too late (they had gotten used to some other type of health food, and you have lost them.)

Of course, with a marketing database, you can devise and apply structured tests with these numbers until you think that you have got it just right. Important to this process are the views of the telemarketers. They are very close to the customers. They can tell you whether the latest offer or marketing wrinkle is working or not. The company was very open to suggestions from everyone participating in the program: customer service, inbound telemarketers, warehouse staff, creative and even computer programmers.

The Product Manager

This brings us to the role of the product manager. The manager serves as the director of the entire process, much like the captain of a large ship. The company was fortunate that their manager was very much a hands-on manager. Every day he scrutinized forty pages of reports that the database cranked out. There were constant telephone calls from his office to telemarketers, to customer service, to the database service bureau, to the warehouse, to accounting, to the creative agency. "Why has the average order size dropped?" "Why are people in the South recommending our product to neighbors, but that is not happening in New England?" "What is the reason for the dropoff in third-time buyers?" "When will you have the revision in the sales tax routine ready?"

A dozen calls a day. A dozen projects launched not only to answer the questions, but to fix what went wrong that prompted the question. It kept everyone on their toes: but it would not have been possible if everyone had not had the database as a pool of common information to use in finding out what was happening and what should be done to fix it.

As a result of this constant hands-on management, the programmers had to change the software just about once a day, five days a week, for the first year. Changing the software was not easy. The service bureau maintained two databases: a production database and a test database. All new software was written for the test database. They would introduce the change, and then run several sample orders through the test database to be sure that the changes did not cause some unforeseen and unexpected change in some other part of the database or ordering system. When the programming staff was

Figure 19-4 40 Different Reports Produced Daily

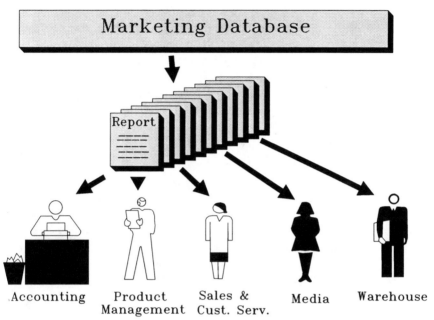

confident that the new change was correct, they would shift it to the production database *between three and four in the morning.* They had to operate at night because those were the only hours when no one was on the system. Colorado operators stopped taking calls at 11:00 P.M., which is midnight Texas computer time. At that hour, the credit card verifications were sent to the bank. They came back one hour later. Beginning at 4:00 A.M., data was transmitted to the company's central accounting unit for retransmission to the warehouse.

Also taking place at 3:00 A.M. was a nightly extract from the system for the standard reports. The database reports could, of course, be run all day long, but that produced a problem. During the day the database was being updated and changed every minute. As people called in their orders, questions, cancellations and such, the information went into the database. Any report run at 10:00 A.M. would have different totals from a report run at 11:00 A.M. It was impossible to check one fact against another. As a result, they discovered that they had to run all reports from an extract that the system ran the night before, so that all 40 pages of reports would be consistent and show the same totals.

Then there was the problem of down time. Computers are always going down for one reason or another. When the computer did go down, 40 screens would go blank all at once in the telemarketing operation. Telemarketers' telephones keep working, but the operators had to take notes on paper, waiting to enter the information until their screens came back on. Of course, as soon as the screens went blank, the telephone calls started from the telemarketers, and then from product management. "How soon will we be back up?" That is usually an almost impossible question to answer, because at first you have no idea why you have gone down. If you knew why you had gone down, you probably would not have gone down at all, because to know why is also to know what is happening and how to prevent it from happening. To provide what later proved to be trouble-free and permanent service, they installed an uninterruptable power supply with a back-up diesel generator. They installed redundant communications gear. But most of the down time was due to software: database overload.

Database Software Overload

Relational databases are very complex. The company was maintaining *indexes* on about 40 different items in the database. (For a more complete discussion of indexes in the database, see Chapter Four. This meant that every time they updated a customer's record as a result of an order or a telephone call, they probably updated 40 different indexes.

Each index is a disk record; a little database of its own. Space needs to be provided for all the records in the database and all the indexes. Sometimes inadequate space is available for one of the many indexes as a result of some unforeseen development. When an index is compromised, the database nucleus registers this fact and brings the entire database down.

Unfortunately, the database is not always able to tell you where the problem is. Diagnostic software must be run to find that out, and this takes time. Sometimes you have a good idea where to look, and you find and correct the problem in a few minutes. Sometimes it takes hours or days. Of course, while you are down, customer calls continue to come in which cannot be processed normally; orders do not go to the warehouse; credit cards do not get verified. Everyone is edgy and angry. But after a few months' experience virtually all of these early software problems are solved, and subsequent years have been virtually trouble-free.

Program Errors

The company's program did have its share of errors. The software for such a database is extremely complex and interrelated. Sometimes a programmer would make one simple little change, something as simple as changing the system for generating automatic reorders to correct some small problem. Everything seemed fine in the test database. It was tested several ways. Fine—no problem. The next day at 3:00 A.M. the change was put on the production database. No problem—everything was normal. The next morning, scanning the daily reports, it seemed that there was an unusually large number of automatic orders, many more than normal. The software was generating bogus orders. Fortunately, they were able to spot and correct these problems before any serious damage was done. They learned that anything unusual must be examined instantly. When it turned out that the minor change in the software resulted in some customers getting double shipments automatically generated, they were able to stop the whole process and not ship anything at all until the problem was corrected.

This type of problem did not happen often. But whenever it happened, it was a crisis. Of course it is easy to say that it happened because not enough testing was done or the software change was not thoroughly thought through. All true. But the dynamic nature of marketing databases means that it is going to happen again. There is seldom time to write perfect software and test it in every conceivable situation before it becomes part of the production system. Product management is constantly making changes, improvements, experiments. Database managers have to be responsive to the market; they have to take the heat or else get out of the kitchen.

Customer Service and Follow Up

All customers who had product delivered received direct mail follow-ups with personal laser letters directed to the householders: "We hope that you and your family enjoyed your latest shipment of _____." Automatic follow-ups also took place for failure to renew. At first, everyone was so busy getting the product out the door that there was no time to plan the direct mail follow-up or the telemarketing to those who did not buy a second time. A marketing database is so complex that it is extremely difficult to plan all the actions in all details in the beginning, faced as you are by constant shifts and changes in marketing strategy as you see that one thing works and another does not.

Because everyone involved in the program across the country was tied in to the database, this database became the heart of the whole program. Creative staff were able to see the effect of their latest TV advertisements as the calls came in; the effect of print ads and direct mail could be clearly spotted. In addition to standard reports, all of the various participants were able to carry out ad-hoc queries, to find answers from the database to specific questions:

- How many customers in Tennessee called up to order in the last forty-eight hours?

- What percentage of people who responded to TV were renewing as opposed to the percentage who came through print or direct mail?

- How many people in Illinois had complained about late deliveries?

All these queries and hundreds more could be directed at the database while it was doing its basic recording and fulfillment job. In addition, the database was used to predict sales and staffing requirements in telemarketing on weekends, holidays and odd hours. The company was able to conduct studies of customer attrition and retention, and to measure the success of various promotions and marketing changes on a daily basis.

Expansion of the Product Line

One inevitable effect of database marketing is the growth in the number of different products that you handle. By talking one-on-one with each customer and by studying your daily reports, you come to realize rapidly what people want in the way of modifications in your service and product line. The company's program started with a few standard products of the mix-with-milk variety. It wasn't long before customers began to ask for more: cookies, a dry cereal and a special formula for people who were trying to put on weight. They even added electronic scales, since weight was considered so important by the customers. Why did they introduce these new products? Because they could retain some customers that way. Not only were they the best health food on the market, they were also the only one with all those special features. Fighting for shelf space for all those varieties in a supermarket would be a hopeless battle. Finding space in their warehouse for these products was a pleasure.

Check Customers

From the beginning, the program relied on Visa and Mastercard as the main payment options. In fact, without these two ubiquitous cards, database marketing would not exist. After a year they added American Express. But also, from the beginning, they accepted checks as payment. But checks were a problem from the start.

The problem is twofold. You take the person's order on the telephone, and then you wait for the check to arrive. When it does arrive, you must match the check to the outstanding order, and then release the order after being sure that the check is good. The result is a lot of waiting, and slow delivery to the customer. The other problem, of course, is that many people call to order but never get around to sending in the check.

One answer is to send an invoice for the order as soon as the customer calls: don't wait for the check. This gives the customer a reminder to send in the check along with a correctly addressed return envelope. This is fairly effective, but it is expensive and slow.

Another answer is to take a chance and ship the product on schedule, with invoices after the fact requesting payment. This works very well for those who agree to automatic deliveries.

Check handling is expensive because as each check arrives, someone in customer service has to find the customer in the database and post the order to show that the check has arrived. Once the order has been "released" in this way, it will be shipped the next day.

LESSONS LEARNED

At the beginning, no one anticipated the complexity of the software needed to make the database function. Ultimately there were up to forty telemarketers talking to customers at the same time. Each operator had a computer terminal with direct access to the database. Product management really managed the program with day-to-day hands-on management of every aspect of the operation.

Product management made changes in the prices, the offer, the inducement, the shipping method, the sales tax system, the products offered. The wonderful part was that since they were working with a live database, it was possible to make a management decision to make a change, tell the programmer what to do, have it done, test it thoroughly on a test database, tell the telemarketers about the change and then introduce it, all in the space of a week. For the first year this happened constantly, week after week.

The customers were very loyal. The Nutrition Advisors were very understanding, and quick to pick up on the changes needed.

The reports showed very quickly which media were working and which weren't. As a result the company was able to make fairly rapid media shifts. The reports enabled the company to make beneficial changes in the telemarketing script and the offer.

The result of all of this change was that the management was able constantly to fine tune the program and engineer a dramatic increase in customer retention levels. Because of the database and the fact that everyone was plugged into it, everyone knew what was happening. Everyone was able to make suggestions: the warehouse, the accountants, the programmers, the customer service reps, the database service bureau. The company was able to build a marketing team that made an outstanding success of what was an entirely new experimental program.

It was possible to compute the lifetime value of a customer, to deal with each customer in a truly personal way, both in outgoing letters and in telemarketing, since each nutrition advisor had the complete details of every customer contact on the screen while she was talking. This was database marketing at its best.

Chapter 20

The Business-to-Business Marketing Database

While there are many similarities, marketing business-to-business is fundamentally different from marketing to consumers. So that we can concentrate on the unique aspects of a business-to-business marketing database, let's begin by listing the differences from consumer marketing.

HOW BUSINESS-TO-BUSINESS DIFFERS FROM CONSUMER MARKETING

- Most business-to-business involves company salesmen. Much of the work of the database thus becomes lead tracking rather than direct marketing.

- Geodemographics does not work. Census data about block groups (income, age, home value, etc.) has no relevance to the businesses located in that block. Businesses are not counted in the regular census. There is a quarterly government survey of businesses which is run by the Commerce Department, but it does not provide information on individual businesses.

- For the same reasons, clustering and psychographics cannot be applied.

- In consumer marketing, you write to the head of the household. In a business mailing, you often want to reach someone special within the organization who may not be available on any list you can rent.

- Business merge/purge is fundamentally different from consumer merge/purge. Be sure your service bureau understands the difference, and has special software.

- Businesses are classified by SIC (Standard Industrial Classification) codes, a very inadequate system developed by the Department of Commerce many years ago, and updated periodically. It is inadequate because products and services are constantly changing. The government classification does not keep up. SIC attempts to define the products or services that the business supplies. Most businesses, even small ones, are covered by several different SIC codes. But, on the whole, many SIC codes are so broad that they cover hundreds of somewhat unrelated businesses.

TYPES OF BUSINESS MARKETING

Let's distinguish the various types of marketing that use a business-to-business marketing database.

Lead Generation and Tracking

In this type of operation, direct mail or advertisements result in the generation of leads. These leads are entered into a database and *qualified* by telemarketing. Those that are qualified are sent to salespeople for action. The salespeople report back to the database on their success with the leads. The database, in turn, keeps track of what has happened to the leads: contact, sale or no sale. The successful customer is posted in the marketing database and is called up periodically by telemarketers or salespeople to cross-sell or sell upgrades.

Product Launch in the Pharmaceutical Industry

An important marketing niche in ethical drugs exists because the Food and Drug Administration does not allow drug companies to advertise prescription drugs directly to the public. Instead, they must inform physicians about their new products, who, in turn, will prescribe the drugs for their patients. The role of the marketing database is to keep track of the physicians' reaction to and reception of the new drug. As part of the whole system several hundred salespeople call on the physicians, providing information back to the database on the results of their visits.

Direct Sales

Some marketing databases are used for direct sales to businesses by telemarketers. One example is providing information to customers. Customer service representatives, manning 800 numbers, receive thousands of calls from business customers. They can tell them what is available and how things work, and they can place orders directly, adding the order to the company's corporate account.

SURVEYS

What do you want to know about your customer? Most pharmaceutical firms are interested in getting their message out to a select group of physicians who specialize in treating the malady that their medicine addresses. Their salespeople make personal visits and distribute samples and monographs. What they want to know about their physicians is:

"Does the physician see many patients with this particular disease?"

"Is he or she a heavy, medium or light prescriber of the kind of medicine that we sell?"

"Does he or she prescribe our medicine, or the competition's?"

"What can we do to get physicians to change their minds and favor our medicine?"

The first three questions are factual. We might get the answers from the physician or from the nurse or receptionist. We might get the answer from a survey, from telemarketing or in a personal visit.

But that last question is the most important question. It will be difficult to get the answer from the doctor, because even he or she may not know the answer. However, the answer may be found in the database if enough relevant facts are available. Suppose that analysis shows that doctors who like your medicine are over 45, while your competition is favored by younger doctors. Or suppose that your competition is favored on the West coast, while your strength is in the East. Suppose that liberal Democrats like their product and conservative Republicans like yours. It may simply be a matter of perception: the image of your company or product in the doctor's mind which may result from his or her background, or from something that your company has done or said. There may be hundreds of different factors that are influencing the choice, some of which you can act upon.

To find out what physicians are thinking, you will have to use focus groups or other detailed analytical techniques. But to apply the ideas from this analysis to individual physicians and to change their minds, you need to use surveys and your database.

DATA YOU CAN LEARN ABOUT BUSINESSES

When you acquire a new customer or a prospect you can refer to several reference sources to add information to their database records, such as:

Where they are; telephone numbers.

What they make.

Their annual sales.

Their number of employees.

The growth in their sales from prior years.

Whether they are a division of another company.

Their principal officers.

This information is available to you from several sources including Dun's, TriNet and TRW. TRW is based on credit information. TriNet is based on the yellow pages, but it, like the others, also obtains information from surveys and other sources so that you can usually get all of the above information from any of the sources.

Matching Difficulties

A difficulty arises in matching information you may have about a business prospect or customer with any of these compiled service lists. We were called in by a major bank which had matched its customer file of 400,000 businesses with the Dun's list for the area, and only achieved an eight percent hit rate. This they thought, and we agreed, was dismal. Even in the best of situations, however, you can't expect much better than a 40 percent hit rate on business lists. And often when there is a match, the information is unreliable. Why is that?

- Businesses have many different telephone numbers and addresses. The chances of the number or address you have being the same as the one on the list you have rented are usually not much better than 50 percent.

- Some businesses don't bother to list themselves with any of the major services. They assume correctly that they are unlikely to gain any business from being listed—only solicitations.

- Many businesses who do answer Dun's or other's survey forms will lie. There is no federal law requiring truth on a business survey. If your sales are $2 million, why not say $5 million? It sounds better, especially when the bank considering your loan application may call on Dun's as a reference.

BUILDING YOUR OWN BUSINESS DATABASE

When you first decide to create a marketing database of your customers you will probably start by going to your mainframe for a list of past customers. This should be a starting point, but from the beginning you will have problems.

For instance, there is usually a ship-to address and a bill-to address. Which should you use? The answer probably is, neither! The ship-to address is often "Loading Dock 7, Warehouse Number 15." How much business you will get by mailing to that address? The bill-to address may be "Accounts Payable Department, Attn. Janet Roach." Upon investigation, you will find that Ms. Roach has no authority to buy anything, and knows nothing about the products that you sell.

The actual individual who ordered your product in the first place —and this is the person to approach for a repeat order—probably does not appear on any of the official documents. He or she is probably listed on the Rolodex of the salesperson who handled the account.

Thus, one of your first steps will be to take the list of customers from the mainframe and try to ask the salespeople to help you out in checking real contacts and telephone numbers against them. Unless you have done your homework very carefully (see Chapter 26), getting these contact names will not be easy. Yet, without them, your database won't be worth much.

If you cannot get the names from your salesforce, the next best place to try is a rented list.

RENTING BUSINESS LISTS

It is actually amazing what you can find in business lists. The information is much more specific than what you find in consumer lists. Look at a sample of what is available:

Obstetricians and Gynecologists

Office and Building Cleaners

Oil Industry Executives

Orthopedic Prosthesis Stores

Aircraft Owners

Plastics Engineers

Many of the people on these lists are just the ones to contact for a sale. Many of the lists rent for $45 per thousand for one-time use. Unfortunately, you cannot really use these names to create your database of prospects since they are for one-time use only, but if they are already your customers you can rent the list and match the company names against your customer list to find out contact names. In many cases, list owners have a second price for unlimited use which may permit you to add their names to your marketing database, providing you agree not to sell or rent the names to others.

Dun's and competitors can be used to identify the chief corporate officers of most large and some small companies.

Dun's SIC 2+2

To attempt to solve the SIC code problem, Dun's Marketing Service has developed an eight-digit (rather than the government's four-digit) SIC system, which does a much better job of pinpointing the type of industry. For example, consider the government SIC code 5084, *Industrial Machinery and Equipment.* This number actually applies to thousands of totally unrelated industries. Consider the way Duns applies its eight-digit system within code 5084 to several industries:

5084 0108 Milk Products Manufacturing Machinery

5084 0301 Chain Saws

5084 0404 Oil Refining Machinery

5084 9910 Tire Recapping Machinery

You will never find technicians, marketers, salespeople or executives from any one of these four industries at a convention attended by any of the other three. The industries are fundamentally different, but they are all classified as 5084.

Duns has rendered a great service by coming up with this new classification system. Unfortunately, the U.S. government is far behind the times and hasn't made it official. There is, therefore, still no really useful universal way to classify American businesses. We badly need such a system.

Using the DUN's SIC 2+2 system, a brewer introducing a new product wanted a sampling of people and restaurants in several particular ethnic groups for which his new beer was designed. Under the SIC code, restaurants are 5812. Dun's SIC 2+2 breaks restaurants down into:

American

Cajun

Chinese

French

German

Greek

Indian

Italian

Japanese

Korean

Lebanese

Mexican (etc.)

A poultry producer sought to acquire a poultry feed manufacturer to help to integrate his operation. The SIC code is 2048 Prepared Feed Manufacturers, which includes dog food, fish food, pet food and so on. Using Duns SIC 2+2, he was able to locate the 122 poultry feed manufacturers from amongst the other 2000 feed manufacturers in SIC 2048.

The trouble is that the Dun's system is unique to Dun's, and is not yet an industry standard.

WHO ARE YOUR BUSINESS CUSTOMERS?

One of the most difficult philosophical questions concerning business lists is trying to decide who your business customers are, and, therefore, who should be on your marketing database. Should it be:

The president of the company?

The vice president for R & D who is looking for new ideas?

The vice president for the division that uses your products?

The branch manager?

The engineer who recommended purchase?

The finance director who approved the purchase?

The operators who actually use your product?

The purchasing officer who placed the order?

The branch manager in another branch that doesn't use your product, but has a function that sounds as if it should?

What a problem! Some companies agonize over this problem and never reach a satisfactory conclusion. It is the problem faced by every salesperson. How do they handle it?

Chances are they make one contact, and then get this contact to suggest other people in the company who are probably interested. The next step is to call on Mr. B, saying, "Mr. A suggested that I see you about your possible need for our product." Eventually, using this technique, they find their way to Mr. W, who is actually interested and in a position to make a recommendation. But Mr. W has to get Mr. Y's approval and final signoff from Mr. Z before a purchase can be made. A couple of more calls are probably in order.

So which names go in the database? My inclination would be to list them all. You want your company and products to become household words throughout the company. Mailing to all of them accomplishes something. Even if they don't even open the envelopes, a piece of mail with your company name on it passes through their hands once a month or so on its way to the wastebasket. By this process your company name has probably registered on ten or twelve officers of the company. When you finally strike home with someone who then asks around about you, he or she will find that everyone has heard of you, and that they are probably disposed to approve a purchase with such a well-known supplier.

A business-to-business marketing database must have room for many different names, and a coding system for their function in the organization.

THE CORPORATE CULTURE

An important marketing problem develops from what Ernie Schell, president of the Communications Center, calls the "Corporate Culture." As Ernie describes it:

> A customer you think you know very well, whom you've sold to for years, moves to another company in the same field, and within six months, the customer seems to be a different person. He isn't buying the same things in the same ways, even if his job is identical and his responsibilities the same. The reason is simple: he is now operating in a different corporate culture.
>
> Thus, within every organization there is a Spectrum of Needs defined by how that company does business. Some of these may be generic to the industry they are in, others will be specific for that company, while still others will be determined by the personal or professional judgment of specific individuals.
>
> Within the Spectrum of Needs, each company demonstrates a Range of Behavior. This will be a function of company size, purchasing policies and practices, manufacturing methods, inventory requirements, competitive position, and other specific factors related to the business activity of that company or organization. Some companies require formal bids, others don't even use purchase orders. Some buyers have a discretionary fund that exceeds the entire annual purchasing budget of other companies in the same business. A growth company in a hot new industry is going to have a different range of behavior from a mature company in any industry.
>
> Within the Range of Behavior for each company, there are in turn certain "Points of Leverage" that determine when and how a sale is made, and what type of sale it will be. An individual can be a Point of Leverage. Location can be a Leverage Point. But so can Corporate Culture. For example, some companies want to be as state-of-the-art as possible. If you can sell them something that will give them a technological edge, you've got an excellent Point of Leverage. Other companies won't buy things until they are almost obsolete.

Finally, each company falls into some kind of Life Cycle Category, based on the company's own growth cycle and the growth cycle of the industry. The company's Life Cycle will have a major impact on the Spectrum of Needs, its Range of Behavior, and its Points of Leverage. So when direct marketers talk about Life time Customer Value, and Life Cycle Marketing, it pays to sit up and take notice.

What all this means for the business-to-business database is that you will have to start collecting information on your business customers in a new way. Some intelligent thinking needs to go into defining the relationship between the products you are selling, and the companies who you are trying to sell to, in terms of all of these factors. It is not just a matter of collecting the right names and addresses. Segmentation in business-to-business marketing is a question of finding out just how each company in your prospect and customer pool stacks up in the above categories, then determining where and how common elements occur, or what groups these customers can be divided into.

WHERE TO SEEK CLASSIFICATION DATA

Successful business-to-business marketing, therefore, depends on getting and using a lot of information about customers and prospects. Much of it can be compiled internally from your salesforce, but the richest sources are the customers and prospects themselves. It is amazing what people will tell you, if only you will ask. Short surveys, often accompanied by a crisp new dollar bill, or a sweepstakes entry or a premium, bring in a wealth of the kind of information you will need for your database. The inducements are personal. Few companies would require that the officer who filled out the questionnaire has to contribute the premium to the company petty cash fund. The premium sets up a personal link between you and the responder—a link that you can use to build a further dialog and eventual sales.

The questions should be interesting, challenging, fun to answer and useful to you in your marketing program.

Car Telephone Case Study

In one such survey a service bureau helped a cellular telephone company build a customer database to use for profiling. A copy of the customer list was spun off from the billing records. Included besides the name, company, and address were key usage data including:

- number of car telephones
- number of hours per month of usage

The list was matched to a D&B file which inserted into the records:

- SIC code
- number of employees
- annual sales
- corporate and subsidiary relationships
- companies with large sales forces

The database used software similar to *MarketVision*, a software system that permits multiple users to make instant counts, reports and selects working from a PC or terminal on their desks. Both Marketing and Sales, as well as the creative agency, had access to the database.

Working with this database of about 36,000 customers, marketing developed a profile of the ideal customer. The first step in the profiling is to determine who are the profitable customers and who are not so profitable by RFM analysis.

With this data in the database, they matched the scores of profitability against occupational classifications to find which type and size of company provided the highest number of profitable customers. The best categories proved to be:

- realtors
- construction companies

- transportation companies
- banks
- utilities
- government

Obtaining Prospect Names

Using the profiles developed from the customer database, they rented lists of matching prospects. The sources included D&B and other compiled lists, plus lists from trade associations of people in real estate, construction and others. Before the promotion could begin, the dealer problem had to be faced.

Defining Dealer Territories

When cellular telephones first became available, it was fairly easy for any auto-radio or electronic store to become a cellular dealer. For many such dealers, the cellular business was a minor sideline. No effort had been made to determine the boundaries of a dealer. When the cellular company decided to begin database marketing in a big way, therefore, they had to decide which leads would be sent to which dealers.

The effort forced them to set up a category called "Authorized Dealer" with a contract, sales territory, and lead tracking responsibilities. The database was coded with Latitude-Longtitude codes, and software was used to determine the distance of each customer from each authorized dealer. Using this software, a series of computer maps were drawn and the dealer areas plotted in such a way as to give each dealer a territory that corresponded roughly to their size and annual telephone installation and maintenance history.

The final outcome of the process was a zipcode definition of each dealer's territory. At the same time, each dealer was required to have a FAX machine, and to agree to act promptly on leads, reporting regularly to the database.

Large accounts were handled by an inside sales team—rather than by dealers. They built into the database software a classification system that would instantly classify any lead by inside vs dealer.

The Prospect Survey

The promotion method selected by the creative agency was a survey, conducted by an independent market research bureau. The survey was designed to get from prospective customers a great deal of information to pre-qualify leads before any valuable salesman's time was expended.

There were about 110,000 prospects targeted, all of whom were in the high-probability group as determined by the profile. The first step was a teaser post card telling them that they would be receiving a very important survey the following week.

They began with a test mailing 4,000 which tested two types of survey forms: A long form (four legal sized pages) and a short form: (two letter sized pages). The detailed questions asked many things about their business and their need for commu nication.

The long form took about 20 minutes to fill out. The short form could be completed in five minutes. Strangely enough, they got the same response from both forms, but much more information (of course) from the long one. So that was the one selected for the rollout.

Each survey form had a crisp new $1 bill folded inside. The response was amazing. There were more than 23,000 returned—a 21 percent response rate.

As soon as the forms were returned, they were immediately keypunched and entered into the database. Each respondent was coded by dealer territory and qualified by an algorithm that determined if the respondent was hot, warm, or cold as a lead. The data for the algorithm was derived from the boxes checked on the survey form. As each lead came in each respondent was classified into one of six groups:

- Internal Sales Hot, Warm, Cold
- Dealer Sales Hot, Warm, Cold

Cold leads were mailed a simple promotional piece and kept in the database for later use.

Warm leads were mailed a special offer endorsed by a leader in their profession (realtor, banker, etc.)

Hot leads were called immediately by the telemarketers to set up an appointment with the internal salesman or dealer. This call served as an additional qualification step to assure that the lead did not go away (buy from the competition), and to be sure that it was really as hot as the survey indicated. There is nothing worse than giving salesmen or dealers a group of leads which you say are "hot," only to have them find out upon investigation that the leads are not hot, and not as productive as whatever they had to stop doing to call them.

How to Get Salesmen to Report the Status of Leads

The most difficult problem for any lead management system is finding out what happens to leads. Salesmen hate to be micro-managed. "How many calls did you make today?" "Why did you wait three days before calling XYZ?" Most salesmen would rather have you look at their sales record instead. "If I am selling, then leave me alone", is their philosophy.

On the other hand, just sending out leads and never knowing what happened is a very frustrating exercise for the marketing manager. In some companies, sales has a very low opinion of marketing, and refuses to call marketing's prospects even when they cry out for attention.

So what is the answer? It is really very simple. Marketing has to give up ownership of the database. It has to belong to the sales force. Give immediate and direct access to the database to the sales managers from the beginning with PC's on their desks.

There were about 6,000 leads sent to in-house salesmen. Of these, about 60% or 3,600 were converted to customers during the ninety days following the survey. The net effect for the client was a 10% increase in their customer base from the program.

Warm leads were given a special treatment. Sometimes the sales staff was unemployed and looking for ideas. The database was designed so that salesmen could "turn on" warm leads when they needed them and "turn them off" in busy periods. By giving the sales staff control, the reasoning was, they would appreciate the database more, feel that it belonged to them, and make more productive use of it, instead of fighting or ignoring it.

Database Maintenance

At the conclusion of the campaign, the database consisted of customers and prospects. At that point it was available to the sales force for selecting existing customers by number of phones and usage to provide fodder for internal upselling promotions. The most productive use of the database proved to be corporate and trade association relationships. They could go to an association and say, "400 of your 2,000 members are using cellular phones. If you can help us to promote the other 1,600, we will work out a special offer of benefit to the members and the association."

Salesforce Automation

Most companies are now looking seriously into automating their salesforces. Some have gone so far as to equip all their salespeople with laptops with special software that keeps track of their appointments, stores data on each of their customers and helps them to know the product line by keeping all the products on disk, instead of in a thick catalog.

Several companies write software for field sales applications. The Upjohn Company bought some of this software to install in 1,400 laptops which it has purchased for its salesforce. The software has several features:

- Return on investment software with margin and lifetime value calculations to help evaluate prospects, figure pricing, structure proposals.

- Customer sales histories going back several years.

- Order entry, order status, replenishment orders, product return status and graphic previews of the products movement over several years.

Most of these laptops are equipped with modems which permit salespeople to send in orders automatically from any telephone. The salespeople can also use the laptop and telephone to query the company mainframe to get information necessary to make a sale. Portable PCs allow valuable company information to be accessed from the field, sent to the corporate office for interpretation and immediately dispatched to everyone who needs it.

A large insurance company equipped its agents with portable computers and printers which could calculate and print out custom insurance policies while they made sales calls. Closing rates improved dramatically. Eastman Kodak found that "Prospects who can sign on the dotted line when their attention and interest are highest have resulted in increased closing rates of 40 percent or more," according to Geoffrey Smith, Manager of Marketing and Sales.

What does salesforce automation mean for the database marketer? Plenty. While the salesforce is plugged into the company mainframe to transmit orders and obtain data, it can also be exchanging information with the marketing database. You can include them in your information loop. The results can be dramatic—not only in terms of giving the salesforce more information, but also in enriching the database with live daily information of what is going on in the field. The salesforce, which is often the last group to get aboard the marketing database concept, will become a functioning part of the database system once it has become automated.

SUMMARY

- A business-to-business marketing database differs from a consumer database in several important ways:
  - ➤ salesmen are usually in the loop
  - ➤ geodemographics do not apply
  - ➤ it is hard to tell the right person to address
  - ➤ merge/purge is different
  - ➤ businesses use SIC codes.
- There are at least three different types of business marketing database:
  - ➤ lead tracking with salesman or dealers
  - ➤ physician database for the pharmaceutical industry
  - ➤ direct sales

- You can gather a lot of information for your database (some of it false) from outside services such as Duns, TRW and TriNet-Net.

- Match rates for business lists hover around 40-50 percent, while consumer match rates are in the high 90s.

- The hardest part of building a business database is finding the correct names to list.

- There are amazingly useful business lists for rent. The exact list you need could well be available.

- The SIC code is usually too broad to pinpoint the type of businesses you are seeking. Duns has a better system, but it is not universal in industry.

- Even when you have signed up a customer, it is hard to know which person in the company should be on your database. My recommendation is to list all relevant names, and mail to them all.

- In structuring your database, you need to consider segmenting your business customers by "Corporate Culture," including Life Cycle, Needs, Purchasing Behavior and Points of Leverage.

- Salesforce Automation can and should be linked to your marketing database to improve corporate communications and enhance information and sales.

Part Six

Economics and Corporate Relationships

Chapter 21

The Economics of Building a Marketing Database

In this chapter we are going to get right down to specifics. We are going to discuss how much it costs to create and maintain a marketing database, and how to estimate the benefits you will get from it.

Database marketing is totally quantifiable. You can and must prove everything you do to be at least theoretically cost effective before you start, or you should not start it. This chapter will help you to do that. Don't let the concept of the old corner grocer overwhelm the objective of database marketing: to build *mutually profitable* relationships with your customers.

Before we begin, some explanations of the model to follow.

■ Prices are based on an on-line, interactive database of about one million customers, complete with a customer service operation with every customer's record accessible for viewing and updating while the customer is on the telephone. The numbers assume that much of the data about customers is entered *in batch*. That means that customer purchases, direct mail responses, outgoing direct mail source codes and so on will be entered into the database from data tapes prepared off-line in point-of-sale devices, or from keypunching or the company's existing billing system. (An example of the latter would be a bank, a utility or an insurance company.) As you know from reading the rest of this book, it is not a good idea to try to add marketing database functions to a company billing system. It will take several years longer, cost many times more and not provide any demonstrable gains.

■ Prices are based on the marketing database being maintained by an outside service bureau, rather than in-house on the company's mainframe. As already explained, this is the least-cost solution. For inside maintenance of a marketing database, multiply the start up times and costs by three or five, and the monthly maintenance by about three. Also, if you do it in-house, be prepared for marketing to take a back seat and low priority as compared to all the other functions being run on the company mainframe.

■ We are assuming one million customers on this database; if you have more, or less, add or subtract about five percent from the costs for every 100,000.

■ We are assuming that the software used is similar to *Market Vision* in which on-line ad-hoc counts and selects from the 1,000,000 name database can be completed in less than 30 seconds.

START-UP COSTS

There are four steps in getting any marketing database up and running:

1. The initial plan.
2. The design.
3. Software development and data conversion.
4. Testing and training.

As you know from Chapter Five, all these steps should be completed *within one year*. If you are serious about getting into a marketing database, you should do a comprehensive and thorough job of

Figure 21-1 Steps in Building a Marketing Database

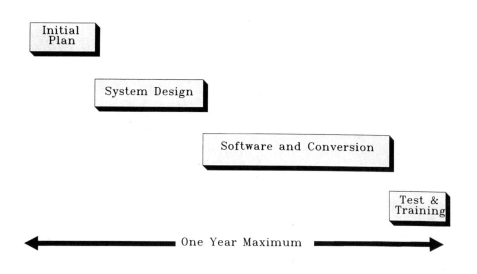

preparation, but do not dawdle and waste time. The valuable experience comes *after* it is up and running, not before.

Initial Plan

Initial planning is a team effort headed by the marketing staff, but involving many others including the service bureau you have selected, your outside direct creative agency, customer service, sales, brand and someone from top management to assure you will have the budget for all that follows. If you are going to have an outside telemarketer handle some functions, include them in the planning phase.

What the creative agency charges is up to them. It is not strictly a part of the marketing database. You should not pay your service bureau more than $10,000 for the initial planning phase. Two months is maximum for this step. Planning includes on-site interviews with all company units that may be involved in the process, including customer service, sales, billing, delivery and marketing. The end product of the planning phase is a set of specifications: a document which describes the objectives of the database, what data will flow in and out of the database, what functions the database will be used for during its first year of operation and what reports are expected from it.

Towards the end of the planning phase you should have a formal conference to review the plan, with all participants represented.

As a last step in the planning phase the service bureau should provide a fixed price cost breakdown of the subsequent steps, based on the approved plan. If they cannot do this, then the plan is not complete and requires additional work before you proceed.

The Design Phase

Most of the design work for the database will be done by your service bureau. If the initial plan is comprehensive, the design will spell out in detail exactly what the database format will be, the menu screens to be used, the exact reports to be produced, the hardware configuration, the conversion problems and the software required. There will be little need to consult anyone outside the service bureau during design, assuming that planning has gone well. Design should take about two months, and should cost between $10,000 and $30,000.

The design should be reviewed in detail by the Database Administrator, who is normally someone in the company marketing staff who, by this point, has been put in charge of the operation. He or she should have authority to spend money from an approved budget set up by the company in the planning phase, after the service bureau's fixed cost estimate was received.

Software Customization

Again, this is all done in the service bureau. The service bureau will be working from existing database software which must be customized for your application. The time and cost will vary depending on:

- how complex the functions are which are assigned to the database;

- how many users will be on the system, and their varying demands for software; and

- the various sources of data which will be coming in to the database, and the complexity of converting and using the data.

You will want to be able to conduct ad-hoc queries, on line, of your databases once it is set up. The software should provide for this. You can expect this step to take from one to three months, and to cost from $20,000 to $200,000. Not included in this figure is the hardware cost. You will need PCs or terminals for every user, and several printers, controllers and line installations. As a rule of thumb, estimate about $2,500 per user for non-telemarketers with PCs, $3,000 for every printer and about $1,000 for every telemarketer using a terminal. Add about $10,000 for controllers and line installation.

Data Conversion

While the software is being customized, your data must be converted. This means taking all of the tapes of customer names that you have collected from various sources, converting them to the new database format and loading them onto the new database. In the process, names and addresses should be cleaned, NCOA should be applied to the old addresses so they can be made up-to-date, the file should be de-duped and any enhancements (demographics, psychographics, cluster coding, etc.) can be added at this time. Each function will have its costs. Reformatting, cleaning, de-duping and loading should cost less than $10 per thousand names. The entire process should be completed in a few weeks at most.

Testing and Training

Don't begin until you have run tests with some of the actual people who will be operating the system when it has been set up. In addition, everyone who will operate the database should receive formal training. Allow one month for testing and training, and budget from $5,000 to $15,000 for this step, depending on how many people are involved.

MONTHLY MAINTENANCE COSTS

Your database is set up. Everyone is trained. You have begun operations. How much will it cost you, every month, to run your marketing database?

The best way to pay monthly maintenance costs in a marketing database is a fixed monthly fee which does not vary with usage. That means that the fee should be the same every month, whether the company is using the database eighteen hours a day or only twice a week. Why is that? Because a marketing database, to be useful, must be used extensively at all levels in the company and in the direct creative agency. It is very important that everyone begin to know the customers, to begin to understand them, to segment them, to plan marketing strategies, to run reports, to try out new ideas, to test and count. The marketing database must become the heart of your company marketing and sales effort.

With a price schedule pegged at so much per hour of use, your inclination will be to use your database as little as possible to save money. With a fixed monthly cost, your inclination will be to use it as much as possible to get your money's worth. The second is the correct attitude for a marketing database.

The monthly cost assigned by the service bureau will vary with the number of users, the size and complexity of the file and the complexity of the batch operations. For a database of a million customers, you can expect to pay anywhere from $5,000 to $50,000 per month depending on the application. This should cover preparation of all your standard reports, updating your database at set intervals from batch data, nightly backup and off-site storage and keeping the system up and running at all times.

In addition, your service bureau will add a monthly management fee. This is the cost of the bureau's customer service operation, which will be the link between your staff and the programmers who are keeping the system running. The management fee will be from $1,000 to $8,000 per month.

If your customer service and sales telemarketers are located at some distance from your service bureau, you will need a leased line connecting them, which you get from the telephone company. The cost depends on the distance. This could vary from a few hundred dollars a month, to $6,000 per month for a cross-continental line.

Production Costs

In addition to your monthly costs, you will have some database costs which vary depending on usage. You will have keypunching, mailing, telemarketing, merge/purge of prospect lists and programming charges for changes that you will be making in the database and system. Most of this can be estimated during the planning phase. Some of these costs cannot be planned in advance, and must be left to later justification based on the need on a project-by-project basis.

Telephone costs: Customer Service and Sales

One direct result of a marketing database is an increase in telephone traffic. Customers will call you much more than they used to, and you will be calling them. This function can be costly or profitable, depending on how you handle it.

You should give very serious consideration to using a 900 number for much of your telephone traffic (see Chapter 17). Technical support in many companies can be made to pay its way. Depending on how you handle it, telephone sales can also be conducted on a pay-per-call basis, if you keep the costs down. This is the direction that the industry is going, and you would be well advised to move along with it. In addition, for those functions that are used with an 800 number, you may want to add automatic equipment ("push 1 for sales") at the front end which, in some cases, may save you thousands of dollars in agent cost.

Balancing all of these factors, let us estimate that your telephone costs per customer per year average about $2.00.

Direct Mail

You will be communicating much more frequently with your customers with a database than you used to do. This is because you both will have more to say to each other. You will be sending out and receiving back surveys in addition to the extra orders you will be getting. If we assume that you communicate with each customer four times a year, at a cost per communication of about 50 cents, you will spend $2 per customer per year on direct mail. In addition, you will have to enter data as a result of survey questions, and to redeem checks, honor rebates and so on. The cost of these items will vary widely.

Total Costs

Putting all of this together, and amortizing your start-up costs over three years, you will have an annual cost for keeping customers and prospects on your database of something between fifty cents and a dollar and a half per name per year. On top of that will be another four dollars in telemarketing and direct mail costs. These are the costs that you must justify to determine whether the marketing database will pay off for you.

Estimating the Benefits

Let's begin by listing the possible benefits, before we try to put a price tag on them:

- Increased customer retention: reduction in attrition.
- Increased conversion of one-time buyers into loyal customers.
- Increased opportunities to cross-sell and up-sell.
- Reduction in acquisition costs through modeling, improved prospect screening and qualification and better targeting.
- Opening up opportunities for niche marketing of special products and services to special groups.
- Inexpensive introduction and testing of new products with rapid feedback.

- Revenue through list exchanges and rental.
- Gains in new customers through referrals by your loyal customers.
- Direct sales from Customer Service.

Customer Acquisition Costs

The first cost you should try to estimate in your cost/benefit analysis is your current customer acquisition cost. To get this number, add up all your advertising, promotion and sales costs in a year, and divide that by the number of new customers you have acquired. This is not easy to do—without a database, you don't know if your customers are constant, or whether you are acquiring the same ones over and over again. Certainly if your effort is concentrated in coupons plus TV and print ads you will have to guess how many customers you have, how many you are losing and how many you are gaining every year. Consider some hypothetical figures based on annual sales of enough product for a million households. In the absence of any reliable survey data (which you should certainly try to get) you can probably assume that of the million households:

- One third are loyal customers who stick with you from year to year. (Group A)
- One third are switchers who buy your product if the sale price, coupons, cash back or rebates are better than your competitors. When they drop out, you replace them with other similar switchers. (Group B)
- One third buy once or twice and then become loyal to someone else. These people are constantly being replaced with other, similar people. (Group C)

Your real customers are only Group A. Groups B and C are not really customers; they are one-time buyers whom you are trying to acquire as customers. Under this definition, the customers you are acquiring would represent your annual growth in Group A, which is probably a small number. Against this you must list the attrition from Group A due to death, disaffection or other causes.

Figure 21-2 One Third Are Loyal to You

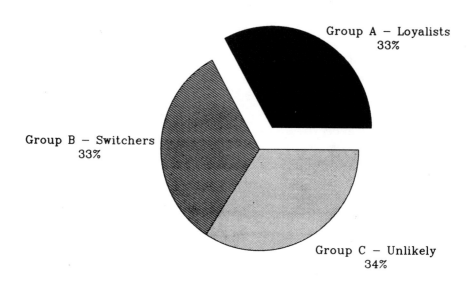

Group A – Loyalists
33%

Group B – Switchers
33%

Group C – Unlikely
34%

In any event, you will have to determine your customer acquisition cost, based on your own industry and situation.

When you have done this, you will need to make an estimate
of the number of customers that you can retain and keep from
dropping off due to your database activities. Here is where Groups
B and C become important. If they have become buyers, they are
also on the database. Turn on the charm. Make them feel important. Ask their opinions. Bring them into the family. How many of
them can you persuade to move into Group A from B or C? Put
this number into your analysis.

Determining Lifetime Value

You will want to determine the lifetime value of your customers.
We will not go into this further here, since we have devoted a

whole chapter (Chapter 10) to this subject. But it is an important part of the economic analysis.

Estimating Gains Through Database Activities

Here is where estimates of gains through cross-selling and up-selling come in. You now have a captive audience: your database customers. What other products and services do you have which they should be buying? If they have $50,000 worth of life insurance, how many can you persuade to take out an additional $100,000? If they have an eighth-page ad, how many will take a half page? If they bought a sofa, how about new dining room furniture? If you are supplying them with envelopes, why not take over all their printing needs?

Devise a plan for your database. Make some realistic assumptions about gains from cross- and up-selling, once you have customers on a true marketing database.

Gains From Understanding Your Market

At last you really know who your customers are. You know what clusters supply most of your business. You can identify those who have bought recently, who buy frequently and in large amounts. You may learn the psychographics of these heavy users. What is this worth to you?

The answer, of course, depends on what you do with the information. If you file it away on a bookshelf, it will not be worth much. If you redirect the information into your media selection program, your direct marketing list selection activities, the positioning of your creative copy and the redesign of your product, you may be able to project real economic benefits from the database.

The knowledge gained from the database may also permit you to carve out one or more unique niche markets which would have been impossible without this insight. Add this possibility to your calculations, if you think that it exists.

Referral Programs

One unique marketing database advantage is the ability to reward
loyal customers for their loyalty and for their referring new
customers to you. Once a customer has referred someone, you will
be able to track that new prospect's purchases, and give your loyal
customer a gift or a rebate. If your customer acquisition cost is $25,
you can afford a nice gift. If the acquisition cost is $100, you can
afford a handsome one.

List Rental and Exchanges

You may encounter strong internal resistance to the idea of list
rental or exchange. In many cases the very people who were saying
that a marketing database is not worth creating, will be the first to
say that the database, when set up, is too valuable to rent or exchange. You may have a fight on your hands. But if you exchange
lists with a complementary non-competitor (baby food and diapers;
life insurance and savings accounts; computers and software), you
will save the cost of renting new outside prospect lists, at $65 per
thousand, and go a long way towards paying the costs of your marketing database. Until you have built your database, you have nothing to exchange or rent.

Customer Service Sales

Customer service personnel are part of the whole database operation.
They help, they advise, they explain and they sell. I love the sign on
the side of a Domino Pizza delivery car that says "Yes, the driver
will sell you a Pizza." Somewhere, somehow, some customer service
people got the idea that they were *above* selling, as if selling was not
the purpose of the business in the first place. The customer talking
to you knows that he or she is conversing with a profit seeking enterprise which is in the business of providing goods and services for
just renuneration. Customer service can and will help sell your
product.

PUTTING IT ALL TOGETHER

For the sake of analysis, let us assume that you have determined the lifetime value of a customer (profit after expenses) is $40. Let us assume that the cost of acquiring a new customer is $25. Let us assume that the cost of the marketing database per year per name breaks down as follows:

Direct Costs:

Database (service bureau) cost	$1.00
Telemarketing (inbound)	$2.00
Direct mail outgoing and incoming	$2.00
External surveys and data enhancement	$0.20

Figure 21-3 Direct Costs of a Database
(In Dollars Per Name Per Year)

Total: $5.30

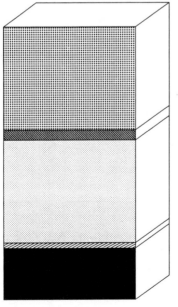

Direct Mail $2.00

Surveys & Data $0.20

Telemarketing $2.00

Premiums $0.10

Database Cost $1.00

Every database is different.

| Premiums for referrals | $0.10 |
| Total cost per name per year | $5.30 |

Now let's try to estimate some benefits to place against that.

Reduction in Attrition

Let us assume that of your base of 330,000 Group A customers, you were losing about 20 percent or 66,000 per year. With the help of the database, you cut that to 10 percent (33,000). Each customer you lose costs you $25 to replace, so the reduction in attrition is a gain of $0.85 cents per name (33,000 times $25, divided by a million names on the database).

Increased Buyer Conversion

Before the database, you were converting only about 66,000 one-time buyers into loyal customers (the level of attrition). Let us suppose that, with the database you can convert 10 percent more of the one-time buyers to loyalists (10 percent of 667,000 is 66,700). The lifetime value of these 66,700 is $2,668,000 (66,700 times $40). Divided by 1,000,000 names this becomes $2.67 per name.

Cross-Sell and Up-Sell

If we assume that you can persuade 20 percent of your Group A and 10 percent of your Group B and Group C customers to cross-sell or up-sell, and the lifetime value of the increased profits from these conversions is $20 (for Group A) and $4 (for Groups B and C), then the annual benefit per name is $1.60 (333,000 Group A times 20 percent times $20 plus 667,000 Groups B and C times 10 percent times $4 divided by 1 million).

Referrals

Five percent of your loyal Group A customers and two percent of your Group B and Group C customers will suggest someone else who will become a customer. This brings in $1.20 per name (.05 times 333,000 plus .02 times 667,000 times $40 [lifetime value] divided by 1 million).

List Exchange and Rental

Some people have an exaggerated idea of the value of lists of customers. Your Groups B and C may not be worth much, but with luck you can rent them all. Let us say that in a year you bring in $1 for every Group A and $0.50 for your Group B and C through rentals or exchanges. Together, these will bring in $0.67 per name (333,000 times $1 plus 667,000 times $0.50 divided by 1 million).

Reduction in Acquisition Costs

It is costing you $25 now to get a new customer. Suppose that because the better targeting of media, message, positioning and product which comes about through better understanding of your customers and the market, you reduce your acquisition costs by 15% or $3.75. Assume that you are now acquiring 133,000 customers per year (balancing the attrition of Group A plus your conversion gain of 67,000). This improvement will save you $498,750 per year, which comes to $0.50 per name.

Customer Service Sales

Assume that these sales bring in an extra five percent sales which were not counted on from other sources. The net profit from these sales is $4. The benefit per name therefore is $2.00 (5 percent of 1 million times $4 divided by 1 million).

Niche Marketing, Product Introductions

These are obvious benefits, but they are hard to quantify in advance. Let's leave them out for now.

Direct Benefits:

a. Reduction in attrition	$0.85
b. Increased buyer conversion	$2.67
c. Cross-sell and up-sell	$1.60
d. Referrals	$1.20
e. List exchange and rental	$0.67

f. Reduction in acquisition costs $0.50
g. Customer service sales $2.00

Total benefits $9.49

The Bottom Line

Direct benefits of $9.49 less direct costs of $5.30 leaves $4.19 per name ($4,190,000 per year) in excess of benefits over costs of database marketing in the example shown here.

The figures will be quite different for your business. You may find greater profit. You may not find a profit at all. If that is so, perhaps your costs are too high. Maybe you are spending too much on telemarketing or direct mail. Drop your losing groups. Target your message better. Or maybe (horrors!) you cannot prove that

---

Figure 21-4 Benefits From a Database
(Dollars Per Name Per Year)

Total: $9.49

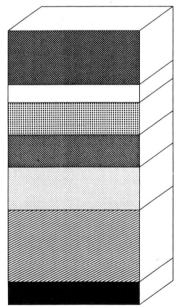

Cust. Service Sales $2

Lower Acquisition $ $0.67

List Exchanges $1.2

Referrals $1.2

Cross & Up Sells $1.6

Increased Converts $2.67

Lower Attrition $0.85

database marketing will save you any money at all! If so, don't do it. Database marketing is an article of religious faith to the converted. They believe that it *has to work*. Right; but if it doesn't, don't use it. After all, this is business. Our goal is to improve the bottom line. Keep your eye on the main objective—making a profit—and don't get led astray by the glory of a marketing database.

What to Do With a Loss

You are all through your analysis, and the costs of your marketing database outweigh the benefits. There is no way that it is going to pay for itself as you have structured it. You have gone over all the figures, and you have made no mistake.

One option is to drop the idea. The other option, which usually makes more sense, is to scale back your plan to something more manageable. Set up your marketing database only for those customers in Group A. Do your customer service, direct mail and other activities only for your best and most loyal customers. Prove and test the database concept on this group. Then, later, extend it to the others *if your experience shows that it will be profitable.*

A Database Checklist

Chapter 28 contains a checklist of most of the things that you need to consider in building a marketing database. You should review this checklist before concluding your study of the costs of building a database to be sure you have not left something out.

SUMMARY

- Your database should be run by an outside service bureau which has the professional software and experience to do the job. They should be able to quote you exact figures for costs during the first year, after the initial planning phase is completed.

- Start-up costs for a marketing database include the initial plan, design, software and conversion and testing and training. Altogether, start-up costs can run from $30,000 to $200,000 in 1990 dollars, and require a passage of up to six months for a database of one million customer names.

■ Monthly maintenance includes updating, reports, management and leased lines. The costs for a one million name database should run from $5,000 to $50,000 per month, depending on the number of users and the complexity of your system. You should pay a fixed monthly fee rather than a fee dependent on usage. This will encourage you to make maximum use of your database.

■ The benefits of a marketing database should be reduced to quantifiable numbers at all times. The benefits include:

■

> Increased customer retention

> Increased conversion of one-time buyers to loyal customers

> Increased opportunities for cross-selling and up-selling

> Reduction in customer acquisition costs

> Opportunities for niche marketing

> Opportunities to introduce and test new products

> Revenue from exchanges and rentals of the list

> Gains through referrals by customers

> Increased sales by customer service

■ Database marketing is introduced because it will have a positive effect on the bottom line. If you can't prove that it does, don't create one. Scale back your plan until it is profitable. Concentrate, at first, only on your best customers.

Chapter 22

Selling the Database to Top Management

Why aren't there more marketing databases in existence today? There are several reasons:

- The concept is new. Most people don't yet understand how a database could be helpful in their particular product situation.

- A marketing database requires a high level of creative leadership to develop a practical plan to put it to work in building loyalty and repeat sales. This kind of creative leadership is rare.

- The marketing staff may understand database marketing, but they find it difficult to sell top management on the concept.

The purpose of this chapter is to provide some assistance to a marketing staff in marshalling arguments and persuasive powers to sell the database idea. I have used an actual case study as an example of how to put the ideas together. Your particular corporate culture may dictate an entirely different approach, but this chapter should at least stimulate your imagination.

Marketing databases don't do anything by themselves. They are only useful and effective if they are a part of an overall system designed to improve sales and customer retention. Some people get so absorbed in the excitement of creating a marvelous database and providing customer service that they lose sight of the main objective. I have heard more than one top executive of a major corporation who has responded, when pitched the marketing database message, "That's a great theory, spending a lot of time and money on customer relations. But will it really have a positive impact on the bottom line?"

Years ago, I worked as an editorial trainee on *Businessweek* magazine. One day, one of the senior editors gathered several of us young men together for a training session. "What," said he, "is the purpose of a business magazine?"

Each of us volunteered great answers: "To keep businessmen informed on what is going on in their industry, and in the country" . . . "To cover the impact of government on the business community" . . .

Figure 22-1 The Marketing Database Unites All Sources

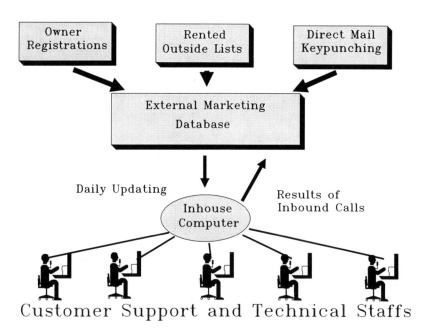

"To describe new ideas and techniques of use to businessmen," and so on.

The old editor listened for a while, and then said, simply:

"You are all wrong. The purpose of a business magazine is to make money. Don't lose sight of that objective."

We might make the same comment about marketing databases.

Before you go too far, prepare a coherent business plan to assure that all your activity is pointed in the right direction and is going to end up making a profit. You may do it for that reason, or to convince top management that your project is worthy of the budget assigned to it. But you have to do it.

HOW TO BEGIN

The techniques can be summarized into:

- Goals
- Objectives
- Strategy
- Methods
- Outputs
- Inputs

Goals

Goals are overall company bottom-line indicators which you hope to influence by the database system. They could be as simple as: "To bring in a measurable profit of $X million during 19XX which can be shown to be attributable to the database system." Another might be: "To introduce a new product K and achieve sales during 19XX of $Y through the database."

In all cases, in this plan, we should stick to objectively verifiable and quantifiable goals and objectives. A poor objective would

Figure 22-2 Business Plan Organization

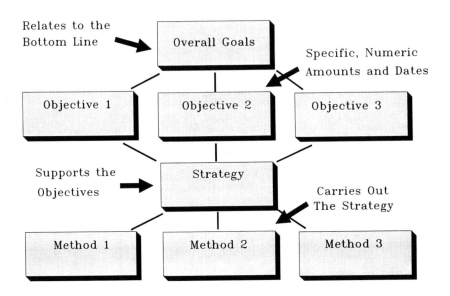

be: "To improve the image of our company in the customer's mind," unless you have a way of measuring what that image is. Particularly bad would be: "To establish two-way communication between our customers and our company so as to build loyalty and improve sales." How can you verify or quantify that?

So we begin with a bold, practical, hard-headed bottom-line goal which says what will happen, by what amount, by what date. If you can't do that, successful database marketing will remain but a dream.

The goal should be supported with reasoning which shows how you will reach the goal, as a result achieving objectives, which you then go on to state.

Objectives

Objectives are the important benchmarks and events that are essential to the achievement of the goals.

For example, a software company realizes that the market has matured to the point where it is more and more difficult to come out with an entirely new product. Thousands of small and large entrepreneurs are working on that same objective. Only a fraction will achieve success. This company, fortunately, has an established base of well-accepted software on which it can build to expand its profits. It could pick such objectives as:

- To sell $X worth of software updates to registered customers through the database during 19XX.

- To cross-sell products to existing customers to a value of $Y during 19XX.

- To add XX,XXX to our registered on the database customers during 19XX.

The last objective is listed because objectives one and two are a function of the size of the database. You can only sell to people you know of. During the formative years, when software was selling like hotcakes, most companies did not have a very active program of registering owners. So when they got around to creating databases, they found that they had less than 20 percent of the customers registered.

As a company begins to use the database to sell, it becomes obvious that:

Sales = D • A • P
where D is the number of names on the database, A is the amount of the average purchase and P is the percentage of customers who respond to your offer to buy additional products. The bigger the database, the bigger the sales. Somehow companies have to find and register the elusive 80 percent of customers who own their products anonymously, never having

bothered to send in the owner registration card. As each lost
sheep returns to the fold, it will then be possible to multiply
them also by A and by P and increase sales still further.

Computing the percentage P (percentage of customers who respond to your offer) is very important to any company. It lies at the
core of the reasoning behind any marketing database. It can be calculated with some precision after the fact, when a year is over, and
then projected into the future to calculate next year's objectives. Of
course P is dependent on a lot of factors, some of which are under
your control. Your pricing, offer, package, sales methods, timeliness
and persistence affect P. Your other customer services and loyalty
building programs affect P. You must test and count.

A, the average order size, may or may not be under your control. In fundraising, it is a much manipulated element. If a contributor gave $20 last time, the next solicitation will ask him to give "$20
or $40 or even $50," trying to nudge him gently into a higher HPC
(highest previous contribution) category. In effect they are telling
him that the amount he gave—whatever it was—was really a *minimum gift*. Many will respond by giving the middle value next time
(which is usually twice what they gave before). If they do so, the
next letter will ask for "$40 or $80 or even $100."

Can you use this philosophy in commercial database market
ing? Why not? Once your customer has earned "gold card" status,
you should always have a platinum card available for her to aspire
to. *Never let the customer feel that he or she has done enough.*
Work to manipulate "A" to a constantly higher level.

Strategy

Once you have the objectives defined, you can launch into your
strategy. Strategies consist of the things that you plan to do to meet
the objectives. Here you get to the essence of what the database is
designed to accomplish. There are several possibilities:

- Establish a fee-based technical assistance program.
- Establish an owner's club for the best customers.

- Develop a series of personalized newsletters.

- Develop a series of surveys and telemarketing scripts that will capture needed information for the database.

- Install a check rebate program to build dealer loyalty and acceptance of the direct marketing program.

- Permit callers to register as owners by telephone.

- Establish a sweepstakes for new owners filling out the owner's registration form.

Methods

Methods spell out exactly how you will carry out your strategies. There should be a method for each strategy. Let's see how our mythical software company could develop its methods.

Fee-Based Technical Assistance. Most companies today have 800 numbers for customers to call. It is generally true that initial owners have some problem in the first few days after purchase. They call up because they do not know how to load or begin to operate the software, despite what the company thinks are complete instructions both in the manual and in the help screens built into the software. After the first couple of weeks, companies seldom hear from the majority of their customers.

But there are some who keep calling. They fall into two categories. Some seem a little thick: they really can't get the hang of how to operate the software. They can't read the manual, nor understand the screens. They want someone to hold their hand for a half hour at a time.

The second group are advanced "techies" who want to do things with the software that it really isn't designed to do. They are on the growing edge of technology; they want to know what is inside the product so they can modify it to do something important to them, but irrelevant to the software company.

Most companies try to get rid of both types of callers. They tie up technical personnel for hours on the telephone with no profitable result. "Just tell them that we do not provide assistance with applications," are the instructions provided to the technical staff.

However, there is a way to turn these nuisances into a profit center. The concept is to set up a 900 telephone number for technical assistance. With a 900 number, the price of the call, including a fee, can be billed to the caller's telephone. The fees can be set to pay for the technician's time and make a handsome profit to the company as a whole. In this way, the callers can talk as long as they want to, and every minute is golden for the company.

At the same time that the technical staff is providing this technical assistance, they can also be entering into the database information about the caller which can be used for future upgrades or cross sales: occupation, application, age, size of company and such. In some cases they also will be able to learn about flaws in the software itself which they can turn over to the product development group for remedial action and the creation of a new, profitable upgrade.

With the new pay-for-information system, all technical calls can be switched to the new 900 number. For those who have just purchased the product, the first few calls involving how to load or start the software would be free. After that, the meter would start running on the 900 number, and the profits would begin to kick in.

Obviously, software companies are not the only ones who can profit by a fee-based technical assistance program. The trick here is to have the marketing database itself become a profit center.

Owner's Club. When PC's first appeared, hundreds of Apple and IBM PC owner's clubs sprang up spontaneously in cities across the country. People wanted to get together and share experiences about how to work these new machines. At every meeting people would bring new software routines that they had written (or otherwise acquired) which they wanted to share with others. They proved to be lively groups, with monthly meetings, newsletters, officers and special committees. Many of them are still functioning.

However, as PC's became more ubiquitous, their novelty wore off. PC's were no longer the province of the bright hacker, but the workhorse of industry: standard equipment on all young workers' desks. Why go to a meeting at night to discuss what you were using all day?

Nevertheless, the central idea behind the owner's club remains a valid one. People like to belong to something. They like to share experiences. They like to learn of new things. How can this idea be adapted to a marketing database to provide group satisfaction and mental stimulation to the customers and profit to the company?

This is the core idea behind an owner's club. After paying a membership fee, members receive informative newsletters *written by the members themselves* with company sponsorship. Annual conventions and quarterly meetings can be held in regional centers. Part of the idea is for people to band together to knock the company—to complain about faults in the software and demand improvements or modifications.

Of course, the net result is a growth in awareness by club members of the total product base of the company, more cross-selling of products to club members, and also a better esprit *within the company* as the enthusiasm of the club percolates through the organization.

Owner's clubs are particularly appropriate adjuncts to marketing databases for such products as automobiles, guns, dogs, cooking equipment, video and photographic equipment, boats, farm equipment, flowers, herbs, antiques and so on.

Personalized Newsletters. I read the newspaper every day. I read scores of magazines. Most of the articles are of little interest to me, but several times a week I see an article whose subject makes me want to read every word. It may be about Eastern Europe, or medical research or outer space. Finding an article of interest to you makes all the hunting through headlines worthwhile. Imagine reading a magazine in which *every article* was interesting to you. It almost seems too good to be true, and it probably is. But it might be possible to get closer to that kind of a magazine or newsletter with a marketing database.

The concept springs from two new developments: the database and modern laser printing technology. Customer surveys make it possible to find out exactly what every member is interested in, in exhaustive detail. It is possible to code a hundred different subjects and store these codes in the database. Newsletter editors can code news articles and features by the same system. When a member receives a newsletter, he finds that *all* the articles in *his* newsletter are on one of his coded subjects. His next door neighbor, who is a member of the same club, looks in his newsletter which he gets the same day and sees an entirely different group of articles, because his interests are very different. This is personal publishing. Of course, tucked in with the interesting articles is the company message about the products, upgrades, discounts and other programs which the database is designed to propagate.

It used to be that to produce different newsletters, you would print five or six versions, and each member would receive one of them. There would be a separate press run for each, and a separate mailing. Today that is not necessary. The presses keep running and each newsletter is produced one after another in the combinations of interest to the particular reader who will receive it. With 100 different interest codes, it is possible to produce and mail one million newsletters in one week and have every single one different from all the other 999,999. It is more expensive to print this way than a straight press run of newsletters that are all the same, but if this method results in the newsletter being read instead of being tossed aside, the results in terms of sales can make this kind of information exchange very profitable to the publisher.

Check Rebate. Another method listed in our software company's business plan is the check rebate, designed to keep the dealer happy. I won't cover it further here, since it is already outlined at length in Chapter 27 ("Database Marketing and the Dealer").

Telephone Registration. When software was new, everyone worried about pirating. After all, copying a diskette takes a couple of minutes. It is almost impossible to trace. The copier won't have the manual, but will have the software, and will have paid nothing for it. Software companies tried to make their product copy-protected, and they refused to help any caller who could not provide them with a valid registration number.

Since then, things have changed. Most of the products sold today are not copy protected. The technology is now moving so fast that most products are obsolete within a few months of their arrival on store shelves. Sales are brisk, and there is much less pirating than had been previously thought. Yet some companies still cling to the notion that owner registration is something to be guarded carefully. Why register someone who has stolen the product, and provide free telephone consultation? What an outrage!

The trouble with this type of thinking is that the name of the PC owner on the database is more valuable to the company than it is to the PC owner! If Sales = D • A • P, then the database needs to grow. You may have missed individuals on the first sale, but maybe you can sell them updates.

This means that every caller should get a warm welcome and become registered, then and there. Don't let anyone talk to your customer service or technical people for even one minute without surrendering name, address and telephone number, plus whatever else you have decided you need to know. After all, they called you to get information. Why shouldn't it be a two-way exchange?

Sweepstakes. Sweepstakes are easy to do, inexpensive to operate and very effective. Give away something big every quarter. Make everyone who has communicated with you in the past three months eligible to win. They can become eligible every quarter if they send in owner registration cards, or join the club, or ask for technical assistance or complete a survey. Publicize the winners throughout your system in newsletters and advertisements. Your database manager can run the selection program in fifteen minutes every three months and provide you with the winner. This is probably the least costly way to build business with a database.

Inputs and Outputs

Inputs. The inputs section of the business plan simply lists everything that you have to do to make the methods work. Outputs are the small benchmark products that prove that your methods are effective.

Examples of the scores of inputs listed on a software business plan could be:

- Add to the size of the database by buying lists of PC owners from magazines and PC hardware companies.

- Set up and train a corps of technical specialists to operate the 900 number technical assistance program. Make a full profit center out of this operation.

- Provide a series of links to assure that all the data coming into the system gets rapidly into the database and is available to all users. Figure 22-1 shows some of the relationships in the database process. In this case, the company has an in-house computer that provides about 100 customer service and technical people with direct access to customer records. The system lets them record the results of calls without actually modifying the customer records that they are viewing. Arrangements can be made to have the marketing database feed a complete new set of data to the company computer at regular intervals. In this way the data the customer service reps are working with would never be more than a week old. The results of telephone calls could go back into the database to close the loop.

At the same time, on a batch basis, new registrations, rented lists and the results of direct mail could be keypunched and added to the database on a regular basis.

- Train customer service reps in the newest scripts designed to present the new company image, increase registrations, increase use of the technical assistance, gain members for the club and make direct sales of products and upgrades.

- Set up a series of insightful marketing reports for the marketing staff and top management which shows, on a weekly basis, exactly how the database system is doing on achieving its objectives through strategies and methods.

- Experiment with test mailings and telemarketing to segmented groups of the database to sell upgrades, products, technical assistance and club memberships. Review the results of the tests, and test some more.

- Set up a staff to prepare the technical newsletters. Encourage club members to furnish information for the newsletters. With any luck, most of the articles can be written by members. Code the articles for field of interest, and set up a matching system of surveys to get the field of interest codes into the customer's database records.

- Of course, the big input is money. How much will it all cost: the club, the newsletters, the database itself, the direct mail, the surveys, the technical staff and the customer service representatives? Profits are what we are seeking here, not just sales. Each part of the plan has a cost, and it all adds up.

The idea is to get authorization for the money you will need to accomplish your objective. Company politics will dictate whether you can ask for everything you want, or only part of it. But at least you, the designer, should have an idea what it will cost you, whether you ask for it all now or not.

Outputs. On the output side, you must find a way to quantify the revenue resulting from each of the initiatives. The total revenue has to exceed the input, either on a quarterly basis or after a given period of time which you will have to determine. This revenue output is achieved by the realization of a number of specific quantifiable products of the inputs:

- Database to grow to so many names by November 19XX.

- Club to have so many members by October 19XX.

- Technical Assistance revenue to reach so much per month by last quarter of 19XX.

These outputs are similar to the other data in the plan: they are objectively verifiable numbers with target dates.

A Caution

We have been reviewing an ambitious business plan for a marketing database. There are few companies which cannot develop such a plan, and would not benefit from it. There are also few companies which have actually done it. One reason is that it is difficult—or dangerous—to stick your neck too far out. Database marketing is revolutionary. It will have many enemies within the company. If you present a grandiose plan which states boldly what you will accomplish by a certain date, and then you fail to achieve your planned results, your program could be killed.

My suggestion is this: start your marketing database system off modestly and slowly, and gather momentum as you go. Start with your top customers and gradually expand to all customers. Get your database working fast—within a year. Show some results. Convince yourself that your concepts are sound. Test and prove that your ideas work. Then go for it.

SUMMARY

- There should be a business plan drawn up for every marketing database. Whether or not you present it to top management, you should have it clearly in your own mind.

- Marketing databases should rapidly become profit centers, not "nice to have" frills.

- The business plan consists of a series of interrelated targets:
  - ➤ Goals
  - ➤ Objectives
  - ➤ Strategy
  - ➤ Methods
  - ➤ Inputs
  - ➤ Outputs

- Each goal, objective and output should be quantified by an objectively verifiable number with a target date.

- Sales = D • A • P. This means that, if you develop sound, effective programs to sell your customers products and upgrades, the bigger your database is, the greater will be your sales. Names are money.

- Some of the strategies explored in this chapter include:
  - ➤ A fee-based technical assistance program.
  - ➤ An owner's club.
  - ➤ Personalized newsletters.
  - ➤ Using surveys and telemarketing scripts to build up information on customers.
  - ➤ Encouraging any caller to register by telephone for inclusion in the database.
  - ➤ Use of sweepstakes to increase the database size.

- All inputs to the database system should be listed and quantified. In particular, there should be a recapitulation of the overall budget cost of the database which can be compared to revenue to determine the profitability of the database.

- Outputs are objectively verifiable measures of progress towards objectives. You can set them forth boldly for yourself, but decide later, after you have gained confidence, how many you want to make public within the company.

- A word of caution: don't make your initial database plans too grandiose. Start small. Get meaningful results the first year. Add to your program step by step as you gain confidence that your methods are working.

Chapter 23

The Privacy Issue— and Other Philosophical Problems

"Modern civilization has given man undreamt of powers largely because, without understanding it, he has developed methods of utilizing more knowledge and resources than any one mind is aware of." (F. A. Hayek, *New Studies*, University of Chicago Press, 1978.)

Database marketing is one of those methods. Proponents of database marketing are advocating a revolution in marketing technique. It goes by many names: individual marketing, relationship marketing, database marketing. The concept is that you try to learn more about your customers, to become friendly with them, to understand them, to develop two-way communications, to remember what they say and to use it in building rapport. As a result, the theory goes, you can build a lifetime relationship with these customers instead of just making a sale or two.

Compared to other methods of marketing, such as mass marketing and direct marketing, database marketing represents the development of a new philosophy of marketing. As with any philosophy it is partly faith and partly reasoning. In any case, if it is a valid phi-

431

losophy it must stand up to rigorous scrutiny. Let's look at it and raise some fundamental questions.

Question: Isn't database marketing really phony or fake? A computer doesn't care about customers. Building a database system which seems to care, complete with personalized letters, is really a fraud on the consumer, right?

Answer: It can be. If all a company does is collect information from consumers and feed it back to them without modifying behavior in the company, then it is a fraud.

I visited the offices of a major non-profit corporation one spring. The organization had modified their renewal forms to include a space for members to indicate their preferred program activities. Hundreds of thousands were completed and mailed in to the group together with their membership contributions. Unfortunately, the corporation had not done its homework. They had not modified their database to receive and report on contributor preferences. Their database programmers were way behind on their software development and simply could not fit this new information into the database. They were in fact throwing away the contribution forms after depositing the money and recording the name and address. The favorite program information was not recorded or tabulated.

Did the failure to capture this information and use it bother management? No one seemed much concerned. In fact, some expressed the belief that the very act of having an opportunity to tell the group what programs they preferred probably made the contributors feel better about the organization and helped contributions. The fact that their responses were thrown away would not be known and was unimportant.

Some even expressed a worry to me about what to do with the information if they did actually capture and record these preferences. Suppose for example that the survey showed that a majority of contributors were opposed to some activity favored by the board of directors. Should they take that into consideration in their program decisions? Some said that that idea would be contrary to the whole philosophy of a public interest group, which should be run for the public good, not for the *contributors,* who, after all, make up only a small faction of the general public who would receive the benefits.

We must leave this controversy to the high-minded public interest sector, and worry here about the reaction of a profit-making company to customer views and desires. Here the objective is clear: giving people exactly what they want should be good for both the business and the customers. The company that discovers what its customers are thinking and then *modifies its behavior* as a result, gives these customers better service and, in the long run, has more sales and more profits. The only fraud, it seems to me, is in collecting quantities of information and then not acting on it.

Successful database marketing will change the behavior of a company. It will have to grant a higher status to customer services. It will have to figure out how to include customer preferences and customer profiles in the design of products and services, the design of advertising, the marketing strategy, the pricing policy, the design of manuals and packages, the billing and delivery methods, the repair and replacement policies, the colors, shapes, sizes, fragrances and weights.

Conclusion: It is true that a computer doesn't care about anyone. But a company can, and should. The database is an information gathering and processing device. The information that it collects and serves up to marketing management should be acted upon. This information tells what the customer wants in the way of products and services. Acting on this information to modify the products and procedures of the company is not a fraud. It is in the highest interests of both the consumer and the producer.

Question: Isn't database marketing really advocating a return to older methods of marketing which the public has already rejected?

Answer: In this book there are constant references to bringing back the old corner grocer. Why are we trying to bring him back? After all, in 1950 there were tens of thousands of them all over America. Today they are virtually extinct. There was a free marketplace, and they lost out. They were swept aside by the supermarkets.

Doesn't that tell us something? If he lost out in the market once, why do we think that we can bring him back now?

Let us see why he lost out. He was not economically viable. His small store was labor intensive. Besides the grocer, there were many clerks waiting on customers. There were stock boys and delivery boys. The selection in his small store was limited. He could not buy in bulk, so his prices were high. One could argue that he lost out not because people didn't like his personal friendly style, but because they did not want to pay high prices at a store with a very limited choice of items.

I am reminded of the look on the faces of visitors from Eastern Europe who get their first experience in a modern American supermarket. Row after row of fruits and vegetables piled high in the middle of winter; an endless variety of meats, fish, bakery goods, dairy products, canned and dry foods. It is overwhelming, even for an American used to such things. You wheel an immense shopping cart down aisle after aisle, taking things from the racks as if you already owned them and piling your cart high with wonderful looking, clean, wholesome food and household products. There is no way that the corner grocer could compete with that. He lost; he is gone.

But with his departure we lost something that many of us miss. We lost the warmth and friendship which he provided. When you are in a supermarket or any large discount, department or hardware store and need help, it is usually very hard to find any employees, other than the overworked cashiers facing lines of people trying to get out. When you ask employees for assistance, you always feel that you are interrupting their regular work. They are there to replenish stock or do something else, not to answer your questions. And they may not know anything about the merchandise you are asking about. In any event, they are strangers who you may never see again. They don't know who you are, and they don't care. You are an anonymous shopper alone in a warehouse.

What database marketing promises to do is to retain the efficiency, low prices and tremendously wide variety of the modern product delivery service, but to add to it some of the warmth, individual concern and understanding that was provided by the old corner grocer. This is possible because the dramatic drop in the price of computer storage has made it possible to retain hundreds of facts about each customer, and to call them up to use in communicating with them on a daily basis. It is possible to recreate by computer some of the thoughtfulness of the old corner grocer without having also to recreate his inefficiency, high prices and poor variety of stock.

Conclusion: Yes, we are advocating bringing back something good from the past, but we are bringing it back in an entirely new, contemporary way which builds on modern marketing methods and practices that the public wants to retain.

Question: Aren't there some people who will be turned off by database marketing? Do people really want to become buddies with their suppliers? Don't people just want to be left alone?

Answer: A valid question. Certainly, back in the heyday of the corner grocer, there were plenty of people who resented his commercial heartiness. They just wanted to slip into a store, buy what they wanted and get out without a lot of conversation. Those people were thrilled when the impersonal supermarket came along. They don't want to go back to the old days. They resent today's telemarketers, who interrupt their evening meal with importunate demands. Can database marketing accommodate these people?

It can, and it must. Some people don't want a lot of mail or telephone calls. They will tell you that. This is information that you must tuck away in their record in the database. Every customer record should have a place for a "No mail," "No phone" and "No visit" code. Listen to what people say, accept it graciously, and respect their wishes. Thereafter, don't bother your customer with unwanted messages. The beauty of database marketing is that you can treat everyone differently, individually, as they want to be treated. The public is no longer at the mercy of a computer-driven mass marketing machine.

Conclusion: Yes, some people will be turned off by too much togetherness with vendors. Database marketing is ideally suited to recognize this and to respect it better than any other system.

Question: Isn't database marketing an invasion of privacy?

Answer: In America, everyone is free to be against everything. No sooner does a manufacturer come out with a great new product or process than some group springs up to point out that the innovation might damage the environment or could kill mice if they consumed megadoses of it. Database marketing is new, but already has its opponents. The question is: do we want private commercial concerns to be building up huge dossiers on us which can, in the future, be used to take away our privacy?

The average corner grocer was, essentially, harmless. We told him things about ourselves, and he acted like a friend. But not all of them were saints. Some were gossips. They chatted with the banker about people's overdrafts and bad debts. They discussed medical problems with the doctor, and asked the bartender and the policeman about people's drinking habits or police records. Such gossip in a small town could be dangerous.

Database marketing is a powerful tool which, in the wrong hands, could seriously invade people's private lives. How do you, as the designer and proponent, guard against that?

First, you should steer clear of building up secondary data in customer's records. Keep facts that your customers have told you about themselves, but not what you have learned about them from others. If they have passed you a bad check, you are entitled to remember it. If you are thinking of making them a big loan, you should request their permission to consult their credit references. If you are selling insurance, a physical examination is in order. But you should not store external data (like credit information, medical problems or arrest records) in a marketing database. If you do, you are laying the groundwork for a future legal challenge that could seriously damage the whole marketing industry.

Second, you should think twice about exchanging sensitive information with other companies. Elsewhere in this book I have advocated the renting of customer names as a valuable way to keep a customer list clean and useful. But watch what you are renting. If you are the keeper of credit information or medical histories, you have a responsibility to be sure that the people who use your data are doing so in a responsible way. If industry does not regulate itself, government will step in and spoil the party for everyone.

Third, you should set up an ombudsman for your database. It is easy for proponents of a database to build in everything that can be learned about prospects and customers which could conceivably help in the marketing process, but the company needs to think of broader issues. Just as the corner grocer had to watch his mouth if he wanted to stay in business, you have to watch your database. One way of doing that is to have someone within the company who is not actively involved in marketing who reviews, periodically, the information being kept on customers and how it is being used. This person should have a pipeline to the top of the company, and the responsibility to assure that the marketing database does not end up being like the CIA. The ombudsman needs to be on board from the beginning, with a definite charter and recognized status. Database marketing is too important to be left to the marketers.

Conclusion: Yes, database marketing can easily become an invasion of personal privacy. You as a database marketer have a responsibility and a civic duty to see that that does not happen. You must take active steps to prevent it.

Question: How do we know that database marketing will actually increase sales?

Answer: Any new technique has to prove itself in dollars and cents. You begin database marketing because of a hunch, but that hunch can be and must be tested before you throw millions of dollars into it.

From the start, you need to do two things: *test* and *count*. Every marketing effort with your database should be a test. Even the ten million name rollout should be a test. As a part of the test, you build in methods of counting. You build in *controls*: people who *were not* exposed to the new technique, against whom you can compare the results.

One of the objections to database marketing is that it is too expensive: millions of dollars must be spent building up the database before you know if it works. Not necessarily. Start small—use it for your best customers only. Test and sharpen your techniques before you spend big money. Do not embark on a five-year plan to build up a database, embark on a one-year plan. In that one year, build in several tests. All during the year, review the results of the tests before going on to bigger and better things.

Remember, database marketing is one-on-one; you and your customer alone together. You can try one thing with one customer and something entirely different with another customer. That is ok—it is one of the beauties of database marketing. Every customer can be a test. But be sure that you really are testing and counting. If you are not consciously trying to learn something from your database you will learn nothing, and you will be swept aside by competitors who are learning more.

Some techniques will work better than others. Some will not work at all. Database marketing does not guarantee results. It is a technique which you can use to get results, but it requires creative imagination, innovative experimentation, rigorous analysis of the results and modification of your approach based on your analysis.

Conclusion: Database marketing is one of the most verifiable techniques in any company's marketing arsenal. Unlike general advertising or direct marketing, you can audit your results and validate your techniques with rigorous scientific accuracy. If you are having an effect on sales, you will be able to prove it.

Question: What will happen when everyone has a marketing database? Won't the selling advantages cancel each other out?

Answer: Cash back. Coupons. Green Stamps. Four-page ads. Once one company uses them, the others have to follow suit. Soon you find yourself spending a fortune just to maintain market share, with no hope of increasing it. Philosopher Emmanuel Kant foresaw it all in 1770 in his *Critique of Pure Reason:* "Always act so that you can will that everybody shall follow the principle of your action." He developed the concept of the *categorical imperative* which commands that "every rational being ought to act as if he were by his principles a legislating member of a universal kingdom of ends." He foresaw a perfect society conducted by rational spirits. Following Kant's idea, cash back as a universal principle, becomes absurd. If everyone offers cash-back it will lose its punch as an inducement and become an accounting nuisance.

What Kant's categorical imperative means for us is that we should not start an expensive innovation, like database marketing, unless we have looked ahead to see what will happen when everyone has adopted it. Is it just another cash back trap?

Database marketing may have little impact on the first sale. You may still have to offer some dramatic gimmick to get the public's attention in the first place. All gimmicks are easily copied. The public becomes bored with them. You will have constantly to come up with new ones to attract new customers.

Database marketing aims not at that first sale, but at the second, the third and the following sales. It aims at building up a lifetime relationship with a customer. It aims at establishing a mutually profitable dialog in which customers tell you what they want, and you modify your behavior *towards them* to give them what they want. It involves modifying your products and services, your delivery methods and billing practices, your customer support and your prices. If you follow it rigorously, it will involve everyone in your company in some way. It will transform the way you create and deliver products and services.

Suppose everyone had a marketing database? Would that be good or bad? If we follow the logic of Kant's categorical imperative, it seems to me that it would be ideal. Every company would be trying to give their customers the particular kind of individual service and attention that they ask for. People would stick with your company not because of the wonderful advertisements, the deep discounts or the celebrity endorsements, but because you are giving them real service, personalized attention, responsive performance.

It is much cheaper to sell to existing customers than to beat the bushes to find new ones. If all companies had a larger repeat business, and could count on it, prices could come down.

For more than ten years, I bought Subaru station wagons. I love the color gold, and all of them were gold. When I came to buy my third wagon, I asked for gold. "Oh, they don't make gold Subaru's any more," the sales lady told me.

"Weren't they popular?" I asked.

"Oh, yes. We sold a lot of them. But this year we have a new designer and a whole new line of colors."

This was my third visit to Stohlman Subaru to buy a car in ten years. I was dealing with a new salesperson. In each of the previous visits I had new salespersons, since the old ones no longer worked there. That is the nature of the business. I had had all my required servicing done at Stohlman. But no one there knew me or remembered me. I had driven to the lot in my gold Subaru, which I parked out in front. As the salesperson walked me to a new station wagon for a test drive, she said, "I can't let you drive it off the lot. Subarus are a different driving experience. I will drive it out into the country, and then you can take over."

Needless to say, I bought a gold Dodge Colt Vista that year, and have never gone back to Subaru. Would a marketing database have helped Stohlman keep me as a customer, despite their constantly changing salesforce? I don't know, but I think so. Whatever feeling of loyalty I had towards the brand was dissipated by the attitude of the staff towards me.

This was many years ago, before the computer revolution. Today it would be fairly easy to keep track of Arthur Hughes and to give him the recognition he wanted and felt he deserved when he came in to buy his third Subaru. Yet few companies today are doing anything about this. The database marketing revolution is still in the future. But it is coming, and companies that have it should see a measurable increase in repeat business. When all companies have it, it will provide all consumers with a higher level of recognition, service and ability to influence the providers of products and services to give them what they want.

Conclusion: If every company had marketing databases it would help them to keep customers, and it would provide to all their customers better service than they would otherwise get. It would probably reduce prices. Universalizing database marketing would probably help both companies and customers.

SUMMARY

■ Database marketing is fraudulent if the company that practices it does not listen to its customers and act on their suggestions. If used to find out what customers want, and give it to them, database marketing is wholly meritorious.

■ Does database marketing involve returning to a rejected method of marketing—the old corner grocer? Yes. What was rejected was his inefficiency, high prices and poor selection. Database marketing brings back his service, recognition, friendship and loyalty, while retaining modern efficiency, low prices and wide variety.

■ Won't some people be turned off by database marketing? Yes. Code into the database not to telephone them or otherwise intrude in a manner offensive to them. Database marketing is ideally suited to respect customer's wishes.

■ Isn't database marketing an invasion of privacy? It can be. Companies setting up databases must take steps to see that they are used for marketing and not for snooping.

■ How do you know that database marketing will actually increase sales? Database marketing lives by counting and reports. If it increases sales, you will be able to prove it. If it doesn't, you should cut it back.

■ If every company had a marketing database, would that not tend to cancel out the advantages? Not at all. A successful marketing database increases repeat sales and customer loyalty. It should improve service to customers and reduce costs and prices. If every company had such a database, it would improve overall customer satisfaction and reduce the general level of prices.

Chapter 24

The Creative Agency

Somewhere behind every *successful* marketing database is a man or woman with a genius for marketing. Anyone can collect a list of customer names and call it a marketing database, but to make it successful requires several important talents and skills:

■ The creative imagination needed to conceive it in the first place; to figure out how it could work and how all the pieces could come together.

■ The leadership qualities to sell it to all the people who have to be sold, and to push it through, despite opposition from an established and ongoing operation which, at first, cannot understand how this new creation could possibly be of any use, but can well visualize how it could cut into their operations and cramp their style.

■ The administrative ability to follow all the pieces through; to see that everything gets done and nothing is left to chance.

■ The courage to face disappointing delays and mortifying errors which occur during the first two years.

People with these talents are rare. Sometimes they are found within an established company. Perhaps you, the reader, are such a person. As you look around your company and contemplate the steps necessary for you to build a marketing database, you will eas-

ily be able to write down a list of all the problems and difficulties
you will have. You must:

- convince marketing, sales, customer relations and management
  that it is a good idea;

- get the budget to carry it out;

- keep it away from those who want to smother it with kindness
  by burying it in a long range plan, and

- maneuver yourself into a leadership position to push it through.

John Stevenson was one of those unique people. In 1978 he
was the first direct marketing professional to manage the American
Express Card Division. As Vice President, he was in charge of the
consolidation of direct marketing for AMEX and responsible for the
application of new systems and advanced technology. He managed a
multi-media communications program which included over one million pieces of direct mail per day.

John was one of the earliest inventors of the concept of
"database marketing" in 1978 through his innovations at American
Express. At that time, AMEX had one of the few huge computer
operations available to build a marketing database. John had the
dream and the resources. He was given sufficient latitude by AMEX
management to mobilize outside advertising agencies, service bureaus and AMEX internal staff talents in statistics, marketing research, operations and systems. The successful concept he created at
that time has spread since then throughout the country.

You may be able to do something similar. Some databases have
been created by inside managers, supported by far-seeing top management. Those who have been successful have risen fast within
their organizations, and gone on, like John Stevenson, to spread the
word throughout the industry.

But in many cases the type of person who has these qualities
and is in a position to exercise them effectively is someone in a
creative direct agency: either of the large direct agencies which are
being built up within the big advertising agencies like Ogilvy &
Mather, McCann Erickson or Chiat/Day/Mojo, or someone in the

scores of independent creative direct agencies like Biggs/Gilmore, that have grown up in cities across the country. Why have they been so successful?

I think that it is because they bring to the table some additional qualities and abilities that are hard to find within an established company:

- an independent spirit, willing to try out new ideas, to pioneer with something new;

- a creative team used to developing creative direct mail and advertising copy;

- (occasionally) an ongoing direct program for the company which can be expanded into a database idea;

- access to the top tiers of management in companies which is sometimes difficult for managers working from within;

- experience in creating databases in other companies which they can transfer directly to use in thinking through and starting up a database in a new environment;

- wide contacts throughout the direct industry which permit them to know where to go for a service bureau, for lists, for modeling capability, for consultants; and

- an entrepreneurial attitude towards the database. They stand to make money by setting up a successful system. To a manager within a company, the database is a risk. If he pushes it and it fails, it could blight his career. If it is successful, he could be promoted. But to the creative agency it is a client relationship — they will be paid for their work either way. They have the drive and the independence to push the idea and sell it.

There are about 500 U.S. advertising agencies actively involved in direct marketing in 1991. Surprisingly few of them have significant computer knowledge and skills. Some of them have acquired their own service bureaus to create integrated operations, but most of them look to the growing number of database-minded service bureaus that can provide the hardware, software and analytical skills needed.

Altogether, there are only a handful of agencies and service bureaus today which are actively creating real marketing databases as we have defined them. It is a massive growth industry today. Anyone who can become successful at it will have a very profitable lifetime career ahead.

Agency Role

The essential idea is that the database is not a free-standing entity, but an integral part of a *creative program* designed to use the database to accomplish a specific objective. Databases don't do anything; they help creative people to accomplish an objective by:

- providing a communication vehicle with customers;
- providing something of value to customers so that they benefit by the communication;
- permitting selection and segmentation of the customer base by RFM principles;
- permitting tests and measurement of success;
- paying their way through proved purchase behavior;
- telling the sponsor and the agency something about the audience for the product which they could use to go on to develop something bigger and more permanent.

Qualities Required

There will be exceptions, of course, but in general it can be said that there cannot be a successful marketing database without the assistance of a really creative direct agency. What does this agency have to do? What are the qualities that it must have which will make a marketing database a success? I believe that there are six, as follow.

1. Ability to Dream Up Winning Concept for a Database. Any successful marketing database is built around an idea or concept of what it will accomplish for the customer and for the company. The idea may be to build loyalty, to promote repeat sales, to sell upgrades or complementary products, to improve service, to qualify and track leads. There must be an idea, and it must be so logical and compelling that it can be sold to other members of the company. To dream up this idea, a creative direct agency needs a man or woman with the kind of vision that will produce just the right idea for the company and product. It is not easy to find such people.

2. Leadership and Salesmanship. An idea alone is not enough. It must be sold to a tough, bottom-line conscious management in a company which probably contains many successful people who do not see the value of a marketing database. The genius who comes up with the creative concept does not have also to be the salesman — the two roles are easily divided. But both abilities must be lodged in the creative agency at the same time and linked together in a winning team to get the marketing database off the ground.

It is much easier to sell a marketing database from the outside than it is to push it from within. For this reason, the creative agency is in an ideal position to make such a concept happen. But without a man or woman with leadership and salesmanship abilities committed to the concept, the database will not fly.

3. Creative Depth. Depth is something that most creative agencies have. By depth, I mean the ability to provide:

- excellent direct mail creative;
- first class magazine, TV, radio ads;
- canny choice of media and placement;
- imaginative telemarketing script ideas;
- close attention to little creative details: the membership card, the welcome kit, the thank-you letter, the long service award.

These are the strengths of creative direct agencies. Many such agencies are superb at providing them.

4. Quantitative Skills. Marketing databases are very different from general advertising. They are *profit centers*. Their purpose is to make money for the company that creates them. Many advertising agencies don't really grasp that concept. In the design, in the execution and in the reporting mechanisms built up for any marketing database, there should be a clear understanding of how the activities under the database will be tracked, reported and related to the bottom line. There must be a clear financial plan from the beginning (which will be constantly revised, of course) which shows the relation of each activity to increasing sales and profits.

Creative people are sometimes vague when it comes to accounting and finance. To be successful at database marketing, a direct agency has to have these financial skills in addition to its other skills.

5. Administrative Ability. It is one thing to sell an idea, and provide great creative to support it for the first few months. But a database needs constant attention to administrative details. This is an area where most creative direct agencies are woefully weak.

Harry Truman used to describe the presidency in this way: "All I do, all day, is to sit in my office and try to persuade people to do what they are supposed to do without my telling them. That is all the powers of the president amount to."

He was right about the presidency, and it applies to the marketing database. Consider this:

- Are the samples being delivered on time?

- Are the telemarketers saying what the script says they should be saying?

- Does the delivered mail look like what the creative designers thought it was going to look like? Or has some flaw in the execution spoiled the package— sloppy folding, poor addresses, late delivery?

- Are there enough customer service telephone lines manned at peak periods, or does the customer always get a busy signal or get put on hold for long periods of time?

- Are we capturing the information for the database that was planned? And are we using the information that we have in the right way?

- Are we updating the database properly and in a timely fashion? Do people throughout the system rely on it for correct information, or is it late, and often wrong?

Running a marketing database is a huge administrative burden with thousands of little details to be attended to. "Fine," I can hear you saying, "but surely these details are the responsibility of the marketing staff within the company, and not the external creative agency."

Yes and no. The marketing staff must take leadership. If it is headed by a strong person who has this administrative ability and exercises it, the creative agency can relax. But what if marketing is not as strong on administration as the situation requires? In this case, it is not enough to sit back and say "We came up with a great idea, but they dropped the ball. Too bad."

The creative direct agency is in an ideal position to see what is happening, and to point it out. It must do this, or the program could fail through lack of follow-through on administration. In many cases this is exactly the situation.

6. *Long-Term Follow-Through.* Here is the greatest weakness of most creative direct agencies. They are great for the big push; selling the new idea; winning the new contract. But after a few months, they lose interest in it. They are dreaming about the next exciting concept. Worrying about the success of the last one is someone else's job.

Marketing databases don't go away. Once you begin them, you must keep them going. You have to feed them new ideas, and little twists and adjustments and tests to keep them alive. For some reason, the personality that is ideal for creating and selling a new idea is very poor at long-term follow through. Maybe agencies need to be staffed with an offensive team to sell an idea and a defensive team to keep it going. This is something that needs to be addressed by anyone who heads a direct agency.

Are Agencies Up to the Challenge?

We have set out the conditions for a successful direct agency. How many agencies out there measure up? I would say that there are very few creative agencies that have sufficient depth in the six qualities I have set forth.

It is possible to develop these qualities. Intelligent and careful staff selection and training can group together a winning team. Unless more agencies do develop this depth, however, the database marketing revolution will never get off the ground. That is the challenge.

Summary

- A successful marketing database comes about only if someone with a very creative idea involving a database is matched with someone with the leadership ability and position sufficient to push the database through in the organization.

- In many cases, the leadership of a creative direct agency coming to a company from the outside is necessary to make a database concept a reality.

- There are six qualities which any creative direct agency must have to succeed in the database marketing support arena. They are:

  1. Ability to dream up a winning concept for a database.
  2. Leadership and salesmanship.
  3. Creative depth.
  4. Quantitative skills.
  5. Administrative ability.
  6. Long-term follow-through.

Most agencies have the first three qualities. Few of them have the last three. Without these last three, the marketing database idea will ultimately fail.

Chapter 25

The Database Administrator

The company is running as usual. Products are being manufactured and readied for sale. The sales staff is signing up contracts with the dealers. Advertising is placing ads through their general agency. Somewhere, off in an unlikely corner, marketing and their direct agency have gotten the approval, and enough money to start a marketing database. Few think that it will ever amount to much, but why not give it a try?

Slowly, the marketing people begin to get their act together. Their business plan was approved and they have signed up a service bureau to create the company's first marketing database. While the service bureau is reformatting the customer tapes and the software is being written, marketing is spending half the time with the direct agency watching the creation of some exciting new direct mail and DRTV commercials. The other half of their time they are working with a new telemarketing firm that has been hired to take the sales calls. The demand on their time is almost more than they can cope with.

They know that they should be working closely with Customer Service, and figuring out an accounting interface between the database and the MIS general ledger system, plus checking that the product fulfillment system is laid out properly, but there really is no time. Launch of the new program is set for three months away, and it seems as if they will never have everything ready.

451

Every day the calls come in. Where is the telemarketing script? What are the SKU's that will be offered, and how much does each sell for? In what states do they have to pay sales taxes, and who do they pay them to? How many telemarketers will they have to have on duty the day that the ad in Better Homes and Gardens hits the stands? Should they accept the excellent bargain offered for spots on national cable? And what kind of response will there be? Will the calls flood the system?

Gradually, panic sets in. Marketing has become the Database Administrator, and it is a little scary. No one who has not experienced it can really understand what it is like to launch a major database marketing operation in a large company. It is like the opening of a Broadway play, but more hectic and unnerving because with a Broadway play, at least, most of the producers, directors, stage

Figure 25-1 Getting Ready for Database Launch

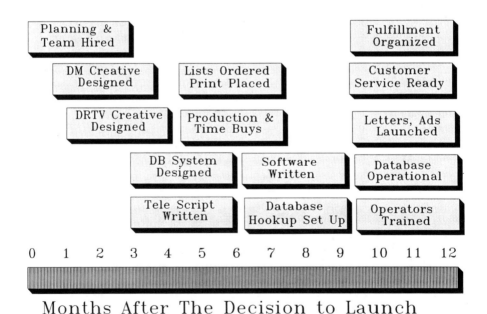

Months After The Decision to Launch

hands and actors have all been through it before in other plays on other nights. Not so in database marketing. It is usually new for everyone: the company, the telemarketer, the service bureau, the direct agency, the fulfillment operation, customer service and the marketing staff. All are experienced and professional in their fields, but few of them have put it all together in a major operation like this one. There is no one to turn to for answers, so you just have to make them up as you go along and hope for the best.

It is a situation that calls for forceful leadership. Marketing must provide it in the form of a Database Administrator (DBA), a man or woman who will be working sixty-hour weeks for the first two years until the project is well-launched. The pressure is brutal. (See Figure 25-1, the schedule for a launch.)

Let's return to the beginning, and get some idea of the pitfalls that exist in each step.

1. Planning

Database marketing involves at least half a dozen different organizations that must work together to achieve a common end. The system requires strong central direction from the DBA. The planning has to be systematic and organized. As much as possible, details need to be worked out once the project is launched because there is seldom enough time to do so. The DBA has to form a planning team which consists of:

- The Direct Agency
- The Database Service Bureau
- The Telemarketers
- The Fulfillment Staff
- Customer Service

Figure 25-2 The Database Management Team

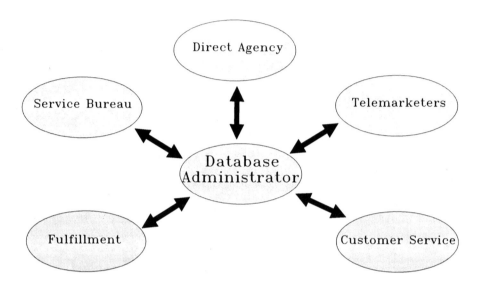

The plan must look forward to the launch, and figure out what has to happen hour-by-hour, day-by-day during the first month. There is a lot of money riding on the ads. Thousands of people will telephone. Everyone—telemarketers, database and fulfillment—has to be ready to meet the challenge.

2. Contractors

Who do you hire to do the work? Some companies have tried to work with an in-house team. I know of few successes. You are better off with professional telemarketers, a responsive service bureau, a very imaginative, thorough direct agency and a resourceful fulfillment staff. With skilled outsiders, the DBA has much more leverage to get the job done properly and on time. If they don't shape up, he can replace them with others. But if he has in-house staff who also work for other persons in the company, he cannot replace them. If they are not responsive he is stuck, and his database marketing project may fizzle. The only area where an in-house crew can possibly handle the work is in Customer Service.

Some questions to ask:

- Is the telemarketer big enough to put on twenty or thirty extra people on heavy days? Do they have the equipment and the trained people available?

- Does the direct agency have staff skilled in creative design, list selection, media selection; and do they have the management capability to follow through on all the details? Do they work well with others?

- Does the service bureau have a large enough mainframe and disk capacity to meet your challenge? Do they have nightly backup and an uninterruptable power supply? Do they have a modern relational database software system? Do they guarantee three-second access time for 50 or more telemarketers simultaneously? Do they have a responsive programming staff that is willing to put up with constant changes in the software during the opening weeks of your campaign? Do they have a quality control system that will catch errors before they become disasters? Do they have the management ability to serve as system integrators for your entire database system? Can they help you to integrate the operations of your telemarketers, your direct agency and fulfillment? Finally, can they produce daily reports and ad-hoc queries on exactly what is going on throughout the system?

- Does the fulfillment operation have the warehouse and shipping staff to get the product out the door on the same day that the order arrives? Catalog marketers are satisfied with six- to eight-week deliveries. But that does not work with database marketing. You are trying to establish a dialog with your customers and keep them for life. That means *response*. When they call, you jump. Will your fulfillment operation jump?

3. Creative Design

How much rides on good design of the offer and the package? A great deal. But more than that, with database marketing, the printed material must conform to other standards: people will be calling your 800 number with the ad in their hands. Telemarketers are waiting to respond with a script worked out in advance. *The ad and the script must correspond.* How easy it is to forget that, and design a great creative ad or direct mail piece that does not fit the telemarketer's plan.

Of course, telemarketers' scripts can be changed and will be changed constantly during the campaign. However, there is another purpose that the creative copy must serve. The database itself has been planned to receive certain information from the customers. Are the right questions asked in the direct mail piece?

One major campaign recently asked customers to recommend friends as customers. A place was provided on the response device for the name and address of the friend. But the agency forgot to include a space or code for the customer —so an expensive promotion was largely wasted.

One key in the plan is the cell code. This is a source code that identifies each direct mail package, each list, each offer, each TV ad, each print ad. By looking at the cell code you should be able to know exactly what induced this customer to call. Creative has to set up a system for these cell codes early in the program. There should be a printed list of them all, so that telemarketers, the service bureau and the copy designers are aware of them.

The problem with cell codes is getting customers to volunteer them. It is relatively easy to print them properly on the direct mail reply forms, but how do you get television respondents to remember them? You are lucky that they wrote down your 800 number. Telemarketers will have to trace the code through the callers. Good planning and design of the ads will help.

4. List Selection

In the rush to do everything else, list selection is often left to the last minute. It is a technical matter that most people don't know much about, yet it is *the single most important factor* in determining the size of the response: more important than the package or the offer. The DBA cannot afford to leave this subject to the direct agency without review.

If there is an existing customer base, some modeling is definitely in order. Do RFM analysis to pick your best customers, and then determine their dominant characteristics. Go after lists that match these characteristics. Proper selection of names, segmentation and merge/purge can save thousands of dollars that will be needed elsewhere.

5. TV and Print Ad Placement

What is your audience? Who is likely to respond? Analysis of your existing customer base can tell you a great deal. If you do a cluster analysis, you can then use Simmons or MRI to pick the media that reaches that audience the best. Time of year is important, as is geographic area. All of these are the province of the direct agency. What is usually overlooked is the impact on the whole system of a successful ad. Somehow you have to decide how many thousand people will call your 800 number on any given day, and have enough trained telemarketers on duty. If you don't, thousands will get a busy signal and you will lose them.

The main problem is that ad placement takes place several months before the actual air or publication date. Media people are looking for the best deal. Somehow, after they have made the deal and placed the ads, they forget to sit down with the telemarketers and estimate daily response. The DBA has to assure that that happens.

6. Fulfillment

Fulfillment is the weak link in any database marketing operation. Here is what you will have to look out for and plan for:

Next-day response on all orders. This is not as simple as it sounds. In database marketing the daily requirement may shift from 800 to 8,000 in one day. This means picking, packing, labeling and shipping. It is very labor intensive. Does the fulfillment house have enough space, enough temporary staff, and the management capability to expand temporarily to meet your peak demands?

Out-of-stock. The best database operation in the world can be sabotaged by poor planning for stock availability. Does the warehouse have enough capacity to keep a month's supply on hand? Do they have a good inventory planning system to let them, and you, know when they run low on certain items? When you run out, what will the customer receive? A post card? A letter? A phone call? What is the system, and is it in place? Finally, when you get the stock back in, what happens? Is it automatically shipped? Does the system keep track of unshipped items?

Quality control. It is easy to send the wrong item. It is easy to send out damaged goods. The DBA cannot check on this. He or she must depend on the fulfillment house having good management and excellent quality control.

7. Customer Service.

Customer service is where two-way dialog really has to happen. Whatever the company did in this area in the past, it will have to do much better with a marketing database. Here are some of the things that the DBA will have to check up on:

The customer records. Has the service bureau equipped all customer service staff with terminals so that they can call up any customer record instantly, and see everything that has happened to them up through yesterday? Can they tell if product has been shipped, and when? Can they see billing errors, and fix them? Do they have a record of all prior calls?

The staff. Are the customer service personnel properly trained for the work? Can they operate their screens? Have they absorbed the new philosophy of customer service: that it is the establishment of a two-way dialog which involves them adding data to the database and giving out helpful information? Do they know that they are *salespeople* as well as information suppliers?

The telephone system. Are there enough lines to prevent customers from getting a busy signal? Is there an interchange between customer service and technical assistance whereby customers who need technical help can get it without dialing back (unless the company has installed 900 number fee-based technical assistance)?

Authority. The most important thing to give customer service is the authority to resolve customer problems on the spot. Replace defective or damaged merchandise, resolve billing discrepancies, find and speed up delayed shipments and issue refunds where necessary. If we are going to recreate the old corner grocer, we have to give our customer service employees the authority that he had to solve customer problems.

8. The Database System

It will take you about six months, minimum, to get the database system up and running prior to your launch. Allow eight months if you can. Here are some features that the DBA has to assure work properly:

The Design. There should be a formal conference when the service bureau has designed the system. Present should be the DBA, the direct agency, the telemarketers and the fulfillment staff. Every aspect of the design should be reviewed to make sure that everyone understands and supports what is going to happen.

Conversion. If you have an existing customer base, it will have to be converted to the new database system. When this happens, the DBA should review the records. He or she should call up customers on the screen and see how their records look. If the records don't come up immediately, this is a danger sign. How will the system react when it is really loaded, after launch?

Are the records clean and presentable for direct mail? Are there any duplicates? You can discover this by asking for a printout of 200 records, arranged alphabetically, beginning at any given point in the database. Scrutinize these records closely. Can you detect any duplicates? Are the address and the spelling of the names correct? The service bureau may object that they did not create the names and so cannot be held responsible for the quality of them. A good argument, but are you satisfied with it? Was there nothing that they could do? How will these people react in the thick of battle?

Keypunching. Who is going to open the direct mail envelopes, cashier the money and keypunch the orders? What capacity are they geared for? Can they handle 1,000 a day? 2,000? 3,000? How about their resources and ability to put on temporary staff?. What is the quality control on their keypunching. The DBA should insist on seeing some of their work done for other clients. Your whole campaign could bog down if you cannot keypunch rapidly and accurately. Do not assume quality without proof.

Letter quality. In most direct agencies, "production" is a separate function assigned to someone accustomed to working with laser mailshops. This may be good enough for direct marketing, but it does not work with *database marketing.* Letters to customers are not "production." They are communications which cannot be shopped around by the job. Your service bureau must be equipped with first-class laser printing and mailshop facilities so that your communications with customers can go directly from the database to the post office in a high-quality, personalized letter. What happens to your two-way dialog when the letters are delayed for a week and the printing is sloppy?

The DBA should investigate the method of producing letters to customers to be sure that the output is timely and reflects the image the company wants to project. Letters can be the weak link in your whole system. A good way to check on quality on a continuing basis is to have the service bureau include the DBA as a "customer" on some customer files every other day. The DBA will receive, at home, a letter which is representative of what all customers are getting. He should look closely at these letters, checking the quality and the timeliness. Even if he doesn't check the letters every day, just knowing that he might will keep the service bureau on their toes.

While the DBA is checking the quality of the letters to customers, he should also investigate the quality of direct mail letters to prospects. (The ones that the direct agency will insist are "production" and will be farmed out to some mailshop.) How good is the appearance of the name on the envelope? Is it a poor quality label? Are there duplicates? The DBA should not just *assume* that the direct mail will be done correctly. Without proper checking, it won't. Yet how many hundreds of thousands of dollars will be spent on direct mail?

Menu screens. The system which the service bureau sets up is the heart of the whole database marketing operation. They prepare the screens that the telemarketers use in answering calls from the customer and the customer service screens that form the basis of the two-way communications. How good are these screens? Will they move as rapidly as the conversations on the telephone move? If not, reprogram them so they are fast. It can be done — the DBA must insist that it is done.

Reports. Database marketing requires that all parts of the marketing team get daily reports on what is going on: sales broken down by cell code, telemarketing operator, SKU, type of customer, sales region and such. You need reports on the average order, the repeat orders, the refunds, the complaints, the suggestions, the referrals. Will this service bureau be able to deliver these daily reports when the orders are coming thick and fast after launch?

Responsiveness. How fast will this service bureau react when you ask them to make an important change in the software? Can they turn things around in a week? If it takes longer, is it because the change is very complex and they want to make sure that no errors creep into the system? Or does it take longer because the service bureau does not have enough programmers devoted to your work? Or because their management is sluggish and uncooperative? The DBA must dig into these matters early because once the program is launched, it is too late. An unresponsive service bureau will doom the project.

Telemarketers

Finally, the DBA will be spending a lot of time with the telemarketers. He must personally be present at some of their training to be sure that they are going to present the right image of the company. These operators are not order-takers. They are the first part of a new company selling program that emphasizes personal attention to each customer. Whatever training they had before is not enough. They need to know all about the company, the products and the database. They need to know how to get information from the customers without being too pushy. They need to sell. They need to be helpful.

Even though the telemarketers are working for a private service bureau, they have to realize that, like actors in a play, they *are* the company. They should be able to refer customers to customer service or technical assistance when necessary. They should have the authority to commit the company to occasional extraordinary kindnesses: "Yes. I will see that you get that sweater by Saturday, in time for the birthday party." And they should have the ability to make good on their promises.

The DBA in the Company Hierarchy

From the above, you should have a pretty good idea of the responsibilities of a Database Administrator. He or she is very busy. The DBA must pay a lot of attention to detail. The DBA has to form an interactive team, and consult the team regularly for help in moving the database forward. The DBA also must wield a lot of authority.

The DBA's supervisor must understand that if the marketing database concept is to succeed, considerable authority will have to be delegated to the DBA to discipline contractors, to resolve disputes, to spend additional money when necessary to get the job done. The DBA must decide on Friday night that the telemarketers should call in twenty extra operators for the weekend because of the new TV spot. He shouldn't have to go somewhere else for approval. If you have a DBA who is not really strong enough for this role, get a new one or postpone your entry into the world of database marketing.

Some marketing databases fail for just this reason: weak administrators in the DBA slot. It is a crushing responsibility. Very few people have the required qualities. If database marketing fails in the long run, it will be because American industry has failed to attract the kind of hard-driving, detail-minded, resourceful decision-makers that it takes to run these systems.

Summary

- There must be a Database Administrator (DBA) in charge of every marketing database within a company.

- Planning a database requires a team consisting of the DBA, the direct agency, the service bureau, the telemarketers, the fulfillment staff and customer service.

- The DBA must pick outside contractors who are up to the job.

- The telemarketers' script, creative design and database design must all mesh.

- The DBA must look into list selection and ad placement.

- Fulfillment can be the weak link in database administration.

- The DBA should assist in training customer service and seeing that they comprehend the philosophy of database marketing and the authority to do their job.

- Database design is important. The DBA must review it and be sure that it meets his or her needs. The service must be responsive to changes and shifts in strategy.

- Any company that commits itself to database marketing must delegate enough authority to the DBA so that he or she can get the job done.

Chapter 26

The Sales Staff and the Marketing Database

One obstacle to successful database marketing is often overlooked: the vice president for sales. Why is it that sales almost always tries to fight the installation of a marketing database system? There are several reasons. Let's begin the discussion by listing some of them.

Why Salespeople Fight Marketing Databases

- A marketing database implies direct sales, which means that no salespeople will be needed. Sales will be cut out of the loop and the commissions. Salespeople are usually asked to provide the database with a list of their contacts. Salespeople live by their contacts. To surrender them is to give up their livelihood. Once they are in the database you will write letters to them and call them; the next thing you know, the database will be selling to them, not the salesman. Goodbye, commissions. One of the main functions of a marketing system is to develop leads. These leads are usually turned over to salespeople for action. But with a functioning database system, complete with telemarketers, you may decide to pursue the lead yourself. What happens to the salespeople?

- Even worse, you may supply all your leads to sales. In the past, salespeople have ignored the leads that they didn't think were worth bothering with. But now your database has a lead tracking system which asks for reports on the status of each lead. The salesperson feels Big Brother breathing down his or her neck.

- In fact, the database can become a management tool for evaluating the effectiveness of each salesperson. Whereas in the past a salesperson could say that sales were poor because the market was not good, today, with a steady flow of leads, the salesperson will have to hustle and dance to someone else's tune. The database may actually reduce commissions. In the cable TV industry, for example, individual cable services are often paid a bonus for the percentage of coverage that they can achieve. For example, if the cables have been run past 100,000 houses in a city, the goal is to have 100,000 subscribers. There are bonuses for 80 percent, 85 percent and so on.

Along comes the marketing database, and through close study of the service area it may be possible to discover that the cables actually are serving 120,000 possible homes, not 100,000. What was 80 percent now becomes 66 percent overnight. Goodbye, bonus.

Look at it from the salespeople's point of view. They are out on the firing line, trying to find leads, win them over, make sales and get commissions. Marketing people think that they can do the same thing by direct mail and telemarketing. This is threatening. Suppose they are correct? They will force salespeople out of their jobs. Even if the marketers are not correct, they will waste a lot of time, get credit for half of the sales and cut into salespeoples' opportunities to make commissions. What good can possibly come out of cooperating with them?

To top it off, marketing departments are often staffed by MBAs who have learned all the theory, but have never, in fact, closed on a sale themselves. They consider themselves above the crass business of asking for a sale. They want to conduct marketing with computers, producing reams of fine reports and statistics.

You may smile at these differences, but they are real differences in most companies, and unless you recognize the problems and deal with them *your marketing database will be a failure.*

Janet Park, President of Marketing Frontiers, tells an interesting story which illustrates this point. "I was having lunch one day with several executives from a leading business-to-business list compiler. They were describing to me in detail the intricacies of their three-year database research project for one of the largest and most sophisticated marketing companies in the United States. Millions of dollars had been spent on surveys, data overlays and analytical models to refine the 'perfect' business list for supporting their brokers in the field offices.

"That same afternoon, I had a meeting with a friend of mine who just happened to be a broker for the same sophisticated marketing company mentioned above. I asked him how he got his leads. 'Yellow Pages,' he said. 'I look in the Yellow Pages and call them up. Sometimes,' he added guiltily, 'I just resort to smokestacking. If I see an interesting looking building while driving around, I'll just stop and make a cold call to see if there's anything worth pursuing.'

"It seemed ironic to me that the sophisticated results of the home office database marketing projects had not yet 'trickled down' to benefit the street soldiers of sales. Smokestacking, not linear regression, was still the default method of research in the field. And this happened in 1988."

The problem is a natural one. As long as marketing people are thinking up new types of direct-mail pieces to generate new leads, their activities are not threatening. But when they try to include *my* customers on their marketing database, I can see the hand writing on the wall, and I am going to fight it.

Remember: the database aims at the lifetime value of a customer. Repeat sales, cross-selling, upselling, referrals — these are the lifeblood of a marketing database, but they are also the meat and potatoes of the sales staff. Who wants constantly to hunt down new customers when the old customers are so much easier to service? Salespeople will see the database as a threat to force them into the harder work of new customer acquisition, while the marketing database gets all the credit and honors for the easy work of servicing existing customers.

Possible Solutions

In most companies sales is strong, marketing weak. In a head-to-head contest, the marketing database will lose. So if you can't beat them, join them. Let's start with the theory, then proceed to practice.

What you want to achieve is a system in which the salespeople feel comfortable with your database. They feel that it is their baby; that they can play with it, feed it, get information out of it and *get credit for its success*. The main concern will be the threat to their compensation method.

This means that if you have a strong salesforce that works on commission, you have to see that they continue to get their commissions once the database is installed. This may be tricky to do with a telemarketing and direct mail program cross-selling and upselling to customers directly. If you have to pay a salesperson a commission on sales he or she did not make, the economics of the database may come into question. Where is the money for the telemarketing and direct mail programs?

Some companies have solved that problem by installing the telemarketers right in the sales divisional headquarters. The commissions earned go partly to the telemarketers and partly to the salesperson of record for the account. The telemarketers are under the supervision of the division sales manager, and come to all the meetings with the salesforce. The salesperson is encouraged to feed the telemarketers work since, in many cases, they can cover more ground in a day than salespeople can cover in a week.

In this arrangement, the telemarketer talks first to any new lead and qualifies it before it is given to a salesperson. Meanwhile, the salespeople are handling the big accounts which need their special attention and clinching ability. The telemarketer handles the less likely accounts, the smaller ones, the long shots. Direct mail is used for the cold calling, followed up by telemarketing. If an account looks really promising, it is then turned over to a salesperson.

Working thus as a team, salespeople can accept and work well with a marketing database. Somewhere in the background is the marketing manager, who is still in charge of the database and is directing the effort from the sidelines. The manager is the coach; the sales division manager is the quarterback. The salespeople are the running and passing backs and the ends; while the marketing database serves as guard, tackle and center: fighting off the unqualified leads and passing the ball to the quarterback for the scoring plays.

HEWLETT-PACKARD EXPERIENCE

Here's how Karen Blue, President of Advanced Marketing Solutions in Oakland, California, went about successfully solving this problem at the Hewlett-Packard Company. It is a wonderful example of marketing and sales working as a team.

A few years ago Hewlett-Packard, facing a tough competitive situation, created a new Customer Information Center to improve customer satisfaction and increase field productivity. The Center was intended to handle the entire Hewlett-Packard line of computers and electronic equipment. Ms. Blue was Direct Marketing Manager for the new center. She established three objectives:

- to fill the sales funnel with timely, qualified leads;
- to integrate and improve the productivity of all direct marketing activities; and
- to automate the feed-back and promotion evaluation process.

The internal customer lists that they started with were difficult to use. They were designed for sales analysis and order processing, not marketing. They contained account numbers, order statistics and invoice addresses, not user names, shipping locations or the profile information they needed for an effective marketing program.

The salespeople initially were very resistant. They didn't think that a marketing unit could effectively qualify leads. They especially didn't want anyone else to contact their accounts - through mail or telephone.

To turn things around Ms. Blue directed two important steps:

- She set up a training program to educate the marketing and sales managers to show them how they would benefit from proper use of marketing tools. She used an outside consultant who had helped to set up the marketing database: Victor Hunter of Hunter Business Direct of Milwaukee.

- The Customer Information Center, when set up, would support the company's sales and marketing strategy with five components:

Figure 26-1 Changing Sales Force Time Allocation

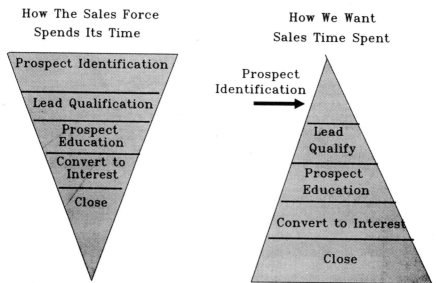

Telemarketers should identify and qualify prospects. Salesmen are needed for last three steps.

---

1. Lead generation.
2. Inquiry management.
3. Lead qualification.
4. Lead distribution and feedback.
5. Promotion campaign measurement and market analysis.

1. *Lead Generation and Inquiry Management*

Lead generation became the responsibility of the direct marketing program managers in each of six marketplaces. They reported both to national field management and to the marketing communications manager in their respective sections.

Inquiries were centralized. There were previously more than fifty toll-free numbers to handle customer inquiries. The center began to handle all of these on a single inbound toll-free number that fulfills all requests for both mail-in and telemarketing literature.

All inquiries, plus additional profile and qualification information, are stored in the inquiry management database. Customer support, telemarketing and sales reps all have direct access to this database.

Customers were encouraged to call, rather than to write in with their inquiries. They found it was less expensive to have customers call on a toll-free number than to try to reach them with outbound calls as a result of a mail-in.

2. *Lead Qualification*

A key to Ms. Blue's success in this area was the direct involvement of salespeople in the process. They contributed to telemarketer training; they defined what constituted a qualified lead; and they helped in designing the feedback and analysis loop.

The salesforce began to believe that trained professional telemarketers could evaluate sales opportunities properly and save field reps much time in the qualification process. Here is what some of them said:

"I really was concerned about someone else getting involved in my selling relationship, but in four of the six qualified leads I received in the pilot program, it looks like I will close sales for more than $600,000."

"With the telemarketer's comments on one of my leads, I was able to go in prepared to talk about a leasing option and save myself an additional visit."

The telemarketers are well-educated, service oriented communicators. Their job is to identify real sales opportunities, and free up the salesforce for its primary job: selling.

3. *Keeping the Leads Hot*

A frequent complaint of salespeople is that leads are "cold" by the time they get to them. To solve this problem, the Hewlett-Packard Customer Information Center developed a Qualified Lead Tracking System (QUILTS) that electronically sent inquiries to telemarketers

---

Figure 26-2 Lowering Sales Costs
Through Pre-Qualification of Leads

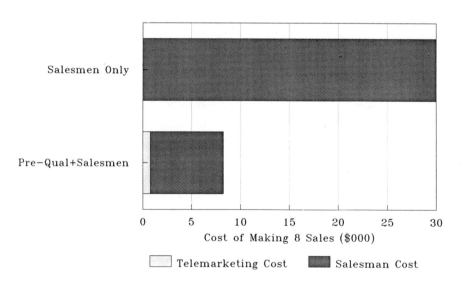

Telemarketers Screen Out 75% of Leads

---

in the Midwest. The telemarketers qualified, ranked and electronically returned leads to the appropriate sales office. QUILTS reduced turnaround time from as much as 14 weeks to 48 hours. Hot leads were telephoned directly to the sales office.

A pilot program was developed to tie this system into the portable PCs of some sales managers, which were integrated into the QUILTS system with leads being transferred electronically every evening.

4. Feedback

A strong selling point of the new system from the field point of view was its capability to feed back quantitative information to product divisions on win/loss statistics.

Previously, when a sales rep called a research and development manager to point out a missing feature on a product or complain about the pricing, his or her views were set aside. Now they were entered into the database, which later reported back percentages of wins and losses from field-generated ideas. The feedback system helped the product divisions to respond better to customer ideas and helped sales reps beat the competition.

5. Results

How well did the Hewlett-Packard system perform? Some answers were provided by Russell McBrien, Application Marketing Manager at Hewlett-Packard. He pointed out that before the new system, studies had shown that salespeople were with customers only about 26 percent of their average day. Using laptop portables, with 130 reps participating and logging over 8,000 hours in a test, they were able to increase customer contact to 33 percent, a gain of 27 percent in selling time due to the new system. Why did this work? The database information kept the reps on the road and out of the office. Remote access to the database meant fewer trips back and forth to the office and less time lost in *ad-hoc* meetings or chitchat.

Before the system, responses to ads in magazines had taken six weeks to arrive at Hewlett-Packard, and another eight weeks before they got to a sales rep. Most of the leads were thrown away as being too old. The ratio of good leads to bad was about twenty-five to one. With the new system, qualified leads are distributed overnight to the sales reps. Customer satisfaction had measurably increased, with inquiry fulfillment being completed in one week rather than six. Over 90 percent of questions are resolved over the phone from the Center, since the 800 number was a gateway to the entire HP Installed Base Center.

Installed Base Center

While the Information Center primarily deals with prospects, Installed Base Center is the Hewlett-Packard name for their marketing database of existing customers. Data collected on these customers includes:

- inventory
- contacts
- buying plans, cycles and habits
- call patterns
- account history
- response to product information and promotions
- contracts
- competitive information provided by the customer

Customers are identified by name, title, buying power and sales history. Such customer knowledge helps to target direct mail programs usually announcing new products or promotions.

After the mailings, telemarketers call customers to check their response to the mailing and to learn if they are ready to buy. These "tele-sales reps" are assigned to specific accounts, therefore giving the customer a regional contact if questions arise. This sales team works together closely to be aware of customer needs, and only when the customer has been qualified is the field sales rep sent to call, making the sales reps' time more productive.

The goals of the Installed Base Center database system are to increase sales volume by 15 percent, increase the number of contacts per account by 50 percent, reduce the cost per order dollar by 10 percent and the number of field sales calls per order by 25 percent while increasing customer satisfaction and creating a customer profile on the database. Another goal of the Installed Base Center is to reduce the new product introduction cycle time by 67 percent.

Using this new system, Hewlett-Packard freed itself from the MIS-generated static reports which proved untimely and inflexible in their search criteria. Product managers using the database and laptops could get win/loss reports, customer histories, sales analyses and forecasts, product profitability and information about the competition.

SELLING XEROX MACHINES IN ENGLAND

Michael Violanti of Phone Marketing America, Inc., a New York based telemarketing agency, describes his work in helping Rank Xerox, UK, to build a database to sell low-cost Xerox® machines profitably.

In the system which he helped to set up, Xerox used telemarketing to screen and qualify large prospect universes, compiling information such as:

- the decision maker by name and title;
- the type of copying equipment now in use;
- the terms of the current equipment (own, lease, rent);
- the copy volume; and
- the replacement cycle.

Sales and marketing worked together to instruct the telemarketers on criteria for qualified and non-qualified leads. Once a decision on qualification was made, the database system provided fulfillment for all levels, including:

- an equipment demonstration;
- a sales appointment;
- literature fulfillment; and

■ the scheduling of a future call-back.

By integrating telemarketing, salesforce and a lead tracking database system, Xerox was able to:

■ Reduce the cost of selling by eliminating cold prospecting activity by the salesforce.

■ Increase the average sales representative's performance by 200 percent.

■ Sell low cost copiers profitably, which opened up a large new market segment.

■ Put in place an ongoing marketing and sales opportunity which provided additional leads as non-qualified segments became qualified.

YELLOW PAGE MARKETING

Sometimes salespeople are able to kill off marketing efforts in their cradle. In one case, a service bureau developed what seemed like an excellent system for the yellow page directory of a major telephone company. The company had been mailing notifications of the due date for placing ads in forthcoming directories to all holders of business telephones (both advertisers and non-advertisers). In the case of advertisers, the notice was intended to get them thinking about the possibility of increasing the size of the ad and expecting the call of a salesperson (since all ads were sold by salespeople). In the case of non-advertisers (which were a high percentage of all business telephone subscribers), the mailing was designed to stimulate subscribers to think about placing ads, and encourage them to call an 800 number or write to the telephone company.

The system wasn't working very well. Salespeople worked on commission: they always called the big advertisers, but rarely wasted even a call on the non-advertisers unless they called in of their own volition.

The service bureau suggested a novel system to increase sales. It involved creation of a marketing database which would provide each advertiser and non-advertiser with a personalized report which showed graphically how his ad (or non-ad) stacked up against his competition. All plumbers in a given area, for example, were ranked against all other plumbers, so that each could see for himself what his competition was doing in regard to:

- how many directories their ads appeared in;
- under how many headings (sewer and drain, heating and air conditioning, kitchen and bath remodeling, plumbing, etc.) they were listing themselves; and
- the size of their ads.

Previously, the plumber could see the size of the competition's ad only in his local book. The other information was new, and promised to prove a powerful selling inducement. Marketing thought the system would be an excellent opportunity.

In fact, the company never adopted the system. The sales force is unionized. A part of the system was a lead-tracking vehicle which would show how well individual salespeople were doing with the leads generated. This was one strike against it from sales point of view. The blow that finally killed the idea was that the central MIS staff decided to adopt it and install it themselves. Three years later, they were still in the design phase.

Summary

- In many companies, the salesforce will oppose a marketing database as a threat to their commissions.
- The salesforce may look on a lead tracking system as a management intrusion into their business.
- To have a successful marketing database in a company with a large salesforce, you have to find a compromise which brings sales and the database together in the same organization.

- One method is to locate the telemarketers working with the database right in the sales division, under the supervision of the regional sales director.

- Telemarketers pre-qualify leads, passing on only those which sales has agreed are qualified. Sales should train the telemarketers and develop the qualification criteria.

- As a part of the system, the database should be used to track leads, and speed them through qualification to a salesperson for action. No time should be lost.

- Hewlett-Packard's experience shows how a sales staff can work closely with a marketing database and telemarketers in an integrated system which can pre-qualify leads, increase salesperson contact time with customers and improve sales productivity.

- Rank Xerox used the system to sell low-end copy machines with a database, a telemarketing staff and salespeople.

Chapter 27

Database Marketing
and the Dealer

Not everyone is hailing the advent of database marketing. Dealers especially view it as a mixed blessing. To them, database marketing is just another name for direct marketing, which means that the company is trying to go around them directly to the consumer, cutting them out of their livelihoods. You have to have some sympathy for their position.

This is a serious problem for any company that relies on retail sales for the bulk of its business—a wide spectrum. It is no problem at all in the case of services or big-ticket items. For hotels and car rental, restaurants, fast food chains, stock brokers, automobiles or real estate, database marketing poses no threat. But if you are selling software or computer hardware, books or transportation, your company has to come to grips with the issue.

As your direct business grows, you must ask yourself how important dealers are to you. Could you go it alone? There are thousands of catalog marketers out there that have no store at all. Sears Roebuck successfully managed both catalogs and stores for a century. But in the case of Sears, the stores are all owned by the parent company. IBM also straddles the fence with direct sales and authorized dealers. The problem occurs in situations in which the dealers are independent. They can handle your product or they can switch to someone else. In most cases, the company will decide that it is too risky to rely solely on direct sales. It will want to retain and support its dealers. Does this mean eliminating database marketing?

INCLUDING THE DEALER

It is definitely possible to develop a database marketing program which includes the dealer as an integral part of the system. Many companies have realized that. A few have begun to experiment with it. When properly done, the database can make the dealer feel more a part of the company team than before, instead of feeling abandoned. But it generally means that you have to put behind you the tempting idea of selling direct and avoiding that commission. You have to set up a system that achieves direct contact with the customer with all the lifetime value that that brings, but still keeps the dealer as the only authorized delivery mechanism. This means that your company has a policy of acting like an automobile company even though your product could be sold direct. To illustrate how it can be done, lets look in some detail at a three industries: the liquor business, cruise lines and package goods.

The House of Seagram

Ogilvy and Mather Direct worked with the House of Seagram to help them to develop a profitable database of scotch and other liquor drinkers. Since most radio, TV and many print ads were restricted and unavailable, Seagram was anxious to experiment with a marketing database as a way of reaching their consumers.

Their first campaign in 1986 (as reported by Phyllis Feinberg in *Database Marketing*, a DM News Special Magazine, from which the following information was developed) was a failure, largely due to the poor list source used. In 1987, they tried again with a major program for Glenlivet scotch - a high-unit margin, low awareness and low penetration product. They sent a broad-based, expensive (70 cent) package to a well-developed group of lists of previous respondents and prospects selected by modeling the current customer base.

The offer involved gifts and a $5 rebate. It also encouraged recipients to send a gift and rebate to friends to increase their referral rate. A year later they sent a second mailing including a cassette tape. An estimated 24,000 bottles were sold as a result of the campaign—two percent of the entire sales volume for the year. Of those redeeming coupons, 70 percent recommended a friend who was added to the database.

Their program did not rely on direct mail alone. They used impact programs and survey cards in magazines. The database now consists of known drinkers, specified by category and brand. If they find out that someone who drinks Chivas Regal also drinks vodka, they send a message promoting their vodka.

Chivas Regal presented a special problem for Seagrams. It has a 95 percent awareness in its category, and 90 percent of scotch drinkers have tried it. But many feel guilty buying it because it is the highest priced scotch. Seagram's solution was to create a "Chivas Class" as a synonym for first class.

The Chivas campaign consisted of direct mail, direct response print advertising and upgrades in air travel and hotel accommodations through tie-ins with TWA and Hyatt Hotels, which added value to Chivas Regal.

Success with this program led them to develop more than 10 similar efforts with other high-image brand products, including a "Royal Watcher's Guide" for Crown Royal and selected programs for Martell cognac, Meyer's Rum and Mount Royal Light. Using their database, Seagram was able to predict the number of drinkers in a category six times over what the normal incidence of drinkers in the population is said to be.

Citibank worked with Seagram to provide information from their point-of-sale program in retail stores. The information gathered from scanners used at the checkout point helped them to build their database and understand the profit impact of communicating with their customers. Seagram sees the decade of the 1990's as the "battle of the databases." If they are correct, Seagrams may have a head start over many others.

Database Marketing for Cruise Lines

There is intense competition in the cruise line business. Most lines have luxury ships which go to exotic places. Rates are relatively high. Most of the lines provide prospective cruisers with expensive brochures and videos which they either send free or sell for a modest price.

- Fact: very few people take a cruise as a result of receiving a brochure or a video. As nany as 99 percent of people who send away for or purchase a brochure or video *do not subsequently take a cruise with that line.* Most cruise lines do not realize this and continue to waste millions of dollars on these inducements.

- *Fact:* two thirds of the people who send away for a brochure or video, and who are listed as passengers of the cruise line, *send away for the inducement after the cruise is completed.* The inducement is ordered by the passenger as a memento of a com-

---

Figure 27-1 Cruise Line Facts:
(Brochures, Videos Don't Persuade)

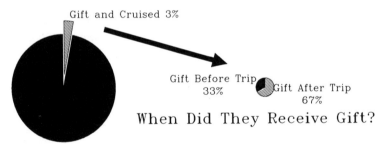

Gift and Cruised 3%

Gift Before Trip 33%

Gift After Trip 67%

When Did They Receive Gift?

Gift, No Cruise 97%

Did They Cruise?

Conclusion: Most Videos & Brochures Are Mementos

Gift=Video, Brochure

---

pleted voyage, rather than a part of the pre-booking decision making process. This, too, seems like another waste of money. But within this simple fact lies the key to increased sales for the cruise line. Read on.

■ *Fact:* in cruise lines that go to one location only, such as the Caribbean, most people take a cruise with a given line *only once*. Ninety percent of passengers will never cruise with that line again. They either go with some other line next time or never cruise again. Repeat business is rare. A marketing program based on the premise of repeat business will probably fail. How can you have a lifetime value when you know in advance that the lifetime is one cruise, period? Read on.

■ *Fact:* most passengers cruise with a given line because of word-of-mouth. There are only two referrals that count with most people: their travel agent or a friend who went on a cruise recently and recommends it or is going on a cruise soon, and wants company.

■ *Fact:* most travel agents are highly suspicious of cruise lines' direct marketing activities. They believe that cruise lines are interested in selling direct *in order to cheat the agencies out of their commissions.* Many agents will boycott a cruise line that appears to have an active direct business with an 800 number.

■ *Fact:* commissions to travel agents vary depending on the amount of business sent to the cruise line. There is much room for maneuver.

■ *Fact:* few cruise lines are doing the kind of database marketing being done by hotels and airlines. There is a wide-open opportunity for a company which quietly develops an effective marketing database and uses it to generate sales that might otherwise go elsewhere. But this has to be done without alienating the dealers. How is this possible?

The Database Plan

Cruise lines can definitely benefit from a modern marketing database system. A database marketing campaign for a cruise line should have these features:

- Include the travel agency in the loop as a part of the system. Let them know that they are included.

- The database should contain five interrelated files:
  - Passengers (booked, cruising, and past cruisers)
  - Cruises (passages booked)
  - Travel agents (there are 35,000 in the U.S.)
  - In-house regional sales officers
  - Prospects (people referred by passengers, or developed from other sources, who have not yet booked).

- Database marketing activity should focus on two objectives:
  1. Convince passengers to recommend others who they think would want to cruise.
  2. Convince travel agencies to recommend the cruise line to their customers.

Referral Program

A referral program should have these features:

1. *On-Board Survey.* Develop a comprehensive survey form to be filled out by passengers while on board the cruise ships. Make the collection of the survey form an obligation of the cruise director. In this survey, collect all the information needed to do intense marketing analysis and database building. Input all the results into the database *within a few days after the ship reaches port.*

2. *Referral Incentives.* Establish a significant reward for recommending someone who subsequently takes a cruise. It should be pegged at $50 or more, and be paid *only when the referred per-*

Figure 27-2 Building Cruise Line Referrals

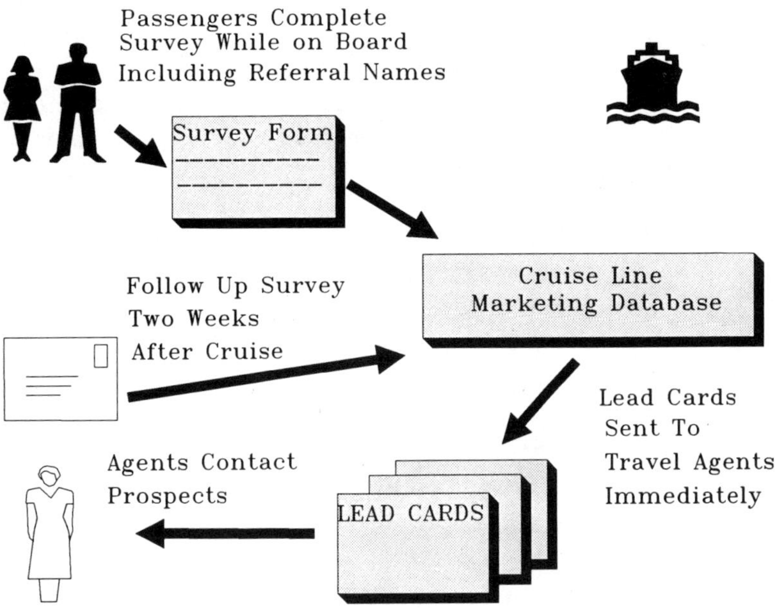

Passengers Complete
Survey While on Board
Including Referral Names

Survey Form
—————————
—————————

Follow Up Survey
Two Weeks
After Cruise

Cruise Line
Marketing Database

Lead Cards
Sent To
Travel Agents
Immediately

Agents Contact
Prospects

LEAD CARDS

---

son has embarked. The marketing database should be set up to keep track of who has referred whom, and to initiate payment when the referred person embarks.

3. *Referral Names.* The on-board survey is the first and best place to get the names. People have time, they are in the mood, they want others to share their joy.

    The second best time to get the names is within two weeks after the cruise is over, when they are telling all their friends how great it was. A post-cruise mailing can help to supplement the on-board names. It has to be fast; a month after the cruise may be too late.

    A third time to get names is between booking and embarkation. This may or may not work. There may not be time to get out the letters. It requires some fast footwork on the part of the database system.

4. *Lead Cards.* As soon as names are received, lead cards should be sent out *to the travel agent who booked the passenger.* Three copies of each card should be sent. The first should be sent back as soon as the travel agent has made contact with the referred person. The second should come back as soon as the prospect has agreed to cruise, or definitely rejected the idea. The lead cards are in the form of pre-printed, return postage paid post cards, addressed to the database P.O. box, and inputted directly into the database the same day they arrive. Time, here, is absolutely critical. Every day you delay can mean lost names and lost sales. A lead tracking report system can monitor exactly what is happening to each lead.

    All passengers should be booked through a travel agent.

Figure 27-3 Tracking Cruise LineReferral Leads

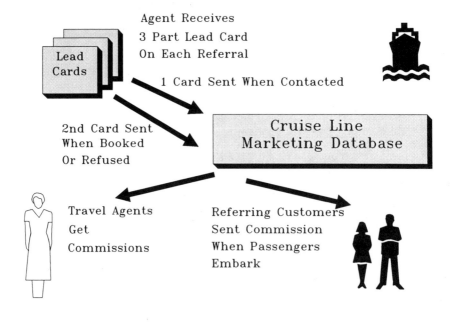

But if some are not, and if these people suggest leads, the lead cards should be sent to the regional sales representative of the cruise line for distribution to a travel agency that rep wants to reward.

5. *Follow-Up on Lead Cards.* Some travel agencies will drop the ball, and not take action on the lead. The database will know that, since the first card is not turned in. In that case, it should be *printed right on the lead card* that if the first card is not received within two weeks, the lead will be turned over to another travel agency for action. The database will make up new cards, and send such "dropped balls" to the regional sales rep for action.

6. *Welcome Kit for Referrers.* Anyone who does refer a prospect should receive a prompt welcome kit, thanking them for the lead,

Figure 27-4 Follow Up on Cruise Line Leads

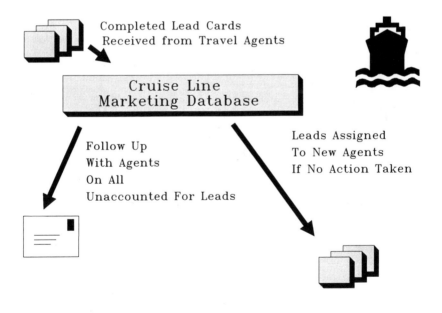

Completed Lead Cards
Received from Travel Agents

Cruise Line
Marketing Database

Follow Up
With Agents
On All
Unaccounted For Leads

Leads Assigned
To New Agents
If No Action Taken

specifically mentioning that the "Carr Travel Agency" has been asked to contact Mrs. McIver directly, mentioning that she has been referred by Mr. and Mrs. Warren. The welcome kit will encourage Mr. and Mrs. Warren to make additional referrals, and may also include inducements such as a brochure and a video. The kit may suggest that Mr. and Mrs. Warren might want to invite friends over to see the video, and place these people on the referral list.

7. *Complete Reports.* The database system should provide the cruise line with complete reports on a weekly basis of what is happening with the referral program, including names re-

---

Figure 27-5 Welcome Kit System for Cruise Leads

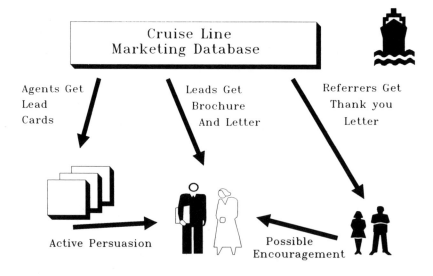

---

ferred, travel agency actions, percentages of success and failure. The system should provide statistics on the cost of the referral program and the increased sales generated, culminating in a return on investment in the referral program.

Travel Agency Cultivation

In general, travel agents decide which cruise line will get their customers' business. Unlike airlines, where everyone builds up a personal history of flight experiences and can form an impression of the level of service and dependability of an airline from past flights, most people take a cruise only once. When they decide to take a cruise, they go to a travel agent. They are confused by what appear to be a dozen different lines, all offering similar luxurious and expensive cruises to exotic islands and ports. Unless they have learned about a specific cruise line from a friend, if the travel agent says, "Well, most of the lines are good, but I think that the best one is ...," then that is the one that most people will choose.

How do travel agents decide which cruise line to recommend? Basically they suggest the ones who have done and will do the most for them.

The standard commission is 10 percent. But for agents who send a cruise line a lot of business, it is customary for the line to pay 12 percent. If the volume keeps up, they will add another percent or two. Cruises cost from $500 to $2,500. Most people travel with someone. The commission, therefore, is substantial.

Cruise lines often sponsor cruise nights at a travel agent's office. They provide the door prizes, the movies, the refreshments and half the cost of the ads. They offer free cruises to the travel agent's staff.

Travel agents become very angry at any cruise line that is suspected of trying to "sell direct." Several lines have tried this, and suffered the agents' wrath as a result. The effect can be devastating on a cruise line, since the agent's ability to choke off business is legendary.

What can a cruise line do to build up good relations with the travel agent? The answer is the travel agent database.

Travel Agent Database

There are 35,000 travel agencies in the United States. Only a few of them handle cruise lines as a major profit center, but they are all potential sales sources. Most cruise lines keep track of their passengers and have tape records of former cruisers. Most of these records also record the name of the travel agent. The first step, therefore, is to set up a functioning travel agent database which, initially, should have the names and data on the 35,000 independent travel agencies.

Plenty of space should be reserved for this database. It will be the most active part of your whole system. You will be constantly updating it from surveys forwarded to you by travel agencies, and with actual cruise and commission information from passenger travel. You will learn, of course, the name of the head

Figure 27-6 Database Helps Cruise Line Sales Force

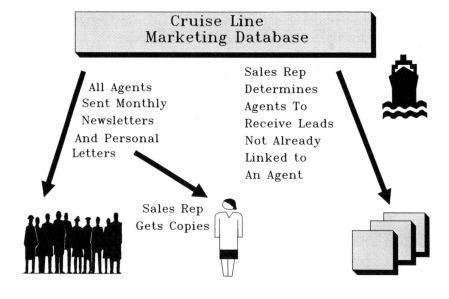

Cruise Line
Marketing Database

All Agents
Sent Monthly
Newsletters
And Personal
Letters

Sales Rep
Determines
Agents To
Receive Leads
Not Already
Linked to
An Agent

Sales Rep
Gets Copies

of each agency, and in many cases, the cruise director. You will learn which lines they favor, so you can reward the loyalists, as well as direct special attention to those on the fence.

As soon as you can, you should try to segment your database into these categories:

A. Loyalists who send you most of their cruise business.
B. Opponents who are committed to some other line.
C. Switchers who send customers to your line and to others.
D. Non-cruise agencies which do not handle cruise business.
E. New agencies, just starting out, which haven't decided what their policies are on handling cruises or which line is the best.

From the beginning, your major attention should be focused on categories A and E. You must find ways to reward the loyalists, but

---

Figure 27-7 Passenger Mailings From the Database

1. File Segmented by Recency, Frequency, $

2. Surveys Sent to Recent Non−Respondents

3. Respondents Get:

    Thank You Letter

    Video, Brochure

    Follow Up Mailings

4. Test Mailings Made to Older Segments

5. Prospect Mailings Based on Passenger Profile

---

you should make major efforts to welcome new entrants into the travel business and to get them thinking your way. It is possible to find out early who these agencies are, and to develop a warm welcoming system involving both direct mail and visits by your regional sales representative.

Once you have a program for loyalists and new agencies, you can go to work on the switchers. You have to learn why they switch: is it the commission, or a perception that, somehow, some other cruise line offers better service? There is a lot to learn about these switchers, and a great opportunity for creative programs to alter perceptions.

Data Indexes

From the agent file in a cruise line marketing database, an index to every passenger and every cruise booked by that agent can be generated. From the passenger file, an index to every cruise that that passenger took, and an index to the travel agents used for the cruises can be generated.

Therefore, from the agent's file it is possible to know:

- how many passengers, by year and month, he or she is booking for the line;
- how many cruises and dollar value per month he or she is booking;
- what the line is paying the agent in commissions and percentages; and
- what the line is doing for the agent in terms of free travel, free movies, cruise nights and such.

The Regional Sales Representative

All lines have regional sales personnel whose job it is to meet with travel agencies, distribute literature and videos, and build up business. These regional sales personnel need support in their work. Even a large line will have only a few dozen such sales personnel. This means that, with 35,000 agencies, most regional sales personnel are trying to cover more than a thousand agencies in two or more states. They cannot hope to make active contact with more than 200 in any given year. The balance cannot be visited or actively cultivated without central assistance from the database. Before the database, most of these agencies were simply ignored.

The database can support several related functions:

Monthly or Quarterly Newsletters. The newsletter not only reports on cruise events, it also lists inducements available to the agency. It is written as an insider publication for the travel agency, with news of interest to the agent beyond the cruise line itself. Included in many of the newsletters are survey forms or coupons which invite agency staff to send in for cruise caps, buttons, brochures, videos, take-one displays and to qualify for free cruises and such. An active newsletter program can do a great deal to change minds about the cruise line. It should not be neglected.

Personal Letters: "Mr. and Mrs. Stein left on May 22 on the Princess Grace. We much appreciate your assistance in booking the Steins."

"You have booked 43 passengers with us so far this year. Your commission is being increased to 13 percent retroactively. We will be sending you a check for $632.50 in addition to your regular commission check on current cruisers. If you can book as many as sixty before the end of the year, we can increase this to 14 percent for the year."

"Here are lead cards for three prospects who have been suggested to us by one of your clients, Mrs. Joseph Mills of 123 Maple Drive, Scarsdale, NY. We are sending them literature and your name. Please contact them as soon as you can, mentioning Mrs. Mills' name. If they do cruise with us, Mrs. Mills will receive a $50 check from us for each person who cruises."

Use of Inactive Cruisers

The fact that most people do not cruise again with a given cruise line can actually be turned into an advantage by a skillful cruise line's marketing database system.

Most cruise lines have on their records a million or more names and addresses of people who once slept on their ships, and will never sleep there again, no matter what they do. But most of these people are still alive. Many of them enjoyed the cruise, and would like to cruise again somewhere else. Some of them would like to go to Spain, or Italy or Japan. They are a resource in the hands of the right person. Who is that right person? A travel agent.

Before these names get too dated, they should be used as an additional inducement and incentive to encourage travel agencies to recommend the cruise line to their customers.

For all intents and purposes, once these people have provided all the referrals that they are willing to provide they are useless to the cruise line for any direct purpose. But the names are legitimately owned by the cruise line, and they have a market value. They are people with the wherewithal necessary to take a cruise or a foreign trip, and, clearly, the get-up-and-go necessary to actually do it. They

Figure 27-8 Use of Inactive Cruiser Database

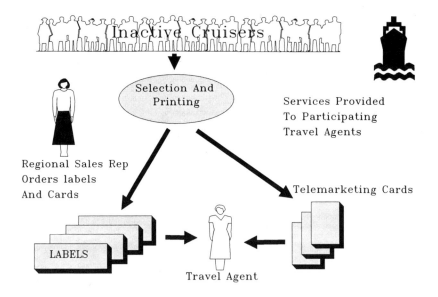

represent a special niche in the American public—not more than two to five percent of the population.

These names can be very valuable to a travel agent if used properly.

To make use of these names, the cruise line can develop an active cooperative mailing program used to reward helpful travel agencies. On the request of a travel agency, the cruise line can segregate its inactive file of cruisers by zipcode, date of travel, class of travel (luxury, economy, etc.), and prepare either gummed mailing labels or telemarketing cards—free of charge—to the travel agent. The use of the names would be placed at the discretion of the cruise line's regional sales representative who can establish criteria for provision of free labels or telemarking cards.

Database Marketing for Package Goods

Why should a package goods manufacturer invest in database marketing?

For an automobile manufacturer, an airline or a catalog merchant, the answer is easy: their margins are high and their customers are easy to identify. Since they can easily find out who the customers are, they would be foolish to pass up the chance to communicate with them to influence them to buy again. They put the names into a database, and build relationships with them.

But package goods manufacturers have small margins, and customers tend to be anonymous visitors to retail stores. Trying to get their names and addresses is difficult; trying to communicate personally with them can be expensive in relation to the profit margin.

So why would a package goods manufacturer invest in a consumer database?

There are some compelling strategic reasons which will be outlined in this chapter.

The Changing Marketing Climate

Things never stay the same. As we know, mass advertising is giving way to individual relationship marketing.

Kimberly Clarke, Kraft General Foods, Quaker Oats, The House of Seagram and RJR/Nabisco, to mention a few package goods manufacturers, have invested heavily in relationship marketing through building consumer databases. What have they seen to lead them in this direction?

The Lifetime Value of a Customer

When you look at marketing from a free standing insert (FSI) perspective, which most package goods manufacturers use, you think of individual sales, not individual customers. You have to realize enough from each sale to pay for the promotion.

There is another way to look at marketing. Once you get someone to start eating RiceChex® for breakfast, you may keep her for years. The total sales to this customer may amount to $100 or more. What is it worth to you to get her to start eating and keep eating RiceChex? With a database, you can identify your customers and develop creative strategies to keep them loyal and buying. You can build a relationship with them which will not be based on price: it will insulate them from the competitor's coupons and the retailer's ads.

Furthermore, the database will be *accountable*. You will be able to *know* the effect of your activities and the ROI from your efforts. You will be able to tell what is working and what is not working. You will be able to perfect your strategy and tactics. This is why Quaker, Kraft and Nabisco are deeply into database marketing.

To understand their strategies and tactics, let's begin by examining the two inter-related directions in which package goods marketing strategy is trying to operate:

- marketing to the consumer;
- marketing to the trade.

Through database marketing it is possible to do a good job of achieving both of these goals.

Marketing to the Consumer

There are four objectives in marketing to a consumer:

1. Create *trial* of a product
2. Induce competitive brand users to *switch.*
3. Promote *cross-selling* within the brand family.
4. Develop *loyalty* to the brand family.

Creating Trial. There are scores of ways to promote trial. Depending on the product, promotion managers will constantly have to innovate with a variety of creative methods. Using the database to promote trial will normally be helpful only as a part of a mix of different tactics. But as one tactic, the database can be helpful in:

- reaching special niche markets for special products (new babies, senior citizens, vegetarians...);

- reaching known innovators or known heavy users;

- reaching people who are already loyal to another product of the same brand.

In these situations, the database may be the most cost effective method of promoting trial.

Promoting Brand Switching by users of competitive brands. Why do people switch brands? Price, coupon availability, whim, creative ads, unhappiness with their last brand.

A better question: why do most people stick with their current brand? Satisfaction, familiarity, resistance to change, fear of the unknown and a sense that this is "my" cereal or soap. How can database marketing turn these people around?

- A database can deliver a list of users of competitive brands. Offering an inducement directly to these users (instead of to everyone) can often be more effective and cost efficient.

- A survey of *non-switchers* can tell us their reasons. We can design individual targeted messages to them to allay their fears.

■ For many people, price is a secondary consideration. They want *the best*, or some special feature that makes products especially desirable for them: packaging, low calories, high fiber, health qualities, environmental purity. FSI's won't reach these buyers. If you know who they are and what they are looking for, you can convince them. A database may be the best way to do this.

Promoting Cross-Selling. The biggest problem facing package goods database marketers *is what to do with the names they generate*. It is hard to justify the cost of a solo mailing to an english muffin buyer. The economics just aren't there.

This is why most of the package goods databases have been built by giants of the industry who have a *wide range* of products which they can promote to their customers. An across-brand mailing which promotes the interrelated healthfulness and nutritional qualities of a group of cereals, muffins, breads, crackers and cookies can be highly successful.

Putting such a promotion into effect in a large corporation can be difficult. The internal incentives built into the organization work against cooperative activities. The corporation must identify the cultivation of corporate brand loyalty in the consumer as a corporate marketing strategy. Some strong central direction is essential.

Once that direction is achieved, the rewards for individual brands through cooperative database marketing can become mutually reinforcing. Ivory Liquid—a detergent with no soap content—was built on the Ivory name. Quaker has extended the famous Quaker Oat name to scores of different products which have no oat content at all.

With a database, the known data about each household can be used to promote selective and individual cross-selling. Individual checks, lasered for different products in different redemption amounts, can be included in a corporate mailing. Known buyers of RiceChex get checks for muffins, crackers and cookies. Known Twinkie buyers are targeted for cereals, bread and, if appropriate, baby food. The result is a mailing to a million households, *each one with a different and individually targeted group of promotions enclosed*. As they cash their checks, the database learns more information about each household and the stores they shop at. Cross-sales have been built, and the database is richer with more household data. The next promotion will be even more targeted, individualized and profitable.

Building Corporate Loyalty. It is easy to become loyal to Dannon® yogurt or Crest® toothpaste. It is harder to become loyal to Proctor and Gamble® or Kraft® General Foods. If a package goods manufacturer is to get the most out of its database, it has to develop a marketing strategy that builds *corporate* loyalty in the mind of the consumer by extending the product loyalty to the corporation that provides the product. The reason is that, as already noted, the economics for a single-product database do not exist.

A database of loyal customers offers advantages:

- New product launch to loyal supporters is far easier.

- Cross-selling is built automatically.

- The database can be used to identify heavy users for special attention.

- The database can be used to profile users. The resulting profiles (age, income, lifestyle, occupation, education, children, race and so on) can be used to:

  - sharpen and redefine the product image;
  - target the advertising message; and
  - identify competing brand users from outside lists.

- You can use the database to build a user's club. By providing newsletters, frequent buyer points, health hotlines, customer service and such, you can build relationships which will last a lifetime.

Marketing to the Trade

The consumer is one target. The trade is the other. Unless stores stock your products and display them, your sales will suffer.

Stores are building databases of their own. Already, four retail chains have store databases of more than three million households, each household equipped with a card which gives it monthly discounts on purchases. Within a few years, almost half of the households in America will be in some retail buyer's club. The store knows *exactly* what these people are buying, day by day. From demographics, the store knows more about the purchasers of manufacturer's products than does the manufacturer.

A package goods manufacturer trying to get shelf space in one of these chains will have to know as much as the store knows about its customers. Without a database, that will be impossible. Chain managements are becoming increasingly sophisticated in their knowledge of consumers' activities and motivations. A manufacturer without a database comes to a chain in a weak position to counter negative arguments.

A database will tell a manufacturer what type of customers are buying and where they are shopping. The manufacturer will know their demographics, psychographics, lifestyles and, from that, what else they buy. The manufacturer will be in a position to point out to a chain that people who come to the chain seeking product A are likely to buy $X worth of B, C, D and E while they are in the store.

The manufacturer can even offer to lead a certain number of customers to the chain's stores through carefully targeted individual promotions.

In the 1990's, such knowledge of the consumer, and database power, may be the key to survival.

Summary

- The travel industry is one in which databases really got their start. In such industries, most large companies find that they cannot operate without independent dealers. In such cases the marketing database should include the dealers in the loop to reward them and make them feel part of the team.

- Cruise lines are covered as an example of the techniques involved. The cruise line example has these features:

1. A referral program including:

    a. On-board survey questionnaire designed to provide names.

    b. Post-cruise mailing designed to elicit more names.

    c. A substantial incentive to the passengers to refer names.

    d. Prompt action on all leads by furnishing them directly to the travel agency.

    e. A follow-up system to be sure that the travel agency has followed through promptly on the lead.

2. A travel agent marketing database which supports:

    a. A monthly newsletter to all travel agencies designed for two-way communication with agencies and to get them to promote the cruise line.

    b. A series of personal letters to travel agencies doing business with the cruise line to let the agencies know that the cruise line is aware of the good work they are doing in referring names and is providing compensating rewards.

    c. An active program of using inactive customers' names to provide labels or telemarketing cards for travel agencies as an additional reward for providing cruise passengers.

■ Package goods manufacturers have a difficult time understanding and justifying expenditures on a marketing database: their margins are too low to support the direct mail which is often the heart of database marketing.

■ Despite this difficulty, many large package goods manufacturers have invested heavily in this medium. Why? They see several important trends today:

    ➤ the cost of data storage and manipulation is coming down every year;

    ➤ they perceive the *lifetime value* of a customer who buys their products over several years, not just once;

    ➤ they realize that retail chains are building their own customer databases, which will mean that they know more about the customer than the manufacturer does.

- Marketing databases can be used to assist in promoting trial, getting competitive users to switch, promoting cross-selling within the brand family and building loyalty.

- Building loyalty and cross-selling requires creation of across-brand loyalty in consumers. But most package goods manufacturers have organized their internal incentives so as to work against internal cooperation between brands. To make effective use of a marketing database for such manufacturers requires strong central direction establishing corporate brand loyalty as a corporate strategy.

- Once that strong central direction is achieved, a package goods marketing database can be one of the most effective tools for:

  - retaining and increasing shelf space;
  - promoting cross-selling;
  - building customer loyalty and profitable lifetime relationships.

Part Seven

Concluding Words

Chapter 28

The Future of Database Marketing

Someone reading this chapter years from now may smile and say, "How naive he was. He was way off the mark." I'll accept that. Virtually no one in the world correctly predicted the collapse of Communism, yet this massive structure virtually disintegrated before our eyes within one year.

With this as a humbling backdrop, I don't want to presume to tell you that database marketing will be everywhere in 10 years. It probably won't. But it seems clear to me from the intense interest in this subject, and the number of companies that are experimenting with it, that it will grow a great deal and will change the way business is conducted in many fields.

Someone was giving advice to economists on forecasting. He said, "By all means, specify a figure. By all means, specify a date. But never specify both."

Rather than giving you a set of numbers that will probably be proved to be wrong, I will list those things that have to happen in industry for database marketing to become pervasive.

The Importance of Genius

As I have already said, a marketing database by itself will not accomplish anything. It won't make money or increase sales. It can waste a lot of resources. For it to be successful, it must be part of an

503

ongoing program with a viable marketing concept. Behind that concept is an idea person who dreams it up and sells it to whoever needs to be sold. Unfortunately, there are few people who have the imagination and drive to dream up such ideas and to push them through. The growth of database marketing will definitely be limited by the number of creative leaders in advertising and industry. What has made America a beacon to the world is that we have provided opportunity for people of vision to rise to positions of power so that they can realize their dreams. The top managements of most companies are looking for such people, even though the bureaucratic structure within the companies is constantly impeding their rise. The opportunity is here; we will just have to wait to see what happens.

The Importance of Risk Taking

Not all creative ideas will ultimately be successful. Many of them will fail. When this happens we write them off and go on to the next thing.

Database marketing is new. It represents a shakeup in the relationships inside a company, and often a change in selling methods. With all that against it, success depends on a company management willing to experiment and take a few risks. Many will say, "We are content with a 28 percent market share. Let's not rock the boat." Database marketing may be tried by those who have only a three percent market share or those who see their market share eroding.

For this new selling medium to work, management has to budget funds for a couple of years at least, and be willing to accept the internal shifts and disruption that it is likely to produce. Top management really has to get religion about a new relationship with customers; and then put their money where their mouth is. Unless someone high up is interested and willing to take the risk, forget database marketing for that company. It cannot come about as a result of the committee system or a branch manager's initiative.

The Importance of the Creative Agency

Certainly one of the most important chapters in this book is the one on the creative agency. I really don't see much possibility of creating a successful marketing database without the assistance of a really effective external direct agency which has the leadership, the ideas and the follow-through to make the whole project work. Looking around, I see very few such agencies in existence. There are plenty of isolated individuals within agencies who have what it takes to create this type of marketing. But for the revolution to get off the ground, these individuals have to rise to positions of leadership, and take their agencies off on a new path. This will take time.

The Role of the Service Bureau

As you know well by now, marketing databases are seldom successfully mounted on in-house MIS computers. They should be set up on outside service bureau mainframes, using the most modern relational database software, on-line access and custom reporting. How many service bureaus are capable of providing that type of support? Probably not more than a dozen. The number will have to grow with the industry. I see no impediment to this happening. The opportunities are there. Service bureau managements are beginning to open their eyes, acquire larger mainframes, hire systems engineers, attend the right conferences and read books like this one. They will be ready when the agencies are ready.

The Role of Customer Service

Sometimes revolutions begin in the strangest places. When a company installs an 800 number and begins to listen to what the customer is saying for the first time, something can happen. Reports can filter up. The possibility of using this information function as a direct sales support vehicle may occur to someone, and the germ of an idea for a marketing database may take root. It seems clear to me that customer service today is a growth industry. More and more, management is beginning to understand just how significant a development it is. It could be that the database marketing revolution will ride on the back of an expanding customer service explosion.

A Checklist for Launching a Marketing Database

A marketing database, by itself, will do nothing good for the bottom line. To be successful in bolstering customer loyalty, reducing attrition, creating repeat sales and building profits, the database must be constructed properly and combined with a comprehensive marketing program which extends throughout the entire company. The following list presents most of the elements necessary for a successful, functioning marketing database. If you leave too many of these elements out of your design, you will not be successful.

Not all databases will require everything on the list, but all of them will probably need most of what is listed. You will have to judge for yourself which features are required on your database.

1. Database Management

Database Administrator. There is a DBA on the marketing or product management side of your company who has the authority and the resources to make central decisions concerning the data base.

Marketing Team. The DBA has created a marketing team which oversees the operations of the database. The team includes personnel from sales, dealer support, customer service, the creative agency, product management, marketing, the telemarketing agency, the outside service bureau, MIS and any other part of your company which has customer contact (delivery, technical support, billing). On the team are represented both "constructors" (people who like to build databases) and "creators" (people who like to design marketing plans using databases). The importance of both functions is understood.

Construction Time. The process of designing and building the database takes place in *one year or less.* If the scope of the total project requires a longer time frame, the scope should be scaled back so that an active, functioning database can be created in one year.

Your learning curve and return on investment begin *after the database is up and running,* not during the planning phase.

Database Size. If this is your first marketing database, it should not be too big. Make a small one as a test from which you can learn; make your grand database later, after you have made all your serious mistakes.

2. The Database Location

Service Bureau. The database is resident on a powerful mainframe at an outside service bureau with relational software which permits two simultaneous functions:

- batch updating; and

- on-line ad-hoc counting and reporting.

Stand Alone. The marketing database is separate from any general ledger or operational database. It is periodically updated from the company mainframe on a regular planned basis.

Programming Staff. There is a programming staff that understands that it will have to make rapid changes in the database structure and software as marketing strategy evolves. This staff should be experienced in database marketing, have a significant array of relevant software and be able to be expanded on short notice to meet marketing deadlines. They must be responsive to the DBA.

3. Customer Information

Duplicate Elimination. All customer records have had the names and addresses cleaned and corrected. Duplicates have been eliminated, and an ongoing duplicate detection program has been set up.

Edit Checks. There are software edit checks built-in to assure that all new data going into the system is correct.

Database Captures All Data. The system captures all relevant information about all customers: their product registrations, purchases, coupon redemptions, letters and telephone calls, complaints, returns, survey results.

Universal Access. All customer information is available to everyone in the company and to dealers with a need to know. This includes both individual customer records and standard reports on the database as a whole (how many called yesterday, how many responded to offer X, who are our "Gold Card" customers).

Record Enhancement. Customer records have been enhanced, as appropriate, with demographics, cluster coding, modeling results and RFM analysis to identify the best and the not-so-good customers. These data enhancements are used as a basis for active programs for interaction with customers and for developing a customer profile for acquiring new customers.

Protecting Customer Privacy. In all that you set up, you are conscious of and aware of the problems of *invasion of privacy.* You build in steps to assure that the database does not become the CIA. You make sure that the database contains "don't mail" and "don't telephone" flags, and that everyone knows how to set the flags on and how to assure that they are adhered to.

4. The Marketing Program

A Creative Leader. Somewhere in the company or the creative agency, there is a man or woman of genius who is masterminding the marketing activities developed for the database. This person has not only the creative ideas to launch the database, but the follow-through to stay with it during the first two years overseeing operations, correcting the embarassing mistakes and making the dynamic shifts which will be necessary due to actual hands-on experience.

Learning from Customers. There is a clear understanding throughout the company that the database marketing program is a responsive system. That means that it involves finding out from customers what they want, and changing company programs and policies as a result of what is learned.

First Year Funding Assured. When the database is launched, there is a dynamic marketing program approved and funded for at least the first year of operations. This program includes plans and dates for all mailings and customer responses, for surveys, for telephone calls.

Lifetime Value Analysis. Work has begun on analysis to determine the lifetime value of groups of customers, together with efforts to act on this information to improve acquisition, attrition reduction, loyalty programs and so on.

Your Own Satisfied Customers Are Your Best Prospects for Future Sales. This is the guiding principle of your database and its associated marketing plan. This may require a review and modification of your existing program of general advertising, coupons, rebates, cash back, owner registration, order forms and such. The database anticipates when customers are due for a refill, a new model, an upgrade, an update, and reminds them and your dealers or your salespeople.

5. Interactions with Customers

Two-Way Communication. here is a recognition throughout the company of the value of two-way communication with customers. This means that your company uses customer contacts both to *provide helpful information* to the customer and to *receive helpful information* back from the customers. Methods are set up for all employees involved in customer contact enabling them to enter the results of their contact into the database.

Needed Information Has Been Planned in Advance. The information you want to capture from customers has been determined, and space has been set aside in the database for it. Surveys are designed, and telemarketers have been given scripts which ask for the needed information.

Information Is Collected. Every contact with a customer has been thought through, and has been designed to gather more information. Each outgoing letter, newsletter, product delivery, service or telephone call, is matched by an incoming survey, response or order. All existing order forms, monthly statements, catalogs, registration forms and such have been reviewed and modified to play a role in building the database.

6. Customer Service and Direct Sales

Incoming Lines. Customers can call an 800 or 900 number where your agents capture their names, addresses and phone numbers. The agents have a checklist of information that you want to obtain from customers for the database.

Database Access by Telephone Agents. The agents have access to the database and can retrieve a customer's record while on the telephone; the agents can enter information directly into the database while talking. The agents have the ability to get information from technical people within the company, if necessary.

Follow-Up Correspondence. There is a planned and automatic system for follow-up letters to every person who calls, thanking them for the call and requesting additional information from them (a simple survey—Were we helpful? Did we give you what you wanted?).

Sales by Customer Service. Customer service has a philosophy of selling! They have been trained to know what you sell, and how to go about it. They have all the information they need on your dealers, your salesmen, your products, the good and bad features, what new products are coming.

Modern Equipment. Your call center (which may be at an outside telemarketing bureau) has an ACD telephone system so that callers are quickly routed to the proper people. If callers must be put on hold, they listen to something useful about your product or company. You have arranged for enough equipment and enough agents so that customers can get through to you in busy times.

7. Rewarding Loyal Customers

Recognition. The database has been set up to provide recognition and special services to your best customers. A method for identifying them has been developed. They receive a special card or other token so that *they know* that they are special. All your employees with customer contact are aware of who these special customers are.

8. Acquiring New Customers

Customer Referral Program. The database is seen as a method for acquiring new customers. One important method is asking customers to recommend other customers. The database is set up to keep track of who recommended whom, and to provide suitable thank-you's and later activities.

Customer Profiling. The database is used to build a profile of your customers which is used to determine criteria for finding new customers. These criteria may include demographics, cluster coding, geographic areas, age, automobiles, responsiveness to direct marketing and so on. In the case of business customers, the criteria can include line of business, products, number of employees, sales and such.

Lead-Tracking System. The database has been designed as a lead- tracking vehicle. All leads from prospecting are monitored to make sure that timely and appropriate responses follow each lead identification through to rejection or closing.

9. Salespeople and Dealers

Salespeople Are Included. Company salespeople are part of the database system. It is not a threat to their commissions. They feel that it is "theirs." Telemarketers whom they train are used to qualify leads before the salespeople get them. Salespeople can access the database and use it in their work to acquire new customers and service existing ones.

Dealers Are Part of Your Team. Dealers play a role in the database system. They may have terminals, reports and lead cards permitting them direct access to customer information. They provide information to the system and get information out. Dealers feel that the database *helps them to get more business*, that it does not compete with them.

10. Quality Control

Direct Mail. A system has been set up to monitor quality on a regular basis. This means that there is a review of the quality of all outgoing mail, including the appearance of the name and address, the correctness of the information, the proper selection of the list, the proper placement of items within the envelope.

Personal Contacts. A system exists to monitor the quality of telephone and personal contacts with customers, including such methods as surveys back from customers which are read and entered into the database and rewards to employees for especially good jobs of customer contact and sales. Employees include delivery and service personnel, accounts receivable and complaint department employees—everyone gets into the act.

Teamwork. The database has created a community of users who are interested and concerned with making the whole process work. A method has been set up whereby all users can make suggestions on how to improve customer contact, service and sales. Suggestions and ideas are encouraged, welcomed and rewarded.

11. Reports

A Constant Information Stream. A dynamic set of reports is designed and programmed to provide daily or weekly feedback for marketing, sales, product management, top management, dealers, customer service and everyone else, on how they are doing, what the customers are thinking, buying, rejecting. These reports are printed and distributed by the database service bureau, but are also available to everyone in the company who has a terminal or a PC.

Special Reports Generated Easily. A method has been set up to generate new reports as the need arises. *Ad-hoc* reports and what-if scenarios are possible for marketing planners with one minute response time. Everyone with a need-to-know should be able to get information out of the database without getting permission or asking anyone else to do anything. Everyone who needs training should have received it.

12. Return on Investment

Keeping Your Eye on the Bottom Line. The purpose of a marketing database is to make money. At the time the database is launched, there is a definite plan for how you will use it to increase profits and how you will *demonstrate and prove* that you are generating profits. There is a clear statement of goals and objectives, and benchmark milestones at definite points of time where you can measure your progress. The database is quantifiable.

A Test for the Reader

Let's try an experiment. You have finished this book; you have learned much about database marketing. I will describe a great creative concept; see if you can find the potential flaws in it.

A successful candy company had always sold through stores. It had a substantial national reputation through its line of higher priced collections of hard candy and chocolate. It had never sold direct.

The vice president for marketing had a great creative idea: sell direct to consumers with this gimmick—the candy company would help each household to compile a "Family Register," a list of birthdays and anniversaries of everyone in the household and all their relations, including all the parents, aunts, uncles, nieces, nephews, grandparents, children and grandchildren.

To compile the register, customers call an 800 number and, free of charge, the candy company's gift counselors would take information from them. Every quarter, customers are sent a printed list of all the birthdays and anniversaries coming up, together with addresses and telephone numbers. For most of these birthdays, the candy company would be asked to send automatically an attractive gift of candy on the correct day, charging the gift to the credit card of the householder.

If the prospect is a business, the recipients would be clients who would receive their candy at Christmas or on some other suitable occasion.

In addition to gifts, customers could have candy shipped to themselves once a month.

You can call the 800 number at any time to add or delete or cancel gifts, or just to find out what birthdays are coming up in the next few weeks.

With any luck, the Register could produce an average of ten or more sales per year for several years in a row. At an average sale of $15 per box plus delivery, the average total sales over a year might be $150, with total per household over three years averaging perhaps $250, considering attrition and cancellations.

The vice president for marketing sent the proposal up the line for approval.

Is this a workable idea? Should the candy company risk a few million dollars on developing the idea? Let's now use some of the concepts in this book to analyze it and see what the vice president has left out of his plan that could cause it to fail.

What the Vice President Forgot

1. The Direct Agency. The company has a history of sales through stores only. No company should try to shift to direct without some outside help from a creative direct agency with experience. Before the VP goes up the line with his idea, he needs to find the right agency and get their help and advice.

The agency will discuss his concept, and if it makes sense, will develop some creative ideas and copy to go with it. They will help him to decide just who he is going to target with this concept: people in their 30's, 50's or 70's? People making $40K, $60K or $80K? Focus groups may be needed, and tests, tests, tests.

What media is he going to use? Where can he find lists of candy lovers? Of gift givers? Are there really several markets out there? What about the corporate market? All these things will be the province of the direct agency.

The agency will also have to write the script for the telemarketers. What you say when people call can make all the difference in a single sale, or multiple sales or no sale. Agencies should know how to write the script.

2. The Telemarketers. No one who has not done it can appreciate the impact on an organization of 1,000 telephone calls a day. How many people does it take to handle that number? How many lines? What training is needed for the staff? The vice president really needs to find an outside telemarketer who can staff up an operation to receive the calls; expecting the company's employees to man the phones spells disaster.

The VP will need very skillful telemarketers trained as gift counselors who are adept at extracting birthdays, telephone numbers, addresses and other information over the telephone, and who are good at selling candy as the ideal solution to the birthday and holiday gift problem. Can you find and train such telemarketers, and can they do the job at a reasonable price?

3. The Warehouse. Warehouses accustomed to shipping in skid lots cannot be converted overnight to shipping one box of candy at a time. Your costs will go through the roof. No one will know how to handle these little shipments efficiently.

What kind of packages are available that will arrive undamaged after delivery? Will the product spoil if left out in the sun all day? What about rain or freezing? How much will the shipping and packing cost? How does that enter into the profit picture? Before the VP goes further, he has to talk things over with the warehouse manager or an outside fulfillment staff.

4. The Sales Staff and the Dealers. How will stores take to the idea of the company selling direct? There is a lot of competition in the candy business. It is not that hard to get into it. If a store thinks that the national ads that they see for the candy will help total sales, but possibly hurt theirs, they may drop the line. Your sales staff will be quick to spot that. Unless you get their cooperation, they may fight the VP's plan from the beginning. What can be done?

One possible solution is a gift certificate for candy good at any retailer who carries the company's products. Printed on the back of the certificate would be the addresses of the stores in the vicinity of the recipient. The VP had better talk to sales before he goes too far.

5. The Service Bureau. Who is going to set up this system for automatic delivery of candy all throughout the year? Who is going to generate the orders, the shipping documents? Who is going to provide the equipment and screens for the telemarketers to enter, change and cancel orders? Before the VP goes much further, he should contact some service bureaus to find one that has the experience and the creative drive to put his idea into operation quickly.

He will need an on-line marketing database which permits telemarketers to call up any household instantly on the screen so that they can read off and change information on birthdays and gifts. The database has also to generate the automatic orders, credit card charges and shipments on the correct days; handle bad cards, cancellations, out-of-stock items and so on.

While he is at it, he will have to steel himself against the possible opposition of MIS to his building a computer database outside the organization.

6. Economic Analysis. The VP needs to think the project through for the first two years and get top management used to the idea that it won't pay off in the beginning. He has to calculate the lifetime value of his customers and balance that off against the acquisition cost. He has to set up some goals and benchmarks for himself so that he can determine when the program is a success or when it is a failure and losses had better be cut.

The message from this exercise is this: successful marketing databases will evolve as a result of little brainstorms like the one the VP had. A creative agency, telemarketers, a service bureau and inside staff—that is the only way that database marketing is going to move ahead.

A Farewell to the Reader

You have now graduated. You are ready to go forth into the world to make customers happy and your company profitable. As we part, recall the words that we began with:

Database marketing offers us a chance to make America a better place to live. It is not just a better way to sell products and services. It is a way of bringing back something that we have lost during the mass marketing fervor of the last 30 years. It is a way of restoring the personal contact with customers that we all enjoyed in the early years of America when you knew your merchants, and they knew you, recognized you, appreciated you and did personal favors and services for you on a regular basis. Database marketing, when done properly, will bring back loyalty and personal recognition as an important part of the business relationships which we all will come to experience and enjoy.

Summary

- Marketing databases don't accomplish anything unless they are a part of an ongoing program with a viable marketing concept.

- The growth of marketing databases will be limited to the availability of men and women with ideas and leadership capability either in advertising or marketing.

- Marketing databases involve risk. They will flower only in companies that are willing to take a chance on something new and potentially risky.

- No marketing database can succeed without the support of an effective creative direct advertising agency.

- An outside service bureau is essential for a successful marketing database. There are not enough such service bureaus with experience today, but their number will grow.

- Outside telemarketers are another vital ingredient of successful database marketing.

- The database marketing revolution will make America a better place to live. It will bring back loyalty and personal recognition as an important part of business relationships in the years to come.

Glossary

Abandonment. As in the phrase "call abandonment." This refers to people who, being placed on hold in an incoming call, elect to hang up ("abandon") the call. Call centers monitor closely the "abandonment rate" as a measure of their inefficiency.

ACD. Automatic Call Distributor. A complex machine used in modern call centers for incoming calls. It routes calls to available agents, holds overflow calls, gives and takes messages, provides reports. A must for modern database marketing.

Address. A computer term for the location on a disk or in memory of a piece of information. Addresses help the computer to find things rapidly, and to store them for later retrieval.

Ad-Hoc Report. A reporting method which permits you to ask questions like: How may women over 60 have bought more than $200 from us in the last 4 months?

Affinity. People who are similar in lifestyle.

Affluents. Households with 30% or more than the cost of living plus taxes. 25 Million (out of 87 Million) households.

Agent. The word for a telephone operator in a modern inbound call center in a company that takes a lot of customer service and sales calls.

Analog. Regular telephone service comes over analog lines. Modern improved service (often used for data lines) comes over DIGITAL lines in which all the sounds are converted to 1's and 0's. For database marketing computer communications, digital is better.

ANI. Automatic Number Identification. A system whereby you can learn the number of a person who is calling you on the telephone. Can be linked to a database to find the person's name and address.

ASCII. American Standard format for data storage on magnetic media (tape or disk).

Autosexing. A computer process for finding the sex and appending titles (Mr. Ms.) to a file of names.

Back End. As in phrase "back end analysis" refers to the results of actions with people who have responded to your initial offer.

Batch Mode. If you have received 10,000 replies to a mailing, you can update your master file with these replies in one batch. This is the fastest and cheapest way to update records. The opposite is On-Line updating.

Baud Rate. A measure of line transmission speed. 9,600 Baud is a good speed for terminals and PC's connected to a marketing database. Speeds can go up to 56,000 or more.

Bits. If a byte is like an atom in computer language, a bit is like an electron. A bit is either on or off. It is either a 1 or a zero. Eight bits make up one byte.

Block. The smallest reported unit in the 1990 Census. About 14 households in a block.

Block Group. The smallest reported unit in the 1980 Census. About 340 households on average.

Bounce Back. The practice of sending another identical (or similar) catalog back to someone who has just ordered something from one of your catalogs.

BRC or BRE. Business Reply Card or Business Reply Envelope.

Brokerage Commission. The commission (usually 20%) paid by a list owner to a broker to handle the rental of a list.

Bugs. Errors that crop up in software. Caused by inability of programmers to predict all possible ways that the code in their programs will be needed to process data.

Byte. A unit of computer memory. One letter or number is a byte. A byte is usually composed of eight bits.

Call Center. The word for an inbound telephone division in a company. The operators are called Agents. The call center uses an ACD (automatic call distributor) to manage the calls efficiently.

CD. A banking term for certificate of deposit. Also: a compact disk, a form of digitized data storage. (as in CD-ROM)

Cell Code. After completing RFM analysis, every customer is assigned a Cell Code which identifies her recency frequency and monetary level of buying. The cell code is often used in mailing. Sometimes used interchangeably with the term Source Code.

Channel. An input-output device as part of a mainframe computer.

Cheshire. A type of plain paper label used in mailing. Requires a Cheshire machine to affix to mailing material. The most common computer label.

Chip. The thing in the center of a computer that makes it work. On a PC a 286 chip is a fast chip. 386 is faster. The fastest chip in 1991 is a 486. Chips are the size of your fingernail, and hold millions of circuits shrunk by photographic methods to tiny size.

Cluster. A way of dividing all households in the country into about forty different types, such as "Blue Blood Estates" and "Shotguns and Pickups." Usually called lifestyle groups. Useful for file segmentation. Clustering systems are provided by Claritas, Equifax, Donnelley, CACI.

Continuation. A mailing to the same list following a successful test of a portion of the list. A continuation becomes a "rollout" when the entire list is mailed.

Controller. A device for managing the data input and output from several devices which are connected with a mainframe. These devices can include terminals or disks or tape drives. Controllers usually have a small computer inside them which permits them to manage the flow of instructions from the computer to the units in an organized way. They make the computer more powerful.

Conversion Rate. The percentage of responders who become customers.

Copy. The text of your direct mail piece.

CPI. Cost per inquiry.

CPO. Cost per order.

CPU. Central Processing Unit. The heart of a mainframe.

Creative Agency. It is hard to conceive of a company that could mount a successful marketing database without the help of an outside creative direct agency. They plan the programs, design mailings, create concepts.

Custom Report. A database report designed by the marketing staff which exactly meets the marketing needs of the company. Once programmed, it can be run daily or weekly for very little cost.

Data Entry. Also called Keypunching. Entering names and addresses and other data into magnetic media such as tape.

DBA. Database Administrator. A person who controls a marketing database. The DBA should be someone from marketing or sales who has the budget for the database.

DDA. A banking term for checking account balances.

Decile. One tenth of a mailing, usually divided by percentage of response.

Demographic. Demographic data usually refers to the data which the Census Bureau collects on a neighborhood such as income, education level, etc. This data can be be *appended* to a household record. It isn't necessarily accurate for any particular household since it is the average for households in that block. But it is usually the only data available.

Digital Line. A type of telephone transmission service that is much more reliable than the normal analog line. All data is converted into bits before it is transmitted. A regular telephone line is called an Analog Line.

Direct Access. A disk is a direct access device. Tape drives are not direct access because to find data on them, you have to read all the way through thousands of records to find the one you want. With direct access, you have all data stored at particular addresses. You can access each piece of data directly.

Disk. Magnetic disks are attached to computers. They hold information (records) which can be retrieved very rapidly if the computer knows the address of the information on the disk (Direct Access). In relational databases, the address of records and information within records are kept on indexes which make access to the records very rapid.

DNIS. Dialed Number Identification. A system whereby you can learn in a call center what number the incoming callers dialed to reach you. Important because many call centers handle calls from many incoming numbers for many purposes, but use the same bank of agents to take the calls. They have to know what number people were dialing so they can react properly to the call.

Duplicate. The same name occurring twice or more on the same file. All very large databases contain duplicates because name or address spelling may vary slightly.

Duplication Factor. The % of names on one list that are also on another list. It is a measure of affinity in the lists.

EBCDIC. A protocol for putting data on a tape. All IBM mainframes use EBCDIC. Most others use ASCII.

Edit Check. A software process whereby data to be entered into a marketing database is checked for logic before it goes into the database.

Enhancement. Appending demographic or lifestyle data to a list.

Extract. A system for creating a sequential file from a relational marketing database. The extract can be used for preparing reports, or for sending data to other companies for their use.

Flat File. Another name for a sequential name file. Contrasted with a database file (not flat because of the indexes).

Focus Group. A group of customers who are assembled together by an advertising agency in a conference room to discuss a particular product. Useful for learning what the public thinks of your product or message or company.

Format. The way data (name and address) is organized on a disk or tape. There is no standard format. Every company has their own.

Frequency. A term for how many times a person buys from you.

FSI. Free Standing Insert, a coupon inserted in a newspaper or magazine which offers a discount if the user buys a certain product. Billions of FSI's are distributed and 4% are redeemed every year. With FSI's you seldom capture the name of the consumer. They are seldom useful for database marketing.

Geocoding. A system for assigning a census code to any name and address. Once a file is geocoded, you can append census data (income, race, etc.) to the records and assign cluster codes.

Geodemographics. Census data that can be appended to a household file once it has been geocoded. Includes such factors as income, education, home type, etc. Derived from the neighborhood of the household.

Hardware. Computers and disks, tape drives, printers, and other gear that are plugged into computers.

Householding. A process in which all people and their accounts are grouped by the house that they live in so that they only get one letter per house in a promotion.

ID Number. A number assigned to a record to help to relate it to other records in the computer which have the same ID.

Index. 1) used in relational databases to help to find common data in thousands of records. An index for income could help find all the customers whose income was between $25K and $35K. Using an index you can query a file of 10 million customers and find out how many women aged 60+ bought more than $200 in the last 6 months, and do it in 15 seconds. 2) A statistical term for relating the value of two sets of numbers. If one group had a response index of 100 and another had 120, the second group had 20% more replies than the first one. The average of any group always has an index of 100.

Influentials. In business-to-business, executives who have the authority to make or influence a purchase.

IVR. Interactive Voice Response a piece of equipment connected with an ACD which permits inbound callers to a call center to choose their own routing of the call ("Push 1 for Sales, Push 2 for Service...")

Keyline. Or Match Key a combination of numbers and letters usually begining with the zip code, which is used as a rough household duplicate eliminator.

Keypunching. The process whereby someone enters names and addresses and other data from hard copy (paper forms) onto a computer tape or disk. It is done on a typewriter-like keyboard into a small computer.

LAN. Local Area Network, a way of joining PC's together.

Laser Letter. A letter produced on a Laser Printer. Very clean and neat looking. Possible to have unlimited personalization of the text of the letter.

Lead. A prospect who has responded is called a Lead.

Lettershop. An independent company that handles all the details of printing and mailing letters.

Lifestyle. Lifestyle data about a neighborhood comes from clustering. If a significant number of people in a given cluster have taken a foreign trip, it is assumed that all similar households have done this.

It is a lifestyle attribute. Included are magazines read, TV programs watched, etc.

Lifetime Value. The contribution to overhead and profit made by a customer during her total relationship with your company.

Lift. The improvement in response from a mailing due to modeling and segmentation. Divide the response from a segment by the overall response, subtract 1 and multiply by 100.

List Broker. A service which brings list owners and prospective list renters (users) together.

List Maintenance. Keeping a mailing list current through correcting and updating the addresses and other data.

List Rental. The process of renting (for one time use, or other periods) a list of names of customers owned by some other organization for an agreed upon cost per thousand.

Mailing List. A list of customers or prospects used to mail catalogs or sale announcements. It is not a marketing database because it does not provide for a two-way communication with customers.

Mail Shop. An independent company which specializes in preparing materials for mailing. They affix labels, sort for bulk rates, prepare bagtags, insert in postal bags.

Mainframe. The largest computers used in business applications. They require raised floors, special air conditioning. Mainframes are recommended for marketing databases because of their power, input-output capability and speed measured in MIPS.

Market Penetration. The percentage of buyers you have as compared with the total households or businesses in the area you have selected as your market.

Match Code. A keyline. An extract of the name and address used to identify a specific record. Used in de-duping.

Megabyte. A million bytes. Disks are rated in megabytes.

Memory. The amount of information that a computer can hold in its head while it is doing work. The more memory, the faster a computer can work, and the more complicated programs it can handle. Most PC's today have 640,000 bytes of memory. Many have several million. Mainframes usually have 16,000,000 or more bytes of memory.

Merge/purge. A software system used to merge many different input tapes in differing formats and put them into a common format for a mailing. Merge/Purge detects duplicates.

Micro. Micro-computer. Another name for a PC.

Mini. Smaller than Mainframe computers. They may also need raised floors and air conditioning. They are less expensive than Mainframes, and, generally do not have the power or input-output capability to manage a large marketing database.

MIPS. Millions of Instructions Per Second. A measurement of the relative speed of a Mainframe computer.

MIS. Abbreviation for Management Information Systems. This term is used in many companies to refer to the data processing staff that runs the central company mainframe computer.

Modeling. A statistical technique whereby you build a model of your customer from a database of customers. With modeling you are looking for common factors which help to explain behavior.

Modem. A device permitting a PC or terminal to send information over a telephone line. You have to have a modem at both ends. Modems are rated in Baud rate.

Mouse. A small switch on a wheel used to control a PC.

MRI. Mediamark Research, Inc. is a nationwide survey organization that distributes consumer purchase behavior data.

Multi-Buyer. A person who crops up on two or more independent rented lists. Multi-buyers usually respond better to a direct offer than other buyers.

Multiple Regression. A statistical technique used in modeling whereby you develop a formula which explains the relationship between several variables of consumer lifestyle or behavior.

NCOA. National Change of Address, a US Postal Service system under which a few service bureaus nationwide have exclusive use of the change of address forms filed by persons or businesses who are moving. These forms are keypunched, and can be used by the service bureau to update your tape of prospects to obtain their correct current address. A worthwhile service for mailers.

Net Names. The actual names used in a mailing, after removing he duplicates and matches to your customer list. In some cases, you can rent names on a net-name basis.

Niche Market. A way of finding a special product that appeals to only one group, and selling that product very profitably only to that group, ignored by others.

Nixie. A direct mail letter which has been returned to the sender because the address was wrong. Also, any undelivered piece of mail.

Nth Name. A software system whereby you can pick every 3rd or 4th or 250th name out of a file to use as a valid test of the file. To test a file of 400,000 with a test mailing of 40,000, you would pick every 10th name. If the test is successful, you mail next to every name except the 10th names.

Offer. What you are offering in your direct mail: 10 for only $19.95.

Off-Line. An off-line database is kept on magnetic tape. You cannot call up a record instantly from an off-line database.

On-Line. An on-line database is one in which all the customer records can be called up on your screen instantly when you want them. On-line databases are kept on disk. The opposite of on-line is off-line which usually means that the database is kept on magnetic tape.

Package. The envelope or container or look of your outgoing direct mail piece.

PC. Personal Computer. The versatile desktop workstation used for hundreds of applications. They can be used to access a marketing database resident on a mainframe.

Penetration. Your customers as a percentage of the universe that defines your customer's type of household or business.

Personalization. The process of including personal references in an outgoing mail piece such as "Thank you for your order of Feb. 23 for six boxes of hard candy, Mrs. Williams." With laser letters, personalization does not cost more than non-personalized letters.

Postal Pre-Sort. Sorting outgoing letters in a special way to take advantage of postal discounts.

Production. A function in an advertising agency of producing letters and other direct mail pieces.

Profile. A way of describing your typical customer. You create a profile by modeling your database. The profile could tell you that your typical customer was a woman of 35-54 with an income of $25-$50K.

Prospect. A potential customer who you have targeted.

Prospecting. Mailing or telemarketing to prospects who are not yet your customers.

Psychographics. A way of grouping people by wealth, orientation, hobbies and interests. See VALS 2. Examples are Achievers, Fulfilleds, Strivers.

Pull. The percent response to your offer by mail or phone.

Purge. To eliminate undesirable names from a list.

Qualify. In business-to-business, a process whereby respondents to an ad or a mailing are determined (usually by a telephone interview) to be worth a salesman's time and attention. In efficient operations, a telemarketer will qualify an incoming lead before the name is sent to a salesman for action.

Quintile. One fifth of a mailing, usually divided by percentage of response.

Recency. A term for how recently a person has bought from your company. It is well established that people who have bought most recently are *more likely* to buy from you again on your next promotion than people who bought from you longer ago.

Reformatting. Changing the format of a rented list to a new record format that matches a desired arrangement.

Regression. Used in the phrase Multiple Regressions. It is a statistical technique, part of modeling, whereby you try to discover a mathematical formula which will explain trends in a set of data, and which variables determine response. A multiple regression will tell you that your best customers live in condominiums, have no children, and have income over $75K, for example.

Relational. A relational database is what is needed for database marketing. Such a database is kept on disk and consists of related files (name and address, orders) which are related to each other by ID numbers and accessed by indexes.

Respondent. Someone who has answered a direct response letter or advertisement.

Response Rate. The percentage of people who responded to your offer.

Response Device. On every outgoing direct mail piece, there is included a response device which usually shows up in the "window" in the envelope to provide the name and address. The response device is an order or donation form. It is important because it always contains the prospect number, and a source code that identifies the offer, package, list, segment, etc.

Return on Investment. A key measure of the success of any direct marketing activity. It is the total net profit from a direct marketing initiative, divided by the total cost of the entire operation. ROI from an initial offer is often negative. But when customer lifetime value is taken into account, it often becomes positive.

RFM. Stands for Recency, Frequency, Monetary. It is a method for segmenting or rating your customers. The best customers are those who have bought from you recently, buy many times, and in large amounts.

Rollout. After a direct mail test of a few thousand letters, a rollout is the mailing to the rest of the names on the successful lists. It may be preceded by a second test or "continuation."

SAA. System Application Architecture. An IBM term for a system whereby PC's can be connected to and used to run mainframes by cooperative processing.

SCF. Sectional Center Facility. The first three digits of the Zip Code.

Seeds. Names of yourself, friends, relatives, or employees inserted in a direct mail mailout to track delivery and quality, and to safeguard against unauthorized mailings. Also called "decoys."

Segmentation. To divide outgoing direct mail into coded groups for testing or to improve response.

Sequential. The way records are arranged on a tape. The opposite is random order, or a relational database.

SIC Code. A coding system designed by the Department of Commerce for classifying the products and services produced by companies. It is a very inadequate system, but it is the only one around.

SKU. Stock Keeping Unit: a warehouse term for the products that a company produces. Each different product has its own SKU number.

Software. Programs that run on computers. Programs tell the computer what to do in a step-by-step fashion.

Source Code. A series of letters or numbers affixed to an outgoing advertisement or promotion that identifies the list, the offer, the package, and the segment (as well as the media) in which the promotion was made. Essential to testing the success of any direct marketing effort. The source code must appear on the response device (or in the case of telephone orders, must be asked for by the telemarketers).

SQL. A query language used with the IBM software DB2 Often pronounced "sequal."

SRI. Stanford Research Institute. A leading research institution which pioneered Psychographics.

Statement Stuffer. An offer or newsletter included with a monthly invoice or statement to a customer.

Storage. The capacity which a computer has for storing names addresses and other data. Storage is usually on magnetic disks, and is measured in megabytes.

Stratification. Adding demographics to a name and address file.

Suppression. Using names on one tape (a customer file) to suppress or drop names from another tape (a prospect file).

Sweepstakes. An offer promising a randomly drawn prize to all respondents, regardless of whether they buy your product. Those who do not buy, but still respond to the sweepstakes are often valuable names for rental or for other offers.

Tape. Magnetic tape is 1/2 inch wide, and holds about 300,000 customer records (depending on their size). Tape records are sequential (one after the other) whereas disk records can be in random order. Tape is the cheapest way to store information, but the data is hard to get at. Tape is used for backup and for sending information from one computer to another. Direct marketing tapes are 9 track, and 1600 or 6250 bytes per inch. They are ASCII or EBCDIC.

Telemarketing. Talking on the telephone to prospects or customers. Inbound telemarketing is usually customers or prospects calling your 800 number. Outbound telemarketing is when you place the call to a prospect or customer. Telemarketing can be done by your in-house staff or by an external telemarketing company.

Terminal. A device that looks like a television screen with a keyboard which, when hooked up to a computer, enables to enter data into the computer, and receive data from it which you see on the screen. The alternative to a terminal is a PC.

Test Database. All marketing databases should have a companion test database which programmers use to write and test new software before it goes on the production database.

Third Class. Over 85% of all mail carrying advertising or promotion is sent by third class. It is much less costly than first class. It usually requires postal pre-sort. Over 790,000 businesses and non-profits have third class mailing permits.

Tiger. A Census system for mapping the entire United States by Blocks, complete with roads and other landmarks. Customers and prospects can be shown on a map using codes to represent where they are.

Update. To modify a database record to insert new information into it, or to delete it. Updating is either done in batch mode (fast and cheap) or on-line (slow and costly).

UPS. 1) Uninterruptable Power Supply. A system of batteries that permits a mainframe to keep going even when the power fails. It is usually connected to a diesel generator that kicks in as soon as the batteries have begun to be needed. 2) United Parcel Service, a vital delivery service for database marketing.

VALS 2. Values and Lifestyles. A psychographic technique used by SRI.

WATS. Wide area telephone service. An "800" number whereby the call is free to the caller.

White Mail. Mail received from a buyer or donor who has not included the response device, so you cannot determine the source code of the offer which promoted his purchase or gift.

How to Keep Up with Database Marketing

Database marketing is new. Most people don't know what it is. There is no central bureau that records its successes and publishes information. For this reason, to keep up with the many new innovations and developments in this field, you will have to read, talk to people and attend conferences. This chapter offers you some guidance, and a suggestion on how we can stay in touch once you have finished reading this book.

Publications

Magazines that you should subscribe to:

Direct Marketing, 224 Seventh Street, Garden City, New York, 11530, (800) 229-6700

Direct, Six River Bend Center, Stamford, CT 06907, (203) 358-9900

American Demographics, P.O. Box 68, Ithaca, New York 14851 (800) 828-1133

Target Marketing, P.O. Box 12827, Philadelphia, PA 19108, (215) 238-5300

DM News, Mill Hollow Corporation, 19 West 21st Street, New York 10010, (212) 741-2095, FAX 212-633-9367

Inbound Outbound, 12 West 21 Street, New York, NY 10010, (212) 691-8215

Books you should read:

The Complete Direct Mail List Handbook, Ed Burnett, Prentice Hall, 1988.

The Truth About Database Marketing, John Stevenson, Gill Winograd, Gary Beck and Craig Walker, Krupp/Taylor 1989.

MaxiMarketing, Stan Rapp and Thomas L. Collins, McGraw Hill, 1986.

The Great Marketing Turnaround, Stan Rapp and Thomas L. Collins, Prentice-Hall, 1990.

The New Direct Marketing, David Shepard, Dow Jones- Irwin, 1990.

Market Segmentation, Art Weinstein, Probus, 1987.

Direct Marketing Success, Freeman F. Gosden, Jr., Wiley, 1985.

Secrets of Insurance Direct Marketing Practices Revealed, Donald R. Jackson, Napoly Press.

Successful Direct Marketing Methods, 4th Edition, Bob Stone, NTC Business Books, 1989.

Database Marketing, Robert Shaw and Merlin Stone, Wiley, 1988.

Guide to Catalog Management Software, Ernest Schell, The Communications Center, Annual, 5th Edition, 1990.

Business-to-Business Direct Marketing, Tracy Emerick and Bernie Goldberg, Direct Marketing Publishers, 1987.

The Business-to-Business Direct Marketing Handbook, Roy G. Ljungren, ANACOM, 1989.

Conventions you should attend:

"Database Marketing," The National Center for Database Marketing, Suite 888, 14618 Tyler Foote Road, P.O. Box 2044, Nevada City, California 95959, (916) 292-3000

This convention probably offers the best two-days learning experience about database marketing. The sessions are held every six months in Chicago and Orlando. Attended by over 700 people each time, with about 70 speakers, they provide an opportunity to hear about new developments, and to meet all sorts of people in the business.

"Direct Marketing Association." Several conferences and exhibitions each year, at least one of which features Database Marketing. 11 West 42nd Street, New York, NY 10036, (212) 972-2410

"Direct Marketing to Business and Industry." National Conference sponsored by Federal Express and Dun's Marketing Services. P.O. Box 1161, Ridgefield, CT 06877, (203) 438-2318

This conference is also of great interest to database marketers in the business-to-business arena.

An excellent reference book for obtaining prospect names is:

Direct Mail List, Standard Rate and Data Service, 3004 Glenview Road, Wilmette, IL 60091, (708) 256-6067.

However, you should not order names without the advice of a list broker who is a part of your marketing team.

Sharing *Your* Opinions

I would like to hear from you regarding your reaction to this book and your experiences with database marketing. Information in our industry is very hard to come by. You can help by filling in the following questionnaire and sending it to the publisher, Probus Publishing Company, 1925 North Clybourn, Avenue, Chicago, IL 60614.

Your response will be entered into a *marketing database!* We will stay in touch with you, telling you about new publications and events of interest to database marketers. We will put you in touch with others in the field who would like to share their experiences with you or to offer you their services, and including creative agencies, telemarketing firms, service bureaus, conference managers. We will try to use the database to build a network of supporters of the marketing database revolution.

So please photocopy the questionnaire and send it in!

To Probus Publishing Company

I have read *The Complete Database Marketer* by Arthur Hughes. My opinion of the book is:

_____

_____

_____

Chapters I particularly found useful and why:_____

_____

Chapters I particularly didn't like and why:_____

_____

How I obtained this book: [ ] Bought from bookstore [ ] Bought by mail [ ] A friend or office copy [ ] Library [ ] _____

I work in: [ ] An advertising agency [ ] A service bureau [ ] A company with a marketing database [ ] A company that should have a marketing database [ ] A consulting firm [ ] Telemarketing [ ] Catalog house [ ] Fulfillment [ ] _____

My Position:_____
I am [ ] new to [ ] experienced at database marketing.

The type of database I am interested in: [ ] Consumer [ ] Business-to -business [ ] Medical support [ ] Other:_____

We [ ] have [ ] are thinking of creating a marketing database. The size is (would be)_____ thousand names. The basic purpose of this database is (would be):

[ ] Product launch [ ] Upgrades [ ] Cross selling [ ] Lead tracking
[ ] Direct sales [ ] Dealer support [ ] Buyer's club
[ ] _____

The principal product or service of our company is:_____

Where is the   [ ] In-house mainframe
database now?   [ ] At service bureau
                   [ ] _____

What do you plan to accomplish with the database during the next
twelve months?
    [ ] Analyze and profile current customers
    [ ] Mail promotions to current customers and record response
    [ ] Telemarket to customers
    [ ] Direct access for customer service
    [ ] Segment customers into specialty groups/ RFM cells
    [ ] Score customers using statistical models
    [ ] Set up a lead tracking and qualification system
    [ ] Project sales, branch locations, marketing programs
    [ ] Furnish leads to dealers, salesmen, telemarketers
    [ ] Build repeat sales, loyalty, cross sales, upgrades
    [ ] Build points or credits for premiums or discounts
    [ ] Use profiles to select prospects from rented lists
    [ ] Market research for product design, media selection
    [ ] Set up direct marketing/catalog program
    [ ] Newsletter/magazine
    [ ] _____

    Where will you get data to update your database?
    [ ] Responses to promotions/coupons/checks/800 calls
    [ ] Direct sales
    [ ] Warranty/registration cards
    [ ] Salesmen/dealers
    [ ] Surveys
    [ ] Customer service calls/ Inquiries/ Tech support
    [ ] _____

What technical features do you have/would you like in your database system:

Have Now	Would Like	
[ ]	[ ]	Users make instant ad-hoc counts from their desks
[ ]	[ ]	Users download data/print reports on their PC's
[ ]	[ ]	Customer service view/update any customer record
[ ]	[ ]	Telemarketers call up records/enter sales on-line
[ ]	[ ]	Many users work simultaneously with database
[ ]	[ ]	Users do selects and segmentation at their desks
[ ]	[ ]	All past promotions/responses/purchases retained
[ ]	[ ]	_____

[ ] I have an interesting case study that I would like to share.

Name_____

Company_____

Address_____

City, State Zip_____

Telephone_____

Send this questionnaire to Probus Publishing, 1925 North Clybourn Avenue, Chicago, Illinois 60614. You will receive an answer.

Index

About the Publisher

PROBUS PUBLISHING COMPANY

Probus Publishing Company fills the informational needs of today's business professional by publishing authoritative, quality books on timely and relevant topics, including:

- Investing
- Futures/Options Trading
- Banking
- Finance
- Marketing and Sales
- Manufacturing and Project Management
- Personal Finance, Real Estate, Insurance and Estate Planning
- Entrepreneurship
- Management

Probus books are available at quantity discounts when purchased for business, educational or sales promotional use. For more information, please call the Director, Corporate/Institutional Sales at 1-800-PROBUS-1, or write:

Director, Corporate/Institutional Sales
Probus Publishing Company
1925 N. Clybourn Avenue
Chicago, Illinois 60614
FAX (312) 868-6250